PENGUIN BOOKS

FOUR HOURS IN MY LAI

Michael Bilton was born in South London in 1947. While working for *The Sunday Times* (London) he was named Reporter of the Year in 1981, and is the author of *Speaking Out*, an oral history of the Falklands War. He left journalism in 1983 to make award-winning documentaries for Yorkshire Television.

Kevin Sim was born in Liverpool in 1946 and began writing for newspapers and periodicals in 1972. In recent years, he has made several internationally acclaimed documentaries, including *Kitty—Return to Auschwitz*. He is the author of *Women at War*.

Michael Bilton and Kevin Sim

FOUR HOURS IN MY LAI

PENGUIN BOOKS

PENGUIN BOOKS
Published by the Penguin Group
Penguin Books USA Inc., 375 Hudson Street, New York, New York 10014, U.S.A.
Penguin Books Ltd, 27 Wrights Lane, London W8 5TZ, England
Penguin Books Australia Ltd, Ringwood, Victoria, Australia
Penguin Books Canada Ltd, 10 Alcorn Avenue, Toronto, Ontario, Canada M4V 3B2
Penguin Books (N.Z.) Ltd, 182–190 Wairau Road, Auckland 10, New Zealand

Penguin Books Ltd, Registered Offices: Harmondsworth, Middlesex, England

First published in the United States of America by Viking Penguin,
a division of Penguin Books USA Inc., 1992
Published in Penguin Books 1993

1 3 5 7 9 10 8 6 4 2

"The Battle Hymn of Lt. Calley" written by James M. Smith and Julian Wilson.
© 1971 Shelby Singleton Music, Inc., and Quicket Publishing Co.,
Nashville, Tennessee. Used by permission.

Other permission acknowledgments appear on pages viii–ix.

Illustration credits appear on pages xi–xii.

LIBRARY OF CONGRESS CATALOGING-IN-PUBLICATION DATA
Bilton, Michael.
Four hours in My Lai/Michael Bilton and Kevin Sim.
p. cm.
Outgrowth of a documentary film made for Yorkshire Television's First Tuesday
program in Britain and Station WGBH in Boston.
Includes bibliographical references and index.
ISBN 0-670-84296-6 (hc.)
ISBN 0 14 01.7709 4 (pbk.)
1. My Lai Massacre, Vietnam, 1968. I. Sim, Kevin. II. First Tuesday
(Television program). III. Title.
DS557.8.M9B55 1992
959.704′342—dc20
91-47651

Printed in the United States of America

Contents

Acknowledgments

This book grew out of a documentary film made for Yorkshire Television's *First Tuesday* program in Britain, and Station WGBH in Boston, part of the American public broadcasting system. For the film and the book we were very fortunate to have Sheldon Himelfarb at our side as a consultant. A former foreign policy advisor to a member of the Senate Foreign Relations Committee, Dr Himelfarb is now a freelance writer, novelist, commentator for National Public Radio, and an independent film producer. We drew heavily upon all his many talents as well as his friendship during the last four years.

In the telling of the My Lai story we were assisted in some measure by very many people but we would particularly like to record our thanks to the following:

In North America: *Alabama*: Wayne D. Thorne; *Illinois*: Tom Glen; *New York*: Jerry Walsh of the law firm of Lane & Mittendorf; Nan Graham of Viking Penguin; Harvey Klinger, our American agent; Nicholas Capezza, James Dursi, and Sarah Granato of the Bronx Library Reference Center; *Virginia*: Joe Lazarsky and Mary B. Dennis, Deputy Clerk of the Court of Military Review in Falls Church; *Florida*: Mrs Dorothy Barker, Andre C. Feher, Colonel William V. Wilson (Ret.), and Michael Bernhardt; *Georgia*: Lawrence Colburn, Eugene Kotouc, Kenneth Hodges, and Lawrence Smith of the *Columbus Ledger-Enquirer*; *Maryland*: Henry Mayer, senior archivist at the Federal Records Center at Suitland; Richard Boylan of the National Archives, Suitland; Samuel W. Koster and Major General Kenneth Hodgson, former Judge Advocate General; Erica D'Andrea, Robert Brisentine, former director of the US Army Crime Records Center, and his assistant, Barbara Parker; *Ohio*: Ronald Haeberle and Mrs Christina Peers Neely, daughter of the late Lieutenant General William R. Peers; *Indiana*: Fred Widmer, Darlene Grant, Lawrence Congleton, and Paul Meadlo; *Wisconsin*: Ernest Medina; *Texas*: Carl Creswell; *Mississippi*: Harry Stanley, Roy Newman of the Newman Lumber Co., Varnado Simpson, and Rita Marie Dearman; *Louisiana*: Hugh C. Thompson Jr, Mona Gossen, Ronald Ridenhour, and Charles Hutto; *New Jersey*: Robert Maples and Allen Boyce; *Oregon*: Gregory Olsen; *California*: Art Findlay of Station KCBS, San Francisco, and Carl Eifler; *Massachusetts*: George Esper of the Associated Press; *Vancouver*: Clare Culhane and Dr Alje Vennemma; *Washington, DC*: Chris Thomas of the London

Times, Val Thomas, Mark Hosenball of the London *Sunday Times*, Colonel Bill Mulvey of the US Army Public Affairs Office, Seymour Hersh, and Danny Coleman; *Colorado*: Joan Howard, formerly of the National Archives Nixon Project; *Pennsylvania*: Colonel William G. Eckhardt.

In Vietnam: Duong Duc Hong, Ministry of Culture, and Vuong Thinh of the Ministry of Foreign Relations. During our stay in Vietnam our interpreter, guide, and mentor was the redoubtable Tran Thi Thuc, former war correspondent and more recently civil servant in the Press Department of the Ministry of Foreign Relations, based in Hanoi. During the latter stages of the Vietnam War she walked the entire length of the Ho Chi Minh Trail, sending back dispatches to the *Hanoi Daily News*, which took her away from her two young daughters and journalist husband for many months. We also owe a special debt for their kindness, courtesy, and hospitality to the people of the hamlets and subhamlets of Truong Dinh, Tu Cung, My Lai, and Co Luy, which made up the villages the Americans called My Lai 4 and My Lai 1.

In England: Do Van Thuc of the Vietnamese Embassy in London; David Robson, Robin Morgan, and David Grossman, our agent; Peter Carson and Caroline Muir at Viking Penguin; freelance editor Miles Litvinoff; Sheila Fitzhugh and Sue Croft at the Yorkshire Television reference library in Leeds; John Willis, who first commissioned our film; Grant McKee, head of documentaries at Yorkshire Television and editor of *First Tuesday*, who gave the project his wholehearted support and then allowed us leave of absence to write this book; our colleagues at Yorkshire Television, Barry Spink, Howard James, Andrew Hartley, Christine Sharman, Lee Corbett, and especially Frank Pocklington, perhaps the finest lighting cameraman of his generation, a former *Picture Post* photographer who picked up his still camera once more to take some of the photographs used in this book. Finally we would thank our respective children, Thomas, Sam, and Hannah, and our wives at home, Sarah Fletcher and Jill Sim, who put up with our long absences from domestic life while this book was being written.

We would like to acknowledge the following for permission to reproduce published material:

Oxford University Press for passages from *America in Vietnam*, by Guenter Lewy;

Penguin Books Ltd for a passage from *On War*, by Carl Von Clausewitz, edited by Anatol Rapoport;

Random House Inc for passages from *Everything We Had*, by Al Santoli and *Observing the Nixon Years* and *The Real War* by Jonathan Schell;

Faber and Faber for a passage from *War Without Mercy*, by John Dower;

Presdio Press for passages from *On Strategy*, by Harry Summers Jr, and *With the Old Breed in Peleliu and Okinawa*, by E. B. Sledge;

Bantam Doubleday Dell Publishing Group Inc. for a passage from *A Soldier Reports*, by General William C. Westmoreland;

Henry Holt and Company Inc., for a passage from *A Rumour of War*, by Philip Caputo.

List of Illustrations

Maps

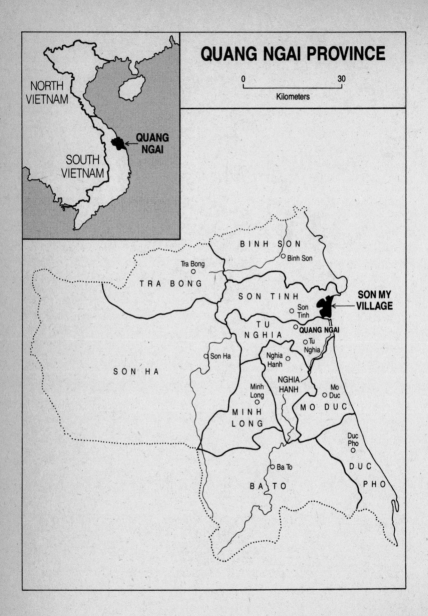

QUANG NGAI PROVINCE

0   30

Kilometers

NORTH
VIETNAM

QUANG
NGAI

SOUTH
VIETNAM

BINH SON

Binh Son

Tra Bong

TRA BONG

SON TINH

Son
Tinh

SON MY
VILLAGE

QUANG NGAI

TU
NGHIA

Tu
Nghia

Son Ha

Nghia
Hanh

SON HA

NGHIA
HANH

Mo
Duc

Minh
Long

MO DUC

MINH
LONG

Duc
Pho

Ba To

DUC

BA TO

PHO

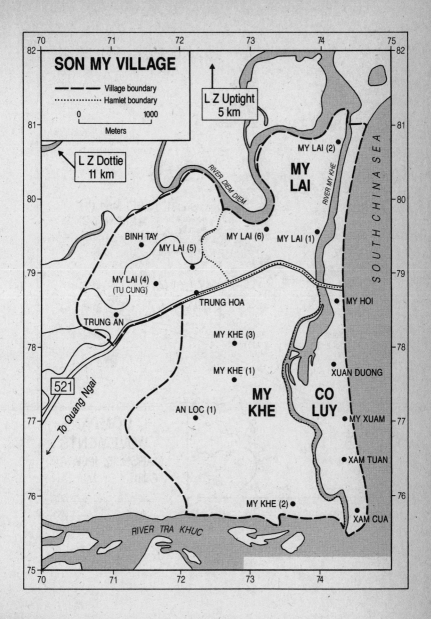

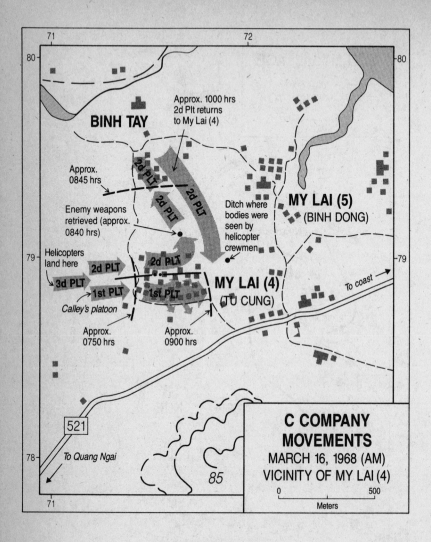

BINH TAY

Approx. 1000 hrs
2d Plt returns
to My Lai (4)

Approx.
0845 hrs

Enemy weapons
retrieved (approx.
0840 hrs)

Helicopters
land here

2d PLT

2d PLT

2d PLT

2d PLT

3d PLT

2d PLT

1st PLT

1st PLT

Calley's platoon

Approx.
0750 hrs

Approx.
0900 hrs

Ditch where
bodies were
seen by
helicopter
crewmen

MY LAI (5)
(BINH DONG)

MY LAI (4)
(TU CUNG)

To coast

521

To Quang Ngai

85

**C COMPANY
MOVEMENTS**
MARCH 16, 1968 (AM)
VICINITY OF MY LAI (4)

0   500

Meters

71   72

80   80

79   79

78

71

1. Introduction

During the period 16–19 March 1968, US Army troops of Task Force Barker, 11th Brigade, Americal Division, massacred a large number of noncombatants in two hamlets of Son My Village, Quang Ngai Province, Republic of Vietnam. The precise number of Vietnamese killed cannot be determined but was at least 175 and may exceed 400.

Peers Commission Report, 1970

If we learn to accept this, there is nothing we will not accept.

Jonathan Schell, 1968

At 5:45 PM every working day, in Columbus, Georgia, a middle-aged businessman locks up his jewelry store, strolls across the parking lot to his Mercedes sedan, and heads for home.

This small, paunchy figure who keeps such regular habits is America's most infamous war criminal. His name is William Laws "Rusty" Calley, the same Lieutenant Calley whose name was once inseparable from the massacre at My Lai. It was of him that Brigadier-General Al Haig warned in a memo to White House staff concerning the case: "There is no individual under investigation, charged or convicted in any case [resulting from the Vietnam War] whose crime can *even remotely* be said to equal that of Calley" (original italics). It was Calley who, weeks before My Lai, threw a defenseless old man down a well and shot him. It was Calley who, seeing a baby at My Lai crawling away from a ditch already filled with dead and dying villagers, seized the child by the leg, threw it back in the pit, and shot it.

"No one," Haig's White House memo concluded, "should undertake to advise the President, who is not fully informed of the sordid facts."

Calley was by no means the only one responsible for the massacre at My Lai—but he was the only man ever found guilty of any offense committed there. In 1971, he was sentenced to life imprisonment with hard labor. Within three days, President Nixon ordered that he should be released from jail pending appeal.

Following this presidential intervention, Calley became the most privileged prisoner in America. He spent the next thirty-five months in his "bachelor apartment" at Fort Benning accompanied, it was reported at the time, by his dog, a myna bird, and a tankful of tropical fish. To pass the time he took up cooking and enjoyed regular visits from his girlfriend, who told the press: "I know that deep down he wouldn't hurt anyone. Just look at the way he takes care of his pets and how gentle he is."

In 1974, Calley was released on parole. Judge Robert Elliott, explaining this decision, observed: "War is war and it's not unusual for innocent civilians such as the My Lai victims to be killed." By way of further elaboration, the judge explained that when Joshua took the city of Jericho in biblical times, no charges had been brought against him for the slaughter of the civilian population.

On his release, Calley moved into a new apartment in Columbus, Georgia. He drove around the streets in a white Mercedes sports car on loan from a sympathizer. At Murray State University in Kentucky he made the first of a series of appearances on the college lecture circuit for $2,000 a time. In 1976 he married—not the girlfriend of his captivity, but Penny Vick, the 29-year-old daughter of a local jeweler. "I don't want to talk about the past," he told reporters at the wedding.

His silence has held to the present day. Historians and journalists are unwelcome at the jewelry store at the Cross Plaza Shopping Mall. When they arrive in the cool bright showroom the small, balding manager of his father-in-law's store looks trapped and impatient behind the counter. He starts to sweat a little. His chubby hands smudge the display cabinets. "This is a place of business," he whispers. "Don't you understand? This is my place of business."

The three days Calley spent in the stockade at Fort Benning, together with the weeks he spent much later imprisoned at Fort Leavenworth, were the harshest punishment served by anyone connected with the My Lai massacre. Everyone else responsible for the most inexcusable act of American arms during this century had got clean away with it. No one remembers them. And now the jeweler from Columbus would also like to forget.

The second moon landing was on the front pages when the news from My Lai broke late in 1969. For a time the two stories vied side by side for news space: one story revealing the new horizons opening for mankind; the other, a ghastly slide into horror. Until My Lai, it had been possible (although perhaps not quite accurate) to believe that the authors of the twentieth century's greatest atrocities were to be found among distant, primitive, or at least deluded peoples. With My Lai the heart of darkness came home to America.

"I think there is a good deal of evidence that we thought all along that we were a redeemer nation," wrote the distinguished Protestant theologian Reinhold Niebuhr. "There was a lot of illusion in our national history. Now it is about to be shattered."

The killers of My Lai were young Americans with an average age of around 20. They had been drawn, enlisted or drafted, from all over America: "A typical cross-section," an official US Army report would state later, "of American youth assigned to most combat units." Official inquiries and investigations put the facts of what they did beyond dispute. At the time of the massacre, Charlie Company, a unit of the Americal Division's 11th Light Infantry Brigade, had been in Vietnam for just over three months. On March 16, 1968, they entered an undefended village on the coast of Central Vietnam and murdered around five hundred old men, women, and children in cold blood. The killings took place, part maniacally, part methodically, over a period of about four hours. They were accompanied by rape, sodomy, mutilations, and unimaginable random cruelties. "It was this Nazi kind of thing," we were told again and again by men who were there—an observation underscored by a single unassimilable thought: How could we have behaved like Nazis?

And how could they? These young boys, 18, 19, 20 years old, who belonged to what was materially the most privileged generation in history; cradled by the theories of Dr Spock and the wealth of the mightiest and most advanced nation on earth? "We were supposed to be the good guys in the white hats," said someone who witnessed what happened.

National consciousness consists of what is allowed to be forgotten as much as by what is remembered. Germany, even a united Germany, is not free of the implications of its terrible past. At the moment of the country's reunification in 1990, German politicians and commentators hastened to reassure themselves and others that Germany had learned the lessons of history—utterances of a people who still remembered what they had been capable of, who still understood that a high level of culture was not a guarantee of civilized values. My Lai suggests that this is more than a German lesson.

My Lai is now almost completely forgotten, erased almost entirely from the national consciousness. What was once an image of incandescent horror has become at most a vague recollection of something unpleasant that happened during the Vietnam War. Even in the newspapers of the time, a process of eclipse can be traced clearly. What was first a "massacre" quickly became a "tragedy" and was then referred to as an "incident." General Peers, whose exhaustive inquiry into the events at My Lai remains the best source for what really happened there, was warned by his superiors not to use the word "massacre" at the press conference held on the publication of his report.

After the initial shocked outcry, My Lai soon became a political and ideological football—with bizarre results. By the time William Calley, the only man found guilty of crimes committed at My Lai, was put on trial before a court-martial of his military peers, public opinion had swung overwhelmingly in his favor. Reporters at the later trial of his immediate superior, Captain Ernest Medina, were agreed that the whole procedure had simply become tedious. The massacre had outlived the nation's attention span. The political, judicial, and media institutions of the United States, at times acting quite deliberately, had succeeded in deflecting attention from the nagging anxiety at the heart of the massacre—what caused Charlie Company, "a typical cross-section of American youth," to commit such an atrocity in the first place? "Was Vietnam responsible for this national degradation," asked the writer Louis Heren in a foreword to the British edition of Calley's memoirs, "or did that country only provide conditions for the festering sores disfiguring the face of American society to erupt in all their horror?"

The question is as vital today as it was twenty years ago. History makes it easy to distance ourselves from the Nazis. It's harder to dissociate ourselves from Charlie Company. The killers of My Lai were the boys next door. No one had told us that the boys next door could do anything like that. What made them do it? How can we stop it happening again? To want to forget the shame and horror of My Lai might be only natural; to remember only moon landings is more dangerous.

At the end of April 1982, a 34-year-old black "Vietnam era" veteran was admitted to a Veterans Administration hospital in Jackson, Mississippi. His name was Varnado Simpson. He was of average height, around 140 pounds, well dressed, and well groomed. Although he possessed above-average intelligence and a good vocabulary, it was observed that he was nervous as he spoke, smoking continuously and making wringing movements with his hands. He always sat with his back to the wall and would never allow anyone to get behind him.

According to their notes, Varnado Simpson told doctors at the hospital that he had entered military service in 1967 and had been posted the following year to Vietnam. There his company had attacked the village of "Milai" and were "apparently" ordered "not to leave anyone alive." He himself had killed women and children in the village and described "other very traumatic events occurring during this action."

When he returned home from the war, Simpson started work in a bank. But in 1969, with the revelations of what had happened at My Lai, followed by the trial of Lt. Calley, he had left his job. People in the street called him "child-killer" and "baby-killer" and he felt that customers were withdrawing their money from the bank because he worked there. Since then, he had become reclusive, extremely fearful, and "somewhat paranoid." Nightmares had become so frequent that he was afraid to go to sleep. The people he had killed in Vietnam, he said, were not really dead and were going to come back and kill him.

In 1977, Varnado Simpson's 10-year-old son was playing in the front yard of his home on the northern edge of Jackson. Teenagers across the road began arguing and one of them pulled a gun. A wild shot hit his little boy in the head.

I was in the house. And I came out and picked him up. But he was already dead . . . he was dying. He died in my arms. And when I looked at him, his face was like the same face of the child that I had killed. And I said: This is the punishment for me killing the people that I killed.

Doctors could do very little for Varnado Simpson. They described his condition as post-traumatic stress disorder, "chronic and very severe." In the year he remained in the hospital they had the greatest difficulty in trying to get him to talk about his experiences. Any discussion or activation of his memories from Vietnam created such extreme discomfort that he simply could not tolerate it. "Mr Simpson has been one of the most uncomfortable people that I have ever seen," his doctor wrote. His prognosis was considered "very guarded and very poor."

In July 1983, with his doctors' agreement, Varnado Simpson went to live by himself in a small house on the same street where his son had died. He barred the windows and put a battery of locks on the doors. In his own house, he felt better able to control his own fate.

Six years later, in the summer of 1989, he still lived alone in the same house. There were more bars on the windows now, and more locks on the doors. The curtains were always drawn. Not much of bright, hot Mississippi summer filtered indoors.

Inside, the living room was gloomy. Varnado Simpson's hands were still shaking wildly. He tried in vain to rest them on his legs but his legs shook too. His whole body shuddered in distress. There was the same thin moustache he wore in the twenty-year-old photograph taken during the war, though his face was rounder, almost swollen, and there was a puffiness under the eyes as if he had been crying, or was about to cry. He sat in an old armchair, his head a little to one side, with a look of utter resignation on his face and his back to the wall. And he began to talk about what happened in Vietnam.

"That day in My Lai, I was personally responsible for killing about 25 people. Personally. Men, women. From shooting them, to cutting their throats, scalping them, to . . . cutting off their hands and cutting out their tongue. I did it."

Why did he do all that? Why did he kill them and do that?

"I just went. My mind just went. And I wasn't the only one that did it. A lot of other people did it. I just killed. Once I started, the . . . the training, the whole programing part of killing, it just came out."

But your training didn't tell you to scalp people or cut ears off.

"No. But a lot of people were doing it. So I just followed suit. I just lost all sense of direction, of purpose. I just started killing any kinda way I could kill. It just came. I didn't know I had it in me.

"But like I say, after I killed the child, my whole mind just went. It just went. And once you start, it's very easy to keep on. Once you start. The hardest—the part that's hard is to kill, but once you kill, that becomes easier, to kill the next person and the next one and the next one. Because I had no feelings or no emotions or no nothing. No direction. I just killed. It can happen to anyone. Because, see, I wasn't the only one that did it. Hung 'em, you know—all type of ways. Any type of way you could kill someone, that's what they did. And it can happen."

"It can happen." It did happen. One hundred and five GIs from Charlie Company went into the village of My Lai. Almost all of them are still alive, living quietly all over America. Each of them must have their own way of dealing with the things they have seen and the deeds they have committed. But it is in Varnado Simpson's sunless room that the poison of the memory of My Lai seems to survive in its most concentrated form.

"I can't remember—you know. I can't remember everything. I don't want to remember," he says. But the truth is that he never forgets. Remembering has become a compulsion. Suddenly, without warning, he jumps up and pulls a large brown book out of a cupboard. A scrapbook of My Lai. Twenty-year-old photographs and news clippings are neatly preserved in an old photo album.

Why has he kept it?

"This is my life," he answers without hesitation. "This is my past. This is my present, and this is my future. And I keep it to remind me. But it's always there. This is my life. This is everything. This is the way I am. This is what made me this way.

"I have an image of it in my mind every night, every day. I have nightmares. I constantly have nightmares of the children or someone. I can see the people. I can go somewhere and see a face that reminds me of the people that I killed. I can see that vividly, just like it's happened today, right now."

Varnado Simpson remains caught in a trap sprung twenty years ago in Vietnam. He wants to be put out of his misery. He has attempted suicide three times and does not know if he will still be here "the next time you come around." On a table, there are dozens of bottles containing the pills which he takes throughout the day and night. One jar is labeled simply: "For Pain." Nothing prescribed by his physicians seems to have much effect or even relevance to his case. He is stretched out somewhere between life and death, scared of both, convinced that on Judgment Day his will be a hopeless case. For there is little doubt that Varnado Simpson sees himself as a man who has already been damned.

"How can you forgive?" he asks. "You know, I can't forgive myself for the things I did. How can I forget that—or forgive? There's a part of me that's kind and gentle. There's another part of me that's evil and destructive. There's more destructiveness in my mind than goodness. There's more wanting to kill or to hurt than to love or to care. I don't let anyone get close to me. The loving feeling and the caring feeling is not there.

"That was caused by My Lai, the war. My feelings and the way I feel and the way my life is.

"Yes, I'm ashamed, I'm sorry, I'm guilty. But I did it, you know. What else could I tell you? It happened. It can happen if you go to war. Those are the type of things that will happen and can happen to anyone … ."

Late in 1917, the British Prime Minister, David Lloyd George, attended a dinner party given for Philip Gibbs, a respected journalist who had returned from the Western Front. After listening to

Gibbs's account of what was happening in France, Lloyd George said later: "Even an audience of hardened politicians and journalists was strongly affected. If people really knew, the war would be stopped tomorrow. But of course they don't know and can't know ... The thing is horrible beyond human nature to bear and I feel I can't go on with the bloody business: I would rather resign."

After three years of war, when millions of lives had already been lost, what could possibly have caused the Prime Minister of Great Britain such a measure of shock and distress? What was it about the nature of the conflict that people didn't and couldn't know, that was "horrible beyond human nature to bear"?

Most people who would agree that war is hell know very little about war or hell. Very few experience war at the sharp end. Even among soldiers, only a small percentage ever find themselves in close combat with the enemy. Around 3 million American servicemen served in Vietnam but the number of combat troops with their "ass in the grass" remained at about 10 percent. These "grunts," the small fraction who knew best of all what men can do in war and what war can do to men, also knew how their experience was sanitized and falsified for the folks back home. Like soldiers from earlier wars, Vietnam vets returned home to find the history of the war already written. "No one can understand who wasn't there," was one common reaction to this predicament. "Nothing you've read in newspapers comes even close to describing what happened," was another. But vets quickly discovered that there was no place at the table for soldiers who wanted to tell what it was really like. The popular imagination strongly resists reality. Faced with the idea of war, it comes up with John Wayne, or Rambo. Certainly, twenty years after My Lai, there is little or nothing in the popular image of war that prepares anyone for the sheer horror of spending half an hour with Varnado Simpson. His is the unacceptable, hidden face of war, his file marked "Don't Know and Can't Know."

When *Four Hours in My Lai*, the film which was the starting point for this book, was shown in the United States in 1989, some critics complained that it seemed cruel to remind people of such a terrible happening after twenty years. Cruel to whom? To the victims? To the perpetrators? Or cruel to those who would prefer a more comforting view of war? Delusion has always played a big part in war, and the cruelest delusion of all is the tempting idea that war can be something other than it is, or that modern war is something other than what war has always been.

> The gates of mercy shall be all shut up,
> And the fleshed soldier—rough and hard of heart—
> In liberty of bloody hand shall range
> With conscience wide as hell, mowing like grass
> Your fresh-fair virgins, and your flowering infants.
> What is it to me, if like impious war—
> Arrayed in flames, like to the prince of fiends—
> Do, with his smirched complexion, all fell feats
> Enlinked to waste and desolation?
> What is't to me, when you yourselves are cause,
> If your pure maidens fall into the hand
> Of hot and forcing violation?

For this nightmare vision of war in *Henry V*, Shakespeare had only to draw on the evidence of real wars as they had been fought throughout history. Why should twentieth-century wars be any different? Why should it be surprising that it is also recognizable as a fair description of what happened in My Lai? The idea of progress is very powerful; there is great appeal in the notion that as a race we have advanced, become more human, passed beyond the stage when war involved gratuitous and unnecessary slaughter.

When it comes to warfare, mankind has always been in danger of considering the position hopeful. "Silent enim leges inter arma," was Cicero's chilling assessment a hundred years before Christ: Laws are silent in time of war. Yet Roman skepticism has not prevented the creation of a whole edifice of international law and rules of warfare built around the ideas of minimum force and the rights of noncombatants. Legislators sit far from the battlefield, and their laws testify more to their humanity than their experience. Philanthropists, von Clausewitz observed, imagine a skillful way of overcoming an enemy without causing great bloodshed, but this is wrong: "for in such dangerous things as War, the errors which proceed from a spirit of benevolence are the worst." Clausewitz continued: "it is to no purpose, it is even against one's own interest, to turn away from the consideration of the real nature of the affair because the horror of its elements excites repugnance."

Yet Vietnam was riddled from top to bottom with measures calculated to obscure "the real nature of the affair," and at every level, from the Pentagon to the "common grunt," America paid the price for not heeding Clausewitz's advice. It was useless for generals to complain—after the event—that Vietnam was no more horrible than the Korean War or World War II; that people should have known that carnage was inseparable from war; that civilian casualty rates were no higher than in other wars; that pictures of scared children turned by napalm into human torches and all the other awful images of death and destruction represent an inevitable reality of war—because the American people had not been prepared for this reality. "We in the military knew better," one colonel of infantry wrote later, "but through fear of reinforcing the basic antimilitarism of the American people we tended to keep this knowledge to ourselves and downplayed battlefield realities . . . We had concealed from the American people the true nature of war."

An army with its head in the clouds had been sent to war by a nation with its head in the sand. Of course, when the American people woke up, they turned against the war in large numbers. Just as the troops in Vietnam did when they discovered that war was something different from what they had been led to believe, that while they were losing real blood, real lives, at home the myth makers were still spinning the familiar yarns. They experienced a disillusionment best summed up by the ex-grunt who wrote tersely: "Fuck you, John Wayne."

The idea that war *really is* hell played a paradoxical role in the story of My Lai. For while a clear-eyed view of the nature of war is indispensable for understanding what happened, it is not enough for an explanation. Indeed, by itself, it provides the seductive and quite corrupting logic that war itself is somehow to blame. If war really is hell, the argument goes, then massacres like My Lai are inevitable: there is nothing that can be done to stop them and therefore it is unreasonable to blame individual officers, or soldiers, or a particular strategy or policy. The terrible nature of the war in Vietnam—revealed to its full extent by the disclosure of the My Lai massacre—came first as a shock but quickly became an excuse.

Within days of the news breaking in November 1969, the London *Times* correspondent reported from Washington:

there has been remarkably little reaction, either from the Congress or from anyone else. Congressional sources say . . . that senators have not reacted in public to the reports since they are not really so unexpected. People have known for a long time that Vietnam was an especially nasty war and that there have been plenty of incidents of brutality involving the American army. One more is merely one more.

What prevented My Lai from being shrugged off as "merely one more" incident was the peculiarly dramatic way in which the news of the massacre reached the public. At first, Seymour Hersh's dispatches which broke the story caused more sensation abroad than in America itself. But they were followed by the appearance on prime time television of former GIs who gave harrowing accounts of their part in the massacre, and then the publication, first in the *Cleveland Plain Dealer* and then in *Life* magazine, of the truly atrocious color photographs taken by an army stills cameraman who had accompanied Charlie Company's attack on the village. Faced with the graphic and grisly accumulation of evidence, horrible and incontrovertible as it was, there was public outrage, shame, remorse, and a fit of national self-examination. There was talk of "moral disaster." "There is a sickness in the land over the My Lai massacre," wrote one columnist. It was at this point, only in response to a public outcry, that the White House chose to announce that the slaughter was "abhorrent to the conscience of all American people," and Richard Nixon made a pledge that those responsible would be brought to justice. The violent public reaction had been unexpected. The Washington correspondent of the New York *Daily News* wrote: "Above all, there is tangibly evident in the nation's capital the recognition by the politicians that the impact on the public of My Lai cannot be reduced *through the usual political devices for diverting the interests of people*" (our italics). Washington need not have worried. Only weeks later, a *Time* magazine poll showed that 65 percent of Americans thought that incidents like My Lai were "bound to happen in war." By the time of Lt. Calley's trial, in 1970, the balsamic attraction of this argument had done much to persuade most Americans that it was wrong to prosecute American soldiers for "doing their duty."

For the US Army, however, the "war is hell" argument carried dangers. Soldiers march off to war to become heroes, not to become murderers. While increased public awareness of the perils of their day-to-day work might in some circumstances flatter the military, the Army could obviously not allow the idea to go unchallenged that their day-to-day activities involved massacre—even in the most brutal of wars. My Lai was a disaster for the Army. "Your dismay could be no greater than mine," Army Secretary Resor told the press. "It is an appalling story."

In the Army's view, My Lai was not an inevitable outcome of the war—but an aberration. "What occurred at My Lai," Resor went on in a review of what he termed the "tragic events," "is wholly unrepresentative of the manner in which our forces conduct military operations in Vietnam . . . Our men operate under detailed directives which prohibit in unambiguous terms the killing of civilian noncombatants under circumstances such as those of My Lai." The clear aim here was to isolate the My Lai "incident" from the war as a whole, and strangely, although it seems exactly opposite to the "war is hell" argument, the end result is remarkably similar. The Army itself was unimpeachable. There was no need to look for an explanation in the way this particular war was being run. Charlie Company was a rogue outfit, a freak unit, whose conduct was outside the scope of acceptable military behavior. Calley was an inadequate soldier who in normal circumstances would never have been made an officer. If Charlie Company were uniquely to blame, it was unreasonable to blame anyone else up the chain of command, or any strategy, or any policy.

However, not everyone agreed. George McGovern, the antiwar Senator of South Dakota, declared: "We put these men in a situation where it was inevitable that sooner or later events of this kind would take place." Richard Falk, professor of international law at Princeton, argued that My Lai was the culmination of the sorts of policy that were being pursued: "It was perhaps an exaggeration and an extreme case, but not discontinuous with the way war was being waged and the climate that was created in the minds of the soldiers as to what was permissible and what was not permissible."

The journalist Jonathan Schell, who had reported from Quang

Ngai Province, where My Lai was situated, in the months before the massacre, wrote: "there can be no doubt that such an atrocity was possible only because a number of other methods of killing civilians and destroying their villages had come to be the rule, and not the exception, in our conduct of the war."

In reports published even before the massacre, and nearly two years before the massacre was made public, Schell had revealed that 70 percent of villages in Quang Ngai had been destroyed by aerial bombardment or artillery fire. The military were "already fighting a war completely different from the war that our policy-makers told the American people they were fighting." For Schell, and others who thought like him, "war" was not to blame; nor, except in the most obvious way, were the men of Charlie Company. What was to blame was the *particular* way this *particular* war was being fought. Clearly this was as irreconcilable with the posture of the Army as the view of the soldier of the Americal Division who told *Time* magazine: "The people back in the world don't understand this war. We are here to kill dinks. How can they convict Calley for killing dinks? That's our job." According to this view, My Lai was not an aberration of the war, but its apotheosis.

In warfare, it is a mistake to think that morality stands still. Thinking about the ethics of war shifts frequently to accommodate technological change. At the beginning of World War I, submarine warfare was considered cowardly and inhuman. At the start of World War II, both sides agreed not to bomb civilians. In both cases the sphere of the permissible widened to accommodate the realities of the conflict. After Vietnam, some attempt was made to incorporate the wholesale slaughter of civilians within a more agreeable perspective.

In *Why We Were in Vietnam* published in 1982, Norman Podhoretz acknowledged that the lavish use of firepower by the United States in Vietnam undoubtedly caused destruction of property and civilian casualties. "The American way of war," he wrote, ". . . was based on the motto 'Expend Shells Not Men.' Was it immoral of American commanders to follow this rule?" Such an idea, wrote Podhoretz, was "bizarre." The Viet Cong themselves killed many civilians and their tactics of "clutching the people to their breast," disguising themselves as civilians, fortifying villages, and using "villagers of all ages and both sexes—little children, women, old men" to plant mines and booby traps resulted in the deaths of many more. Besides, he reminds his readers, civilian casualties in Vietnam, counted as a proportion of total numbers killed, were no greater than in many other armed conflicts of this century, and far less than in the Korean War. In fact, the civilian population of South Vietnam actually increased during the war. Podhoretz is bothered that what had passed unremarked in World War II or Korea caused so much public consternation in Vietnam. To believe that the Vietnam War was more brutal than past wars was, in his opinion, to indulge in an "absurdly unhistorical view."

In a similar vein, General Fred C. Weyand, whose troops had defended Saigon during the Tet Offensive and who later became Army Chief of Staff, later advocated that future wars demanded not so much a change in American tactics as a change in American attitudes:

The American way of war is particularly violent, deadly and dreadful. We believe in using "things"—artillery, bombs, massive firepower—in order to conserve our soldiers' lives. The enemy, on the other hand, made up for his lack of "things" by expending men instead of machines, and he suffered enormous casualties. The army saw this happen in Korea, and we should have made the realities of war obvious to the American people before they witnessed it on their television screens. The army must make the price of involvement clear *before* we get involved.

But while apologists rationalize the immense firepower, with its inevitable implications for civilians, they do not attempt to justify what happened at My Lai. Podhoretz, for instance, had no hesitation in calling My Lai a "massacre" and an "atrocity." It "was justified by no military necessity," was "carried out against unresisting and unarmed persons," and "the executions ... therefore constituted acts of murder." It is difficult to avoid the conclusion that the indiscriminate killing of civilians by aerial and artillery bombardment is to be placed outside moral consideration because in the conditions of modern warfare it has become inevitable and necessary. This license, however, is not to be extended to the soldiers on the ground who are most at risk. The distasteful irony is that in Vietnam it was impossible for the people who controlled the "things" that constituted the "American way of war" to discriminate between the Viet Cong and civilians and in practice there was very little pressure on them to do so. Instead, the onus of discrimination, of restraint, ultimately of humanity, devolved upon the "common grunt."

Wars are not fought by jurists—they are fought by boys. The average age of an infantryman in Vietnam was 20. Most were away from home for the first time. They were adrift in a lethal environment experiencing horrors that those who were not there can hardly imagine. Was it realistic to expect these combat troops to make moral choices?

There is little in past history to suggest that decent, humane behavior can be taken for granted in combat situations. Shakespeare and his contemporaries understood this:

> What rein can hold licentious wickedness
> When down the hill he holds his first career?
> We may as bootless spend our vain command
> Upon the enraged soldiers in their spoil,
> And send precepts to the Leviathan
> To come ashore.
>
> (*Henry V*, III, 3)

Enraged soldiers. Vain commands. Army Secretary Resor had insisted that Americans operated "under detailed directives which prohibit in unambiguous terms the killing of civilian noncombatants." It is true that at any one time in Vietnam there were mountains of such "detailed directives." An Army survey showed no fewer than fourteen were "in effect and available" to US troops throughout Vietnam at the time of the My Lai "incident." Telford Taylor, the former chief prosecutor at the Nuremberg trials, found these rules of engagement to be "virtually impeccable." But these directives merely displayed the good intentions of those departments of the Army responsible for good intentions. There is little evidence that they were widely disseminated to troops at combat level, or that strenuous efforts were made to see that they were implemented. There is, on the other hand, abundant evidence to suggest that the rules of engagement, in which Resor and the

Army command put so much faith, were flouted or simply ignored. GIs didn't need directives to find out how the Army treated the Vietnamese: they only had to look around. If the higher command did not see what was going on, it was because they didn't want to. When doctors and nurses, serving in voluntary hospitals in Quang Ngai City heard that American troops had slaughtered around five hundred people in the nearby village of My Lai, they were shocked, but not surprised. If all the "detailed directives" had any real meaning, why weren't they surprised?

Again, one of the great unexplained questions of the massacre at My Lai is whether the men of Charlie Company were actually ordered to kill everyone in the village. The company commander has always denied giving his men such an odious instruction. Opinion among the men is divided. Many remember hearing the order clearly and explicitly. Others think that the instruction to kill everyone, including "the old men, women, and children," was unspoken, only implied. It is an argument that will probably never be settled, but it begs an important question. What had happened to lead the vast majority of men in Charlie Company to believe that the slaughter of a whole village could even be considered by American officers? Why weren't *they* surprised?

There was blindness or disingenuousness in the command's stubborn refusal to see what was really happening in the combat zones. Perhaps it was inevitable. The generals spoke with two voices: they demanded aggression and restraint; high kill ratios and fine courtesies; victory and respectability. Into one side of the equation they poured billions of dollars; into the other, hot air. "We are here to kill dinks" had a clearer ring about it for many soldiers in Vietnam than the wish lists issued by the Army command. In the real war—in the jungles and paddy fields—the latter meant little or nothing. They were vain commands—"precepts to the Leviathan."

Throughout the crisis provoked by My Lai, the Army used its directives as a shield to protect its honor and the reputation of the senior officers involved. During the course of the trials and inquiries it successfully prevented any examination of the relationship between My Lai, such established tactical concepts as search and destroy, body count, or free fire zones, and the behavior of Charlie

Company. To do otherwise was to take a line of reasoning that took responsibility for the massacre far up the chain of command. But to trace My Lai back to the psychology of a single inadequate officer, or to the delinquency of some of his men, was simply perverse. Philip Caputo, a marine lieutenant, was only a more articulate witness among the many fighting men who saw that there was something more than the absolute savagery in which the war was fought that prompted many American fighting men—"the good solid kids from Iowa farms," he calls them—to kill civilians and prisoners:

General Westmoreland's strategy of attrition also had an important effect on our behavior. Our mission was not to win terrain or seize positions, but simply to kill: to kill Communists and kill as many of them as possible. Stack 'em up like cordwood. Victory was a high body count, defeat a low kill ratio, war a matter of arithmetic. The pressure on unit commanders to produce enemy corpses was intense, and they in turn communicated it to their troops . . . It is not surprising, therefore, that some men acquired a contempt for human life and a predilection for taking it.

Yet even accepting that policy played its part in the massacre, policy alone cannot provide a full explanation. Not all American soldiers became brutalized. Not every company on a search and destroy mission murdered all the villagers they encountered. The culture of war did not *compel* troops to commit atrocities, it created circumstances in which atrocity was possible, maybe probable, but not inevitable. The culture of the Vietnam War created opportunities. How they were used depended on who was involved. Which soldiers became brutalized, which companies went on to massacre villagers, cannot be explained by tactics or policy alone. What marked out Charlie Company and made it capable, if not of a unique atrocity, of an atrocity on such a scale, and in such a manner?

When you're in an infantry company, in an isolated environment like this, the rules of that company are foremost. They're the things that really count. The laws back home don't make any difference. What people think of you back home don't matter. What matters is what people here and now think about what you're doing. What matters is how the people around you are going to see you. Killing a bunch of civilians in this way—babies, women, old men, people who were unarmed, helpless—was wrong. Every American would know that. And yet this company sitting out here isolated in this one place didn't see it that way. I'm sure they didn't. This group of people was all that mattered. It was the whole world. What they thought was right was right. And what they thought was wrong was wrong. The definitions for things were turned around. Courage was seen as stupidity. Cowardice was cunning and wariness, and cruelty and brutality were seen sometimes as heroic. That's what it eventually turned into.

That, in 1988, was how Charlie Company's regression into barbarism was described by Michael Bernhardt. In 1968, Bernhardt had been a "tunnel rat" at My Lai, but he had joined the company late and had an ambivalent attitude toward the unit. They were his buddies, but he was always an outsider. He understood, but did not share, the mentality that drove the company toward massacre.

Bernhardt did not kill anyone at My Lai. There were others too who refused to follow orders, or what they thought were their orders, and were not carried away in the frenzied bloodletting that the assault on the village became.

Harry Stanley refused a direct order to kill women and children huddled together in a crater. "We had orders, but the orders we had was that we were going into an enemy village and that they was well armed. I didn't find that when I got there. And ordering me to shoot down innocent people, that's not an order—that's craziness to me, you know. And so I don't feel like I have to obey that."

Despite the brutalizing war, despite the horrendous experiences the men of Charlie Company had shared together, for each and every soldier there was a moral choice at My Lai. The men who refused to take part in the massacre were those who recognized the choice that they were being asked to make. But most men didn't. What had happened to them since they had come to Vietnam had led most of Charlie Company to forget what Bernhardt had said "every American would know"—that killing babies, women, and old men was wrong. And during the time this elementary humanitarian formula was on hold, they committed an atrocity from which there was no way back.

Ronald Ridenhour is a Vietnam veteran who knew many of the men in Charlie Company and who twenty years ago was responsible for revealing the My Lai massacre to the world. Today, he thinks the lessons have been misunderstood. He feels great disappointment but no anger toward the men who made the wrong choice, believing that the real fault lay elsewhere, with a system in which only the extraordinary few could conduct themselves in a moral fashion:

We were kids, 18, 19 years old. I was 21 years old at the time. I was one of the oldest people around there among the common grunts.

Most of them [Charlie Company] had never been away from home before they went into the service. And they end up in Vietnam, many of them because they thought they were going to do something courageous on behalf of their country. Here are these guys who had gone in and in a moment, in a moment, following orders, in a context in which they'd been trained, prepared to follow orders, they do what they're told, and they shouldn't have, and they look back a day later and realize they probably made the biggest mistake of their lives. [There were] only an extraordinary few people who were in those circumstances who had the presence of mind and the strength of their own character that would see them through. Most people didn't. And for most of them—people that I personally just was stunned to discover had made the wrong choice they did—they had to live with it. They have to live with it. And so do I. So do we all.

No phrase tolled more clearly through the dark debate that followed the exposure of the My Lai massacre than the cry uttered by the GI's mother who told the press: "I gave them a good boy, and they made him a murderer."

America grieved for itself and for its own. My Lai focused the nation's regret on what the war had done to its boys, almost to the exclusion of what its boys had done to the Vietnamese. Jonathan Schell picked up the public mood in an article published in the *New Yorker* on December 20, 1969: "When others committed them, we looked on the atrocities through the eyes of the victims. Now we find ourselves, almost against our will, looking through the eyes of the perpetrators." No one need find this surprising. It is an exceptional victim who gets more column inches than his murderer. As victims, the Vietnamese were not exceptional. They were more a statistical, abstract concept—an aggregate—than people of flesh and blood. It may not seem too surprising that Calley's psychiatric report showed that he felt not as if he were killing humans but "rather that they were animals with whom one could not speak or reason." Yet when Calley was first charged even the indictment spoke of "Oriental human beings"—not people. Calley's final speech to his trial, self-serving and no doubt carefully prepared, still appealed to the idea that at the time it had been reasonable to assume that the victims at My Lai were somehow less than real humans:

When my troops were getting massacred and mauled by an enemy I couldn't see, I couldn't feel and I couldn't touch, nobody in the military system ever described them as anything other than Communism. They didn't give it a race, they didn't give it a sex, they didn't give it an age. They never let me believe it was just a philosophy in a man's mind that was my enemy out there.

The attitude of the company as a whole was little different. To the troops of Charlie Company, to American troops in general, all Vietnamese were "gooks," "dinks," "dopes," and "slopes." Soldiers who could not find the Vietnamese who were their enemies soon struck out wildly at the Vietnamese who were supposed to be their friends. "How can you tell the enemy?" Varnado Simpson said. "They all look the same." To which another My Lai veteran added: "In the end everyone in that country was the enemy."

In all wars, it is common for the enemy to be dehumanized, but in Vietnam, American soldiers also dehumanized their allies. Charlie Company had not been in Vietnam long before the pattern of brutality leading to My Lai began. Their own losses and injuries hastened the process. Hatred, fear, racism, and revenge turned to beatings, torture, rape, murder. All these offenses were committed with impunity by individuals and groups from Charlie Company in the weeks before the massacre. Finally, at My Lai, they discovered that having dehumanized the Vietnamese, they had dehumanized themselves.

Today, back in the United States, they live with the knowledge of what they did in different ways, remembering or forgetting. Calley, in his jewelry store, has become a "valued member of his community." Varnado Simpson, in his barricaded home in Jackson, is "totally incapacitated for any type of employment." It is his tragedy that the Vietnamese only became people for him after he murdered them. It is as people that they come back to haunt him today.

Today in My Lai, a new village has grown up around the handful of survivors of the massacre. The rice fields, flooded by salt water during the war, have been reclaimed, and with the resumption of the rice harvest, life has returned to the village. Bamboo trees sway and creak above the rebuilt homes. New wells have been dug to replace those destroyed and poisoned by the Americans. Along the paths between the paddy fields, children pull lumbering water buffalo and tiny women carry impossibly heavy loads suspended in baskets at the end of long poles. Nearby on the estuary of the Diem Diem River on the coast of the South China Sea, fishermen sail out in sampans and canoes, while on the shore women and girls spin rope made from the tough hair stripped from the husks of coconuts. Idyllic pictures but hard lives. Village leaders look forward hopefully to a time when life will be easier. They point with pride to the new village school, and when morning lessons finish, the cries and laughter of children fill the air. It is difficult to believe that the massacre ever took place.

People who remember the old village stare in amazement at an American map of it, pointing out the fields to the west of the village where the American helicopters landed and the homes where their families and neighbors were slaughtered in 1968. Here and there dark granite blocks mark the places where groups of villagers were brought for execution and mown down. At the eastern side of the village, a small museum and a heavily stylized war memorial commemorate the dreadful circumstances in which My Lai became a "hero village." The memorial is the tallest structure in the village: a solid white figure, carved out in the Soviet fashion, unbowed in adversity, a clenched fist raised defiantly toward the sky. Heroic, certainly. Yet like all officially sanctioned memorials, you can't help feeling that it is missing the point.

Truong Thi Le is old now and lives alone. During the massacre she lost nine members of her family including her father and a brother. She herself survived by hiding in a paddy field until long after the shooting had finished. She says:

I think of it all the time, and that is why I am old before my time. I remember it all the time. I think about it and I can't sleep. I'm all alone and life is hard and there's no one I can turn to for help. Then I think of it all the time. I'm always sad and unhappy and that's why I'm old.

I think of my daughter and my mother, both of them dead. I think of it and I feel extremely bad.

I won't forgive. I hate them very much. I won't forgive them as long as I live. Think of those children, that small . . . those children still at their mothers' breasts being killed . . . I hate them very much . . .

I miss my mother, my sister, my children. I think of them lying dead. I think of it and feel my insides being cut to pieces.

The massacre at My Lai and its subsequent coverup stand in the history of the Vietnam War at the point where deception and self-deception converged. If the Tet Offensive of 1968 had mocked America's complacent expectation of an imminent victory, My Lai's exposure late in 1969 poisoned the idea that the war was a moral enterprise. The implications were too clear to escape. The parallels with other infamous massacres were too telling and too painful. My Lai had been on the same scale as the World War II atrocities at Oradour in France, and Lidice in Czechoslovakia, outrages which had helped diabolize the Nazis. Reports now suggested that, if anything, the behavior of the American troops had been even worse. Americans, who at Nuremberg had played a great part in creating the judicial machinery which had brought the Nazi monsters to book, now had to deal with a monstrosity of their own making. "If we learn to accept this, there is nothing we will not accept," Jonathan Schell wrote in December 1968.

How America learned to accept My Lai; how Calley became a hero; how in spite of enormous piles of evidence, and in the face of clear and specific recommendations from the official inquiry set up to look into the massacre, no one, other than Calley, was ever convicted of committing a crime at My Lai—this, in part, is the story told in this book. Here also is an attempt to explain why Charlie Company—a particular group of young Americans operating in a particular place at a particular moment—came to believe that it was their task to wipe out an entire village. And finally, here is a record of the consequences of that task, both for the men of Charlie Company and for their victims—consequences that continue to the present day.

Much of what follows makes disturbing reading. We have sought to follow the advice of the American judge Irving Younger, who said: "The first task of free men is to call all things by their right names." We have tried also to follow the example of another American jurist, Telford Taylor, who told the War Crimes Tribunal at Nuremberg: "The mere punishment of the defenders . . . can never redress the terrible injuries which the Nazis visited on those unfortunate peoples. For them, it is far more important that these incredible events be established by clear public proof so that no one can ever doubt that they were fact and not fable."

This is not a book against war as such, but against the forces that continue to deny the true nature of war. It is a plea for telling things as they are, instead of as we would hope them to be. It is written in the belief that, when the peoples of democracies send their children off to war, they should have a realistic idea of what war is, unclouded by euphemisms and fine phrases. They should know what they are sending their young men and women into. It is written to show soldiers that, as well as physical danger, there are moral traps in war that must be safeguarded against. It is written in the hope, probably forlorn, that there will be no more mothers who will say: "I gave them a good boy, and they made him a murderer."

2. The War

By the time Charlie Company arrived in Vietnam in December 1967, the pattern of the war had already been set. American advisors had been fighting alongside South Vietnamese government troops since 1962. Combat troops had been sent in by President Johnson in 1965. The war had taken on a hard-nosed character of its own. It was getting bloodier. Both sides were throwing more men and resources into a conflict that both sides still expected to win. But no one thought anymore that a decision would come quickly. It was beginning to look like years.

The men of Charlie Company were being sent into Vietnam to do the job of men they were replacing. After their year's tour of duty, those who survived would go home to be replaced by other Americans who would do the same job. The war was becoming a treadmill.

At about this time, General William C. Westmoreland, commander of American toops in Vietnam, was in Washington, DC, giving a reassuring speech to the National Press Club: "With 1968, a new phase is starting," he said. "We have reached an important point where the end comes into view." In the Pentagon, meanwhile, other analysts were taking a more sober view.

Since taking command of the Vietnamese operation, Gen. Westmoreland had overseen the creation on Vietnamese soil of one of the greatest armed expeditionary forces in history. An American military presence, which by late 1967 numbered nearly half a million men, was underpinned by a colossal infrastructure which had transformed South Vietnam. The United States was spending $2 billion every month on the war.

Six thousand miles from mainland America, US engineers had built a road network, deep-water ports, eight major airfields, and ninety other airstrips. More than forty ice cream plants were constructed to "provide ice cream as far forward as possible." A million tons of supplies were being delivered every month—an average of 100 pounds a day for every American in the country.

The war now reached into every corner of Vietnam. The marines alone mounted 1,200 patrols every day. During one operation, Ranch Hand, 4 million gallons of herbicide and defoliant were spilled over the countryside—this was said to be more than four times the annual capacity of all American chemical companies put together. "We seem to be proceeding," wrote one unimpressed critic in the Pentagon, "on the assumption that the way to eradicate the Viet Cong is to destroy all the village structures, defoliate all the jungles, and cover the entire surface of Vietnam with asphalt."

Two years earlier, American officers had confidently predicted that the Viet Cong would quickly succumb "when they see our first team." But far from being overawed, the Viet Cong every day demonstrated their ability to strike targets anywhere in the country. In response, Westmoreland returned again and again to Washington for more money, more men, more weapons. Until late 1967, these requests had largely been met. Yet the only observable result of the extra American commitment was, in the dry assessment of a Pentagon analyst, "to escalate the military stalemate."

By the end of 1967, any analysis of the military situation had become extremely thought-provoking. Fifteen thousand American troops had been killed in the previous two years. A further 60,000 had been wounded. Enemy casualties were said to be four times higher. Millions of Vietnamese had become homeless and one American estimate put civilian casualties at 30,000 a year. America was locked into a land war in Asia which seemed to have no end in sight. Meanwhile, every night on television, the world watched the richest and most powerful nation on earth turn the most advanced weapons in history on an enemy which, with the important exception of bicycles, had hardly a single wheeled or tracked vehicle in the whole of South Vietnam. This was not what the people of America had come to expect from a war.

In 1945, America had emerged from World War II with a powerful model of what a good war should be. The evil of Nazism and the barbarity of Japanese imperialism had been overcome.

Alone among the Allies, America had not been bombed or invaded. Instead America had ended the conflict richer and with an improved standard of living. Good had fought evil and the right side won. A war which had left the United States with prosperity, global ascendancy, and a firm grip on the moral high ground was a hard war to follow. Of course, the unparalleled victory had been won at a price, although, in victory, few stopped to contemplate what had been sacrificed during the racial savagery of the Pacific War or the carnage of the Falaise gap. A war which had climaxed with GIs feted as they liberated the capitals of Europe, and with the unforgettable rapture of the victory parades, was immortalized in movies as yet another step toward America's manifest destiny. A glow of self-satisfaction, undimmed by the more problematic outcome of the Korean War, had left the country entirely unprepared for what was to come in Vietnam.

The first reports from Vietnam drew heavily from this deep well of patriotic pride. President Johnson himself evoked the great crusade when committing combat troops in 1965: "Nor would surrender in Vietnam bring peace," he told the nation, "because we learned from Hitler at Munich that success only feeds the appetite of aggression . . . we have learned the lesson of history."

The following year in Honolulu, Johnson once again returned to this stirring theme:

In the forties and fifties, we took our stand in Europe to protect the freedom of those threatened by aggression . . . Now the center of attention has shifted to another part of the world where aggression is on the march and the enslavement of free men is the goal . . . That is why it is vitally important to every American family that we stop the communists in South Vietnam.

At the height of the cold war, in the years after the Berlin Wall and the Cuban missile crisis, this was a very powerful picture of events. So long as good was on the march against evil again, all was well with the war. It made good copy too. The US Army command in Vietnam greatly approved of stories which compared their operations with Omaha Beach or Iwo Jima. The World War II pedigree of Army units was often mentioned in dispatches. It was noted, for example, that the Americal Division to which

Charlie Company was attached was the first American fighting
unit to go on the offensive in the Pacific War. All this helped to
emphasize continuity of purpose and perpetuate the image of the
American fighting man as a kind of muscular crusader in the war
against evil or communism. At the time, there seemed little difference between the two.

Yet Vietnam never even remotely rivaled World War II as a
great American event. It was always too complicated and difficult.
For years it was a pesky, outlandish little war, a sideshow. Then,
when the crisis came, it revealed itself as a dirty, inglorious affair;
a war without grandeur, and without victories. By the time Charlie
Company arrived, the war had already become unhitched from the
great winning tradition of American arms. By early 1968, after the
Tet Offensive, comparisons with the war against the Nazis disappeared altogether from American television. "It was funny," said
Fred Widmer, a former radio operator with Charlie Company.
"You always had this picture of World War II in the back of your
mind—and that's not the way it really was."

Despite Johnson's high-flown rhetoric, the decision to commit
American troops was taken as a last resort—only after it had
become clear that American dollars alone would not work. In the
1950s, the United States had paid for the French war against Ho
Chi Minh's communists, and the French had lost—disastrously—at
Dien Bien Phu. In the early 1960s, Kennedy had bankrolled the
South Vietnamese to fight their own communists. But the Saigon
government fared no better than the French. Indeed, a perverse and
mystifying rule seemed to apply: the more aid to Saigon, the
stronger the communists became.

From 1961 to 1965, the South Vietnamese, under the tutelage of
their American advisors, put together a simulacrum of the American
way of war. The South Vietnamese Air Force, equipped with
American planes (often flown by American pilots), strafed and
bombed villages with American napalm. *Search and destroy, body
count, kill ratio, air strikes*, most of the concepts which were to be
at the heart of the American war were in place in fact, if not in
name, long before the arrival of the American troops.

But superpower tactics did nothing to impede the advance of the
communists. On the contrary, Saigon's wanton campaigns in the

countryside proved a powerful stimulus to guerrilla recruiting. Over three-quarters of Vietnam's population lived in the villages and their support in the war was vital. Yet government troops treated their peasantry like "an occupied population." Property was looted, women raped, and captives subjected to the most sadistic tortures during interrogation. The Viet Cong meanwhile grew in numbers and confidence and learned how to deal with the tactical innovations of the American advisors. In spite of millions of dollars of US military aid, and the presence of thousands of US military advisors, the Viet Cong had grown steadily stronger.

By 1965, South Vietnam was on the point of collapse. The communist insurgents exercised wide control throughout most of rural Vietnam. There were provinces, such as Quang Ngai, in which only the provincial capital was considered safe for government troops. In some rural areas Viet Cong patrols were the only military units the peasants had ever seen.

In November of 1964, a guerrilla attack on Bien Hoa airport, 20 miles northeast of Saigon, destroyed twenty-seven US planes. The following January, the ARVN (South Vietnamese Army) lost two hundred men in an ambush within miles of Saigon. At Ba Gia in Quang Ngai Province an entire 500-man battalion of government troops was wiped out. Only sixty-five men and five US advisors escaped. When American intelligence reported that Saigon was on the point of abandoning the five northern provinces altogether, President Johnson felt that he had no alternative but to follow the advice of his generals. The generals did not doubt that the American way of war would eventually prevail, so long as Americans waged that war.

With hindsight, it is easy to trace the origins of the catastrophe to the period before 1965. But at the time, those who opposed the official line, like military advisor John Paul Vann, the subject of Neil Sheehan's magisterial biography, *A Bright and Shining Lie*, were squeezed out, their insight and experience counting for nothing.

"This is a political war," Vann told anyone who would listen, "and it calls for discrimination in killing."

Despite his low opinion of Saigon's troops, Vann had no illusions that American forces would do any better—or kill with greater discrimination. If the South Vietnamese had trouble telling the difference between friend and foe in the villages, he argued, GIs would soon start to see the whole rural population as the enemy. "We'd end up shooting at everything—men, women, kids, and buffalo." And so it came to pass. On March 8, 1965, Johnson sent in "the first team": the first American combat troops landed in Vietnam.

American troops arrived in Vietnam looking for the kind of war they knew all about—a war of decisive battles and quick victories. Commanders constantly urged their forces to engage with the enemy, to force him to stand up and fight. The Americans could invest unlimited resources into this kind of warfare which—in its purest form—allowed American commanders the chance to concentrate their overwhelmingly powerful weapons on a lightly armed opponent who could not fight back.

But the Americans had misjudged the situation. They seriously underestimated the extent of opposition to the Saigon government and did not fully appreciate the character of a war which one general would later describe as "a devilishly clever mixture of conventional warfare fought somewhat unconventionally and guerrilla warfare fought in the classical manner." What they faced was, in fact, two armies fighting two very different kinds of war: the NVA, the North Vietnamese Army, which first threatened in frontier regions and the demilitarized zone (DMZ); and the National Liberation Front (NLF), composed of irregular units fighting a guerrilla war in the countryside. Guerrillas saw no obvious reason why they should satisfy the American appetite for conventional warfare. They were experienced fighters who would only stand and fight on their own terms, and instead of offering the Americans pitched battles, they relied on hit-and-run tactics, surprise attacks, and small swift engagements after which they would withdraw before their enemies could deploy their formidable firepower.

A guerrilla war presented a special peril to the US Army because its raison d'être was to stand the conventional art of warfare on its head. The set-piece battles so earnestly sought by the Americans played no part. Instead the guerrillas had their own measure of success which depended on how much they could harass their enemy, force him to disperse his strength, demoralize him, and finally sap his will to continue. These are tactics that have been employed throughout the ages by Lilliputians seeking to destroy those more powerful than themselves. They have seldom been more vividly described than by an obscure nineteenth-century Fenian, Fintan Lalor, who gave this advice to his Irish compatriots about how to deal with the English army of Queen Victoria:

You must draw it out of position; break up its mass; break its trained line of march and manoeuvre—its equal step and seried array ... You must disorganize and untrain, and undiscipline your enemy, and not alone must you unsoldier—you must unofficer it also, nullify its tactics and strategy as well as its discipline; decompose the science and system of war, and resolve them into their first elements. You must make the hostile army a mob ... and oblige it to undertake operations for which it was never constructed.

A case study of what these tactics meant in practice, and just how successfully they were employed by the Viet Cong, can be seen in the destruction of Charlie Company's morale, described in what follows.

"When the enemy feels the danger of guerrillas," wrote Mao, the arch-philosopher of guerrilla warfare, "he will generally send troops out to attack them." How well Mao knew his enemy, and how poorly the Americans knew theirs. The problem facing the general wishing to defeat a guerrilla force backed by large-scale popular support is—where does he find them? In a conventional war, it is clear who are civilians and who are soldiers, but guerrillas wear no uniforms or insignia to differentiate themselves from noncombatants. In action, of course, they will carry weapons; when they withdraw, they become indistinguishable from the rest of the population. In military terms the guerrillas are hiding behind the screen of civilians. But the guerrillas see it differently. They say that their soldiers "came from the people. They were the children of the villages. The villagers loved them, protected them, fed them. They were the people's soldiers." How then can they be attacked without at the same time civilians being attacked? How should the

civilians be treated if they are hiding the guerrillas willingly? In
such a war, how is the line drawn between a civilian and an
enemy?

The aim of American strategy was simple—to kill Viet Cong in
such large numbers that they could not be replaced. But how was
this to be achieved without at the same time killing large numbers
of civilians? This was a problem to which no one on the American
side ever discovered a satisfactory answer. It was the biggest failure
of the war.

It was a failure magnified enormously by American strategic
thinking. For Westmoreland, Vietnam was a war of attrition, a
"meatgrinder" as they called it in the Pentagon. The object, he
explained, was to bleed the North, to waken in the communist
mind the notion that they were draining their population "to the
point of national disaster for generations to come." To achieve this
goal and to win in a war of attrition, Americans had to kill Viet
Cong fighters faster than the communists could replace them. As
befits a great industrial power, the war was to be fought on an
industrial scale. Westmoreland, like Patton before him, intended to
construct a killing machine so formidable as to be irresistible. Its
sheer size and power would pulverize the enemy into submission.
"You don't fight this fellow rifle to rifle," said an American
general in Vietnam. "You locate him and back away. Blow the hell
out of him and police up."

Yet while the use of overwhelming American firepower to crush
the Wehrmacht or the Japanese had simply seemed both effective
and justifiable, its deployment in Vietnam, where there was no
satisfactory means of distinguishing between warriors and civilians,
led inevitably to the loss of large numbers of civilian lives. Referring
to the bombing of North Vietnam in a memorandum to President
Johnson in May of 1967, Secretary of Defense McNamara wrote:
"The picture of the world's greatest superpower killing or seriously
injuring 1,000 noncombatants a week, while trying to pound a tiny
backward nation into submission on an issue whose merits are
hotly disputed, is not a pretty one." After World War II, no one
could seriously doubt that the strategic bombing of populated
areas would lead to great loss of life. The tragedy of Vietnam was
that this was happening in every arena of the war.

From the beginning of American involvement, it had become common practice for patrols to call for artillery or an air strike if they received even sniper fire from a village—irrespective of whether civilians also sheltered there. By the end of 1966, fighter bombers were making up to four hundred such sorties a day. Added to B-52 raids in the country, this meant that around 825 tons of bombs were delivered every day, a figure doubled by the tonnage of high explosive fired off by the artillery. "The solution in Vietnam," General DePuy told a visiting emissary from the Pentagon, "is more bombs, more shells, more napalm . . . till the other side cracks and gives up." And that's what they got. In 1967, an article in *Life* magazine claimed that the cost of killing a single Viet Cong guerrilla was $400,000, which included the cost of 75 bombs and 150 artillery shells. No nation in history had waged war with such little regard to expense. Only days before My Lai, Robert McNamara, the retiring Secretary of Defense, would remind an audience gathered to record his farewell from the Pentagon that more bombs had been dropped on Vietnam than on the whole of Europe during the whole of World War II. Costly in dollars, as McNamara had said elsewhere, but cheap in American lives.

But not Vietnamese lives. There was little to choose between the consequences of the American strategic bombing in the North and US military action in the South. Civilian casualties among the people of the South whom the Americans had come to Vietnam to protect rose from an estimated 100,000 a year in 1965 to 300,000 a year in 1968.

The logic of attrition meant that, in order to kill Viet Cong in large enough numbers, they first had to be found and flushed out of their safe havens in the countryside. "Search and destroy" was Westmoreland's tactical solution to this problem. The idea, outlined in the Pentagon Papers, was "to take the war to the enemy, denying him freedom of movement anywhere in the country . . . and deal him the heaviest possible blows." The search and destroy missions of the Vietnam War have had a bad press. In June 1969, before the revelations of the My Lai massacre, Westmoreland was already complaining that "bad publicity" and "misunderstanding" had "distorted the term in the public mind with aimless searches in the jungle and destruction of civilian property." The concept, he argued, was "designed to find and destroy (or neutral-ize) enemy forces and their base areas and supply caches. This was essentially the traditional attack mission of the infantry." Thus armed, Westmoreland told Washington that he expected that the war would be won in a little over two years—by the end of 1967.

"I never had the luxury of enough troops to maintain an American, Allied or ARVN presence everywhere all the time," Westmoreland wrote in his account of the war, *A Soldier Reports*.

Had I at my disposal virtually unlimited manpower, I could have stationed troops permanently in every district or province and thus provided an alternative strategy. That would have enabled the troops to get to know the people intimately, facilitating the task of identifying the subversives and protecting the others against intimidation. Yet to have done that would have required literally millions of men.

In opting for search and destroy Westmoreland was from the beginning ruling out "getting to know the people intimately." What this meant in practice was that the job of "identifying the subversives and protecting the others against intimidation" was left to raw GIs who were sent into the countryside armed with the most sophisticated weaponry, but with little more than a hunch about who the enemy was. How were they supposed to do this job? No one ever told the "common grunts." This is how Varnado Simpson, then a rifleman with Charlie Company, remembers patrol-ling in 1967–8: "How can you distinguish the enemy? How can you distinguish between the good and the bad? All of them looked the same. And that's why the war was so different. You know, it wasn't like the Germans over here or the Japanese over there. They all looked alike, North and the South. So how can you tell?"

Varnado Simpson was 19 years old when he went to Vietnam, just a little below the average age of US troops. As the war wore on, an increasing number of recruits had scored so low on standard-ized intelligence tests that they would have been excluded from the normal peacetime Army. The tour of duty in Vietnam was one year. Soldiers were most likely to die in the first month after they arrived, and the large majority of deaths took place in the first six months. Just as a soldier began gaining experience, he was sent home. A rookie army that constantly rotated inexperienced men was pitted against experienced guerrillas on their home ground. "How in the hell can you put people like that into a war?" asked Bruce Lawler, a CIA case officer in the north of South Vietnam. "How can you inject these type of guys into a situation that requires a tremendous amount of sophistication? You can't. What happens is they start shooting at anything that moves because they don't know. They're scared. I mean they're out there getting shot at, and Christ, there's somebody with eyes that are different from mine. And boom—it's gone."

"Until now," Westmoreland said in 1965,

the war has been characterized by a substantial majority of the population remaining neutral . . . In the past year we have seen an escalation to a higher level of intensity in the war. This will bring about a moment of decision for the peasant farmer. He will have to choose if he stays alive. Until now the peasant has had three alternatives: he could stay put and follow his natural instinct to stay close to the land, living beside the graves of his ancestors. He could move to an area under government control. Or he could join the VC. Now if he stays there are other dangers.

The peasant farmer soon came face to face with the "other dangers"—though whether he had much choice in the matter is open to doubt. Within weeks of the marines landing at Da Nang the area surrounding the air base became a "combat zone" whose population was persuaded to opt for "refugee status" in safe villages. These people were hesitant to move, the official US Marines history explains, "reluctant to give up their homes." The officer in charge of the operation solved the problem by dropping artillery near their villages for a few nights, "after which their attitude about relocation improved," he said. "I suppose given a free choice, they would not have left their hamlets," he admitted. It took "a hell of a lot of artillery." His commander commented: "The Marines are in the pacification business."

In August, a CBS TV report showed marines using Zippo lighters to set fire to the thatched roofs of houses in a village a few miles to the southwest of Da Nang. "The day's operation burned down 150 houses, wounded three women, killed one baby, wounded one marine and netted these four prisoners," Morely Safer told viewers in America. It was one of the first and, in the early years of the conflict, rare reports to focus on civilian casualties. The marines protested that the report was a one-sided version of a complex mission in which the marines had come under fire.

That autumn, the first big search and destroy operations took place as marines attempted to hunt down the Viet Cong regiment which had attacked the vast new American base at Chu Lai, 20 miles north of Quang Ngai City, closer to the Batangan Peninsula where the My Lai complex of villages was located. In September, marines taking part in Operation Pirana, the first big sweep of Batangan, described the peasants of the villages they passed through as aloof and making no friendly overtures. In most cases these operations made contact only with snipers and booby traps. The main body of Viet Cong had disappeared before the marines moved in.

The impact of American firepower on the people in the countryside was massive. In November, Neil Sheehan, then a journalist working for the *New York Times*, visited the area to find "one fishing village in Quang Ngai Province, on the central coast north of Saigon, in which at least 180 people—and possibly 600—had been killed during the previous two months by aircraft and Seventh Fleet destroyers. The five hamlets that composed that village, once a prosperous community of 15,000 people, had been reduced to rubble." The village had been razed because it was in a VC-controlled area and Sheehan was told of ten more similarly destroyed villages elsewhere.

Sheehan's report of this indiscriminate destruction was published in October 1966. In it Sheehan remarked that "the gun and the knife of the Vietcong assassin are, in contrast, far more selective ... It has been estimated that, over the past decade, about 20,000 persons have been assassinated by Communist terrorists. This is a gruesome total, but the annual average is a great deal lower than the probable yearly number of ordinary civilian victims of the war."

Rules of engagement were designed to limit the risk of civilian casualties. In theory, they were issued to every serviceman: in practice, they might as well have been written on water. Commanders were told that prestrikes and preparatory fire in civilian areas were forbidden. Careful planning and execution of airstrikes and the proper use of artillery, they were instructed, would minimize damage to the lives and property of noncombatants. "Troop indoctrination briefings" were ordered to be held before each operation to remind soldiers of the rules of engagement and their responsibilities toward civilians.

Every soldier was issued two pocket-sized cards, the "Nine Rules" and "The Enemy In Your Hands," which were to be carried at all times. Both were tabulations of almost chivalric exquisiteness. Rule three: Treat women with politeness and respect. Rule seven: Don't attract attention by loud, rude, or unusual behavior. "Treat the sick and wounded captive as best you can . . . he is a human being and must be treated like one. The soldier who ignores the sick and wounded degrades his uniform. The soldier shows his strength by his fairness, firmness and humanity to the persons in his hands."

A US Army survey drawn up in 1972 revealed that there were no fewer than fourteen MACV* directives concerning the prevention and reporting of war crimes available throughout all American units serving in Vietnam at the time of the My Lai massacre. The survey outlines the scores of directives issued by the military command in which avoidance of civilian casualties at all costs is emphasized in the strongest terms. The motivation behind this lavish bombardment of headquarters concern was a mixture of high principle, military necessity, and—public relations. "We must, like Caesar's wife, be above reproach," wrote Westmoreland in 1967. The following is typical of the Army's output:

The principle of the laws of nations, as they result from the usages established among civilized peoples, the laws of humanity, and the dictates of the public conscience obligate those who conduct military operations in populated areas to cause as few noncombatant casualties as possible . . . The rural and small town Vietnamese have suffered greatly with the ebb and flow of war through their fields and homes. This poorly educated, unsophisticated peasant understands little of the reasoning

* US Military Assistance Command Vietnam.

behind the actions of either the Viet Cong or the Government forces as they come and go; his only legacy is one of destruction or pilferage of his property or injury to his family and friends ... The Viet Cong will exploit fully any incidents of noncombatant casualties and destruction of property by Marines.

In addition to the real war, there was the war on paper. On paper, the war was being won; on paper, American troops made every effort to avoid civilian casualties. The Americans, of course, wanted to believe they were fighting a humane war. The sheer volume of these directives would afterward be used to show that the Army command had done everything within its power to prevent war crimes and unnecessary injury to noncombatants. But words are not deeds. In the paddy fields and villages, it was a very different war. Good deeds carried no rewards. Body count meant a lot more than the Geneva Conventions.

Body count—the number of Viet Cong killed—was what mattered most in Vietnam. Killing Viet Cong was what the "meatgrinder" had been designed for and was judged by. Pacification and "nation-building programs" always took second place. In a war that did not offer territory as a reward, body count became the index of success and failure in the whole war. Officers who did not achieve satisfactory body counts were replaced; units who performed well were rewarded with leave. The body count was the key statistic after each firefight and the pressure to produce high figures was enormous. "Our mission was not to win terrain or seize positions but simply to kill: to kill communists and kill as many of them as possible ... Victory was a high body count, defeat a low kill ratio, war a matter of arithmetic," observed Philip Caputo, a young infantry officer in Vietnam. It is hardly surprising that civilian casualties were often included as Viet Cong and there was always a marked discrepancy between the numbers reported killed and the numbers of enemy weapons recovered. A report which included a large number of noncombatant casualties would lead to questions. It would reflect badly on the whole unit and its command. Officers who made such reports were unpopular with the men and with their seniors; and soldiers who could not tell the difference between friend and enemy when they were alive had less incentive to be discriminating when they were dead. A popular expression reflected this: "If it's dead and Vietnamese, it's VC."

US troops met hostility with hostility, suspicion with suspicion. The word "gook"—a racial slur dating back to the Philippines War at the turn of the century and rediscovered during the Korean War—was resurrected once again to refer to all Vietnamese, regardless of what side they were on. Other expressions—"slope," "dink," "slant-eyes"—were commonplace. In combat zones, without clear guidelines on how to identify the Viet Cong, many GIs stopped trying.

In any case, in the combat zones, it was not just that GIs could not tell the difference between Viet Cong and innocent civilians. In many cases, they had ceased to believe in the existence of innocent civilians at all. The "common grunts," infantrymen at the sharp end of the search and destroy missions, found little by way of welcome in the villages and hamlets. Instead the villagers were "aloof," "hostile," or even "superior." The patrols meant heat, physical exhaustion, clouds of flies and mosquitoes, a growing sense of rage and frustration, and constant danger. "More of the same hot walking with mud sucking at our boots and the sun thudding against us from distant tree lines," wrote Philip Caputo, whose memoir, *A Rumor of War*, was intended to show "that war, by its nature, can arouse a psychopathic violence in men of seemingly normal impulses." Days of patrolling would usually end with no enemy contact, but a rising toll of casualties nevertheless. Deaths and injuries from booby traps, mines, and unseen snipers were four to five times higher than they had been in World War II and Korea. Booby traps "cut us down one by one," wrote Caputo of his experience in 1965, just as in 1968 mines and booby traps would rip the heart out of Charlie Company. GIs became convinced that the civilians in the villages hid knowledge of nearby ambushes and booby traps. There was a widespread belief that the Viet Cong used women and children to lay traps and throw grenades.

Fred Widmer of Charlie Company describes the situation as many combat troops saw it. "You couldn't pinpoint who exactly was the enemy," he recalled.

In the end anybody who was still in that country was the enemy. The same village you had gone in to give them medical treatment . . . you could go through that village later and get shot at on your way out by a sniper.

Go back in, you wouldn't find anybody. Nobody knew anything . . .
We were trying to work with these people, they were basically doing
a number on us. . . You didn't trust them anymore. You didn't trust
anybody.

Under the circumstances, what made many GIs decide to shoot
quickly was a dangerous mixture of hatred, fear, revenge, and an
infantryman's rule of thumb. Little was left of the politesse of the
"Nine Rules" or the decency of "The Enemy In Your Hands."
American operations became laced with a generalized racial fury
masked as an anticommunist crusade.

The irony was that many on the American side, including the
commanders of the first troops to be sent to the country, knew that
the ordinary civilian—and in Vietnam this meant the peasant—was
the key to the war. Injure him and you injured the war effort. "The
injury or killing of hapless civilians inevitably contributes to the
communist cause," General Lewis Walt, commander of the III
MAF, the Marine Amphibious Force, told his men shortly after
they arrived in the country, "and each incident of it will be used
against us with telling effect." A fellow commander, Lt. General
"Brute" Krulak, wrote to Robert McNamara in Washington to
explain that, though winning the hearts and minds of the
Vietnamese might take time, "the raw figure of VC killed . . . can
be a dubious index of success since, if their killing is accompanied
by devastation of friendly areas, we may end up having done more
harm than good."

This was a profound challenge to the whole idea of the war of
attrition. Stationed in South Vietnam's most northerly provinces,
where the Viet Cong exercised almost total control in the
countryside, the marines believed that the main task was to win
back the villages to the government's side. They believed that
effort should be concentrated where the people were, *not* where
they weren't. "The Vietnamese people are the prize," declared
Krulak. Attrition, he believed, would not pay off; it was the
enemy's game.

This represented the view of the entire marines senior command.
"Search and destroy means traversing the same terrain repeatedly
against a nebulous foe—while the people were untended,"

maintained General Greene, the Marine Corps commandant. Gen. Walt, who liked to claim that he had learned the fundamentals of fighting guerrillas from "men who had fought Sandino in Nicaragua or Charlemagne in Haiti," constantly stressed the need for pacification and backed it up by putting half the marines' effort into building secure villages free from Viet Cong control.

But Westmoreland was not interested. It was simply not the war he had come to fight. For him, pacification was best left for the South Vietnamese. American troops had come for quite a different purpose and in his opinion the marines weren't pulling their weight. In any case, Westmoreland could argue that the successes of the marines were patchy and their position in the villages was by no means strong. Pacification was one front too many. From 1966, winning hearts and minds took a back seat. Growing numbers of marines were siphoned off to counter the threat of large-scale North Vietnamese incursions in a process that would eventually lead to the nightmare siege of the Khe Sahn. The alternative strategy foundered under pressure of North Vietnamese attacks from the North and the relentless demands of the war of attrition. The hold of the Viet Cong on the countryside remained unbroken because, in the end, the people were vital to them and they courted popular support. All American attempts to put the people first failed because, in the end, the Americans put their faith in their firepower—and went to war with a blunderbuss.

Public opinion asks fewer questions of winning armies. Morely Safer's CBS TV report on the torching of Cam Ne in August 1965 had caused shock and dismay. But the reaction was short-lived. Until the second half of 1967, American press and TV coverage still largely supported the war. Nevertheless, concern was growing about civilian casualties. Neil Sheehan's alarming report from Quang Ngai Province of the wholesale destruction of Vietnamese villages was published in October; and in December, Harrison Salisbury reported from Hanoi on the huge numbers of civilian casualties caused by the bombing of North Vietnam. Martha Gellhorn's articles, written in mid-1966, were deemed too tough for American newspapers and were published in the London *Guardian*. "We are not maniacs and monsters," she wrote, but our planes range the sky all day and night, and our artillery is lavish and we have much more deadly stuff to kill with. The people are there on the ground, sometimes destroyed by accident, sometimes destroyed because the Viet Cong are reported to be among them. This is a new war . . . and we had better find a new way to fight it. Hearts and minds, after all, live in bodies.

As yet, these were voices offstage. Unsettling though they were, they did not have the power to change the course of the war. But those who did have that power were beginning to have second thoughts as well.

Throughout the summer of 1966, Secretary of Defense McNamara grew more disenchanted with the progress of the war. In August, a secret seminar of experts had confirmed his impression that Operation Rolling Thunder, the bombing of North Vietnam, was not working. By November, he was questioning the very basis of Westmoreland's strategy. He expressed the view that American attrition estimates substantially overstated the actual VC/NVA losses. "For example," he wrote in a letter to the President, "the VC/NVA apparently lose only one sixth as many weapons as people, *suggesting that possibly many of the killed are unarmed porters or by-standers*" (our italics).

In March 1967, Westmoreland's request for another 200,000 troops provoked more soul-searching. American casualties were running at a thousand a month and the consensus in Washington supporting the war was breaking down. "When we add divisions, can't the enemy add divisions, and if so, where does it all end?" President Johnson asked Westmoreland. He had no reply, for the truth was that the buildup of American forces in the past two years had been more than matched by the increase of Viet Cong and NVA units.

More damage was wrought upon the concept of the war of attrition by research which showed that the Viet Cong and NVA took the initiative in 85 percent of combat engagements. They started the shooting and had the element of surprise on their side. "Attrition is the enemy's game," Krulak had claimed, and it looked as if he had been right. If the Viet Cong were choosing when and how often to fight, they were the ones controlling the rate of attrition—not Westmoreland. "These results imply that the size of the force we deploy has little effect on the rate of attrition," was the dry comment of the analyst submitting these observations.

In 1946, at the outset of the war of independence from the French, Ho Chi Minh had said: "You would kill ten of my men and I would kill one of yours. But at that rate you would be unable to hold on and I would carry the day." The Pentagon was learning that this was more than an idle boast. Figures issued by the Office of Systems Analysis showed that, even with large additions to American forces, the North Vietnamese could carry on indefinitely.

Indefinitely was too long for American public opinion. The public was unaware of the growing doubts within the war cabinet, but in the Pentagon and the White House, policy makers knew that opinion outside was turning against the war. In May, McNamara received this despairing note from his deputy, John McNaughton:

A feeling is widely and strongly held that "the Establishment" is out of its mind. The feeling is that we are trying to impose some US image on distant peoples we cannot understand . . . and we are carrying the thing to absurd lengths. Related to this feeling is the increased polarization that is taking place in the United States with seeds of the worst split in our people for more than a century.

Opposition to the war was moving from the fringes of American society to the center. Establishment figures began to speak out. Eugene McCarthy's book, *The Limits of Power*, calling on the USA to get out of Vietnam, reached the bestseller lists. In *How to Get Out of Vietnam*, J. K. Galbraith described the war as "perhaps the worst miscalculation in our history."

Robert Kennedy's antiwar stand was winning him growing support. An opinion poll in October showed him ahead of President Johnson by twenty points. Another opinion poll in the same month revealed that 46 percent of the public thought the war to be a mistake; only 44 percent continued to back it. Fifty thousand demonstrators marched on the Pentagon. Right-wing car stickers read: "Win or Get Out." Left-wing students chanted: "Hey, hey, L.B.J., how many kids did you kill today?" *Time* magazine wrote in October: "Until recently most of the opposition has come from intellectuals and the young, from college professors and clerics. But now the ranks have been swelled by apolitical businessmen and

uneasy politicians eyeing the antiwar sentiment in the polls ...
Congress is in a rebellious mood."

Meanwhile, reports of the conflict from Vietnam grew more and
more harrowing. Prisoners were filmed being tortured; terrified
parents and children were seen clearly scared witless as their
communities were destroyed. The Army was becoming worried
about its image.

"There is increasing evidence," wrote Westmoreland in a
confidential letter to his deputy, General Bruce Palmer, on October
16, "that the war in Vietnam is being degraded by a growing
segment of the press and public at large." He demanded that any
activity "reflecting unfavorably on the military image" be eliminated. Among such activities he listed prostitution, excessive drinking, and violations of the Geneva Conventions and the Law of
Land Warfare. "The tensions of the forthcoming election year
will focus to a major extent on virtually every aspect of our effort
here," Westmoreland warned. However, he was not so concerned
about the military operations, thinking they would "speak for
themselves." They did.

A report from Jonathan Schell in the *New Yorker* revealed that
in the two years since 1965, 70 percent of all villages in Quang Ngai
Province had been wiped out. According to officials in this region,
40 percent of the population had passed through refugee camps.
American representatives working for the Agency for International
Development pleaded with the American military command to
stop generating refugees because they could no longer cope with
those already made homeless. In Quang Ngai City, hospital workers estimated that the civilian casualties in the province were running at 50,000 a year. "The Americans are destroying everything,"
one South Vietnamese captain told Schell. "If they get just one
shot from a village they destroy it." A government investigation
into this article reported: "Mr Schell's estimates are substantially
correct."

President Johnson's position was unenviable. Americans required
two things of the war: that they win and that they look good. As
1967 drew toward a close, dark shadows were falling over both of
these objectives. There was dissension in the administration, anger

in the streets, a presidential election the following year and rumors in Washington that the Secretary of Defense himself had turned against the war. Robert McNamara was indeed haunted by doubts. For a man whose pregovernment business life had been spent absorbing statistics, the balance sheets of the war didn't add up anymore. Throughout the autumn he called for restrictions on troop increases and a curb on the bombing. The military read the figures differently. Backed by powerful allies in the Senate, they accused McNamara of defeatism and called for more, not less. "Unskilled civilians," they argued, were preventing the "professional military experts" from doing their job and winning the war. Johnson had to choose, and, on the eve of election year, he went for optimism. In November, he dumped his Secretary of Defense.

The administration then launched the biggest public relations campaign of the war in an attempt to win back public confidence. The message was clear: We are making progress. In Saigon, Westmoreland and his staff briefed journalists, producing maps, charts, and graphs that demonstrated impressively that the war of attrition was working; the crossover point had been reached; two-thirds of the country was back inside government control; half of the enemy battalions were out of action.

In truth, the only triumph was of hope over experience; of the optimism of Westmoreland and the Chiefs of Staff over the gloom of McNamara and the Pentagon's Office of Systems Analysis. It was the apotheosis of the paper war, an exercise in magical thinking. Victory was just around the corner. "The enemy's hopes are bankrupt," Westmoreland told the National Press Club in Washington. "We have reached the important point when the end begins to come into view." It was November 21. In Hawaii, Charlie Company were waiting for transport to Vietnam.

Just two months later, at the end of January 1968, at the time of the Lunar New Year in Vietnam, the Tet Offensive exposed the November briefings for what they were. The Viet Cong launched massive attacks on cities throughout South Vietnam. In Saigon, a Viet Cong commando squad even raided the American Embassy and held the compound for almost a day. Feebly, Westmoreland attempted to portray Tet as the last desperate throw of an enemy at his wits' end, but nothing in the November briefings had prepared America for the "surprise, strength, length and intensity of these attacks." Afterward, although the attacks were repulsed, nothing remained of November's bold assurances. The President and the American public knew they had been deceived. "We are mired in a stalemate," Walter Cronkite told the nation on TV.

"Our strategy of 'attrition' has not worked," wrote assistant secretary of defense Alain Enthoven in a new report. "We know that despite a massive influx of 500,000 US troops, 1.2 m tons of bombs a year, 400,000 attack sorties a year, 200,000 enemy killed in three years, 20,000 US killed, our control of the countryside and the defense of urban areas is now essentially at pre-August 1965 levels. We have reached stalemate at a high commitment." Enthoven called for a new strategy. In particular, he said that search and destroy missions, the key component of attrition, should be abandoned.

By the end of March, Gen. William Westmoreland, the architect of that strategy, had been recalled, and the President himself had told the nation that he would not seek reelection.

And while these things were being considered and discussed, the men of Charlie Company, now an element of Task Force Barker fighting in Quang Ngai Province in Vietnam, were preparing a search and destroy operation against a small village near the South China Sea. No one had told them it was a discarded strategy in an orphaned war.

3. The Company

Before My Lai, before Vietnam, before the Army, before one of his buddies from Charlie Company started calling him "Mr Homicide," Fred Widmer's nickname among his friends was Bones. He was a tall, skinny boy, the only son of the town treasurer of Lower Burrell, a small town just north of Pittsburgh. In the summer of 1965, at the age of 17, he graduated from high school. "To a real sweet boy, who I have just met this year," a girlfriend wrote in his high school year book. Another girl called Jackie Maffeo, the senior class homecoming queen, added: "To a wild kid from Lower Burrell." But there was nothing too wild about Fred.

Nineteen sixty-five was the year Hare Krishna first came to New York; Professor Timothy Leary produced *The Psychedelic Reader* at Harvard; and Mick Jagger and the Rolling Stones were top of the hit parade with "(I Can't Get No) Satisfaction." In Lower Burrell, Fred Widmer was having old-fashioned fun in his first car: "We'd do crazy things like drive around McDonald's backward." Fred had grown used to discipline while he was growing up. He had attended strict Catholic school and been raised with a firm hand. "When it was time to get your butt beat, you got it beat by Dad, and Mom didn't hesitate either. There came a time when she couldn't beat me anymore so she'd chase me with a broom and I'd just stand there laughing at her."

Fred was still living at home, and one night in November he had come back late just one night too many. His mother took away the car keys. The next day, at the Federal Building in Pittsburgh, Fred enlisted in the Army. It was his eighteenth birthday. Later, he went and bought some life insurance to benefit his parents in case he was killed.

*

Kenneth Hodges, from Dublin, Georgia, had enlisted two years before. He was a farmer's boy, born and raised on the "two-horse farm" his father had been alloted under a government program in the 1920s—as much land as a man could farm with two mules. "Plantin' cotton, pickin' cotton, choppin' cotton . . . pullin' corn, raisin' hogs . . . I was happy on the farm," Ken said. "I didn't feel a desperate need to get away." Ken Hodges was lured, though, by the idea of travel and seeing places. He had an uncle who had been in the Army and told him that the infantry was a good way of seeing the world. "My mother and father were proud of me when I joined," he recalled. "They were worried about Vietnam, but my mother was a schoolteacher and very Christian. Strong Christian beliefs. She resigned herself to the idea that the Lord would take care of me, if that was His plan."

In Portland, Oregon, Greg Olsen enlisted right out of high school in 1967. He came from a devout Mormon family from a good part of town and, like all his friends, he was expected to attend college, which would have meant a deferment from the draft. But he was driven by curiosity. Vietnam was the big issue and he wanted to see it at first hand. He had a young, naive, venturesome attitude, he remembers. "I just didn't know what I wanted to do, I just didn't want to go to college at that time." His father was a patriot and seemed to be proud of the choice Greg had made. His mother tried to talk him out of it. "I wanted to know what was going on there. I didn't know what I was letting myself into. I don't think I took much into account. If someone had leveled with me, I could have been talked out of it. I don't think anybody really had a clue." Greg Olsen signed his papers in June. In December, he was in Vietnam—the only member of his high school class to go.

Harry Stanley was from Gulfport, Mississippi, though he had also spent time growing up in Chicago and Florida. There were six brothers and two sisters and at the center of this large family was Harry's mother, Annie Burrell Jones. Most of the time Harry's father was not around, and Annie brought the family up by herself. She believed in hard work, school, and church on Sundays. "She gave us the morals that everyone has," says Harry. "I know it sounds crazy here in Mississippi, but I was brought up to believe everybody's equal. All my mother's children had to believe that everybody's equal 'cause that's what she believed."

At 17, Harry was doing well at school, and he drove the school bus to make money. But he dropped out suddenly after an argument with his father and enlisted the same day. His mother never treated him the same way again. "When I came back from Vietnam . . . she . . . viewed me as a different person, somebody you don't want to trust."

Michael Bernhardt came from a middle-class Catholic family from Long Island. At the age of 13 he told his parents he wanted to go to the La Salle Military Academy, an extraordinary Long Island institution run by Christian Brothers and retired Army officers. He emerged four years later, a boy soldier. No one had to teach him much about the value of discipline and the necessity of obedience. "By the time I had finished there, if they'd taken me right out and put me in a regular unit, nobody would have noticed." In 1967 he signed up as a paratrooper. He was a tough young man, he thought, with few illusions: "I was never apprehensive about a tour of duty."

And then there was William Laws Calley. Who was Calley? In the early seventies, a small industry grew up trying to find an answer. Toilers at this trade looked for a monster but all they found was a nonentity: a bland young man burdened, it seemed, with as much ordinariness as any single individual could bear; and almost too much of the conventional and commonplace to retain what is necessary for human identity. To the press Calley was just about as average an American as ever came out of the nondescript middle-class side streets of Miami. He could be "any young American." He was "The Quiet American." It was noted with astonishment that he had emerged from a background which most would regard as coming close to the American ideal. Elsewhere it was said that his life could have been lifted from the cover drawing of the old *Saturday Evening Post*. His averageness had made him so invisible at one college he had attended that all anyone could remember about him was that he paid his rent regularly. In a similar vein it was reported that he never drove too fast and would often mow the lawn and do jobs about the house. Who was Calley?

By 1971, at the time of his trial, journalists had discovered no scandal; investigators no criminal record; psychiatrists nothing to throw any doubt on his grasp of reality. The many who combed through his life found no shred of deviance nor even a single distinctive feature other than his height: 5 feet 4 inches. He had come from a stable family; he had been neither popular nor unpopular; he had no particular talents and few, if any, enthusiasms. Water skiing was the closest he had ever got to violence. Throughout a long education, he had shown no aptitude for learning. His college career had simply fizzled out. In the end, most would have agreed with the London *Times* that "Rusty" Calley was simply "the nice boy charged with massacre."

At the age of 22 Calley was rejected for military service for being tone deaf. He had worked as a short-order cook, driven cars through a car wash, spent time as a railroad conductor and as an investigator for insurance companies. He was in San Francisco in 1966 when his mail from home caught up with him and in it a couple of notices from the draft board requesting him to attend for a reevaluation of his medical condition. On his way back to Miami for a draft board hearing, his car broke down in Albuquerque. "What do I do?" Calley asked the duty sergeant at the local Army recruiting station. "You enlist," was the sergeant's reply. On July 26, 1966, William Calley tumbled into the Army almost by accident.

Over the next few months nearly all of the 150 or so young men who would make up Charlie Company followed Calley through the doors of recruiting stations and draft offices throughout America and stepped onto the conveyor belt that would take them to Vietnam. In time, they would become the most analyzed Army unit in American history, but nothing about Charlie Company's origins was planned. The random procedures by which the Army assigns recruits to particular units seem to have been working under no greater restraint than the law of averages. Charlie Company was very average. An investigation ordered by the Army Chief of Staff in 1970 revealed that 87 percent of Charlie Company's

NCOs were high school graduates, nearly 20 percent above the Army's norm. The figure for other ranks was 70 percent, again slightly higher than average. In other areas—intelligence, trainability, and aptitude—Charlie Company differed little from the Army as a whole. Only thirteen were from what came to be called McMamara's 100,000, the Project 100,000 men well below the Army average in terms of aptitude and intelligence and deemed unlikely to meet peacetime entry qualifications. Most of the men in Charlie Company were between 18 and 22 years old. Nearly half the company was black. The Peers Report concluded that there was little to distinguish Charlie Company from other rifle companies: "the men were generally representative of the typical cross section of American youth assigned to most combat units throughout the Army ... [They] brought with them the diverse traits, prejudices and attitudes typical of the various regions of the country and segments of society from whence they came." Only with hindsight could such normality appear in any way menacing.

During the winter of 1966–7, while these very normal young men were still completing basic training in the great land fortresses of the United States—Fort Polk, Fort Benning, Fort McPherson, Fort Jackson—the battalion to which they would eventually be assigned was still being formed in Hawaii. The 1st Battalion, 20th Infantry, was an historic unit reactivated to satisfy the demands of an expanding war. Although as yet of only skeletal composition, the new unit reached back to a proud tradition dating from the Civil War when men of the regiment had fought some of the bloodiest battles of the conflict under General George Sykes. Thereafter, known as "Sykes' Regulars," the regiment had fought in the Indian Wars, the Philippine Insurrection, World War I, World War II, and the Korean War. In the words of the official history: "The men of the unit carved their names in history fighting in the battle of Little Big Horn, Caney and San Juan Hill, Manilla, New Guinea, Lone Tree Hill, Luzen, Blue Beach in Lingayen Gulf, Munez, and Purple Heart Valley, the bloodiest 6,000 yards of battle zone in the world."

Sykes' Regulars enjoyed an intimidating past, but at the Schofield Barracks in Hawaii, they were starting from scratch. In the summer of 1966 a nucleus of officers and NCOs was drafted from other units for the demanding task of creating the new infantry unit.

They were joined on December 19 by Captain Ernest Medina, slated as the commander of the battalion's C Company.

By the time of his arrival in Hawaii, Medina had been in the Army for ten years. Coming from a poor Mexican-American family, he had started life in Springer, New Mexico, with few advantages. His father was a farm worker. His mother died of cancer less than a year after he was born, and he was brought up by his Spanish-speaking grandparents in Montrose, Colorado. As soon as he was old enough he joined the Army.

At 30 years of age Medina was a tough, able soldier who had risen quickly through the ranks by his own efforts. He had excelled as an NCO and graduated fourth in his class of two hundred at Officer Candidate School. He had a no-nonsense approach to his job. He was abrasive, sometimes sarcastic, to his subordinates. But he gained the almost universal respect of his men and a reputation as an officer who was hard but fair—an authoritarian who knew what he was doing. In Vietnam, that counted for a lot. Most of his men agreed that he was an outstanding company commander. His job at the Schofield Barracks was to transform the raw recruits who were beginning to filter through from the mainland into a credible fighting force. Medina succeeded brilliantly. Within months his company, Charlie Company, was recognized as the best in the battalion. "We took every award," he remembered afterward.

The Peers Commission, which investigated the background to My Lai, later claimed that "training deficiencies" had played a significant part in the massacre. But in Hawaii, the Army had no reservations about Charlie Company's performance. On the contrary, the company had performed very well. The men had arrived on the islands with little more than basic training, yet as part of Sykes' Regulars they improved so quickly that in one amphibious training exercise in May they left an "enemy" force completely confused and disorganized. "So swift was the unit's advance that the Chief Umpire had to stop the operation," reads the official account of this achievement, a victory so sweet to the commanding officers of the 1/20th that it was recorded for posterity by the regimental historian. In another exercise, Charlie Company's CO earned himself the sobriquet "Mad Dog" Medina. Charlie Company won the "company of the month" award.

Meanwhile, the process of transforming raw recruits from civilians to soldiers continued under the supervision of the company's drill sergeants. By this time, four years after leaving the cotton fields of Georgia to become a soldier, Kenneth Hodges had become one of these sergeants responsible for training Charlie Company:

The transition from civilian to soldier is very distinct. It needs very rigorous training. You have to train him to march, you have to train him which is his left foot, which his right foot, which foot he steps off on and why it's important that he does. So orders are a very important part of a soldier's training from the beginning. They are taught how to drill, how to march with weapons. They are taught how to use weapons, how to use weapons to kill. They are taught to be soldiers. They are trained to be killers. They're trained from their early weeks in basic training. They're taught how to use a bayonet. They're taught the spirit of the bayonet. The spirit of the bayonet is to kill. They are taught hand-to-hand fighting, they are taught close-order fighting. They are taught how to deal with the enemy when they come face to face with him.

Hodges remembers nothing in his training about the possibility that an order might be illegal. "You learn early in your career that you have to carry out the orders you are given to the letter," he said. "There's no time allowed in the heat of combat to question an order. You could be risking the lives of the people around you."

William Calley's training had taken a slightly different course. After basic training, he had transferred to Fort Lewis in Washington State to train as a clerk-typist. From there he had successfully applied for Officer Candidate School and had begun six months' junior officer training in mid-March 1967. Concerning obedience to orders, however, his position was little different to that of Hodges: that "all orders were assumed to be legal . . . the soldier's job was to carry out any order given to him to the best of his ability." Asked at his trial whether he ever felt the need to discriminate between legal and illegal orders, Calley had replied that he had never been told he had the choice. "If I had . . . questioned an order, I was supposed to carry the order out and then come back and make my complaint." On paper, all soldiers received at least one hour's instruction on the Law of Land Warfare and the Geneva Conventions. In practice, it made little, if any, impression on men who were spending hundreds of hours being trained to follow orders and learning how to kill.

In the summer of 1967, the battalion was ordered to prepare for Vietnam. Deployment was to be earlier than expected. Training was accelerated as the men readied themselves for transfer to the war zone. There was a course called "Vietnam Social Environment" in which "intensive effort was made to thoroughly familiarize personnel with the Vietnamese people, customs . . . and the nature and causes of the conflict in that country." At the Jungle Warfare School there was a mock-up of a "typical Southeast Asian village" to familiarize troops with the proper methods of securing, searching, and clearing villages and how best to work with the civilian population. Second Lt. Calley was deputed to give the men a talk called "Vietnam Our Host." "What a farce that was," he said later, claiming that it had taken him only about three minutes to read out. "Items like . . . 'Do not insult the women. Do not assault the women.' . . . 'Be polite.'"

Such courses, however, were little more than cosmetic exercises. They made little impression, given the many hours the men spent during combat training listening to their instructors refering to the Vietnamese as "gooks" and "slants." "We did not have too much training about Vietnamese people," Fred Widmer recalls. "We might have had one or two brief sessions. Most of what I knew was from other veterans, people who had come back. One guy in particular—Sanchez—who was assigned to us in Hawaii had been with the 1st Cavalry. He knew what was going on, and what it was like, and what we were in for."

According to Calley, the only lesson every GI learned was not to trust anybody: "It was drummed into us, 'Be sharp! On guard! As soon as you think these people won't kill you, ZAP! In combat you haven't friends! You have enemies!' Over and over at OCS we heard this, and I told myself, I'll act as if I'm never secure. As if everyone in Vietnam would do me in. As if everyone's bad."

What most Charlie Company veterans remember about the training was its unreality and how little it prepared them for what they had to face in Vietnam. For Fred Widmer, it seemed they had been preparing for World War II or Korea. Calley thought they could go to Vietnam and be Audie Murphys, "kick in the door, run in the hootch, give it a good burst—kill." Varnado Simpson said: "You can't have no type of training can compare with what war's like. None. There's no such thing as preparedness for war . . . We trained and we were so psyched up, and they program you to kill and go to Vietnam, you know. But once you get there, it's a different situation."

From his perspective as drill sergeant, Kenneth Hodges took a different view. "As one of the sergeants who trained the men of Charlie Company, I was very pleased with the way they turned out. They turned out to be very good soldiers. The fact that they were able to go into My Lai and carry out the orders they had been given, I think this is a direct result of the good training they had."

In the light of what was to happen later, this judgment appears perverse, but there's no doubt that at the time Hodges's opinion on the success of Charlie Company's training was shared by his superiors in Hawaii. When the time came for Sykes' Regulars to embark for Vietnam, the honor of selection as the advance party for the 11th Brigade went to the 1/20th's best company: Charlie Company.

Not everyone shared the commanders' confidence, however. For the first time in his life, Greg Olsen, the Mormon boy who had come straight from high school in Portland, found himself living alongside people from other parts of the country. He found the experience depressing, and he kept to himself. "I thought, see, these guys are thugs . . . I wouldn't have seen any of them in my community. I didn't want anything to do with them. I was growing up fast and I knew they existed, but I didn't have to fraternize with them."

Michael Bernhardt was also concerned. Charlie Company did not match up to the high standards of order and discipline he had learned at the La Salle Military Academy. Trained as a parachutist, he was disappointed to have been transferred to a run-of-the-mill infantry company. Bernhardt was unusual for an enlisted man. He was a military animal, a stickler for authority, and was happiest when things were being done by the book. He gained a reputation as a barrack-room lawyer and was not afraid to tell his superiors how things should be run. "You're going to change the Army, aren't you, Bernhardt?" one sergeant challenged him. Bernhardt conceded he was going to try. But it was not the system that bothered Bernhardt. He believed that good soldiers not only needed discipline, but *liked* it. It was the lax discipline in Charlie Company and the fact that officers did not always insist on their orders being carried out that worried him. In an argument with Calley shortly after arriving in Hawaii, he found the young lieutenant callow and lacking in leadership qualities. The men of Charlie Company were a different matter:

Some of the men in the company were a little unusual. There were some who were cruel. But there wasn't anything extraordinary about them. There's going to be that element in any group. Most of the men were just ordinary Americans. They weren't the bottom of the barrel. They were men who would have been accepted for military service at any time. I wouldn't expect them to murder anybody or torture anybody . . . In the United States they would have been friends of mine.

On November 9, the 11th Infantry Brigade, to which the 1/20th Battalion was now attached, were mustered for review at the Schofield Barracks in Hawaii. Charlie Company was ready for action. "Charlie was really made for war! We were mean, we were ugly," Calley said afterward. Three weeks later the company was flown to Vietnam.

"We flew over on a Continental Airlines plane," Fred Widmer recalls. "It was a weird situation—a civilian plane with a civilian stewardess and crew. They were flying both ways, they were flying people out as well as in, so they got to see both ends. I remember getting off the plane and the stewardess just stood there crying as we unloaded . . . They were more attuned to what we were getting into than we were."

By the second week in December, Charlie Company's deployment in Quang Ngai Province in Vietnam was complete.

In 1967, Quang Ngai was one of the most beautiful and dangerous regions in all Vietnam. To the west was the unruly Annamese mountain range. To the east, the white sandy beaches of the South China Sea. Between lay a narrow coastal plain, home to the majority of the population who labored in the rice fields or fished in the plentiful rivers and built their villages in the shade of surprising and vivid outcrops of enormous bamboo and banana trees.

The people of the region were tough and resilient. They were well known in Vietnam for blunt speaking and stubbornness. Among the Vietnamese of Saigon and Hanoi they had a reputation for being coarsemannered and unsophisticated. Yet they had great independence of spirit, and it was said that the rigors of their existence had given them a "leathery will."

Historically, they had proved consistently difficult to tame or bring under control. The people of Quang Ngai and neighboring Binh Dinh had provided the fiercest resistance to the French takeover in the nineteenth century; and in the 1930s they had been the first to rebel against colonial rule. The French, who returned after World War II, had never been powerful enough to regain control of the region, which the Viet Minh designated a "free zone"—that is, a part of the country that had already been liberated. The administrative unit known as the "village" of Son My—of which My Lai was one hamlet—had actually been created by the Viet Minh in 1945. Although many of the Viet Minh fighters had gone north after the partition of Vietnam in 1954, many had stayed behind, and Viet Minh influence continued virtually uninterrupted.

Outside the cities, the influence of the Saigon government never reached far. By the 1960s, a whole generation of young people had grown up under the control of the Viet Minh and, later, the National Liberation Front. With the launching of the Strategic Hamlet Program in 1962, Saigon attempted to win back lost ground. Villagers were driven from their homes into the cities and to new fortified villages in an attempt to separate the people from the NLF and its organizers. But the burning of homes and fields, often involved in these measures, only increased the people's hostility and resentment.

In the early 1960s many former Viet Minh who had gone to the North started to turn up again in their old villages. There they found fertile ground for a new rebellion and quickly harnessed the people's anger against the Saigon government.

By 1965, government troops controlled only the area around the provincial capital, Quang Ngai City. The Viet Cong in the province were strong enough to inflict severe casualties on South Vietnamese units. During the spring and summer offensive, the 1st VC Regiment tore apart a 500-strong Saigon unit at the small hamlet of Ba Gia, just 20 miles south of the huge US base at Chu Lai. The position had become so grave that only American intervention prevented the Saigon government from abandoning Quang Ngai City altogether.

Nearly three years later, when Charlie Company was deployed in Quang Ngai Province, the military situation remained critical. In March of 1967, General Westmoreland wrote in a message to Admiral Ulysses S. Sharp, the Commander-in-Chief of the Pacific Command:

One of the most critical areas in the RVN today is Quang Ngai Province. Even if a major operation were conducted in this area during 1967, the relief would be no more than temporary. A force is needed to maintain continuous pressure on the enemy, to eliminate his forces and numerous base areas, and to remove his control over large population and food reserves.

Until now the US Marines had been responsible for security in the province. But the marines found themselves pulled in two directions. Guerrilla activity was, if anything, increasing. At the same time, more men were needed to meet the growing threat of invasion from the north by conventional units of the North Vietnamese Army. A failure to provide reinforcements, Westmoreland wrote on March 28, would enable the VC to "continue operating unmolested throughout the key Quang Ngai Province."

The result was the formation, in the spring of 1967, of Task Force Oregon: the first US Army—as opposed to marine—unit to operate in Quang Ngai Province. "Task Force Oregon has three big advantages over the marines," a senior American advisor in Quang Ngai City told a journalist in August of 1967. "First, they have had the manpower to do the job. Second, they have had the firepower, which is very important for shock effect. Third, they have had the helicopters."

Almost immediately the conflict reached a higher peak of intensity: higher body counts, more refugees, more civilian casualties reported at local hospitals. Two main thrusts of American strategy were pursued with increased savagery. Large-scale helicopter attacks were launched in an attempt to surround and trap sizable enemy units. These missions generally failed in their main purpose, but invariably devastated wide areas of the countryside. In Operation Benton, a two-week search and destroy mission in August, Task Force Oregon destroyed an estimated 65 percent of the houses of about 17,000 Vietnamese, and announced an enemy body count of 397. Jonathan Schell reported:

Into an area of ten by twenty kilometers they had dropped 282 tons of "general purpose" bombs and 116 tons of napalm; fired 1,005 rockets (not counting rockets fired from helicopters), 132,820 rounds of 20-mm explosive straffing shells, and 119,350 7.62-mm rounds of machine gun fire from spooky flights; and fired 8,488 artillery rounds. By the end of the operation, the Civil Affairs office had supervised the evacuation of six hundred and forty of the area's seventeen thousand people to the vicinity of government camps.

And Benton was only a medium-size operation. Alongside the larger operations, there was a second thrust, the day-to-day process of clearing the countryside of anything and anyone who might provide support or sustenance to the National Liberation Front. In a province deemed correctly to be overwhelmingly sympathetic to the Viet Cong, this meant eliminating the countryside. The villages were bombed, burned down, and pulverized. Sometimes villagers would be warned in advance that their homes were about to be wiped off the face of the earth. Sometimes not. It was common practice to shell or bomb any village from which US soldiers had taken any fire, even small arms fire, without any warning at all. The destruction, detailed in Jonathan Schell's reports from the province, was on an almost unimaginable scale.

This was the reality behind Westmoreland's prediction in 1965 that the war "will bring about a moment of decision for the peasant farmer. He will have to choose if he stays alive." American officials frequently referred to this choice. "The choice is yours," one leaflet dropped on villages proclaimed. "If you refuse to let the Viet Cong use your villages and hamlets as their battlefield, your homes and lives will be spared." A million leaflets a day were being dropped on Quang Ngai Province at this time. The whole exercise assumed that the largely illiterate peasants could actually read them. From 1965 to 1972, 50 billion leaflets were dropped over Vietnam. Fifteen hundred each for every member of the population.

"The VC use villages as protection, the way a gangster uses a hostage. So in the process of getting at Charlie it's inevitable that the village gets it. These people have had a choice," the senior advisor in Quang Ngai told Jonathan Schell. "They've had a chance to get out," a helicopter commander told the same reporter.

To stay and be killed, or to go and join thousands of other refugees in the squalor of the refugee camps or the mushrooming shanty towns around the towns and cities: what kind of a choice was this? Whatever they did meant personal turmoil and possible catastrophe for the Vietnamese. It certainly meant the end of the lives they had lived till now. But for the Americans, the whole point of clearing an area of countryside of its people was so that anyone who remained must be Viet Cong. These areas became free-fire zones. Anything that happened to someone who chose to remain in, or return to, a free-fire zone was their own fault; they could expect the worst. The belief that the people had been given a chance to get out and had made their choice made the strategy morally workable. In a free-fire zone, the pursuit of a high body count could proceed unencumbered by the need to discriminate between combatants and civilians at all.

Nowhere was this breathtaking carelessness of human life greater than in Quang Ngai. No one was actually saying "Kill civilians," but no one strived to keep them alive. Because the killing of civilians came to be seen as unavoidable, less and less time was spent on seeing how it could be avoided. To American spokesmen the death or injury of noncombatants was always "accidental," an "inevitable tragedy of war," and therefore somehow uncorrectable. The bombs and the artillery provided a backdrop of indiscriminate destruction on such a vast scale that individual acts of brutality toward the Vietnamese were frequently overlooked. "No one has any feeling for the Vietnamese," a private from Texas told Schell. "They're lost. The trouble is, no one sees the Vietnamese as people. They're not people. Therefore it doesn't matter what you do to them."

It was an old war by the time Charlie Company arrived in Quang Ngai and they inherited the habits and attitudes of a war culture that had already reached a terrible maturity. The new company learned from the old.

Christmas Day, 1967. For Charlie Company the year ended on "Gilligan's Island," a safe and well-defended island set between the fishing village of Sa Huynh and the Pho Thach Peninsula on the South China Sea. An American Christmas dinner was on the table and Captain Medina provided a Christmas tree and lights which he had brought from Hawaii.

The first month had been C Company's phony war, a honeymoon period during which there had been no contact with the enemy and no casualties. They had built a base camp at Landing Zone (LZ) Carentan near the town of Duc Pho, in the southernmost part of Quang Ngai Province, a part of the country which had known little except Viet Minh and then Viet Cong rule for over a generation. When the marines had arrived at Duc Pho in 1965, they had been unable to travel more than 500 yards from their camp without coming under heavy fire. The marines had corrected that. In 1967 Jonathan Schell reported that the Duc Pho district was one of the most heavily damaged in the province. He estimated that outside a few enclaves "from ninety to a hundred percent of the houses . . . had been destroyed." In Charlie Company there was some disappointment in finding no enemy left to shoot at. "We didn't fire in anger all of December 1967," Calley later remarked, observing with obvious regret that "GIs before us had searched the AO [area of operations] and destroyed it and searched it and destroyed it." Instead, Charlie Company spent December guarding bridges and practicing in the deserted villages of Duc Pho. The Army called it "in-country orientation." An Australian advisor was brought in to instruct the company on how to distinguish between noncombatants, Viet Cong regulars, suspects, and sympathizers. He said it was very difficult. So did other instructors from the South Vietnamese Army. They got the same story from some *chieu hoi*—former Viet Cong. "The Australian emphasized that you should be extremely leery of children," Medina testified later.

In that first month Charlie Company experienced not the shock of war, but the shock of the Third World. "It was like going into the backwoods," one of them remembers. "We regressed five hundred years," recalls another. "We were exposed to something that went far beyond the world as we knew it," said Fred Widmer.

We had just left Hawaii with all its hotels and nightclubs and bars and we wound up in Vietnam where people went right out and shit in the rice paddy in the morning, drop their drawers right along the trail anytime. It was hard to consider people in the modern day and age living like they did. I think it went against our value of what human life is.

Greg Olsen pitied the people he saw around him: "They were in an awful predicament and didn't know what the hell to do. They seemed to be overjoyed at any display of affection. I often thought how neat it would be to see their country in peaceful circumstances and I never did develop a hatred for them." Michael Bernhardt remembered that the Vietnamese, especially those who had had anything to do with American soldiers, were always wary, but Fred Widmer's photographs, taken in the first few weeks in Vietnam, show Widmer and other GIs from Charlie Company posing happily with Vietnamese children.

Calley was always frustrated in his attempts to keep the children away from his men while they were guarding bridges at Duc Pho. "All the men loved them. Gave the kids candy, cookies, chewing gum, everything," he said later. "Not me. I hated them . . . I was afraid of Vietnamese kids." By contrast, Harry Stanley, the black teenager from Gulfport, tried hard to find out more about the lives of the Vietnamese he met around the base camp. Within three months he had taught himself to speak the language better than the company's GI interpreters who had been trained in Hawaii. Being aware that Calley and Medina did not like the Vietnamese, an antipathy shared by many of his buddies, did not change his attitude: "Some of the guys just felt like I was a 'gook-lover.' That's what they called me. And to them this was a slander against the American soldier. But these were our allies . . . Just because I was an American soldier, doesn't make them any less than I am as a human being."

At this early stage, neither Calley's dark fears nor Harry Stanley's open curiosity determined the feelings of Charlie Company. Attitudes toward the Vietnamese were mixed and as yet untested by combat. In fact, at this time, the company still felt good about itself. The esteem and recognition they had earned in training had not yet worn off, and they easily took up their place in a proud military tradition.

Sykes' Regulars 1/20th Infantry Battalion now formed a small unit of the 11th Infantry Brigade that gave itself the sobriquet "Jungle Warriors." In turn the "Warriors" were themselves a brigade attached to the newly reconstituted American Division— "the first US Army unit to conduct an offensive operation against the enemy in any theater during World War II." In Vietnam, all Americal Division troops, including those in Charlie Company, wore a shoulder patch of the stars of the Southern Cross on a blue background. The men of Charlie Company were not overawed. "We thought Charlie [Charlie Cong, the Viet Cong] were afraid of us," recalled Kenneth Hodges. "There's a difference between patrolling and going for a walk in the woods. You got to look like you've come for business . . . You got to look like you're going to do battle. No playing around." So before they had even fired a shot in anger, Charlie Company had taken on the title "Jungle Warriors." Just as later, perhaps with more justification, they became "Barker's Bastards." As they sat down for dinner on Christmas Day, morale on Gilligan's Island was high.

The real business of the war began early in the New Year, when Charlie Company was camped out on a safe haven fire base called LZ Charlie Brown. Two years later, in 1970, a civic action officer, Don E. Fox, based on Gilligan's Island when Charlie Company was there, made a sworn statement to Army Criminal Investigation Division officers about an incident which had taken place early in 1968. "I fully understand how the incident could occur," Fox told the military police, "but I considered the incident most unusual when it happened."

Fox had known Capt. Medina slightly and had a high regard for his abilities as a unit commander. He was reputed to be strong on discipline and brooked no deviation from his orders. However, Fox told the police that in spite of this the men liked and respected Medina. They had an "unusually high esprit de corps." They carried out Medina's instructions as a matter of course, since "his reaction to deviation was well known to all."

One day in January 1968, villagers in Sa Huyhn came to Fox for help in recovering the body of a local fisherman from the main highway just north of the village. The villagers were afraid to go alone for fear of being shot by the Americans guarding the two bridges near to where the body was lying. Fox drove to the scene and discovered that the body was male and had been shot several times in the chest and head. The guards on the bridge were from Charlie Company. They told Fox that they had received a message from Medina over the radio that a VC was crawling up on the highway, having swum across the inland sea. One of the GIs had looked down the road, seen the man, walked up to him. "He put his M-16 rifle against the man's head, and shot him," Fox said. When he returned with the body, villagers told Fox of another man shot while fishing on the inland sea.

That evening on Gilligan's Island, Fox talked to two officers, a captain and a first lieutenant, who had been monitoring the radio traffic between Medina and his men. He was told that the incident had begun when the leader of a Charlie Company platoon, making a sweep of the uninhabited northern part of the Pho Thach Peninsula, had radioed in that two boats had been observed out on the inland sea with two men in them fishing. Medina ordered his men to kill the fishermen. The platoon leader reported back that no weapons were visible, that the men appeared only to be fishing and could easily be picked up. Medina repeated that he wanted the men killed. One of the fishermen was shot by the platoon firing from the peninsula. The other was wounded but escaped by swimming across the inland sea and managed to crawl as far as the highway. It was here that he was killed by the bridge guard. The incident had struck Fox as unusual because the area had been quiet. No VC movements had been reported and no weapons were ever found. Neither Fox nor the two officers who had listened to these events over the radio made an official report. "I think that we all felt that making such a report would get us nowhere," Fox told the military police. Charlie Company had won its first body count. The phony war was coming to an end.

Within days the company was redeployed. On January 26, 1968, orders were received to join a new strike unit of around five hundred men, made up of three rifle companies and an artillery battery carved out of the 11th Infantry Brigade. Again the Army displayed its faith in Charlie Company; each company chosen for the new task force was considered by the brigade commander, Brigadier General Andy Lipscomb, to be the best in its battalion and led by men considered to be "top officers." The new unit, called Task Force Barker after its commander Lieutenant Colonel Frank Barker, was quickly transferred to the north of Quang Ngai Province. This area of operations was codenamed "Muscatine," a name chosen by General Sam Koster, the Americal Division's commander, after a town of the same name near his home in Iowa.

Muscatine was "Indian country"—a Viet Cong stronghold. Despite the none-too-gentle attentions during the previous three years of US Marines, Korean Marines, and the South Vietnamese Army, the National Liberation Front had remained resolutely in control. Booby traps, mines, and ambushes had awaited those who tried to eject them. Medina promised his men action. From their new fire base camps, LZ Dottie and LZ Uptight, six miles from Quang Ngai City, Charlie Company could look out north over hundreds of paddy fields toward Chu Lai, the vast new air base constructed by the marines and now the headquarters of the Americal Division; and, turning south, toward the Batangan Peninsula and the South China Sea. *Batangan* was a French and American transcription of the Vietnamese name: Ba Lang An—Three Villages of Peace.

Inside their fire bases, men of the task force enjoyed as much of the American world as could be flown in by helicopter. They received their mail, American newspapers, cold beers, steaks, ice cream, Coca Cola, and *Playboy* magazine. But all around them was the world of the Viet Cong.

An American intelligence report concluded that there was no substantive evidence that prior to 1968 "the VC had any difficulties obtaining sufficient manpower and logistics support" from the area: "Supply routes appeared to be well established, storage facilities numerous and well stocked with all classes of supplies, and ample civilian labor readily available." The enemy had food, shelter, and freedom of movement. There were even some reports of the local manufacture of supplies and equipment. All of which contributed to "a high incidence of enemy-initiated attacks."

For three years, a key element of resistance in the area had been the 48th Local Force Battalion—a National Liberation Front (VC) unit, which began as an outfit of around five hundred men, activated in August of 1965 in a village not far from where Charlie Company were now dug in. According to American intelligence, the leadership of the battalion had originally been made up of returnees from North Vietnam. The rank and file were either guerrillas recruited from the local villages or young draftees from Quang Ngai or further north, from Quang Tin. Wherever they came from, the 48th proved astonishingly resilient. They had been attacked by US Marines during their first month of operations, with losses, according to the Americans, of fifty men. In three further clashes in 1965, the marines claimed fifty-three more Viet Cong from the 48th killed in action. These were heavy losses, yet throughout the next two years, the 48th continued to be a thorn in the side of the Americans. They fought a series of small-scale operations in and around the Son Tinh district, which had now become the responsibility of Task Force Barker and which, according to American advisors, "was the constant leader in enemy-initiated incidents."

According to an American intelligence profile, the 48th LF Battalion differed little from Viet Cong units throughout Vietnam. Recruits were given political and military training which included forced marches and walking on dry leaves. Prisoners captured in January 1968 told the Americans that the unit held "dry runs" of operations in rice fields, but that they never fired their guns while practicing. All raids and ambushes were carefully planned and discussed before being undertaken. Before attacking a hamlet, another prisoner revealed, a scout would be sent ahead to pinpoint the weakest spot in the perimeter defenses. The attack would then follow at night with diversionary fire aimed at the front gate.

The fighting men of the 48th received support from the villages they controlled; in particular, rice was procured through "village economic committees." Every man in the unit was issued two and a half milk cans of rice a day.

From such small crumbs of information the Americans endeavored to piece together a picture of a VC local force unit that had been giving them the runaround for years. The pattern of their operations in eastern Son Tinh and Binh Son districts in the north of Quang Ngai Province put their home base in the Batangan Peninsula, but every attempt to find and destroy them had failed. Those prisoners who, early in 1968, claimed that the guerrillas were becoming "afraid to fight" or had lost their "fighting spirit" were almost certainly only telling their interrogators what they wanted to hear. Long experience suggested that the 48th remained a resourceful, combat-hardened unit of local men fighting on their own ground and well capable of looking after their own back yard.

Now it was Task Force Barker's turn to try to destroy them. Barker's Bastards—unblooded, inexperienced young men, recently flown in from another world. It was an asymmetrical, unequal contest, and absolutely typical of the Vietnam War.

Tet is the beginning of the Lunar New Year—the greatest celebration and holiday of the Vietnamese calendar. Christmas, Easter, Thanksgiving, and the Fourth of July all rolled into one, was how it was explained to American GIs. It is a time when people return to their villages to pay respects to their ancestors, to celebrate the rebirth of nature and the promise of a new beginning.

During the war, it had become the practice for both sides to declare a truce to celebrate the holiday, and the Tet of 1968 was no exception. A recent lull in the fighting had persuaded the government in Saigon to lift the ban on fireworks it had imposed in previous years. Broadcasts from Hanoi Radio emphasized the need to observe the ceasefire for the duration of the festivities. A 36-hour truce began at 6 PM on Tet Eve, January 29.

In the early evening of the following day, a Viet Cong force led by the 401st Sapper Regiment moved toward assembly areas around Quang Ngai City. There they were met by local VC guides who led the main force across country and through sugar cane fields to their assault positions. At 7 PM, a South Vietnamese regional force outpost reported its position completely surrounded by VC. In Quang Ngai City there was no awareness yet that this was the prelude to a general attack. Tet celebrations continued through the evening.

Quang Ngai City was familiar with the menace of war. In size, it was no more than a small town, an unsettled, raw outpost of government control surrounded by checkpoints and patrols. The dozens of small trading posts, shops, cafes, and engineering workshops strung out along the main street were rattled and shaken constantly by the choking convoys of military vehicles that passed through the center of the town on Highway One. Quang Ngai City was a siphon for the black market and American contraband. Even its corrugated iron roofs had been ripped off from supplies earmarked for the refugee camps. The streets teamed with strangers and foreigners—refugees, soldiers, advisors, aid workers, Catholic nuns, Canadian Quakers, intelligence agents, CIA operatives—the flotsam of the international war effort.

There was a feeling of time running out, of a way of life wearing thin. In 1965, Quang Ngai City had almost fallen to the Viet Cong, and for years, few of the nearby villages had been secure enough to guarantee the safety of government officials in the hours of darkness. Raiders from the hostile countryside made frequent incursions. Most nights the chatter of small arms fire could be heard in the city itself, while from outside the city's heavily guarded perimeter artillery boomed away in the darkness, randomly attempting to obstruct the free passage of guerrillas across the rice fields. Nevertheless, Quang Ngai was a provincial capital, the headquarters of a South Vietnamese Army division, and an important political, administrative, and military center. Its location in the middle of the coastal plain, astride the main north–south routes of communication, gave Quang Ngai a vital strategic importance. A frontier town, an American visitor called Quang Ngai, on the edge of Indian country.

Just after four o'clock on the morning of January 31—somewhat delayed by the late arrival of heavy weapons units—the waiting Viet Cong launched a barrage of mortar, rocket, and machine-gun fire, and simultaneously attacked targets on all sides of the city: to the east, the airfield; to the west, the citadel; a South Vietnamese training center just across the Tra Khuc River to the north; the provincial jail; and the headquarters of the 2nd ARVN Division. The Tet Offensive had begun in Quang Ngai City.

Charlie Company, stationed 12 miles north at the American base LZ Dottie, were put on alert. Through the night they could hear the din of the fighting in Quang Ngai, but more chilling and eerie were the tremendous sights from 60 miles away as munitions dumps were blown up at the gigantic American airfield at Chu Lai. The Americal Division headquarters itself was under attack. The flashes in the west and rolling concussions of explosions brought to Charlie Company a numbing sense of their own vulnerability. The enemy were all around. They were closing in. If the enemy could attack the division, thought Calley, "you don't have any-place to really go home . . . think what he would do to your company if he caught you alone."

In Quang Ngai, the Tet Offensive followed the pattern of the attacks taking place that night all over South Vietnam. Bold, dramatic moves were followed by bloody retreat. The Viet Cong's most dramatic success was overrunning the provincial prison and releasing nearly six hundred prisoners. Elsewhere they were stopped short by overwhelming firepower.

During the suppression of the Tet Offensive, the cities felt the full force of tactics hitherto restricted to the countryside. The American after-action report on the Quang Ngai attack observed: "During the attack the enemy occupied areas where the civilian population was dense and areas the friendly forces might be reluctant to fire upon. These areas included the Provincial Hospital and the Catholic church . . . Damage to civilian buildings was extensive wherever the VC chose to fight."

From LZ Dottie, Charlie Company were moved a few miles south to block the enemy's line of retreat. They dug in at Nui Dong De, marked Hill 102 on Army maps, overlooking Highway One to the west and looking to the east across the hills and streams to the coast. Between Charlie Company and the sea lay the valley of the Tra Khuc River and the villages of My Lai. Strictly speaking, this area was outside the Muscatine area of operations and under the responsibility of the ARVN.

Early in the afternoon of February 1, the Viet Cong's 48th Local Force Battalion which had overrun the training center to the north of Quang Ngai succumbed in the face of an armoured counter-attack. According to American figures they had lost 144 killed and an unspecified number wounded. Under the eyes of Charlie Company, the stricken guerrillas retreated northeast toward the coast. The Americans were powerless, unable to open fire in this area without the permission of the South Vietnamese authorities. "We sat on a hill and watched a battalion of VC come out of Quang Ngai City, and we couldn't shoot them, because they were under ARVN jurisdiction," Fred Widmer remembered two decades later. "I distinctly remember watching them suckers march out of there and we could not touch them." By the time Medina managed to get through the red tape and order up an artillery strike, the guerrillas had escaped down the Tra Khuc Valley in the direction of My Lai and the hamlet the Americans labeled Pinkville on their maps. The 48th Local Force Battalion would never again present such an easy target.

Now began day after day of patrolling. After Tet, officials in Quang Ngai City were jittery. The urgent job of Task Force Barker was to hunt down the 48th Battalion before they could regroup for a second offensive. Throughout February, the three rifle companies of Task Force Barker crisscrossed the Muscatine area of operations in search of the Viet Cong. Sometimes Alpha, Bravo, and Charlie Companies, acting in concert, would attempt to encircle the guerrillas. The traps always closed empty. They were chasing phantoms. There was nothing to show for the long, hot, exhausting days tramping through paddy fields and friendless villages.

Morale became a problem. Once Colonel Barker himself came out on an APC and delivered ice cream to the company in the middle of a paddy field. "I remember him up there on the tank asking us how we were while they were unloading the ice cream," says Greg Olsen. As he watched the sticky ice cream melt, Olsen made a jaundiced appraisal of Col. Barker. "He was like Patton— an egoist. A short guy, with starchy pressed battle fatigues." More commonly, while Charlie Company sweltered on the ground, the commanders flew overhead in their helicopters. For them, the well-stocked delights of the mess. For Charlie Company, another night of dirt and K-rations. After weeks in the field, rising at dawn and digging in every night, Charlie Company began to feel isolated and forgotten.

"To be honest, we felt abandoned by anyone above us," Michael Bernhardt observed much later. "We were abused . . . they wore us down to nothing." The impression grew that Charlie Company was getting a raw deal. They turned in on themselves. "We were a small group isolated in a strange land," recalled Bernhardt. "We had a company of men that all came from one country and were dropped 10,000 miles away and felt close, because there was no one else to feel close to."

In mid-February, the company started to take casualties. The first happened on a night patrol within sight of LZ Dottie. A private in Calley's 1st Platoon stepped on a booby trap at the side of a trail. There had been so little action up to this point that Calley had forgotten to take along a medic and the wounded man only just survived the few hundred yards back to camp.

On February 11, the 2nd Platoon came under heavy small arms and mortar fire, just to the north of the Diem Diem River, about a mile west of My Lai 1—Pinkville. Several GIs were wounded and gunships were called in to cover the 2nd Platoon's untidy retreat. "It was really confusing," Michael Bernhardt said. "Nobody knew what was going on." The Viet Cong were well hidden, but Bernhardt remembered seeing a GI fire his M-16 into a Vietnamese family that was crouching for cover nearby.

The following afternoon, Lt. Calley led his 1st Platoon back to the same location on the Diem Diem River. They were moving along the riverbank when they came under fire. Calley screamed into the radio for artillery support, and the batteries at LZ Uptight a few miles to the north poured shells into the guerrillas' position. Later that day artillery officers told Calley he had used a million dollars' worth of shells.

The men—in their first firefight—were discovering things about each other and about themselves. Greg Olsen recalled: "We were pinned down in a trench taking a lot of fire. Sergeant Cowan was on one side of me putting up his helmet to get some bullet holes in it. Almost like it was amusing. On the other side there was this other guy just sobbing. He'd come unglued. Crawling around like a dog. Just lost it."

The 1st Platoon withdrew under cover of the massive artillery bombardment. According to some of the men, Calley was totally lost. He led them back toward the river. As they broke cover, the snipers started up again. Ron Weber, Calley's radio operator, took a shot which shattered his set and tore his kidney out.

He died a few moments later, Charlie Company's first killed-in-action. His horrified companions lifted him onto the hovering medevac helicopter. A GI in shock blubbered and howled. No one had known much about shock before. "If we got hit much harder, we would all go into shock," Calley told his court-martial nearly three years later. "It was terrifying . . . a terrifying experience."

In later years, Calley admitted that he had been careless. He had led his men into an exposed position. But this is not the impression conveyed in his controlled after-action report, written just after the event, in which Weber's death was set against a VC body count of six. Given the circumstances of the encounter, there is no way Calley could have known how many—if any—of the enemy had been killed. The report is simply evidence that Calley had learned the protocol of body count culture early. Asked later how he arrived at a body count, he had replied:

you just make an estimate off the top of your head. There is no way to really figure out exact body count . . . As long as it was high, that was all they wanted . . . I generally knew that if I lost a troop [soldier], I'd better come back with a body count of ten, say I shot at least ten of the enemy, which was pretty hard when you are only fighting one sniper.

Calley's version of how body counts were actually arrived at contrasts in an interesting way with the procedure described by the 11th Brigade's commander, Col. Oran K. Henderson: "The body count is usually made by a US soldier physically having killed or having come upon a body, reporting it through the chain of command to the company commander."

The next day, February 13, it was Bravo Company's turn to take a beating. The whole task force was committed to an attack on My Lai 1—Pinkville—considered to be the most likely stronghold of the 48th VC Battalion. Charlie Company took up a blocking position as Alpha and Bravo companies attempted to move forward. Near the hamlet of My Lai 4, Bravo Company were pinned down and heavily mauled by an enemy hidden in the hedgerows and tree lines. Only the intervention of a platoon of APCs succeeded in rescuing the Americans, who later reported one man killed and five injured in the operation. The body count for the Viet Cong numbered seventy-eight reportedly killed by the end of the day.

On the following day, Alpha Company met heavy resistance and failed to break through to My Lai 1. On the third day of the operation the task force broke into the village only to find that the VC had slipped away during the night. Captain Patrick Trinkle, the commander of A Company, later graphically recalled what they found:

The area was so thickly covered with booby traps and command-detonated mines that it was impossible to move. There were tunnels every fifty feet ... We recovered three tons of small arms ammunition and some 81 mm and 60 mm mortar rounds. There were no civilians in this area. We had engineers brought in and destroyed the tunnels with explosives.

A body count of eighty was reported for the three-day operation—with no enemy weapons captured. There were five Americans dead and fifteen wounded. Behind these figures the real lesson stood out. The task force had taken a hammering and the VC had escaped.

Frustration and anger ate away at the company's esprit de corps. The men stopped believing that Charlie Cong was afraid of Charlie Company. Faith in Medina was still high, although some of the GIs felt he pushed the company too hard. Calley was another matter. Opinion about him was universally hostile. According to one GI in his platoon, Calley was a "glory-hungry person ... the kind of person who would have sacrificed all of us for his own personal advancement." John Smail, a squad leader with the 3rd Platoon, called him a nervous, excitable type who yelled a lot. "I think that it's important for you to know," Smail told the Army CID, "that Calley was so disliked by members of the unit that they put a bounty on his head. None of the men had any respect for him as a military leader." Greg Olsen thought he was incompetent: "I remember instances when we were lost, one time at night, everyone knew we were lost, but Calley wouldn't admit it." Someone else thought Calley acted like a small guy who had been pushed around a lot by bigger people before he joined the Army. Now that he had authority he didn't know how to use it, and he didn't listen to suggestions. Many commented that there was something about him that rubbed people up the wrong way. Medina gave his junior lieutenant a tough time and ridiculed him in front of his men. "The captain called him Lieutenant Shithead, regularly," one GI remembered; "that tended to minimize your opinion of him." Others recalled that Calley's attempts to win favor with Medina were frequently rebuffed with a sarcastic "Listen, sweetheart . . ."

A few days after the attack on Pinkville, there was a very emotional memorial service for Ron Weber at LZ Dottie. Men were in tears by the end. Weber's death had shaken Charlie Company. He had been killed by snipers that no one had even seen. Injuries from booby traps were beginning to mount. But where was the enemy? More than twenty years later Varnado Simpson's reply still conveys the torment and frustration behind that question: "Who is the enemy? How can you distinguish between the civilians and the noncivilians? The same people who come and work in the bases at daytime, they just want to shoot and kill you at nighttime. So how can you distinguish between the two? The good or the bad? All of them looked the same."

Fred Widmer recalls:

When we first started losing members of the company, it was mostly through booby-traps and snipers. We never really got into a main conflict per se, where you could see who was shooting and you could actually shoot back. We had heard a lot about women and children being used as booby-traps and being members of the Viet Cong. As time went on you tended to believe it more and more. There was no question that they were working for the Viet Cong. But at the same time we were trying to work with these people, they were basically doing a number on us—and we were letting them. So the whole mood changed. You didn't trust them anymore. You didn't trust anybody. Deep down inside, you had mixed emotions. You knew there was an enemy out there—but you couldn't pinpoint who exactly was the enemy. And I would say that in the end, anybody that was still in that country was the enemy.

At the time Fred Widmer and his comrades in Charlie Company were reaching this conclusion, which had so many sinister implications for the Vietnamese, Major General Samuel W. Koster, commander of the whole Americal Division, was issuing a memorandum to his officers entitled "Acts of Discourtesy Toward Vietnamese People." Koster was an austere and authoritarian soldier whose ambitions reached to the top of the military tree. He had been disturbed by reports of misbehavior by troops under his command. Americal troops had been accused of rape, looting, pilfering, and brutality, he charged. Such acts "destructive to our mission and to the image of our great Nation" were not to be tolerated:

Every time an American berates or downgrades the efforts of our ARVN allies, he jeopardizes the efforts of the United States. Every time we joke or poke fun at the manner in which Vietnamese people work or dress, their pride is injured and they dislike us a little more for our lack of understanding. Every time a Vietnamese female is insulted by word, gesture, or touch, the name of the United States is insulted. Every time we carelessly call the Vietnamese people childish and crude nicknames, we heap criticism on the United States. No one appreciates the lack of social and intellectual contact with the people more than a soldier in a combat area, but this lack of contact seems to bring the worst out in a minority of our people.

Incidents of the kind Gen. Koster was referring to are described in the Americal Division's records of courts-martial from September 1967 to June of the following year. The total number of GIs tried in various kinds of courts-martial for offenses against the Vietnamese numbered only eleven. None of the accused was an officer. The value of this slender catalogue is to demonstrate not the scale of the abuse of Vietnamese, but its character. Two soldiers were acquitted on four counts of pulling the pin from a hand grenade and threatening to drop it near Vietnamese they were interrogating. Two others were accused of cutting the hair off the head of a Vietnamese woman with a straight razor. They were fined and reduced in rank. A sergeant charged with killing a civilian by shooting him in the back with an M-16 was jailed for two years. A private who shot a woman was given three years. Another soldier who had struck civilians about the head with his rifle causing grievous bodily harm was also jailed. He was found not guilty on another count of bludgeoning a man to death on Highway One near Quang Ngai City. Only one rapist appears on these charge sheets. He was sentenced to twenty years. Throughout

the entire period covered by the report, which includes most of
Charlie Company's tour of duty in northern Quang Ngai Province,
the record shows that not a single one of Medina's men was court-
martialed for offenses against Vietnamese civilians, nor indeed
was anyone from Task Force Barker. In view of the high standards demanded by Gen. Koster this might seem like a surprising
omission.

In fact, Charlie Company's drift toward brutality took very little
time. It began with beating up suspects in villages and quickly
became more serious. Bernhardt stayed aloof from the process;
Fred Widmer did not:

They had explained the Geneva Convention to us during our training
and in the beginning we did what we thought was right and we turned
them [the prisoners] over. But it was kind of hard after you had been
there a while and you started seeing, learning, finding out what real
experience is all about. Here you are fighting an enemy who doesn't
follow the Geneva Convention but you have to abide by it. It's like being
in a football team where you have to follow the rules to the letter and the
other team can do whatever the hell they like. The voices of authority in
the company—the platoon sergeants and officers—acknowledged that
this [executing prisoners] was a proper way to behave. Who were the
grunts to disagree with it? We supported it.

There was an alternative: "Chieu Hoi," the "Open Arms"
amnesty program instituted by President Ngo Dinh Diem in 1963
to encourage defectors from the Viet Cong to rally to Saigon's side.
But according to Widmer, Charlie Company quickly wearied of
offering sanctuary to captives from the other side:

For a while we tried to absorb these people into the Chieu Hoi
program—but once we figured what was going on, after we'd been there
for a while, we thought it was stupid to take a guy who had been
shooting at us, just because he said: "I surrender." You take him back
and you feed him and nine times out of ten we'd find out he wound right
back out in the field shooting at us again. We knew this from other
people and from being around.

"*We knew this from other people.*" Like the specter of children
throwing grenades, the bogy of the treacherous defector undoubtedly had its roots in reality. But Charlie Company had already

begun to mistreat civilians and prisoners long before they experienced these things directly. They were reacting to a booby-trapped environment according to the prevailing attitudes of American and South Vietnamese troops before and after they arrived in Vietnam. Attitudes instilled from "the guy from the 1st Cav." whom Widmer had talked to in Hawaii. Or the ARVN instructors who had taught Calley when he first arrived in the country. For GIs, the problems surrounding relations with the Vietnamese in the villages were a matter of life and death. In the field, Gen. Koster's headmasterly lesson in etiquette was about as useful as a knitting pattern. Soldiers learned from soldiers. There was nothing about the "normal young men" of Charlie Company to suggest that they would overturn conventional wisdom or current practice. When they arrived in Vietnam, they went along with what they found, partly because they were scared, partly because they didn't know any better, and partly because no one told them differently. The war culture that defined the problem as "gooks" and "slant-eyes" also defined the remedies.

"The first time I saw something really bad," says Fred Widmer,

was the point at which we stopped taking prisoners. We had been there about a month and a half, or two months. There was one guy Medina had to shoot the prisoners. Instead of having everyone around and shoot them, they would walk them down toward the beach, or behind some sand dunes, and shoot them—a couple of shots and they were done. As time went by, things were done, ears cut off, mutilations. One prisoner had his arms tied straight out on a stick. One was a woman and one was a man; there was no question that these two were Viet Cong. The woman was working as a nurse and we found them in a tunnel with all the medical supplies and we knew they were the enemy. Lit cigarettes were put inside the elastic of the guy's pants and we watched him dance around because they were burning his ass. I think it was a bit of making him talk and a bit of venting our frustrations, a bit of both. I don't remember what happened to them, whether they were turned over or shot.

The more it went on, the more you didn't trust anyone; you didn't believe anybody because you didn't know who was who, you didn't know who the enemy was. As we went on, more and more prisoners would be executed. I would say it was a regular occurrence. I did abuse someone—a prisoner—a *papa san*. I found myself doing the same things that had been going on all along. I found myself caught up in it. We cut his beard off him—this was an insult. A *papa san* with a beard is considered as the wise man, and to cut off their beard was a real sign of disrespect to them.

You found yourself punching them around, beating them up trying to get them to talk. I never did hit anyone with my rifle. I have taken a knife to them . . . I never tortured anyone to death. I think I probably saw people tortured to death.

Bernhardt, an outsider as usual, watched the downward spiral: "It started with just plain prisoners—prisoners you thought were the enemy. Then you'd go on to prisoners who weren't the enemy, and then the civilians because there was no difference between the enemy and civilians. It came to the point where a guy could kill anybody."

Esequiel Torres was a sergeant in Charlie Company's 2nd Platoon. He was still only 19 when he arrived in Vietnam. Born in Brownsville, Texas, of Spanish–American parents, he was a small man, thickset with dark features. It was remembered afterward that he always carried a bowie knife. In mid-February, the 2nd Platoon was on patrol in a small village near LZ Uptight, north of the Diem Diem River, not far from where Weber had been killed. During a search of the village, Sergeant Torres discovered an old man lying on a bed. He forced the man off the bed, put a rope around his neck, and together with two other men from his squad began to torture him. Torres shouted at the man, threatening him with his bowie knife, demanding to know where the VC were. The man kept replying: "No bic! No bic!"—he did not understand what they wanted. They punched the old man and twisted and stabbed his leg, which was already injured, wrapped in a crude bandage.

One of the Americans, unable to watch, walked out of the hut, but another witness stayed and saw what happened next. With the rope around his victim's neck, Torres placed the terrified and frail old man on a table and then looped the rope over a bamboo beam, tugging on it to make it tight and secure. Then he kicked the table away. As he left the hut, Torres shouted: "Hey, Makey, I hung the son-of-a-bitch." It is not known whether the victim survived.

During the same operation, witnesses describe another incident in which Torres tortured a VC suspect by dunking him in a well and by hanging him from a tree by his feet. Eventually Torres hanged this man too, but he was cut down while still alive.

Although abuses became more frequent, no action was taken against the perpetrators. By contrast, Medina's dislike of the Vietnamese was clear for everyone to see. GIs who showed kindness to prisoners were rebuked. According to witnesses, Medina himself beat up suspects during interrogation. A GI named Lloyd from the 1st Platoon remembered Medina had told them that if they captured a prisoner and didn't kill him, then they would have to guard him and share their food with him. Lt. Calley, who never pretended to like the Vietnamese, could be pushed to extremes of violence. During an interrogation in one village, Harry Stanley was standing only ten feet away while Calley and another GI, Herbert Carter, interrogated an old farmer:

Lt. Calley asked some questions and then Carter hit the old man in the mouth twice with his fist. Then Carter pushed the old man into a well, but the old man spread his legs and arms and held on and didn't fall into the well. Then Carter hit the old man in his stomach with his rifle stock. The old man's feet fell into the well, but he was holding on with his hands. Carter hit the man's fingers, trying to make him fall into the well. Then Lt. Calley shot the man with his M-16.

For some GIs, incidents like these showed that the official attitude to brutality was permissive. What resulted was a moral vacuum, a moratorium on restraint and self-control. Common decency became optional—a matter of personal inclination. Even those who refused to be drawn in were left morally thrown off balance. Greg Olsen was in the village when Calley and Carter threw the old man down the well:

I was in the village. I remember seeing people butted in the head with rifles. But you start losing your sense of what's normal. You don't give up your morals, but you become a lot more tolerant. We believed this behavior was pretty commonplace. I didn't think we were doing anything different from any other unit. You really do lose your sense . . . not of right or wrong, but your degree of wrong changes.

And Michael Bernhardt, who watched what was happening

from the sidelines, was already viewed with some mistrust by Medina, Calley, and others in the company:

When I saw American soldiers committing acts that would be called atrocities if somebody else had done them, I began to think that maybe I'd been just too naive all my life, that this was the way things really were. Little by little, I began to see that this group of men was getting out of control. Discipline was beginning to wear off. Without military discipline they were there alone in the country with no point of reference. The things that they had brought from their families and schools were far away and beginning to disappear.

Fred Widmer too felt things going from bad to worse and felt himself drawn along with the tide:

I think if it ever occurred to me that things were getting out of hand, or that I was questioning what I myself might be capable of doing, I suppressed it. It did creep up in my mind because you still have those values of what is right and what is wrong that you have been taught all your life.

I think the frustration got to me but I also think I began to enjoy it. That's what is scary because at the time you did find yourself enjoying it. I guess you could term it the superiority we had over them. It's a strange feeling. In retrospect you look back on it and wonder how you yourself could have done it. Twenty years later, when you look back at things that happened, things that transpired, things you did, you say: Why? Why did I do that? That is not me. Something happened to me.

You reach a point over there where you snap, that is the easiest way to put it, you finally snap. Somebody flicks a switch and you are a completely different person. There is a culture of violence, of brutality, with people all around you doing the same thing.

Inevitably, the physical abuses went on side by side with sexual abuse. If life was cheap in Vietnam, so was sex, and despite all regulations, little stood in the way of a GI and sexual gratification on whatever terms he wanted. In Duc Pho, where Charlie Company first arrived in Vietnam, "there were some houses you could go to." At LZ Dottie, "some of the *mama sans* came in and sold themselves." Company medic Nicholas Capezza remembers that he was always giving the men penicillin shots and almost used up his supply. Widmer remembers that he "used to have my hootch maid service me on occasions" in the bunkers at Dottie. At other times girls were shared.

Several of us would give the same girl money and she would screw or blow job us one after the other. I don't think people thought too much about it. It was more or less like going to the toilet. I would rather have done that than rape someone. It would have been the same as someone coming into a rural community like Lower Burrell and picking out women and taking them . . . And of course if it was my sister, I wouldn't like it. And there were increasing numbers of women being raped. Out in the field it was an everyday occurrence for some people. I can remember, vaguely, one or two instances where I saw it happening and walked away from it.

After twenty years most members of Charlie Company remember the talk about rapes. From the beginning of their tour of duty, a group within the company appear to have used the search and destroy operations and patrols as an opportunity to prey on the women of the villages and countryside. Michael Bernhardt had heard "rumors of rape"; Harry Stanley was "familiar with stories of rape and gang bangs." He remembered that nothing would happen to the perpetrators: "You feel this is not right but there's nothing you can do about it." Sergeant Kenneth Hodges had "heard plenty of talk." Varnado Simpson commented: "Rape? Oh, that happened every day." Most people remember Dennis Conti in a village near LZ Uptight cutting the braided hair off a young girl at gunpoint and using it to decorate his helmet. Angry villagers followed the patrol cursing and shouting, one GI recalled. Conti, who had a bad reputation within the company for abusing women, told a later inquiry that he had cut the girl's hair off for a bet. No disciplinary action was taken.

Greg Olsen was sickened. He had seen Conti with the braided hair on his helmet and the following day had seen him again with a Vietnamese nurse hung over his shoulder: "I heard people talking about Conti . . . At the time I wasn't surprised. You stick some jerk over there and give him a gun and very little restriction and you stick him in a free-fire zone, he's going to live out all these things he'd go to prison for in the States."

Leonard Gonzalez, a member of the 2nd Platoon, saw rapes committed every time the company went through a village:

Take one squad say, it's a small village, one squad would go from the back, one goes from the front, and the other is going through. Now the one that is going through is having their fun . . .

One squad got one girl—one lady. Then they told me: "Go in there," and I said: "No, I won't." So what I did is I went inside and she looked real bad. The only thing I can do for the lady is, like, I got the canteen and wiped her. She was awful perspiring. I wiped her forehead. I tried to help her up. She got scared of me, I was part of them. I tried to tell her I don't have nothing to do with it. I helped her up to her feet. I took her to the well, got some water from the well . . .

Then another squad heard about the thirteen guys who did their thing with this woman, and were going to try her out and I told them to leave her alone, and then at that time I just walked off. I said: "Forget it." I don't want to kill my own men. I tried to tell her: "Get out of here—go." She was going to run . . . but, like, after thirteen guys got to her it's hard to walk.

Other GIs remember similarly depressing stories of casual depredation, rape, and murder, although most say that the grosser abuses of women were confined to one section of the company—well known to the rest of the men. Nevertheless the rapes, like the brutalities, continued unchecked. Without clear leadership, even those alarmed by what was happening kept their own counsel. "There was a different set of rules and I don't think any of us quite knew what those rules were," Greg Olsen remembered with regret:

You'd expect if you had knowledge of a murder, it would be incumbent on you to do something about it. But there wasn't an avenue to do it and you certainly had second thoughts about taking that kind of a stand. It isn't likely that anybody would have done anything about it except turn on you sometime. You got to remember that everybody there has a gun . . . It's nice to face your accuser, but not when he's got a gun in his hand. I was probably lacking in courage to do that. Lacking in understanding. You know, this was war. Everything you're taught about war in the movies and what you read is that war is hell and brutal things happen in wars. I wasn't prepared to single myself out at that point. You feel like a pretty small pawn in a great big game.

Fear was one reason for keeping quiet, but another even more powerful motive for not rocking the boat was Charlie Company's growing group solidarity. The company had trained and lived together for nine months, ever since Hawaii. With every new day and night spent in the field, the feeling grew stronger that the men of Charlie Company had no one else to rely on but each other. Medina insisted that orders be obeyed, but in other respects he was one of the boys. Outsiders noticed that relations between officers and men were closer and more informal than in other companies. Medina would "joke around" with the men and pose for photographs with them. Time and again veterans of Charlie Company remembered: "We were like a family." Alienated from the dangerous world around them, for days at a time their only link to the outside world was the helicopter delivering supplies. Even Bernhardt, who had arrived in the company as a late replacement, recognized how close-knit the company had become: "We were all close, the whole company—I had to depend on them and they had to depend on me." It was difficult to tell tales on men your life depended on. Besides, the brutalities, the rapes, the murders were episodes that only happened, as Bernhardt points out, when the company was in contact with the Vietnamese civilians: "Otherwise we were just like a regular society. This was all we had; this was all the people in the company felt they were answerable to. They felt they were answerable to the company commander and the other people around—and nobody else."

Fred Widmer believed the company became too *much* of a family: "You knew everybody; you knew too much about them; you were too familiar with everybody." Medina had done his job too well. For Widmer, his company commander was "the kind of officer that you see in war movies; the men would follow him anywhere." There was, however, a reservation. "Medina's failing," said Widmer, "the failing of the whole company, was that we were too close together. You are not supposed to be."

Charles Hutto, a former sergeant with Charlie Company, made the same point: "We knew each other real well. That's why it was so hard when your buddies started getting killed."

On the Sunday morning of February 25, 1968, the sky was heavily overcast and a fine cold drizzle fell on the village of Lac Son in northern Quang Ngai Province. Capt. Medina was leading Charlie Company through the bamboo thickets and hedgerows of the countryside toward a blocking position just south of the village. Above them, at the top of a small hill, was what was left of an old Korean Marines base. At around 7:30 AM came a huge explosion, followed by screams and more explosions. A minefield. "We had walked into the middle of it before anyone had tripped anything," one GI recalled. "Anybody who moved to try to help someone just got blown up themselves."

Immediately, Medina shouted: "Freeze!" Nonetheless, some men panicked and ran toward one another, detonating more explosions. Varnado Simpson fell to the ground, whimpering, and had to be held down by his buddies to stop him trying to break and run. Widmer was knocked unconscious by the impact of a mine that blew the left foot off another radio operator who was running in front of him. Someone called out mistakenly that Greg Olsen had been killed. Medina kept his head and tried to restore order and get his men out of the minefield and bring help to the injured. Later he was awarded the Silver Star for his "courage, professional actions and unselfish concern for his men." Medina gave his own account of the incident to Calley's court-martial in 1971:

We started sweeping the area as best we could with mine detectors, taking pieces of toilet paper and marking the mines that we found. We had one individual that we could not evacuate, that was dead . . . I took the medic that was with me, the platoon medic from the first platoon, and he and I moved through the minefield to where the individual was lying. He was split as if somebody had taken a cleaver and right up from his crotch all the way up to his chest cavity. I had never seen anything that looked so unreal in my entire life; the intestines, the liver, and the stomach and the blood looked just like plastic. We took a poncho and we spread it out and the medic started to pick him up by the legs. I reached underneath his arms to place him under the poncho and we set him on top of another mine. The concussion blew me back. I fell backward. As I got up the medic was starting to go to pieces on me. I looked at him as if he had stood behind the screen and somebody had taken a paintbrush with red paint and splattered it through the screen. He had blood all over him. I grabbed him as he started to pass me and I shook him and I said, "My God, don't go to pieces on me. You are the only medic I have got. I have got people that are hurt." I hit him. I slapped him. I knocked him to the ground and I helped him to get back up, and I saw on his religious medal a piece of liver and I tried to get it off the individual before he seen it. The individual was very shook up.

Everybody was shaken. Three men were dead. Another twelve suffered ghastly injuries. Few could forget their own fear, or the screams of the wounded, or the gruesome task of loading the medevac helicopters. "When you have been through a minefield and put the remains of friends in body bags, nothing shocks you anymore," Michael Bernhardt recalled. For Widmer it was the first true experience of the horror of war, "the terror of seeing people blown apart." He remembers watching helplessly as an injured friend lay hollering on the ground, the words going round his head: "This is war, this is what it is about, this is what happens to you." Charlie Company's esprit de corps vanished without trace. Morale sagged. What remained of the élan of the unit that had formed the vanguard of the 11th Brigade's deployment in Vietnam was destroyed in the horror of the minefield near Lac Son. Although Medina emerged from the catastrophe with his reputation among the men enhanced, rumors that the minefield had been laid by the Koreans—allies in the war—further undermined the company's faith that their officers knew what they were doing. But most of all, they blamed the Vietnamese—not the Viet Cong who they could not see or find, but the Vietnamese of the villages who did not warn them of the minefields and the booby traps.

The idea that the villagers were "definitely responsible" filled the minds of the chastened and sullen company as they eventually pulled themselves free of the mines. Sgt Hodges summed up the feelings of his men: "Feelings of revenge extended to all the people in the village, because we felt that all of them, whether they were female, military-age male, old men, or kids, they were all part of the problem."

Lt. Calley noticed the change in mood of the men. He had been on leave at the time of the incident and had returned to LZ Uptight in time to meet the helicopters ferrying the dead and injured. From now on, the men in his platoon no longer gave candy to the Vietnamese children they came across while on patrol in the villages. Instead, Calley noticed with some satisfaction, they kicked everybody aside—even "the nice sweet kids." He could hardly refrain from telling them: "Well, I told you so."

*

Meanwhile, frustration in the field was matched by growing frustration at Task Force Command. Two days before the disaster at Lac Son, Task Force Barker had failed in yet another combined operation to trap the Viet Cong's 48th Local Force Battalion. This time the intelligence reports—based, it was claimed, on previous combat operations, visual reconnaissance, prisoner interrogations, and reports of informants and agents—had suggested that the enemy were holed up in a village marked as My Lai 6 on American maps. But before Alpha Company, leading the attack, could near the village, they came under heavy automatic and mortar fire originating from My Lai 4. This was the second time in a month that the task force had encountered resistance from My Lai 4. Captain Patrick Trinkle, the commander of Alpha Company, called in airstrikes and helicopter gunships to dislodge the guerrillas. There was intense fighting all afternoon, during which Trinkle himself was wounded—shot in the leg and the back.

By the early evening when Americans reached their target at My Lai 6, the enemy—who may or may not have included elements of the 48th LF Battalion—had disappeared. According to the American version they "had broken contact by infiltrating with civilians leaving the area or by going down the extensive maze of tunnels which abound the area." One American was killed and fifteen injured. This compared with a body count of sixty-eight for the Viet Cong. These were satisfactory ratios, although, as usual, very few enemy weapons were recovered.

"Well planned, well executed, and successful" was the official version of this scrappy and inconclusive little skirmish. But in private, task force commanders were scathing. General Lipscomb, the 11th Brigade commander, watched the operation from his helicopter and returned to Duc Pho "almost in disgust." Yet again, he thundered, the engagement had underlined the unit's inability to "close with the enemy." Instead of pressing forward, ground troops had wasted too much time waiting for airstrikes and medevac helicopters. Enemy soldiers had been able to escape with their weapons and the weapons of the enemy dead. South Vietnamese soldiers, helping the task force from the south, had been too afraid of the large numbers of mines and booby traps to advance into the area. American troops were not as aggressive later in the battle as they were earlier, although aggression increased again at the insistence of Barker. According to Col. Oran K. Henderson, soon to take over as commander of the 11th Brigade, Alpha Company had sat back and permitted the enemy "to bug out of there." It was understandably disagreeable for an American commander to admit that his men had been guilty of a failure, and Henderson resolved that if the enemy ever escaped another time it would not be for want of aggression on the Americans' side.

No one doubted that there would be another time. Tet was still fresh in everyone's mind. In Quang Ngai City there was a curfew from seven in the evening to seven the following morning. Reports from the American mission expressed anxiety over a "second Tet." In the countryside around the provincial capital the mood was uncertain; most people in the villages were described as "sitting on the fence." Pacification in the villages, or "revolutionary develop-ment" as pacification had come to be called by 1968, could only work if villagers knew that the Americans could protect them from Viet Cong reprisals. After Tet, no one could be sure anymore. By March, little more than half of the Revolutionary Development (RD) teams were back at work in the countryside and of those only a handful dared to sleep in the villages at night. Most Americans believed that the Viet Cong had suffered a severe setback at Tet. Estimates put enemy losses in the Quang Ngai City attack alone at more than 640. Nevertheless reports of the period bristled with apprehension. Charlie Cong was somewhere out there, recruiting, reequiping, regrouping, waiting for a second chance. The problem—as always—was: where?

Eugene Kotouc, a short, overweight, and balding infantry captain, twice passed over for promotion, was Task Force Barker's intel-ligence officer. Kotouc was not a methodical man. He hardly ever took notes, never compiled a written intelligence report, and did not once use a typewriter the whole time he was attached to Task Force Barker. He did, however, have experience of Vietnam, and could speak Vietnamese.

Like Medina, whom he knew well, Kotouc was an enlisted man who had joined the Army in 1955. In the early sixties, he had attended the US Army Special Warfare School at Fort Bragg, North Carolina. He learned Vietnamese at the Presidio at Monterey, California, and trained to be an advisor to the South Vietnamese Army. His first tour in Vietnam began on September 4, 1962, when he was 28, and even included two months in Quang Ngai. But evidently he didn't shine in South Vietnam. He left after only eleven months for a posting with the Army National Guard at Beatrice, Nebraska, not far from his family home in Humboldt.

By chance, the start of Eugene Kotouc's second tour of duty in South Vietnam coincided with the arrival in Quang Ngai City early in February 1968 of a dark and truly extraordinary character. Robert B. Ramsdell was already 45 years old, a large, some said fat, man, who wore jeans, a beret, an army combat jacket, and carried a high-velocity Swedish submachine gun. Earlier in life, Ramsdell had been an army police detective, then a private eye in New York and Florida. He was now starting his first assignment for the CIA and had come to Quang Ngai to supervise the Phoenix Program in the province.

The "Phuong Hoang" or Phoenix Program was a new intelligence offensive designed to identify and eliminate the Viet Cong infrastructure, defined as the political leaders and cadres who formed the backbone of the enemy's superb clandestine organization in the countryside. Its aim was to coordinate intelligence from a national network of informers and strike hard at the estimated 70,000 members who made up the hard core of Viet Cong civilian support. Phoenix quickly became controversial. Although it was fiercely denied by the Americans at the time, the program encouraged the widespread use of assassination, torture, and imprisonment—the mirror image of the "selective" and discriminating terror that hitherto had been the hallmark of the Viet Cong. Although the South Vietnamese carried out the Phuong Hoang follow-up actions in the villages and hamlets, the CIA provided advisors, money, and equipment. Their informants in the villages got paid by results, an arrangement the agency's staff found a far better way of producing information than putting people on retainers.

Nothing about the operation of Phoenix in Quang Ngai under Ramsdell in 1968 belied the program's lurid and sinister reputation.

Soon after Tet, Quang Ngai, in common with population centers throughout the country, set up its own "Phuong Hoang house"— an interrogation center which quickly acquired its own notoriety. Many suspects sent there by the Army were never seen again, and doctors at the prison at Con Son Island complained that prisoners sent on to them from Quang Ngai were frequently victims of severe beatings and torture. Dr Margaret Nelson, who worked for the American Friends Service Committee, told a congressional hearing in 1970 that she had dealt with dozens of cases of torture from Quang Ngai: "Prisoners told me of being tortured by electricity with wires attached to ears, nipples, and genitalia; by being forced to drink concoctions containing powdered lime; and by being tied up and suspended by ropes often upside down from the rafters for hours."

Under Ramsdell, the program quickly gathered pace. By May 1968, Phoenix operatives in Quang Ngai boasted that they had already drawn up a black book—a list of suspects—for every village in the province. In three months, they claimed, an estimated 796 people had been captured or killed under the program.

Skeptics in the intelligence community in Quang Ngai doubted the value of such intelligence. Most CIA men did not condone the extreme violence used by the South Vietnamese forces; indeed, they saw it as counterproductive. In many cases Vietnamese farmers were being fingered as Viet Cong simply as a means of settling old scores. Moreover, under beatings and torture, VC suspects often told their interrogators what they thought they wanted to hear. Experienced CIA officers felt it was far better to turn a VC supporter round, so that they could persuade others to accept an amnesty and work for the South Vietnamese government.

But Ramsdell was a true believer. He paid a lot for his information and never doubted his sources. Where others counseled caution, Ramsdell, who had never been to Vietnam before, exuded confidence to the point of arrogance. In 1970, he would tell the Peers Committee that he knew almost everything of significance happening in the province. "I've gotten word when a GI truck has gone through the village too fast, or run over a cow," he told Peers.

For Task Force Barker, the most important question on the

intelligence agenda was that of the strength and location of the 48th LF Battalion. Historically, the Batangan Peninsula had always been considered by military intelligence to be the battalion's HQ. Its area of operations was known to be concentrated in the eastern Binh Son and Son Tinh districts in which the My Lai villages were found. Task Force Barker had tried twice—and failed twice—to trap them in this area. No one was even sure whether the opposition the task force did encounter consisted of elements of the 48th Battalion or not. What was certain was that the main body of the VC regiment was not where it was supposed to be when the attacks took place.

On February 29, a week after Alpha Company had failed to run the local force battalion to ground, the task force received a confidential "Sphinx" cable from Saigon with the news that analysis of agents' reports suggested that the 48th was deployed in the Batangan Peninsula and was about to combine with other units and initiate an offensive in the Quang Ngai City area.

On March 1, an enemy trawler was fired on and forced aground on the peninsula. The trawler returned fire, but overwhelming allied counterfire forced the crew to abandon ship, which was then destroyed by a self-destruct mechanism. Intelligence reported that the trawler had been supplying the 48th Battalion.

In fact Army intelligence was diffident about pinpointing the whereabouts of enemy units. The chief intelligence officer of the 11th Brigade had only a vague idea of where the 48th VC Battalion was even during February when the clashes with Task Force Barker were taking place. Trying to locate them was "like playing blind man's bluff."

Nevertheless, many Army intelligence officers—including those from the 11th Brigade and the Americal Division—believed the 48th Local Force Battalion was nowhere near My Lai. According to these assessments, the unit, hard hit during Tet when it had lost the battalion commander and two of its four company commanders, was rebuilding in the mountains to the west of the province—far from the coastal plain where the My Lai group of villages were located. Furthermore, whereas Task Force Barker was expecting to meet anything from 250 to 400 Viet Cong, Army estimates put the ravaged 48th's strength as down to less than a hundred fighting men. One Army account, which described how the body of the 48th's commander had been dragged through the streets of Quang Ngai City, claimed that the battalion's numbers had been reduced to around thirty.

An intelligence roundup for March 1968, prepared retrospectively, summed up the state of knowledge thus: "Although Son Tinh District remained relatively quiet during this period, elements of the 48th and existing local force units *probably* roamed the district countryside. The hills north and northwest of the My Lai 4 area were *probable* base camps for elements of the 48th Battalion and it *probably* received supplies by sea off Batangan Peninsula" (our italics).

So where was the task force getting its information from? There is a strange discrepancy between what the Army thought it knew about the Viet Cong and what the task force thought it knew. Army intelligence made only tentative claims. By contrast, Ramsdell and, for that matter, Kotouc were almost pontifical.

There was a kind of perverse destiny that brought the two overweight and middle-aged American captains, Ramsdell and Kotouc, together in post-Tet Quang Ngai City. Both were new boys to the real world of intelligence assessment in a battle zone; both were inexperienced, both desperately eager to establish a reputation. Ramsdell had provided intelligence to Kotouc prior to the My Lai operation and the curious convergence of their views irresistibly suggests that it was indeed Ramsdell who had provided the intelligence for the attack on My Lai itself. The suggestions that the 48th Local Force Battalion was up to four hundred strong, that everyone in the village was Viet Cong or a Viet Cong sympathizer, and that at seven on a Saturday morning all bona-fide civilians would have left the village for the market—all these views were shared by Ramsdell and Kotouc and accepted uncritically by Task Force Barker.

Asked later about intelligence indicating that no civilians would be left in the village at the time of the attack, Ramsdell replied that the civilians went to market early in the morning because of the heat. Eugene Kotouc echoed Ramsdell when he testified to Peers in a similar vein: "In the civilian population area, there were several markets, large markets, where all the people would gather each day because they had no refrigeration or anything like."

With hindsight, it appears naive, even simple minded. Yet early in 1968, this nugget of anthropological insight—along with the corollary that everyone who was not at market was Viet Cong—was deemed unchallengeable by Ramsdell; considered impeccable by Kotouc; and was passed on unamended to the bitter men of Charlie Company seeking revenge for their losses.

Meanwhile, the losses continued. On March 14, while on patrol on Highway One near LZ Dottie, Sergeant George Cox was killed by a booby trap. Cox was a popular figure in the company, with a reputation for looking after his men. He had been leading a small squad from the third platoon when the booby trap exploded, ripping him to pieces and hideously injuring two other soldiers. Dyson lost both legs; Hendrixson was blinded, suffered groin injuries, and lost an arm and a leg. Shrapnel from the blast landed at the feet of other members of the squad resting 200 feet away. It was an appalling sight. After loading their dead sergeant and injured comrades onto a helicopter, the remainder of the squad headed back toward LZ Dottie in a frenzied and wrathful state. Some men were crying. They snatched angrily at the possessions of the Vietnamese in the hamlets they passed through. A villager passing on a bicycle was beaten up, but managed to escape. A woman working in the fields was shot when someone shouted that she was carrying a weapon. When the squad came closer they discovered she was unarmed and still alive. They shot her again and kicked her body to pulp. Somebody stole her ring. They were now close to Dottie, and angry villagers stormed the camp in protest against the murder. Medina managed to hush it up. No one was charged with any offense. Medina said later that the woman had been discovered with a detonator still in her hand. Calley commented that Medina wasn't about to lose men just because they "kicked a Vietnamese kid or killed a damn innocent woman . . . He had to keep a combat effective unit."

Michael Terry was in the squad. That night, his friend and fellow Mormon, Greg Olsen, wrote to his father back in the States:

Dear Dad:
  How's everything with you? I'm still here on the bridge, we leave here

Saturday. One of our platoons went out on a routine patrol today and came across a 155-mm artillery round that was booby trapped. It killed one man, blew the legs off two others, and injured two more. And it all turned out a bad day made even worse. On their way back to "Dottie" they saw a woman working in the fields. They shot and wounded her. Then they kicked her to death and emptied their magazines in her head. They slugged every little kid they came across. Why in God's name does this have to happen? These are all seemingly normal guys; some were friends of mine. For a while they were like wild animals. It was murder, and I'm ashamed of myself for not trying to do anything about it. This isn't the first time, Dad. I've seen it many times before. I don't know why I'm telling you all this; I guess I just want to get it off my chest. My faith in my fellow men is shot all to hell. I just want my time to pass and I just want to come home. I really believe as you do, Dad, there is a cause behind all this, and if it is God's will for me to go, I would rather do it here than home on the freeway. Saturday we're going to be dropped in by air in an NVA stronghold. I'm still hoping I'll be able to get out of here for a few days to go to a conference. Don't expect any letters for a while but please keep writing them.

> I love and miss you and Mom so much—
> Your son, Greg.

With these most recent losses, Charlie Company was down to 105 men. Since arriving in Vietnam three months before, they had suffered twenty-eight casualties, including five killed, three of them in action. All the casualties had come from mines and booby traps and snipers. They had never seen or encountered the enemy in any strength. There had been no heavy contact. They were battle-scarred without being battle-hardened.

At ten o'clock the morning after Cox's death, Friday, March 15, there was a change of command in Task Force Barker's parent unit, the 11th Infantry Brigade. At a formal ceremony at Duc Pho, Col. Oran K. Henderson accepted the brigade's colors from the outgoing commander whom he had served faithfully ever since the brigade had been reactivated in Hawaii in 1966. It was Henderson's first combat command. By one o'clock, he had already flown by helicopter to LZ Dottie for a briefing on a Task Force Barker operation due to start the following day. This was the same operation referred to by Greg Olsen in his letter home to his father—a new attempt to trap the local force battalion. Charlie

Company were to be dropped by air into an NVA stronghold—My Lai 4. It was Charlie Company's chance to get even.

According to Kotouc, the briefings for the officers in the chain of command for Task Force Barker were often haphazard, disorganized affairs. Barker would sometimes speak for five minutes then abruptly leave his command tent to answer a radio call or attend to some other business. He'd return to throw Kotouc or one of the others a question: "What about this? What's up here?" Kotouc would give his report, and the company commanders would listen, whereupon Barker would jump up once more and disappear to his tent, only to come back a few minutes later and continue where he left off. There wasn't much real dialogue or exchange of ideas. Very little was written down on paper.

On this occasion, somewhat to his surprise, the new brigade commander was asked to address the briefing. Henderson was unprepared. He had seen little combat in Vietnam, and up to this point had not been much involved in tactical operations. Nevertheless, he had studied the task force's previous efforts to destroy the 48th Battalion and been unimpressed. The coming attack against My Lai 4 was to be the first combat action under his command. He wanted results and he wanted aggression. "I wanted them to make contact and forcibly move in when they made contact and destroy the enemy as fast as they could," Henderson said later. The 48th Local Force Battalion had been giving the Americans "a hell of a lot of trouble." He wanted them eliminated "once and for all." Forget about stopping and starting to evacuate the wounded, he told the task force officers. "The best way to protect the wounded man so he could get evacuated was to aggressively pursue the enemy and move on out." Medina recalled that Henderson had warned against "men, women, or children, or other VC soldiers in the area" picking up weapons and getting away. None of the others present could remember this aspect of Henderson's briefing.

Col. Henderson was still at the briefing when the division's artillery chaplain, Captain Carl Creswell, joined them:

I had no business there. Chaplains do this—just stopped in to say "hello" and meet the new commander. They had the maps laid out on the board and there was a major in there who was on the task force staff. I remember he said: "We're going in there, and if we get one round out of there, we're gonna level it."

And I looked at him and I said: "You know, I didn't really think we made war that way." And he looked at me and he said: "It's a tough war, chaplain." I left shortly after that and got into my bird and went back to division headquarters. And, of course, they assaulted My Lai the next day.

At 2:15 PM, Col. Henderson left to return to Duc Pho. The briefing continued with Eugene Kotouc's intelligence assessment. By now, Kotouc had been Task Force Barker's intelligence officer for five weeks and he thoroughly approved of Henderson's emphasis on aggression. He had seen Bravo Company mauled in the My Lai area and he expected similar tough opposition the following day. Although no written record of the briefing survives, witnesses all agree on the general thrust of Kotouc's contribution. The 48th LF Battalion was dispersed throughout the area, but the latest intelligence, the assembled officers were told, suggested that VC headquarters and two companies, totalling over two hundred fighting men, were located in My Lai 4. The civilian population were all "active sympathizers with the VC." By seven in the morning most noncombatants would have left the village for market.

Nor is there any documentary record of the contribution of Lt. Col. Frank Barker, the task force commander, which came next. If written orders or maps of the operation were ever made, they no longer exist. Barker himself was killed in a helicopter crash in June 1968, leaving no account of his own version of the events. Evidently his briefing concentrated on operational matters. The three-day search and destroy operation was to begin at 0725 hours the next day. An artillery battery of four 105-mm howitzers located at LZ Uptight would open up on an area just to the west of My Lai 4 to clear a landing zone for the incoming helicopters. According to most witnesses, Barker also ordered artillery and helicopter gunship fire to be directed on the western edge of the village itself to knock out the enemy positions dug into the tree line. No warning was to be given to the inhabitants. Some reference seems to have been made to leaflets that had been dropped on the village warning of an impending attack, and Barker repeated his intelligence officer's view that most civilians would have gone to the local markets. No plans were discussed about what to do with any civilians who remained in the village. Charlie Company was to land by helicopter at 0730 hours and begin to move east through the village. Later Bravo Company would be ferried to another LZ on the coast, south of My Lai 1, but for a time they were to be held in reserve in case Charlie Company ran into trouble.

What was to happen to the village itself? Task force officers left the meeting with the clear impression that Barker had ordered the destruction of all the "houses, dwellings, and livestock" in the My Lai area, although there is some doubt as to whether this was a direct order or something that had been assumed. Kotouc recalled Barker saying that the village was to be destroyed. "He wanted the area cleaned out, he wanted it neutralized, and he wanted the buildings knocked down. He wanted the hootches burned, he wanted the tunnels filled in, and then he wanted the livestock and chickens run off, killed or destroyed. He wanted to neutralize the area." For Medina also, those were Barker's clear instructions.

And what was to happen to the civilians? There is nothing to suggest that Barker explicitly ordered the murder of the ordinary people of My Lai. But the previous failures of the task force and the demand for more aggression; the intelligence picture of a community entirely controlled by the Viet Cong; the bland assumption that civilians would be "gone to market"; the totally unjustified belief that innocent people had been warned to get out of the area—in other words, the entire scorched-earth concept of an operation planned to "neutralize" the area, drove irresistibly to the conclusion that here was a free-fire zone in which even the people were to be eliminated. In the words of the Peers Commission Report: "it seems reasonable to conclude that LTC Barker's minimal or nonexistent instructions concerning the handling of noncombatants created the potential for grave misunderstandings as to his intentions and for the interpretation of his orders as authority to fire, without restriction, on all persons found in the target area."

Sometime in the middle of the afternoon, the briefing broke up. Barker and his company commanders strode across the base camp at LZ Dottie toward the helicopter pads. In moments, they were airborne, heading toward the target area only 12 miles away. They flew southwest over Hill 102, Nui Dong De, from which only weeks before Medina and Charlie Company had watched the battered remnants of the 48th LF Battalion in full retreat beneath them. With the hills behind them, the American commanders peered down to the rolling countryside around Lac Son where the minefield had been; and then the bend in the Diem Diem River where Weber had died. Afterward, turning south, the helicopter circled over the rich patchwork of paddy fields and villages in the wide valley of the Tra Khuc River. They flew high so as not to attract attention, but they could clearly see the road, at times hardly more than a track, which led past the old fort at Chau Thanh and out past the villages of My Lai toward the sea. Below were villages hidden beneath extraordinary outcrops of trees and exotic vegetation, irregular islands moored in rice fields. Narrow yellow tracks, almost causeways, joined one habitation to another. They were villages whose real Vietnamese names the Americans had never troubled to learn: Truong Dinh, Tu Cung, My Lai, Co Luy, collectively marked on American maps as My Lai 4. The helicopter then flew along the coast, over the villages the Americans knew as Co Luy 1, Co Luy 2 and Co Luy 3 and on in the direction of My Khe, which nestled under tall dark coconut trees on the white sand dunes at the very edge of the South China Sea. My Khe was Bravo Company's target for the following day. In the west, the sun was sinking toward the Truong Son Mountains as the helicopter circled back homeward. Below was some of the most beautiful country in Vietnam. In the helicopter sat Medina, the leaders of the other two companies, and Lt. Col. Frank Barker, a task force commander with something to prove.

Later that afternoon there was a memorial service for Sgt Cox at LZ Dottie, another highly charged emotional occasion. The men remembered Cox's wife who had stayed behind in Hawaii when Charlie Company had embarked for Vietnam. Reports of the sickening injuries to the others intensified the men's feelings.

The light was fading as the service for George Cox ended. Medina called Charlie Company together. The men gathered in a dark and vengeful mood and sat or leaned on rusting 55-gallon drums while they waited for their commander to explain what was in store for them the following morning. Here, outside Medina's command post, occurred the inevitable conjuncture of policy and psychology—the time and the place when America's wall-eyed strategy in Vietnam coalesced with the unappeasable bloodlust of "a normal cross section of American youth assigned to any rifle company." A machine out of control joined with men out of control.

Medina grabbed a shovel from a quarter-ton trailer and drew a map of My Lai 4 in the dirt at his feet as he described the coming engagement. Tomorrow, he told them, was Charlie Company's chance to get even.

Medina relayed what he had learned at Barker's briefing earlier in the afternoon. The 48th Viet Cong Battalion were in My Lai 4 with a strength of between 250 and 280. This meant that Charlie Company would be outnumbered more than two to one, but they were not to worry because helicopter gunships would all be on the American side. He told them to expect "a hell of a good fight." He told them that all innocent civilians would have gone to market.

But what was going to happen to the village?

"I told them we had permission, Colonel Barker had received permission from the ARVNs, that the village could be destroyed since it was a VC stronghold, to burn the houses down, to kill all the livestock, to cut any of the crops that might feed the VC, to cave the wells, and destroy the village."

And what was going to happen to the innocent civilians? Somebody at the briefing asked him: Do we kill women and children? It was an astounding question that speaks volumes about the temper of the men—but the fact that such a question was indeed asked is not disputed. Where testimony is divided is what Medina replied. "My reply to that question was: No, you do not kill women and children. You must use common sense. If they have a weapon and are trying to engage you, then you can shoot back, but you must use common sense."

Many of the men got a different message. This is Sgt Hodges's recollection of the briefing:

This was a time for us to get even. A time for us to settle the score. A time for revenge—when we can get revenge for our fallen comrades.

The order we were given was to kill and destroy everything that was in the village. It was to kill the pigs, drop them in the wells; pollute the water supply; kill, cut down the banana trees; burn the village; burn the hootches as we went through it. It was clearly explained that there were to be no prisoners.

The order that was given was to kill everyone in the village. Someone asked if that meant the women and children. And the order was: everyone in the village. Because those people that were in the village—the women, the kids, the old men—were VC. They were Viet Cong themselves or they were sympathetic to the Viet Cong. They were not sympathetic to the Americans. It was quite clear that no one was to be spared in that village.

Sgt Hodges was not alone in his interpretation of Medina's briefing. Many of the senior NCOs left the meeting convinced that the order was to kill everyone. Staff Sgt L. A. Bacon: "We were to kill all the Viet Cong and Viet Cong sympathizers in the village." Sgt Charles West: "It was a search and destroy mission, we were to kill everything." Staff Sgt Martin Fagan: "Kill everyone." Sgt Isaiah Cowan: "To kill everything that was in the village." Enlisted men too, Glimpse, Lamartina, Gonzalez, Lloyd, Partsch, Moss, later testified that this was what they heard. Flynn even remembered the question: "Someone asked, 'Are we supposed to kill women and children?' and Medina replied, 'Kill everything that moves.'"

Harry Stanley said:

Captain Medina had told us that the intelligence had established that My Lai 4 was completely enemy controlled. He described the formations we were to use the following day and told us to carry extra ammunition. He ordered us to "kill everything in the village." The men in my squad talked about this among ourselves that night because the order to "kill everything in the village" was so unusual. We all agreed that Captain Medina meant for us to kill every man, woman, and child in the village.

At his trial in 1971, twenty-one members of Charlie Company testified on Calley's behalf that Medina had ordered everyone killed. This is the version of Medina's briefing that Calley himself gave the court:

We were going to start at My Lai 4 and would have to neutralize My Lai 4 completely and not let anyone get behind us. Then we would move to My Lai 5 and neutralize it and make sure there was no one left in My Lai 5, and so on until we got into the Pinkville area. Then we would completely neutralize My Lai 1, which is Pinkville. He said it was completely essential that at no time [should] we lose our momentum of attack, because the two other companies that had assaulted the time in there before, had let the enemy get behind him, or had passed through the enemy, allowing him to get behind him and set up behind him, which would disorganize when he made his final assault on Pinkville. It would disorganize him, they would lose their momentum of attack, take heavy casualties, and would be more worried about their casualties than they would their mission, and that that was their downfall. So it was our job this time to go through, neutralize these villages by destroying everything in them, not letting anyone or anything get in behind us, and move on to Pinkville.

Calley was on trial for his life, and therefore his version is hardly impartial, but there's a great deal here that echoes Col. Henderson's address to the task force commanders that morning. It was absolutely to be expected that he would not anticipate the import of his advice when translated to men in the field. Henderson had spent his time fighting the paper war. In the real war, however, the logic was quite straightforward: If the intention was to ensure that no one was left alive behind you, and in the absence of any other instructions about what to do with civilians, the only alternative was to kill them.

Someone had asked, Calley told the court, "if that meant women and children." And Medina had said: "That meant everything."

But not everyone agreed that Medina had ordered everyone in the village to be killed. Greg Olsen, whose foreboding letter to his father had been posted only two days before, has a completely different recollection of the briefing:

There clearly, absolutely, wasn't an order to go in and slaughter everybody in that village and anybody that says so is a liar. Medina said that any villagers were to be rounded up and airlifted to refugee camps. That was specifically addressed in the meeting. If I thought I was going to get on a helicopter that morning with clear orders that I was going to slaughter every living breathing human being in that village, I'm sure to

God, it would have been so appalling and unthinkable. I mean, I'm not stupid. I know they couldn't have forced me to do something like that.

Others too denied there was any explicit order. "It was like Medina's benediction," Michael Bernhardt said. "He didn't actually say to kill every man, woman, and child in My Lai. He stopped just short of saying that. He gave every other indication that that's what he expected." Whatever Medina actually said, there can be no doubt about the impression he made on most of the men. To hurt pride he offered satisfaction. To grieving soldiers, he offered a chance to strike back. To bitter and resentful men, he offered an end to frustration. Medina let slip the dogs of war. My Lai 4 was thrown in the path of their vindictiveness and fury. Charlie Company was going to get its revenge. The task force would get its body count. This time there would be no mistake.

"Your adrenalin started to flow just thinking about the next day," Widmer remembered years later. "We were going to get into it—and this is what we're here for. Finally, at last, it was gonna happen."

The meeting broke up. Medina and Kotouc left to eat supper together. The men drifted back to their bunkers. They had a steak and beer. Some watched a strip movie. A few got a little drunk.

4. My Lai, March 16, 1968: AM

Soon after first light, Charlie Company lined up on the landing field inside the defended perimeter of LZ Dottie, waiting for the "Dolphins" and the "Sharks" to appear out of the sky.* Some of the men were bleary-eyed. They had talked long into the night about what the next day would be like, before finally snatching a few hours' sleep, only to be ushered from their bunks before dawn, at 5:30 AM, and told to gather up their gear.

Platoon commanders distributed ammunition. More than a hundred men and several tons of fighting gear were about to be shipped 11 miles in an operation they hoped would take the enemy completely by surprise. The target of their first full-scale combat assault was less than fifteen minutes' flying time away. The troops could hear the distant *whop-whop-whop-whop* of the nine liftships and gunships from the 174th Helicopter Assault Company before the aircraft emerged from behind the tree line. They landed close by, kicking up clouds of fine dust from the downdraft of spinning rotors.

The "Slicks," the troop-carrying helicopters, were to move the company in two lifts. First they would take Medina's command group, the 1st Platoon, and as many of the 2nd Platoon as they could manage. These would then secure the landing zone for the remainder of the company. Also to be carried on the second lift were a few additional men from other brigade units temporarily assigned to Charlie Company for the Pinkville operation. They included Lieutenant Dennis Johnson, a military intelligence officer, and his Vietnamese interpreter. Demolition engineers Jerry

---

* "Dolphins"/"Sharks": radio callsigns of the liftships and gunships of the 174th Helicopter Assault Company.

"Hotrod" Hemming and Calvin Hawkins had volunteered for the operation only the day before. Finally, an Army photographer and a reporter from the public information outfit were being taken along as well.

Weighed down by extra clips of ammunition, machine-gun bandoleers, grenades, flak jackets, water canteens, ropes, flashlights, .45 pistols, medical bandages, grenade launchers, and K-rations, the men on the first lift waited at the departure point. The additional equipment they needed for battle meant an extra heavy load for the liftships. Radio operators stuck close to their platoon command groups; ammo bearers were joined as if by an umbilical cord to the machine-gun teams. When the choppers touched down, the men in the first lift clambered into the vibrating compartments of the doorless cargo holds. Waiting for them on either side of the aircraft were two gunners, crouched beneath a metal covering enclosing the helicopter's transmission and hydraulic system, directly beneath the rotor mast.

The pilots sat in heavily armored seats of half-inch-thick steel wrapped in an aluminum frame. They throttled every last percent of available power on the gauge, making mental notes against checklists of radio call signs and frequencies. They had already made their calculations of the likely weight they were carrying, judging down to the last few hundred pounds how high and how fast they could fly the aircraft, men, and equipment. Behind them turbine fans spun gases from a jet engine and caused the machines to shudder violently. The pilots waited for the point when the 48-foot-long rotors were spinning fast enough to give the aircraft lift. They then pulled on the control stick, adjusted the rotor wings, and allowed the aircraft to rise slowly off the ground.

Watching this at a distance, the remnants of Charlie Company left behind on the ground inhaled the sweet smell of kerosene filtering from engine exhausts. Finally the "Dolphins" and "Sharks" staggered from their parking slots and gradually lifted into the air. They lumbered, nose tilted forward, along the ground until the pilots judged they had enough power to climb higher. Rising above the tree line, they gathered up into a "V" formation before heading south, hugging the edge of Highway One.

On the ground the Army photographer began work. Ron Haeberle had been in the fourth year of college as a photography major in his home town of Cleveland, Ohio, when he was drafted. The Army quickly recognized his talent with a camera and assigned him to the Public Information Detachment at brigade headquarters at Duc Pho. Haeberle and Jay Roberts, a PID reporter from Arlington, Virginia, were assigned to write a morale-boosting piece on Task Force Barker's campaign to root out the Viet Cong from the Batangan Peninsula. Their usual procedure, developed after similar missions with other outfits, was to prepare a press release and photograph that would be used in *Stars and Stripes* and many other Army newspapers. The MACV information office in Saigon circulated their stories, and often they made it onto the AP wire and into the papers back home. Now, Haeberle's service-issue Leica, with its black-and-white film, stayed unused as he focused his own 35-mm Nikon on the slowly rising helicopters. He had captured the first image of the day on Ektachrome color film.

Several hundred feet above, the pilots lined up behind the aircraft they were designated to follow in the formation. By 7:22 AM, the first lift of troops had left Dottie behind and was well on its way. "Coyote Six," Frank Barker's command-and-control helicopter, was already on station. "Skeeter," a tiny bubble helicopter, was *en route* from Chu Lai. During the battle it would skip low over the trees, reconning the battle ground, ferreting out the enemy positions, drawing fire for the high and low gunships to engage. Off the coastline away out to the east on the South China Sea, *News Boy India Two Zero*, a high-powered Swift Boat of the "Brown Water Navy," which operated among South Vietnam's inshore waters and rivers, moved into position. It was all going like clockwork.

In the hamlet, which the Americans had labeled My Lai 4 on their military maps, the day had begun several hours earlier with the lighting of fires. This was women's work. Every household had a fire in their dirt yard, sheltered from the wind and shared with dogs, pigs, ducks, and chickens. With luck the dying embers from the night before were enough to give a flame to a freshly applied handful of dried twigs. A pan of water was boiled constantly on the lighted fire and replaced only when a meal was to be heated up. It was an early morning routine which had gone on for generation after generation. Most of the farmers, who were heads of households, were already out in the fields. Some of the older children had gone to fetch water from wells, or check how many fish they had netted in the river.

Seven kilometers away, the pilots swung their aircraft round in a long semicircle and made their final run-in to approach the landing zone from the southwest. They scanned the horizon, looking for smoke: not the fine wisps of blue smoke from household fires, but thick, heavy, white smoke, the kind that accompanied the booming sounds of surface detonating rounds as high explosive and white phosphorus shells whumped and burst onto the western edge of the settlement. For three minutes, just before 7:30 AM, a small group of artillerymen sweated and strained to deliver their first barrage of the day from four 105-mm guns. D Company, 6/11th Artillery Battalion, had fired thousands of rounds into Quang Ngai Province during its time at the fortified fire base at LZ Uptight, across the Diem Diem River only 6 miles north of My Lai 4. To the artillerymen firing the guns the target was merely a set of coordinates, though they knew perfectly well that when the shells landed they would kill anything within a radius of 35 meters on unobstructed flat ground.

The impact of the artillery fire was being monitored that morning by Lieutenant Dennis Vasquez, an observer aboard Frank Barker's "Charlie Charlie" aircraft. Covering a similar route to the one they had taken on their fly-by recce the day before, Barker's observation team were still several miles away from the LZ. In the distance Vasquez could see smoke popping around what he took to be the landing zone. When the shells thundered in toward their target the people of My Lai 4 fled underground into crude bomb shelters or tunnels dug beneath their homes.

Virtually unobserved, the artillery barrage was tantamount to blind firing. No spotter was close enough to adjust the fire away from the village. What was intended as an artillery preparation for the paddy fields 400 meters northwest of the village turned instead into something else. In those three minutes 120 rounds fell not only among the dikes and fields but also very close to the fragile dwellings spread out around the hamlet. Eventually they strayed over into the inhabited area itself, sending shrapnel flying, snapping trees like twigs, causing terror and panic.

Blind firing was nothing new to the province of Quang Ngai. Hundreds of thousands of rounds had been lobbed across the region, from the mountains in the west right down to the wide coastal plain. Mostly it was harassment and interdiction fire intended to unsettle the Viet Cong and to keep them on their toes at night. Some of these barrages were fired by an artillery unit at a fire base perched on top of a mountain overlooking the Song Ve Valley. In August the previous year, B Battery of the 2nd Battalion of the 320th Artillery celebrated the firing of its 250,000th round with a brief ceremony, complete with pennants flying and a color guard standing to attention.

In his command-and-control chopper, the "Charlie Charlie" ship, Barker sat at a homemade console of radios. At the flick of a switch he could contact the ground troops and the gunships. Sitting next to Barker, Lt. Vasquez didn't bother to adjust the artillery fire which was intended to clear the drop zone for the helicopters. Barker was keen to keep down the heads of any Viet Cong defensive positions. Every one and a half seconds a shell exploded close to the village. So powerful was the roar of the artillery it could be clearly heard several miles away by the members of Charlie Company who remained waiting on the ground at Dottie.

At LZ Uptight, where the rounds of the preparatory artillery barrage were being fired the mortar platoon members left behind manning the direction-finding radar listened in on their radios. Over in Task Force Barker's tactical operations center at Dottie, and further to the south in the operations room of the brigade headquarters at Duc Pho, more radio operators waited to monitor news of the battle.

As the liftships neared their arrival point, the men of Charlie Company were shaken by the sudden fusillade of machine guns pouring tracer fire down onto the landing zone. Martin Fagan, with Medina's command group in the fourth helicopter, sat next to the port door gunner. The deafening clatter as the machine gun opened up scared the hell out of him. To Dennis Conti, who was with Lt. Calley's command group, the gunner nearest him appeared to be firing almost straight down as they dropped through thick smoke low over the landing zone.

The paddy field was bone dry. As they hit the ground Calley shouted: "Let's go!" and everyone but Conti jumped out. He had caught his mine sweeper in the seats behind him. Eventually freeing himself, he jumped down into the long elephant grass. Conti was considered by everyone in the platoon to be a street-smart Italian. Joe Cool. Ladies' man. But now, with the smoke from the fires still drifting around, he became disoriented. He couldn't tell which way the rest of the platoon had gone. To his right he heard a machine gun open up and saw what he thought was a farmer running with his cattle. He fired a round from an M-79 grenade launcher—but the man was too far away.

Machine gunners Robert Maples and James Bergthold jumped out of their "slick" when it was still six feet off the ground. Hitting the paddy, Maples stumbled under the weight of the machine gun he was carrying and lost his helmet. He scrambled around trying to find the steel pot and then ran to the irrigation dike. Bergthold, carrying a .45 pistol, three hand grenades, his pack, and about six hundred rounds of machine-gun ammunition, struggled along behind. Hemming and Hawkins, the demo men from the engineering battalion, also made a dash for the safety of the dike. Hawkins then had to run back to find a roll of detonation cord his partner dropped when jumping out of the liftship. He found the cord and rejoined Hemming.

The "Dolphins" took off again and the leadship announced over the air the landing zone was "cold." The "Sharks" continued pouring all kinds of fire onto the fringes of the village with machine guns, grenade launchers, and rockets. Barker acknowledged the message from "Dolphin Lead" and relayed it back to the operations center at Dottie. The information surprised him. Against all the odds the LZ was cold. There was no enemy fire. Just then the "Warlord" aero scouts took up a chase of several armed men in black pajamas running below them. "We got a couple of dinks with weapons," the pilot of the lead ship radioed as another chopper headed off to block an escape route. From different parts of My Lai 4 villagers were trying to get to safety a few hundred yards away down a road which led in one direction to Quang Ngai City and in the other to the coast. The rest of the villagers stayed hiding in their bunkers or simply took shelter in their homes.

The next twenty minutes saw intense aerial activity as the helicopters continued searching for signs of enemy positions. The fifty troops on the ground spread out and secured defensive positions, running to the bank of an irrigation ditch. Out in the fields another farmer frantically raised his hands by way of both greeting and to show he had no weapon. He was immediately felled by a burst from a machine gun. The first lift held their defensive positions and waited for the rest of the 2nd and 3rd platoons to join them.

The second lift had a quicker journey across country to the LZ. There was no longer any reason to follow a circuitous route; the element of surprise had only been required for the first lift. John Smail, a squad leader with the 3rd Platoon, nearly didn't make it at all. His assigned chopper on the landing field at Dottie quickly filled up. He approached to get on board but there was no room for him and he had a few anxious moments as he quickly raced round searching for another ship to board. As they lifted off at 7:38 AM, the other men began joking with him about almost being left behind before the start of Charlie Company's most important mission.

Soon they were over the landing zone. The door gunners in the "slick" carrying Diego Rodriguez, of the 2nd Platoon, opened up with yet more tracer fire. Already nervous about what lay ahead, Rodriguez sat by the starboard door. Suddenly spent shells flew up from the machine gun and struck him in the face. In another ship, meanwhile, Haeberle took a couple of more shots with his Nikon of the approach to the landing zone.

When the second lift hit the LZ they too quickly spread out as they ran to take up defensive positions with the others. Mortars were set up and a 3rd Platoon squad led by Steven Grimes was sent to recover a VC weapon spotted by one of the aero scouts who had marked it with a smoke canister. Other members of the platoon saw a woman carrying a child in the brush some distance away. A tall soldier from Chicago named Charles West stood up and with his M-16 on full automatic began loosing off a burst of fire from the hip. Smail, his squad leader, got angry and shouted out how stupid the soldier had been to fire in the direction of where Grimes's men had gone searching for the VC weapon. He could have killed their own men.

To Michael Bernhardt what was happening already confirmed his worst fears about Medina's instructions the night before. Along with the gunships, almost everyone in the 1st and 2nd platoons was firing their weapons, and now the 3rd Platoon was joining in. The moment a Vietnamese was spotted, volleys of fire were loosed off, and the "enemy" fell wounded or dying. It was apparent to Bernhardt, as it was to virtually everyone gathered there on the ground, that they were receiving no return fire at all. There was no incoming.

The 1st and 2nd platoons got ready to move into the village in separate groups. Spread out "on line" in a typical infantry formation, they moved forward, over the dike, through another paddy, and entered the village firing from the hip. The 3rd Platoon and Medina's command group stayed behind, forming a defensive perimeter on the western edge of the village, about 150 meters from the tree line. Twenty minutes after they arrived Medina wanted Bernhardt to check out a suspicious looking ammo box someone had found. Among his equipment Bernhardt carried a long rope. To make sure it wasn't booby-trapped he tied the rope round the box and jerked it several times. When it failed to explode, he opened the lid and found inside a small Sony radio and various pieces of a medical kit. Bernhardt kept hold of the box for the rest of the day.

Shortly before 8 AM, Medina radioed the operations center via the "Charlie Charlie" ship that they had fifteen confirmed VC killed. It was his first lie of the day. It was impossible to have a battle and not have enemy killed.

Over the course of the next three hours Charlie Company moved through My Lai 4 and also entered several other subhamlets, small pockets of homes grouped together and known in the neighborhood by a particular local name. The place the Americans called My Lai 4 was in fact called Tu Cung by the Vietnamese who lived there. It had a number of subhamlets—including Binh Tay and Binh Dong. Tu Cung, along with three other hamlets—My Lai, Co Luy, and My Khe—spread over two or three square kilometers as far as the coast to the west and the Tra Khuc River to the south. Collectively this formed an area the locals called Son My village. The whole of

Son My was the target for Task Force Barker over the next three days.

The totality of what happened in My Lai 4 that morning was not known to any single individual who took part in Charlie Company's combat operation. As they assaulted the village each platoon split into separate squads and soon these too became broken down, as numerous groups of men, often in ones and twos, moved through the hamlet. Occasionally they crossed each other's paths and squads from different platoons intermingled. At the end of the day a number of soldiers remarked that it had been a miracle none of them was caught in any crossfire. Parts of the village were covered in thick foliage, bamboo trees, banana trees, and other vegetation. No single group of GIs had the opportunity to see what everyone else was doing. But they could all hear firing, often long bursts of automatic fire from M-16s and machine guns. Hand grenades were thrown and the M-79 launchers hurled small bomblets 100 meters or more through the air.

A few geographical features gave Charlie Company some sense of direction. A main trail ran approximately north–south for the whole of the village. Another ran west–east forming a "T" junction of sorts where the two trails met almost in the middle of the settlement. An irrigation ditch formed in a discontinuous semicircle around the furthest southern fringes of the village several hundred meters beyond the tree line, separated from the inhabited area by rice paddies.

Lt. Col. Barker's plan provided for two platoons initially to sweep through the village, quickly taking out any enemy opposition they encountered. Half an hour later the 3rd Platoon would come in behind, mopping up, killing the livestock, and burning hootches. Capt. Medina and his command group would direct operations from the rear.

Calley's 1st Platoon edged into the southern portion of My Lai 4 in three separate squads, line abreast. Calley and his radio operator, Charles Sledge, held back, maintaining a discreet distance from the troops advancing in front of them. Prisoners or Viet Cong suspects were to be sent back to the platoon commander for screening.

Greg Olsen fired his M-60 machine gun as they moved forward, trying to hit a man running away. The weapon suddenly jammed while Lenny Lagunoy was feeding him a belt of ammunition. Lagunoy grabbed the gun from Olsen, recocked it so as to clear the obstruction, and fired once more on the fleeing villager. All around them troops were firing on anything that moved. Olsen shot at animals, pigs, chickens, ducks, and cows. Soldiers yelled inside small dwellings for people to come out, using hand signals if they appeared. If there was no answer, they threw grenades into the shelters and bunkers. Others didn't bother to find out if the bunkers were empty and threw the grenades in regardless. Small clusters of people were being gathered into one larger group of fifty or sixty old men, women, children, and babies in arms, some so badly wounded they could hardly walk. Olsen noticed one elderly woman shot in the hip. Several of the troops saw their buddies behaving in ways which shocked them.

For Robert Maples it was not the first time he had seen things he disapproved of, but this was something altogether different. A quiet, mild-mannered, and thoughtful Negro from Englishtown, a rural area of New Jersey, he had enlisted almost two years before out of a sense of curiosity about Vietnam instead of waiting to be drafted. Not long after he arrived in the country, Maples and some of the other men saw a personnel carrier with twenty human ears strung like trophies on its radio antenna. Everyone in the company soon heard about it. Then, on one of their first patrols up in the mountains, they discovered they were being followed. A couple of the guys set up an ambush and killed those shadowing them. To prove it, they cut off their ears and brought them back for the rest to see. Maples was disgusted. He thought the episode gross and unwarranted. Now, minutes after they entered My Lai 4, he and Bergthold came across a hut which had been raked with bullets. Inside, Bergthold discovered three children, a woman with a flesh wound in her side, and an old man squatting down, hardly able to move. He had been seriously wounded in both legs. From six feet Bergthold aimed his .45 pistol and pulled the trigger, causing the top of the man's head to fly off. It was a sight that would be forever etched in Maples's memory. Bergthold claimed to have shot the old man as an act of mercy.

Two other members of the same squad, Roy Wood and Harry Stanley, were taken by surprise when a woman came out of a bamboo hut. Wood whirled and fired, creasing the woman in the side, slightly injuring her. The woman had two children, one a baby in arms, the other only just able to walk. They sent her back to Calley for screening. In another hut they found a man, his wife, a teenage girl, and a younger girl. Wood grabbed the terrified man and shouted: "VC?" Holding his hands in the air, as if to plead for his life, the man replied: "No VC." Then Wood saw the pitiful sight of an elderly woman who had been wounded, staggering down a path toward them. She had been shot with an M-79 grenade which had failed to explode and was still lodged in her stomach. An old man wearing a straw coolie hat and no shirt was with a water buffalo in a paddy 50 meters away. He put his hands in the air. Several members of the platoon opened fire as Calley watched. Harry Stanley saw that the fleeing villagers were offering no resistance. His friend Allen Boyce, who lived in New Jersey only a couple of miles from Maples, came up behind him with a Vietnamese farmer, aged between 40 and 50 years, in custody. He wore black pajamas and his shirt hung open so that Stanley could see his chest. Boyce pushed the man forward to where Stanley was standing beside the trail. Suddenly, and for no reason, Boyce stabbed the man with the bayonet attached to the end of his rifle. He fell to the ground gasping for breath. Boyce killed him and then grabbed another man being detained, shot him in the neck, and threw him into a well, lobbing an M-26 grenade in after him.

"That's the way you gotta do it," he told Simpson, who had considered Boyce a close friend during jungle training in Hawaii. This sort of deranged behavior profoundly affected many of those who witnessed it and refused to take part. Maples, who was standing nearby, said to Stanley: "That Boyce has gone crazy."

Even Robert Lee, the platoon medic, joined in the frenzy but confined his efforts to slaughtering animals. He killed a cow that had been injured. Lee was from a farming community and "didn't want to see the beast suffer." Up in front, he and the platoon sergeant, Isaiah Cowan, could see women and children being slain. They were stunned by what was happening all around them. The further they went into the village, the more bodies they found.

Dennis Conti stayed for a while with Calley's command group but occasionally wandered off on his own, zigzagging across the path which ran west to east through the village as far as the main trail. He stuck close to Calley in case the platoon leader needed the mine sweeper. He helped round up people for questioning, a normal procedure when they searched villages. He gave his mine sweeper to an old man to carry while he moved some of the Vietnamese toward the platoon command group. To Conti the men appeared all psyched up when they landed. The shooting, once it began, created almost a chain reaction. He joined in, without killing anyone. Inside the village his comrades appeared out of control. Families had huddled together for safety in houses, in the yards and in bunkers only to be mown down with automatic weapon fire or blown apart by fragmentation grenades. Women and children were pushed into bunkers and grenades thrown in after them. But if Conti discovered anyone alive he brought them back to the trail. He and Paul Meadlo collected a group of about twenty-five people—mostly women and children. Still more were brought over by other members of the platoon. At one point, wandering off on his own, Conti found a woman aged about 20 with a 4-year-old child. He forced her to perform oral sex on him while he held a gun at the child's head, threatening to kill it. Just at that moment Calley happened along and angrily told him to pull on his pants and get over to where he was supposed to be.

Amid all this mayhem the first and second platoons overlapped on occasions when the right flank of Lieutenant Stephen Brooks's 2nd Platoon crossed paths with the left flank of the 1st Platoon. Half a dozen people from both platoons then witnessed a stocky, blond-haired 2nd Platoon soldier from Kansas City called Gary Roschevitz become hysterical when troops from the 1st Platoon were walking a small group of villagers back for screening. Roschevitz, aged 25, was older than most of the grunts in the company. Standing almost six feet tall and weighing close to 230 pounds, he made a surprise grab for Roy Wood's M-16 and demanded the weapon as a trade for his M-79. But Wood wasn't having any.

"Don't turn them over to the company," Roschevitz appealed to those gathered there. "Kill them!"

Wood, who was physically by far the smaller of the two men, held tightly onto his rifle. Roschevitz then snatched hold of

Varnado Simpson's M-16, turned, and shot a Vietnamese farmer in the head. Wood began feeling sick at the sight of the man's brains spilling onto the ground and turned away. Roschevitz shot two more peasants in the head before handing the gun back to Simpson.

As far as the outside world knew, a firefight against a large Viet Cong force was underway in the village. Barker and Henderson were back on the scene briefly in their respective helicopters. By about 8:30 AM, Barker had checked once more with Medina to find out how things were going. Medina told him that the body count was 84 enemy killed, and Barker relayed the additional 69 KIA to the tactical operations center. In fact the death toll was far higher, but still no shots had been fired at Charlie Company and they had yet to kill a single enemy soldier.

In the northern portion of the village the 2nd Platoon had also run berserk. Employing the routine combat assault technique used by Calley, Stephen Brooks's men also approached line abreast in three squads. Firing as they moved, they came to dwellings and yelled out "Lai dai" in Vietnamese ("Come here") at the villagers sheltering in homemade shelters or bunkers. Fragmentation grenades were tossed inside; homes were sprayed with automatic fire. Children aged only 6 or 7 came toward them with their hands outstretched, saying "Chop chop." They asked for the food and candy they had received from other American soldiers on two previous visits to the village. The soldiers scythed them down. After one group of Vietnamese were killed in front of a hut, the first squad leader, Sergeant Kenneth Scheil, began telling the men with him that he didn't like what they were all doing but that he had to obey orders. The villagers had huddled together for safety, but the Americans poured fire into them, tearing their bodies apart, one man firing a machine gun at random, others using their M-16s on automatic.

Dennis Bunning informed his squad leader, Sgt Hodges, he wasn't going to fire on women and children. Hodges ordered him to get right out on the far left flank, beyond the tree line and into the rice paddies. Brooks's radio operator, Dean Fields, witnessed Varnado Simpson shoot a woman with a baby from a distance of about 25 meters. Her right arm was shot almost completely off at the wrist. All that held it on was a fragile piece of flesh. She ran into a hootch and someone yelled an order for her and the baby to be killed.

Max Hutson, the weapons squad leader, formed a machine-gun team with Floyd Wright. As soon as they passed the tree line they were confronted less than 30 feet away by a middle-aged woman climbing out of a tunnel using both hands. She was unarmed but they opened fire and she fell back into the tunnel. Hutson and Wright took turns on the machine gun. Whenever they came across any Vietnamese they opened fire, killing them. Hutson could see people firing all around him—the whole scene was one of chaos and confusion, with people moving, yelling, and shouting. Some of the troops were afraid they would be shot by their own men.

The other machine-gun team, Charles Hutto and Esequiel Torres, were also firing at everything that moved—Hutto with the M-60 and Torres with his rifle. After thirty minutes Torres demanded they swap. By this time Hutto, growing weary of all the killing, was glad to hand over the heavier and more powerful weapon.

Jay Buchanon, the platoon sergeant, was also over on the extreme left flank of the platoon, almost on the edge of the tree line. He quickly realized the whole assault was a complete mess. Amid the thick undergrowth he knew there was no opposition but it sounded like a pitched battle was going on. He yelled: "Keep moving, keep moving—fire when fired upon. Stay on line, keep moving. If you receive fire, return it."

Away to his right, closer to where Brooks was moving forward, a slaughter was taking place. Thomas Partsch, a sensitive soul who made regular entries in his diary whenever the platoon took a break, could see that Brooks had totally lost control. As soon as villagers emerged with their hands held up, the troops shot them down. Partsch and Gary Crossley came to a building. It was a well-made house, 20 feet by 10 with a small extension on the side measuring about 8 feet by 6, which gave it an L-shaped appearance. The dwelling was of good quality, a permanent structure made of mud and clay. It had an elevated floor about one step up from the ground and a roof which overhung the house by about two feet over the entrance door, with bamboo windows either side, providing shade from the tropical sun. An old man appeared dressed in black pajamas. Without hesitating Crossley shot the old man in the left arm, just below the elbow. The shot severed the arm, causing it to hang down. Attempting to put his hands in the air, the old man yelled: "No VC! No VC!" A woman wearing black pajama bottoms and a white shirt came out carrying a baby. She frantically shouted in Vietnamese at the two Americans, then proceeded to drag the man inside. Partsch noticed that Crossley looked physically pale and was shaking nervously. He hadn't fired again. When Partsch asked him why, he said that he didn't know.

"Why didn't you finish the job?" Partsch asked again. Crossley replied that he just couldn't bring himself to pull the trigger a second time, he only wanted to see what it was like to shoot someone. Just then two men—Hutson, the weapons squad leader, and Wright, carrying the machine gun—went in after the Vietnamese couple and opened up with a burst of fire.

Occasionally Partsch was close enough to Lt. Brooks and his radio operator to hear Medina calling: "What the hell is going on over there?" At times the static was so bad that Brooks couldn't make contact. After receiving one such message, the platoon leader ushered Partsch away from the radio. Overhead Partsch saw Frank Barker flying low over the treetops in his helicopter—clearly recognizable in his white flying helmet, sitting in his normal position, right near the edge of the door next to the machine gunner.

When he sat down for a rest, Partsch got out his diary and wrote in pencil his account of the day's proceedings so far:

Got up at 0530 and we left 0715. We had nine choppers, two lifts. We started to move slowly through the village, shooting everything in sight, children, men, women, and animals. Some was sickening. Their legs were shot off and they were still moving. They were just hanging there. I think their bodies are made of rubber. I didn't fire a single round yet and didn't kill anybody, not even a chicken. I couldn't. We are now supposed to push two more villages. It is about 10.00 hours and we are taking a rest before going in. We also got two weapons, one M-1 and a carbine.

Those in My Lai 4 that day had a choice whether or not to take part in what was happening. Many followed what they believed were their orders. Some appeared even to enjoy the activity. Only a handful offered any real help or compassion to the Vietnamese. The platoon medic, a Mexican-American named George Garza, found a little boy aged 6 or 7 with an arm injury and bandaged it. Harry Stanley and another Negro, Herbert Carter, the 1st Platoon tunnel rat, located a second child. Carter admired Stanley, describing him often as a "sharp dude." He believed he cared more for the Vietnamese than his fellow Americans. Stanley urged the boy to keep quiet and stay hidden.

Another who refused to take part in the slaughter, Leonard Gonzalez, was also assigned to the extreme left flank of the 2nd Platoon, beyond the tree line. He patrolled in a rice paddy at the far northwest corner of the village. On the edge of the field Gonzalez discovered a young girl aged 11 or 12, wounded in the chest. She was lying on her back, dressed in black pajamas with a white top, crying and moaning with pain. Gonzalez got his canteen and poured water on the girl's forehead and tried to get her to drink some water. There was little more he could do for her and he got up to leave. Gonzalez had only gone a few paces when he heard a shot; he turned to see that she had been killed.

An order came telling the squad to close up. This meant that Gonzalez and Bunning, who was about 25 meters away, had to move over out of the paddy, through the trees and into the village itself. In a clearing near a small hootch a group of fifteen Vietnamese had been gathered, four women in their thirties, three in their fifties, three girls in their late teens and five children aged between 3 and 14. Standing around were seven or eight soldiers from two different squads including Hutto, Torres, and Roschevitz. Gonzalez heard someone yell that if anyone was behind the Vietnamese to take cover because they were going to open fire. A shot rang out and a bullet penetrated the head of a young child being carried by its mother, blowing out the back of its skull. Others began firing also until the entire group was dead. Gonzalez could stand no more; he turned away and vomited. Few words were spoken until someone said: "Let's move out."

Roschevitz later fired two rounds from his M-79 grenade launcher at a group of Vietnamese sitting on the ground. The first bomblet missed; the second landed among them with devastating effect, but against the odds it failed to kill them all. Someone finished off those left alive. A soldier stooping over a tunnel yelled for the occupants to come out. Gonzalez moved closer and could hear people responding as if they were about to comply, whereupon the soldier threw in a grenade and yelled: "Fire in the hole!"—telling everyone to stand clear.

Behind the 1st and 2nd platoons Medina's command group had formed a security line out in the paddy fields beyond the western perimeter of My Lai 4. Some forty-five minutes had elapsed since the first troops entered the village and Medina was waiting to send in the 3rd Platoon, led by a recent arrival, a young lieutenant named Geoffrey LaCross. This was LaCross's very first combat mission. From Lake Leelanau, Michigan, he had joined the company and taken command of the platoon only three weeks before, on February 26, the day after the minefield incident. Medina hoped the savvy of the platoon sergeant, Manuel Lopez, would make up for LaCross's inexperience. It helped that the 3rd Platoon had been given the less taxing role of mopping up.

For Medina, the best way to clear a village was to send a sweep team through very rapidly, clearing people out of the hootches as quickly as possible. The search teams would then go from hootch to hootch, checking bunkers and tunnels looking for any enemy who might be hiding. One added refinement today was that LaCross's men were also to burn the village. Medina received the instruction to let the Zippo squads loose from Frank Barker directly. Barker said he had arranged for this to be cleared with the Vietnamese authorities in Quang Ngai through the senior district advisor to the 2nd ARVN Division. The truth was that since the area was controlled by the Viet Cong the government officials didn't care what happened to people in the villages. Medina knew Barker regularly met with the Vietnamese and the American province advisors. The burning of villages was supposed to be strictly controlled. As far as Medina was concerned, the burning of villages was always carried out with the approval of the South Vietnamese.

Some distance away Sergeant Grimes's squad from the 3rd Platoon searched for Viet Cong weapons. They set off through the paddy fields and then followed the line of the irrigation ditch which ran around the village. Grimes's men crossed over a bamboo footbridge and saw a tiny bubble aeroscout reconning low over the ground drop a smoke grenade. They recrossed the bridge, moved toward a clump of foliage, and found an M-1 and a rifle.

More rifles were found when the 2nd Platoon located the bodies of two VC killed by the gunships and marked with smoke. The VC, each about 20 years old, were not in uniform but carried an American pack, pistol belts, and ammo pouches. They had been armed with an M-1 and a carbine, which was now full of mud and still loaded.

Deeper into the village the 1st Platoon collected a large group of about sixty Vietnamese. They were made to squat down. An alert Conti spotted a 4-year-old child running away toward a hootch. Dropping his gear, he sprinted after the child, which managed to escape him. He discovered a woman with a baby in a hootch and a much older female he took to be the grandmother in a nearby underground shelter. Conti escorted the young woman and her child back to the holding point and then returned for the old woman, who had refused to move. He then teamed up with Meadlo. Once more they guarded the squatting Vietnamese. Calley appeared with his radio operator, Charles Sledge.

Calley had been called twice that morning on the radio by an anxious Medina. "What is happening over there?" Medina demanded to know, challenging the slow progress of the 1st Platoon. He wanted Calley to get his men back on line and keep moving. This made the young platoon commander nervous. Throughout his time with the company he had frequently been made the butt of Medina's jokes. Medina knew Calley couldn't command the respect of his men. Now, under pressure, Calley replied that the large groups of civilians they had gathered were slowing the platoon down. Never one to accept excuses, Medina told Calley simply to get rid of them. So when Calley came across Meadlo and Conti in the clearing and said: "Take care of them," his intention was clear. It was his way of getting Medina off his back.

Conti thought nothing of the implications of Calley's request when he replied simply: "OK." Like many in the company he regarded the man as a joke and resented the way Calley tried to suck up to the men one minute, calling them by their first names, and then shouted and bawled at them the next. Conti felt his platoon commander had absolutely no leadership ability.

Among the squatting Vietnamese were ten to fifteen men with beards and ten women, as well as a handful of very elderly, gray-haired women who could hardly walk. The rest were children of all ages—from babies up to early teens.

Calley, who was carrying a bandolier of ammunition around one shoulder, said: "I thought I told you to take care of them."

Meadlo somewhat naively responded: "We are. We're watching over them."

"No," reposted Calley. "I want them killed." He moved over to where Conti was standing beside Meadlo. "We'll get on line and fire into them."

Conti and Meadlo looked at each other and backed off, neither of them wanting a part in what was about to happen. Calley, losing his temper, beckoned them toward him: "Come here . . . come here. Come on, we'll line them up; we'll kill them."

Conti, searching for an excuse, pointed out that he was carrying a grenade launcher and he didn't want to waste ammunition. Perhaps he should keep guard over by the tree line in case anyone tried to get away, he suggested.

Calley turned to Meadlo: "Fire when I say 'Fire.'"

Conti stood behind them as Calley and Meadlo, standing side by side, blazed away. They stood only ten feet from their hapless victims, changing magazines from time to time. The Vietnamese screamed, yelled, and tried to get up. It was pure carnage as heads were shot off along with limbs; the fleshier body parts were ripped to shreds. Meadlo had taken twenty-three fully loaded magazines for his M-16 in his pack when they left Dottie. He fired in a spraying motion. He noticed one man dressed in red fall dead as he fired the rifle on automatic until the magazine was exhausted. Then he reloaded. He then switched to semiautomatic fire and loaded the third magazine.

After a minute or so Meadlo couldn't continue. Tears flooded down his cheeks. He turned, stuck his rifle in Conti's hand, and said: "You shoot them." Conti pushed the weapon back: "If they are going to be killed, I'm not doing it. Let him do it," he said, pointing at Calley. By this time Conti could see that only a few children were left standing. Mothers had thrown themselves on top of the young ones in a last desperate bid to protect them from the bullets raining down on them. The children were trying to stand up. Calley opened fire again, killing them one by one. Conti swore at him. Finally, when it appeared to be all over, Calley calmly turned and said: "OK, let's go." Suddenly someone yelled out that more Vietnamese, five women and six children some distance away, were making a break for the tree line. Calley burst out: "Get them, get them! Kill them!" Conti waited until they reached the tree line before letting loose with his grenade launcher, firing above them into the top of the trees. He asked Calley if he should pursue the fleeing villagers, but Calley replied no.

The urgency now was to push on to the far end of the village. Calley cajoled his men forward. They split up once more and continued to come across still more Vietnamese hiding in bunkers, shelters, and their fragile homes, terrified. Gathered in groups they were marched to the far side of the village, toward the paddy fields and the irrigation ditch. By the time Conti arrived at the edge of the ditch there were already a number of Vietnamese standing there, guarded by some of the soldiers, who squatted down and took a rest. Conti approached Charles Hall, from Chicago, a Negro soldier in the first squad who was standing near a small wooden bridge which crossed the ditch. The Italian boasted how Calley had earlier caught him with his pants down and his penis out trying to get a blow job from the Vietnamese woman, while threatening her child with a gun. Nothing surprised any of them about Conti. He and half a dozen members of the company were notorious for fooling with the local women—so much so that medics administered shots of penicillin to him while they were on operations in the field. Nick Capezza, the company medic, used to joke how he nearly exhausted his supplies of the antibiotic drug giving Conti his shots for venereal disease.

Meadlo's face was flushed. His eyes were still full of tears when he arrived with Grzesik at the ditch site and found Calley sitting down. "We've got another job to do," he said looking up at them. About ten members of the platoon were guarding forty to fifty Vietnamese. Babies were crying and crawling around. James Dursi, a heavy-set Irish-Italian from Brooklyn, was looking at a man in white robes with a goatee beard, whom he took to be a Buddhist monk, praying over an elderly woman. She was seriously ill and had been carried through the village on a narrow wooden platform which the Vietnamese use as a bed. Calley was now on his feet. Harry Stanley appeared on the scene and tried to question the monk, who was crying and bowing as he tried to make himself understood. Calley couldn't understand him. Grzesik, who had attended Vietnamese language classes in Hawaii, tried more questions and got nowhere. Calley was getting more and more impatient. Where had the Viet Cong gone? Where were the weapons? Where were the NVA?

When the man shook his head, Calley struck him in the mouth with his rifle butt.

Just then a child, aged about 2 years and parted from its mother, managed to crawl up to the top of the ditch. Dursi watched horrified as Calley picked the child up, shoved it back down the slope, and shot it before returning to question the monk. The villagers pleaded for the holy man's life. Stanley asked the bearded man the same questions in Vietnamese that Calley was asking in English in an effort to defuse the situation. But the monk vainly replied that there were no North Vietnamese soldiers in the village. There were no weapons. Stanley translated these replies. Immediately Calley grabbed the monk, pulled him round, hurled him into the paddy, and opened fire with Meadlo's M-16. As the elderly *mama-san* lying prostrate tried to get up, she too was killed.

More Vietnamese shepherded by soldiers were arriving on the scene, and Calley indicated to Meadlo and Boyce he wanted everyone killed. He began pushing the peasants into the irrigation channel. Others joined in, using their rifle butts to shove the wailing Vietnamese down the steep slope. Some jumped in by themselves; others sat down on the edge, moaning and crying, clearly aware that disaster was imminent. It was a pitiful sight.

Up until the time all the firing started, Herbert Carter had been kneeling beside Dursi, quietly playing with a couple of children. Dursi said incredulously: "I think Calley wants them all killed." Carter said: "Oh, no."

"He can send me to jail but I am not going to kill anybody," said Dursi, beginning to move away, wondering what would happen to him for refusing to fire. Dursi was another one who liked to play with the children. Earlier in the day he had been devastated after he opened fire and killed someone running from the village. It turned out to be a woman carrying a baby and Dursi was horrified and ashamed by what he had done. Olsen had seen he was really cut up about it.

A woman standing next to Robert Maples showed him a bullet wound in her left arm. He felt helpless. There was nothing he could do for her. Calley shoved her in the ditch and told Maples: "Load your machine gun and shoot these people."

Maples shook his head and replied: "I'm not going to do that." Calley turned his M-16 on Maples as if to shoot him there and then. Maples was surprised and relieved when some of the other soldiers interposed to protect him. Calley backed off. Seconds later he and Meadlo began firing. A machine gun opened up and one of the squad leaders tried to usher the men into line so they could all fire simultaneously. Dursi stood completely frozen, watching disbelievingly, as the Vietnamese tried frantically to hide under one another, mothers protecting babies. Screaming at Dursi above the sounds of M-16s on full automatic, Meadlo continued pouring shell into the ditch. Crying hysterically once more, he stopped for a second: "Why aren't you firing?" he pleaded with Dursi. "Fire, why don't you fire?" The onlookers saw the remnants of shredded human beings, hundreds of pieces of flesh and bone, flying up in the air as the shallow ravine was repeatedly sprayed with bullets. Magazine after magazine was reloaded during the mass execution.

On the other side of the village the noise of all the firing had disturbed Medina. For a while he was concerned that his men were engaging heavy enemy resistance. Shortly after 8:45 AM, the 3rd Platoon was sent in to mop up. Immediately they found artillery craters, buildings badly torn up by shrapnel, and bodies scattered everywhere. They began killing every animal they found—some deliberately wounding pigs and water buffaloes, watching them writhing in agony. Haeberle took pictures of hootches being set on fire and grenades being hurled into holes in the ground. A buffalo, shot several times from a short range, just wouldn't die. On top of another beast sat a soldier, bayonet in hand, repeatedly stabbing the animal in a frenzy, riding like a rodeo bronco rider until the buffalo fell to the ground. With his Nikon camera Haeberle photographed a woman dressed in black pants and dark blue blouse lying dead on the ground, her brains beside her head. Haeberle remembered later that his instincts as a photographer took him over:

I knew it was something that shouldn't be happening but yet I was part of it. I think I was in a kind of daze from seeing all these shootings and not seeing any return fire. Yet the killing kept going on. The Americans were rounding up the people and shooting them, not taking any prisoners. It was completely different to my concept of what war is all about. I kept taking the pictures. That was my job as a photographer, to take pictures, a normal reaction I have with a camera, just picking up and keep on shooting, trying to capture what is happening around me. I feel sometimes that the camera did take over during the operation. I put it up to my eye, took a shot, put it down again. Nothing was composed. Nothing was prethought, just the normal reaction of a photographer. I was part of it, everyone who was there was part of it, and that includes the General and the Colonel flying above in their helicopters. They're all part of it. We all were. Just one big group.

Larry Polston could see no sense in killing civilians. Crossing a trail, he noticed two small boys, aged about 5 and 8, who were wounded and crying. Robert T'Souvas, one of the platoon's dopeheads, took aim and shot both children in the chest and shoulders. Polston asked him why he had done this. "Because they were already half dead," said T'Souvas sadly. A man and woman came running down the trail away from the village; a soldier shot them and they fell to the ground.

LaCross's men mopped up in style. The rifle squads roamed over the paths the 1st and 2nd platoons had taken, killing most of the remaining Vietnamese they encountered. The third squad came across several women shot in the back but still alive. William Doherty and Michael Terry, a devout Mormon, discussed what they could do for the injured, who would get no medical assistance and would die a lingering death. They began finishing off the wounded. It took three shots to kill one woman, with two small bullet holes in her back, who at first appeared almost dead.

LaCross brought up the rear with Stephen Glimpse, his radio

operator. The whole place was littered with corpses, lying contorted, sometimes ripped apart by bullets and shrapnel from fragmentation grenades. They came across one pile of ten bodies, then a larger group. The grisly scene was like walking through a charnel house. There seemed to be no end to it. On the single occasion when LaCross tried to fire his rifle at livestock, it jammed and he didn't raise the weapon again for the rest of the day. They had walked 50 feet past a teenage boy who was wounded in the foot when a shot rang out behind them. Glimpse heard a voice say: "Oh, my God." He too felt there was no reason to kill the boy. He became even more upset when they stopped at the L-shaped house, where Partsch earlier witnessed the occupants being killed. A woman lay there with a dead baby aged between six and twelve months beside her. Glimpse found this particularly distressing. There was just no need for it. Patrolling in the northern section of the village in the wake of the 2nd Platoon, LaCross found it hard to accept this was what happened on a combat operation. He felt ill at the numbers and horrendous condition of the bodies, and asked John Smail, his first squad leader, incredulously: "Is it always like this?"

Haeberle took pictures at the L-shaped house, again on his Nikon. With the Army-issue Leica he took black-and-white pictures, innocuous snapshots of the boys in Charlie Company doing soldiering stuff, burning hootches, checking bunkers, interrogating villagers. Someone set the L-shaped house on fire and a huge bamboo tray used for drying rice was hurled into the flames. A Vietnamese interpreter, Sgt Duong Minh, questioned a 90-year-old man who appeared to be extremely deaf. Capezza brought the old man down the steps from his house before setting it on fire. Haeberle carefully framed the shot before taking a photograph.

At the rear of the property Minh found the body of a small boy aged about 4, shot in the head and back. He was greatly concerned by this and many of the other scenes he witnessed. Minh had signed on as an interpreter with the Americans the previous November and now worked for the military intelligence officer, Lieutenant Dennis Johnson. They were only attached to Task Force Barker for the day. Minh was taken completely by surprise by what he witnessed the Americans doing. A passionate anticommunist, he had a virulent hatred for the Viet Cong. During the recent Tet Offensive he had been in Hue visiting his family when the city was attacked by the Viet Cong. He just managed to get himself and his family out of the city to the safety of Duc Pho before the VC killed thousands in a reign of terror. Now he was seeing this small village ravaged by American troops. He quizzed Johnson, a 30-year-old career soldier with six children of his own, and demanded to know why this had happened. When Johnson didn't reply, Minh pressed him further. Johnson was already preoccupied by personal problems with his wife's health back home in the United States. He repeated that he didn't know the answer; he was only a military intelligence officer there to carry out interrogations. Still not satisfied, Minh later found Medina at the village schoolhouse, close to a watchtower at the southern edge of My Lai 4. Nearby was a pile of bodies that Minh figured everyone must have seen. Once again he wanted to know why so many civilians had been killed. Medina said his orders had been to destroy the village: "Sergeant Minh, don't ask anything—those were the orders."

Medina's control over what had gone on since they first landed was negligible. The tough disciplinarian, consciously or unconsciously, had quite simply allowed his men to run amok and he had given Viet Cong body counts to Frank Barker which were clearly false. He had not ventured into the center of the village and did not see what had happened at the irrigation ditch where several mass executions had taken place. However, he had seen plenty of dead civilians—well over one hundred of them—and it was clear there had been no crossfire, because there had been no enemy.

After the 3rd Platoon moved out of their defensive positions around the landing zone Medina's command group set off across the paddy fields and an irrigation gully toward the southernmost portion of the village. Bernhardt was with Medina and saw him twice fire at a woman in a paddy holding a small wicker basket, the kind thousands of Vietnamese women took to market, suspended in front and behind with hessian twine from a sturdy flattened stick carried across one shoulder. A small bubble helicopter flying overhead dropped a smoke canister near the woman to indicate she was injured. Bernhardt and James Flynn, one of the forward artillery observers, walked with Medina over to where the woman was lying face down. She wore a white jacket and dark silk trousers and she was still breathing. Fagan thought she was faking injury. Medina searched the wicker basket and found syringes and other medical supplies. From three or four meters away Fagan watched as Medina nudged the woman and then turned her over with his foot. She let out a moan. Medina turned quickly and shot her several times in the head.

The command group came across scattered corpses and saw a pile of between twenty and twenty-five bodies of men, women, children, and babies lying on the trail. Medina looked grim. The men nearby could see he was visibly disturbed. Jerry Hemming saw him looking at the bodies with a sad expression, as if he didn't like what he was seeing.

The command group met up with small groups of stragglers from the 3rd Platoon. Charles Gruver, who had been one of the very last men to leave the defensive perimeter, was standing talking with Smail. They seemed an odd pair to team up. Smail was the conscientious NCO while "Groovy" Gruver was regarded as being wayward, wild, and undisciplined. One of the other sergeants, La Croix, called him a misfit, too immature to be a good soldier. He had no respect for any rank. If they told him to do something he didn't want to do, his general attitude was: "To heck with it." Before he left Vietnam several months later, Gruver was sent to Long Binh jail for marijuana possession, stealing a 2½-ton truck, and desertion.

Gruver and Smail were talking about a 5-year-old boy who was very badly wounded, holding his arm. His left hand or wrist had been blown away and was bleeding heavily at the stump. His nose had been shot off and he had other head injuries. Smail thought the boy was almost walking dead.

Medina's radio operator, Fred Widmer, lagged 25 meters behind the command group and stopped beside the two men. The child was only three feet away from Smail and Gruver. Widmer raised his rifle, turned his head away so that he could not see what he was about to do, and pulled the trigger. Smail later recalled the child had been the only person in the village he had seen alive throughout the whole day.

The scene has never left Widmer's memory:

The most disturbing thing I saw was this one boy . . . and . . . this was something . . . you know . . . this is what haunts me from the whole ordeal down there. It was a boy with his right arm shot off, half hanging on. I was on the trail going back to the headquarters section and had just turned the corner when I saw the boy. We stared at each other. He had this bewildered look on his face: "What did I do? What wrong?" He just . . . it's hard to describe . . . couldn't comprehend.

I shot the boy, killed him. I fired three shots in the boy with an M-16 I borrowed from someone else. I like to think of it more or less as a mercy killing, because somebody else would have killed him in the end. But it wasn't right. When I shot him I was sick to my stomach over what I'd done. Soon as I did it I realized: "God, what have I done?"

Charlie Company's operation that morning lacked one essential ingredient typical of most combat assaults—the normal radio traffic that went with a firefight. In an operation against an enemy stronghold the radio net was normally overloaded with messages from platoon commanders and squad leaders trying to maneuver their men into fighting positions so they could bring superior firepower to bear. Anyone within listening distance of another of Medina's radio operators, John Paul, would have heard such messages very clearly. He had wired a four-inch jeep speaker to the radio. One message Paul remembered clearly had come from the task force executive officer, Major Charles Calhoun, who asked Medina if any civilians had been killed. He replied that a few had been hit by gunships and artillery fire. It was a question which appeared to trouble the company commander. There had been continuous gunfire throughout the morning, some of it involving very long bursts of automatic weapons fire, so much so that at one point Medina believed the men might actually run out of ammunition. A 3rd Platoon machine gunner, Everett Cayot, handed over his M-60 ammunition to a runner from another platoon because he hadn't used any. While Medina may not have seen mass executions taking place, the evidence of his own eyes told him what everyone else could see—that some kind of massacre had occurred.

In fact it was worse than a massacre. Too many of Medina's men were taking sordid pleasure in sadistic behavior. Several became "double veterans," GI slang for the dubious honor of raping a woman and then murdering her. Many women were raped and sodomized, mutilated, and had their vaginas ripped open with knives or bayonets. One woman was killed when the muzzle of a rifle barrel was inserted into her vagina and the trigger was pulled. Soldiers repeatedly stabbed their victims, cut off limbs, sometimes beheaded them. Some were scalped; others had their tongues cut out or their throats slit or both. Tommy Lee Moss saw Vietnamese place their hands together and bow to greet the Americans, only to be beaten with fists and tortured, clubbed with rifles, and stabbed in the back with bayonets. Martin Fagan saw bodies which had been shot in the head at point blank range. He could tell because the penetration of an M-16 round created a shock wave inside the skull, forcing the brain completely out. Other victims were mutilated with the signature "C Company" or the shape of an Ace of Spades carved into the chest. Fagan figured this had been done as a warning to the superstitious Vietnamese. It was widely believed they regarded the Ace of Spades as a sign of bad luck.

Troops from all three platoons carried out wanton and mindless acts of brutality. The 2nd Platoon were already among the most notorious rapists in Charlie Company. Even the platoon commander joined in on occasions. Several times in the field during previous weeks Stephen Brooks turned a blind eye to the platoon's activities, telling anyone who would listen: "They've got to get it someplace," or "They might as well get it in the village." The platoon sergeant, Jay Buchanon, was not happy about the sheer indiscipline involved. He didn't want the guys messing with women when they went through villages. The normal tactic was for one group of regular rapists to hang back and do their thing while the rest of the platoon continued moving through, searching hootches and questioning people. They often encouraged women to part with their babies by giving them to small children to take care of, while they took the mother to a hootch to rape her. Eleven men from one squad violated a Vietnamese girl in one village and when another squad heard of this they came across to join in. During another patrol in a mountain hamlet the men became bored and agreed it was time they had some fun. Splitting up they chased around looking for women. Someone came back and told Partsch:

"There's a good one down there and everyone's taking turns." He went to look and saw Lt. Brooks queueing up with everyone else.

In My Lai 4, Varnado Simpson watched three men—including Hutto and Hutson—go into a hut with a girl aged about 17. Her trousers forcibly removed, the girl was held down while she was violated. Simpson observed this from the door. Fagan also witnessed part of the girl's ordeal. When they were finished the helpless captive was shot dead—her face completely blown away. Torres stabbed several people with a bowie knife and was seen by Hutto raping a girl. She was crying, fighting and resisting him. Another soldier held her down and when Torres finished, he took out his penis and got on top of her. The scene became something of a public display. Soon several men gathered outside the hut looking in through the window.

For Simpson the crucial moment was when he shot the woman and baby soon after entering the village:

I went to turn her over and there was a little baby with her that I had also killed. The baby's face was half gone. My mind just went. The training came to me and I just started killing. Old men, women, children, water buffaloes, everything. We were told to leave nothing standing. We did what we were told, regardless of whether they were civilians. They was the enemy. Period. Kill. If you don't follow a direct order you can be shot yourself. Now what am I supposed to do? You're damned if you do and you're damned if you don't. You didn't have to look for people to kill, they were just there. I cut their throats, cut off their hands, cut out their tongue, their hair, scalped them. I did it. A lot of people were doing it and I just followed. I just lost all sense of direction.

I just started killing any kinda way I can kill. It just came. I didn't know I had it in me. After I killed the child my whole mind just went. It just went. And after you start it's very easy to keep on. The hardest is to kill the first time but once you kill, then it becomes easier to kill the next person and the next one and the next one. Because I had no feelings, no emotions. Nothing.

I just killed. I wasn't the only one that did it; a lot of people in the company did it, hung 'em, all types of ways, any type of way you could kill someone that's what they did. That day in My Lai I was personally responsible for killing about twenty-five people. Personally. I don't think beforehand anyone thought that we would kill so many people. I mean we're talking about four to five hundred people. We almost wiped out the whole village, a whole community. I can't forget the magnitude of the number of people that we killed and how they were killed, killed in lots of ways.

Do you realize what it was like killing five hundred people in a matter of four or five hours? It's just like the gas chambers—what Hitler did. You line up fifty people, women, old men, children, and just mow 'em down. And that's the way it was—from twenty-five to fifty to one hundred. Just killed. We just rounded 'em up, me and a couple of guys, just put the M-16 on automatic, and just mowed 'em down.

Some of the most bestial incidents occurred 500 meters to the north of My Lai 4 in a subhamlet called Binh Tay. The 2nd Platoon went there after searching the paddy fields for Viet Cong weapons. Sgt Kenneth Hodges, one of the squad leaders, took a young girl into a hootch. She was in there with him for fifteen minutes. When she went in she was wearing a black top and pants. She came out minus her pants. Her blouse was unbuttoned and several people saw Hodges trying to fondle her.

Gonzalez thought the girl running around without pants on was aged about 16. He appealed to her mother: "*Mama san*, please give her some pants . . ." He thought she had understood and appeared to thank him. A number of men violated the same girl. Gonzalez had seen this many times before. When a girl was being raped the others moved in quickly to get some of the action. Several men saw three GIs with the girl. One had penetrated her, one was having oral sex with her, and she was fondling the penis of the third.

Gonzalez had spent the past two hours witnessing scenes of mounting savagery. He then encountered the aftermath of the most grotesque incident yet. Gathered in a pile outside a hootch at Binh Tay he saw seven naked women aged between 18 and 35—their corpses dotted all over with tiny dark holes. The sight really sickened him. Nearby was Roschevitz, the carrier of a "bloop gun"—an M-79 grenade launcher which resembled a sawn-off shotgun that could hurl a 40-mm spherical bomb well over 100 meters. Throughout the day dozens of these grenades had been fired at the Vietnamese villagers. The effect depended on the range over which the grenade was fired. The bomblets, stabilized by fins, were fired through the rifled barrel of the launcher, which caused the grenade to spin and become armed after about 30 meters. They detonated on impact and were capable of killing anything within a radius of five meters. Grenadiers carried special rounds containing buckshot, for close-in use during jungle warfare. Gonzalez realized the women had been killed with several buckshot rounds fired at close range.

Roschevitz was explaining how they came to be naked to a group of men standing nearby. He forced the women to undress with the intention of having sex with all of them. If they didn't strip, he said, he was going to shoot them. He singled out one woman, telling her to "boom boom" him. She became hysterical and the other women panicked, yelling, screaming, and begging for mercy. Roschevitz decided to let them have it. He fired several rounds and killed them all. Later, as they were leaving Binh Tay, Gonzalez saw the young girl who had been raped. Once more she was without her pants, walking alongside some of the men. Gonzalez thought the girl figured out that if she stuck close to them, they probably wouldn't kill her.

In the southern part of the village two soldiers were trying to open the blouses of young girls among a small group of women and children on the main trail. Soldiers were yelling at the women: "VC? VC?" Half a dozen GIs were milling around watching this as the girls modestly tried to keep themselves covered up. They were screaming hysterically and the only thing Harry Stanley could make out, with his limited knowledge of Vietnamese, was that they were not VC.

"VC boom? VC boom?" Someone asked a girl if she was a VC whore. Some of the women carried children in their arms and an elderly, balding woman intervened to protect the girls, crying: "No, no, no." She was repeatedly kicked. Grzesik tried to calm the situation down as Ronald Haeberle walked by. One of the soldiers said: "Hey, watch out, he's got a camera," as the shutter clicked. Haeberle continued walking on down the trail. He had only gone a few yards when someone said: "Let's waste them." Haeberle looked back over his shoulder to see that the group of women and children had fallen to the ground. One of the GIs watching saw a tracer round from a machine gun strike a baby's bare bottom, killing the child instantly. A little boy tried to stand up and was immediately shot.

Haeberle thought the troops were going to question the group:

Just as soon as I turned away I heard firing. I saw the people drop. They started falling on top of each other, one on top of another. I just kept on walking. I did not pay attention to who did it. By that time I knew what the score was. It was an atrocity. I felt I wanted to do something to stop this and, as we were going through the village, I asked some soldiers: "Why?" They more or less shrugged their shoulders and kept on with the killing. It was like they were fixed on one thing—search and destroy, and that meant killing civilians.

I noticed this one small boy had been shot in the foot. Part of the foot was torn off, he was walking toward the group of bodies looking for his mother. I put up my camera to my eye, I was going to take a photograph. I didn't notice a GI kneeling down beside me with his M-16 rifle pointed at the child. Then I suddenly heard the crack and through the viewfinder I saw this child flip over on top of the pile of bodies. The GI stood up and just walked away. No remorse. Nothing. The other soldiers had a cold reaction—they were staring off into space like it was an everyday thing, they felt they had to do it and they did it. That was their job. It was weird, just a shrug of the shoulder. No emotional reaction.

Harry Stanley stayed a few feet away from the group of bodies for about five minutes, looking at the result of the execution. The Vietnamese women and children were a mass of wounds, mostly to the chest and stomach, their intestines and blood spilling onto the sandy trail. There was no more sound and the other soldiers moved away.

A few minutes earlier Haeberle had captured a sequence of pictures of Charlie Company's only casualty of the day. Herbert Carter, the tunnel rat, managed to shoot himself in the foot while clearing his .45 pistol. This was after Widmer saw people still alive among a pile of bodies, some twitching in their death throes. Among them was a little boy, aged about 4 or 5, wounded in the stomach. Widmer went over to Carter and said: "Let me borrow your pistol." Widmer shot into the group with the automatic weapon. He stepped to within two feet of the boy and shot him through the neck. Blood gushed from the wound and the child tried to walk off, but could only make three or four steps before he fell to the ground. He took four or five deep breaths and then stopped breathing. Widmer went to pull the trigger again but the gun failed to fire. "The damn thing jammed," he said, returning the weapon to Carter, who then sat there trying to clear the weapon by pulling the cocking arm back. Suddenly the gun went off, shooting Carter through the foot. He writhed in agony, shouting: "Medic, medic!" Medina quickly arrived on the scene, having heard of the incident over his radio. He wanted to question Carter to see if he had deliberately shot himself. Widmer passed the injured soldier a marijuana joint to ease his pain and explained to Medina what had happened. Stanley helped Abel Flores, a medical aidman, to ease Carter's boot and sock off. It was a clean wound straight through the foot. Flores applied a field dressing. Capezza gave Carter a shot of morphine, and painted the letter "M" on his forehead. A couple of onlookers, Kern and Hemming, shared a beer, while Mauro and Widmer carried the injured GI out into the paddy field.

Frank Barker, flying close by in the "Charlie Charlie" ship, answered the radio call for a "dust-off" medevac helicopter. When he landed, Medina went out to talk with the task force commander. Thomas Kinch and the rest of the weapons platoon maintained a security perimeter while the helicopter was on the ground. Hemming was also there and overheard part of their conversation, particularly the phrase: "These killings have got to stop." Barker could not have failed to notice. The bodies were everywhere. After he had taken off, Kinch overheard traffic on the company radio network. Now someone was demanding to know what all the bodies were doing on the outskirts of the village. A helicopter pilot had reported seeing corpses all over the place.

Medina had already been questioned once that morning about civilian casualties by Maj. Calhoun, the brigade executive officer. Now he was being asked again. He stuck to his story that between twenty and twenty-eight civilians had been killed by gunship and artillery fire. He knew this was a lie. He had seen at least a hundred bodies during the morning, although he never saw the irrigation ditch that was piled high with corpses. There had been no firefight and not a single shot had been fired at his men. The 48th Viet Cong Battalion was nowhere to be seen. Like most experienced soldiers, Medina recognized trouble when he saw it.

*

Hugh Clowers Thompson Jr, aged 25, was a reconnaissance pilot with the 123rd Aviation Battalion aero scouts who flew his helicopter by the seat of his pants, as he skimmed around battle zones hunting out enemy defensive positions. The small plexiglass cockpit of his H-23 observation chopper provided superb all-round vision. It resembled a flying bubble and these aircraft became known as "bubble ships." Thompson was a character. He was known to everyone in his unit for being cocky and aggressive. He was also an exceptional pilot who took danger in his stride. If there were enemy to find he would seek them out and kill them. He did not court danger but was not afraid of confronting the Viet Cong. He never turned tail and he knew when to engage and when to get out of the way. Ruthless in winkling out the VC, Thompson was also a very moral man. He was absolutely strict about opening fire only on clearly defined targets. He did not want to brutalize the enemy or see them endure unnecessary suffering. He wanted to kill them cleanly and made it absolutely clear to his gunners that he wanted to see a weapon first before they opened fire. Then he expected a clean shot. He would not fire at someone simply because they were running away, unlike countless soldiers who regarded a fleeing person as the enemy for sure. Seeing a weapon reassured Thompson that this person was the enemy.

Thompson was a good-looking man. He fitted the image of the hotshot aviator: tall, dark, and handsome. He was also well liked and respected by those who worked closest to him. Brought up in Stone Mountain, Georgia, he was the son of a local electrical contractor. Hugh Thompson Sr had started out as a power pole climber and ended up running his own company. He worked hard and encouraged his sons to do the same. He and his wife ran a strict and fairly conventional family, with Baptist church on Sundays. He served in the US Navy Reserve and his younger son Hugh followed him. Studying for a college degree didn't suit Hugh Thompson Jr and he dropped out of Troy State University, Alabama, and volunteered for active duty in the Navy. He served with a SeaBee construction unit from 1961 to 1964. When he left the Navy he returned to his home state and ran a funeral home. By this time he was married with two sons of his own. The urge to fly helicopters had been with him for some time and with the Vietnam

War in full swing the Army was looking for more pilots. One day at the side of a road in 1966 Thompson saw a US Army advertising billboard which pictured a man standing next to a helicopter. He found the local recruiting office. When he passed the aptitude test for flight training he signed on. The Army trained him to be a helicopter pilot at Fort Walters, Texas, and then Fort Rucker, Alabama. He arrived in Vietnam two days after Christmas Day, 1967.

With Thompson on board the bubble ship as he reconned around My Lai 4 were two young GIs, his crew chief Glenn Andreotta and Lawrence Colburn, an 18-year-old door gunner. Accompanying them over the battle zone were two Huey gunships, providing the firepower to keep the observation chopper out of trouble. A low gunship stuck close to Thompson's aircraft. The other—the "high guns"—flew several hundred feet above. If he drew fire, Thompson had to bank away and allow the low gunship to come in to engage the enemy. This gave Thompson and his crew a chance to get clear. Communication between him and the gunships was through a primitive FM radio system, which meant that Thompson could communicate only with the gunships and not with the ground forces' UHF radios. A message for the ground commander or the task force "Charlie Charlie" ship carrying Frank Barker had to be relayed through the high gunship. Carrying 800 pounds of fuel, Thompson's tiny helicopter could stay in the air about two hours. The gunships, however, carried a heavy load: 6,000 rounds of ammunition for the miniguns, special pods carrying fourteen rockets, and a 40-mm grenade-launching system with 300 rounds. The extra weight meant they had to fly faster to remain airborne, and this limited their fuel consumption. It meant they had to return to Dottie every hour to refuel. Flying in pairs, there had to be an overlap when they broke away to refuel so Thompson was not left without gunship cover.

It was dangerous work but that morning it quickly became apparent to everyone flying around My Lai 4 that they were receiving no enemy fire. Skipping over the ground at treetop height, Thompson spotted the occasional VC weapon and military-aged males, possible Viet Cong suspects, making a run for it. He forced two unarmed Vietnamese men to a standstill. They threw their hands up as his door gunner trained the M-60 on them. Another helicopter landed, apprehended the suspects, and flew them off for a tactical interrogation. Several times before on combat operations Thompson had landed to pick up VC. He virtually grabbed a prisoner off the ground and flew him back to the fire base, the prisoner standing on the skids and hanging on for dear life. Once it had nearly ended in tragedy. Thompson was flying a prisoner for interrogation and discovered the VC had a hand grenade hidden on him. Now if he picked up VC prisoners he made sure they were stripped naked first in case they were hiding a weapon; even a knife could be dangerous. For Thompson the first rule of flying in Vietnam was that pilots didn't live long if they took foolish chances.

However, at My Lai, after the initial burst of activity, there were no more VC suspects or enemy prisoners to pick up. The inhabited areas of the village surrounded by vegetation were partly covered in thick smoke, which made for poor visibility. Thompson marked several wounded people on the ground with green smoke, a signal they needed help. Returning to the My Lai area about 9 AM after the first refueling, Thompson immediately noticed that people who were previously injured were now dead. There were groups of bodies as well as many dead water buffalo. Over the radio he warned the gunships to fire only when they could positively identify an enemy target. They had good visibility as they hovered sometimes only four or five feet off the ground. Gunner Lawrence Colburn, in the doorway, didn't want to look at the corpses. Out in the paddy field beside a dike 200 meters south of the village they watched a small group of soldiers approach an injured woman, aged about 20. Thompson had marked her with smoke. They were flying close enough for Colburn to look at her face as she lay half in and half out of the dike. She made a feeble gesture with her hand and was obviously in need of help. Thompson put the aircraft into a standstill hover, only a few feet off the ground. The high gunship told the ground forces on the radio: "You have wounded over where the bubble is hovering." Thompson and his crew watched as an infantry officer, wearing a captain's bars on his helmet, came up to the woman, prodded her with his foot, and then killed her. Those in the helicopter could hardly believe what they were seeing. Minutes later over on the eastern side of the village they saw dozens of bodies in the irrigation ditch. Movements from the ditch convinced them people were still alive. Not far away a group of infantrymen taking a cigarette break sat around on the ground and relaxed, taking off their steel pots. It was obvious there was no firefight taking place.

Unable at first to figure out how the civilians had gotten into the ditch, Thompson landed the helicopter, unstrapped his seatbelt, and climbed out. The motor was still running and there was a blast of downwash from the rotors. A husky sergeant walked over and the pilot shouted to counter the noise from the engine. Thompson wanted to know if there was any way they could help the people in the ditch. The sergeant replied the only way to help them was to put them out of their misery. A young infantry officer came up and Thompson questioned him about what was happening on the ground. The officer said it was none of his business because *he* was in charge of the ground troops.

Several members of Calley's platoon observed Thompson's intervention. Calley had gone to speak with the bubble helicopter pilot. Stanley overheard Calley telling Sledge afterward that the pilot hadn't liked what was taking place: "He don't like the way I'm running the show, but I'm the boss here." Olsen, who wanted no part in the executions at the irrigation ditch, had moved 150 meters out into the paddy field to set up a perimeter defense. He saw the pilot angrily shaking his arms and gesticulating.

Frustrated, Thompson lifted off again and circled the area for a few minutes. Almost as soon as he took off his worst fears were confirmed. Andreotta reported the sergeant was now shooting people in the ditch. Thompson began thinking about what the Nazis had done in the last war—marching people to a ditch and blowing them away. Furious with himself and everybody else, finally he snapped. He flew low over the northeast corner of the village and spotted a group of about ten civilians, including children, running toward a homemade bomb shelter. Pursuing them were a group from the 2nd Platoon returning to the village from their murderous expedition to Binh Tay. Based on all he had seen in the village that morning it was obvious to Thompson what would happen when the troops got to the fleeing civilians. He landed his aircraft between the villagers and the soldiers and radioed the gunships he needed help. Screaming to his crew that he had to get the people out of the bunker, he issued an instruction that bewildered Colburn. If the Americans began shooting the villagers, Thompson said, Colburn should turn his machine gun on the Americans. "Open up on 'em—blow 'em away," Thompson urged him. Colburn turned his gun around to face the GIs, though he was unsure whether he would be able to open fire on his own men. Concerned for their own safety, Colburn wasn't sure it was a good idea to land in the middle of a combat zone. The pilot confronted the lieutenant in charge, Stephen Brooks. He said he wanted help to get the peasants out of the bunker. Brooks told him the only way to do this was with hand grenades. Thompson shouted that he personally would get them out and told the lieutenant to stay put. With that he went across to the bunker and gingerly coaxed the civilians to come out.

Crew members in the gunships overhead heard Thompson announce over the radio that an old man was sitting in the path of the troops near the door of a small bomb shelter. Thompson's voice was choking with emotion. He swore obscenities, cursed and pleaded with the aerocrew to come down and help rescue the civilians. One pilot initially queried the request and Thompson threatened that if the infantry opened fire on the civilians his machine gunner would turn his guns on the Americans. Danny Millians, a warrant officer on the low gunship, realized the delicate nature of the drama unfolding below and, knowing that Thompson couldn't talk directly with the ground troops, radioed the high gunship to tell the infantry to stop killing. Millians and Brian Livingston, another pilot, landed their ships and flew the Vietnamese—two men, two women, and five or six children—four miles away to the safety of the road which ran west to Quang Ngai City.

By the time the gunships evacuated the Vietnamese, Thompson and his crew had been on the ground for about twenty minutes. They were about to break off and return to Dottie to refuel but Thompson made one last pass of the ditch. As he did so Andreotta shouted he could see something moving. They landed and Thompson covered Colburn and Andreotta with a machine gun as they approached to the edge of the ditch. It was a horrendous sight; a hundred dead men, women, and children filled the channel four or five deep. Bodies were scattered along the edges of the ditch. There was blood, filth, and stench everywhere. The corpses looked completely mangled and torn apart. Colburn took an M-16 and stood on the lip of the ditch about four feet down the slope as Andreotta eased his way down, wading among the cadavers. No one had any doubt that mass executions had taken place. Eventually he found what he was looking for: a child, aged about 3, covered in blood and slime but not seriously injured. He had to move a couple of bodies out of the way to get the child completely free. He then handed the little body up to Colburn by the back of its shirt. It was limp and felt just like a rag doll. Colburn set the child down on the ground and reached out to assist Andreotta back up the slope. All three men inspected the child. There wasn't a scratch on him (they thought it was a boy)—it was a miracle he had survived. Thompson, who had a son about the same age, was crestfallen and decided to fly immediately to the ARVN hospital in Quang Ngai. The child, in a clear state of shock, lay across Andreotta's lap. Colburn noticed the blank look on its face and saw too, for the second time that day, that tears were streaming down Thompson's cheeks. Colburn wasn't going to let himself cry. He could have cried, but he didn't. The journey into Quang Ngai was made in virtual silence. They handed the child over to a nun at the hospital, refueled at a local strip, and made their way back to Dottie.

They arrived back at Dottie at about 11 AM. Thompson got out of the aircraft and threw his helmet on the ground. He told his section leader what had happened, and when Millians and Livingston landed they confirmed it. A group of them sought out their company commander, Major Fred Watke, in the aviation section's operations van. They told him everything they had seen. Watke then walked up the hill to the low-ceilinged tent of the tactical operations center and passed the information on to Barker. He in turn quickly got on the radio to his executive officer, Maj. Charles Calhoun, who was flying in a helicopter over the battle zone. Calhoun was instructed to find out what was happening and get it stopped. There had been allegations that civilians had been shot. Barker wanted assurance from Medina that nothing of the kind was happening.

The order went out to Charlie Company to cease fire. Calhoun had contacted Medina immediately to pass on Barker's concern and Medina relayed the order to the platoon commanders. Brooks told the 2nd Platoon to "knock off the killing" and to round up any more civilians they found in a group. Buchanon, the platoon sergeant, "rogered" the message. Some of those on the ground recalled hearing the words "Stop the killing" or "Stop killing civilians" spoken over the radio. Fagan had earlier heard Medina call on the radio requesting that the mission be changed from a search and destroy operation to search and clear. Everyone knew there were no Viet Cong or NVA forces in the area. Fagan was standing behind the command group when he heard Medina radio the higher headquarters. Permission to change the status of the mission was at first refused but fifteen minutes later Medina was on the radio again talking back and forth with the tactical operations center (TOC). He told them the NVA had got out of the area and only women and children remained.

Several people that day eavesdropped on exchanges over the communications network. The ether had been alive with Thompson's vitriol, and transmissions between helicopters and from the high ship to the ground troops had not gone unnoticed either back at Dottie. Word went around that something strange was happening. Thompson's clearly overheard threat to fire on American forces was one situation that could not be kept quiet. At brigade headquarters in Duc Pho, Sergeant Major Roy Kirkpatrick, monitoring the Task Force Barker net, heard that ground troops were shooting civilians. However, when the duty officer in the brigade operations room, Captain James Henderson, queried Barker's TOC at Dottie to find out more, no one knew anything about it.

At My Lai 4 it was chow time. Charlie Company took a lunch break.

5. My Lai, March 16, 1968: PM

A few yards off the main trail leading into the center of the village, Private David Hein found his skills as a mortar man uncalled for. Instead he began poking around the debris of a house that had been demolished by grenades and set on fire, and was completely surprised to uncover an old man hiding, partially buried, in a shallow trench. It scared Hein and made him jumpy. Recovering his composure he helped the old man up on his feet and handed him over to Roger Murray, a radio operator in Medina's command group. In a nearby hootch Hein made another find. Two small girls aged about 3 or 4 had been abandoned. He led them gently by the hand down to where the command group were eating their K-rations in a clearing beside the trail. John Paul lifted the kids over a concertina wire fence and set them down among the GIs, who shared their lunch with the children. At the bottom of his pack "Hotrod" Hemming found some candy and played with the kids for a while, carrying one of the girls around piggyback fashion. They later left the children with a group of twenty Vietnamese they had encountered in the southeastern corner of the village.

For Hemming and his partner Hawkins it had also been a slow day with only occasional need for their services. Medina had warned them the night before their principal task would be to blow up bunkers and destroy caches of food supplies they might find. Clearly expecting their repertoire of demolition skills to be used to the maximum, they brought with them an extra case of C-4 plastic explosive, ten sticks of dynamite, blasting caps, and other tools of their trade. But it was only when they found a well-constructed house with its doors locked and windows barred that they got to show their real expertise. It was to be a demonstration which ended in farce. Medina wanted to investigate the house further. Twice Hawkins tried to blow the bars off the windows by winding detonation cord around them. When this proved unsuccessful, Medina ordered the demolition men to blow a hole in the wall. A one-pound charge of C-4 was placed near a window. Unfortunately this was exactly that portion of the building that supported the main roof beams. The resulting explosion caused both the walls to come tumbling down and the roof to cave in. There was no one inside. Until the demolition men got there it had been someone's home, kept clean and tidy.

Medina's instructions to Charlie Company were well understood by everyone. The rest of the civilians were to be left unharmed. Moving through the subhamlet of Binh Dong, 2nd Platoon rounded up another fifty Vietnamese. Medina's interpreter, Sergeant Nguyen Dinh Phu, told them to head down the road toward Quang Ngai City. There were ten military-age males among this group who Medina considered possible Viet Cong suspects. He wanted them interrogated by one of the military intelligence (MI) men. By this time Lt. Dennis Johnson had flown off with his interpreter and the team from the public information unit to join Bravo Company over on the coast. The VC suspects were taken into custody and made to walk ahead of the soldiers in case there were booby traps. Another interrogator was coming out by helicopter to question the suspects.

Among the troops there was talk about how many people had been killed during the assault on My Lai 4. Partsch discussed this with Bernhardt, who throughout the entire morning had continually said out loud to himself and to anyone who would listen: "This is wrong. We haven't seen any young guys." Partsch, thinking that all the young men had gone off to join the Viet Cong, had agreed: "Yeah, that's all you do see is old men and women. Every time we go through a village that's all we see." Bernhardt quickly responded: "Then what are we doing this for? It should have been stopped right away when we didn't see any young guys through this village." They had heard messages over the radio saying: "I got ten," or "I got five." Both men realized these were not reports of VC killed—they were including everyone who had been shot, especially women and children. When Bernhardt had mentioned this to Buchanon or Lt. Brooks they ignored him, even though

Bernhardt knew the platoon sergeant was against what was happening. That afternoon as they were leaving the village, Bernhardt angrily summed up his feelings to Partsch: "What did we go through here in the first place for? If it was wrong, why didn't they stop it sooner? We should have stopped it as soon as we went in; as soon as we saw there were no military people we should have stopped it right away."

At about 3 PM, Medina called the platoon commanders together. He wanted to hear their body count for the day. LaCross was completely unsure of what he was supposed to report. He listened to Calley and Brooks as they reported their body counts. Rather than look stupid by saying he had no count to give, LaCross told Medina his men had killed six VC. Everyone standing there knew the body count was a total fiction.

Miles away from this piece of playacting, others also knew civilians had been killed during the operation. These deaths were certainly enough to cause serious concern. Earlier in the day, when he had landed at Dottie to refuel, Col. Henderson had already briefly mentioned to the divisional commander that a handful of civilians had been killed. But Henderson's estimate had to have been on the conservative side. He could not have failed to see what his own radio operator, Michael Adcock, saw as he and the brigade commander flew back and forth over the village: between thirty-five and forty Vietnamese civilians lying dead on various trails. This included one group of about fifteen bodies near an L-shaped junction of an irrigation ditch. Adcock had clearly observed this from his cramped position in the passenger compartment of Henderson's helicopter. He was squeezed between the brigade commander on one side and Colonel Luper, CO of the artillery battalion, on the other.

Many other people including senior officers both at 11th Brigade headquarters at Duc Pho and in the tactical operations tent at LZ Dottie were also aware that something serious had happened during the Pinkville operation. Staff Sergeant Lones K. Warren, assigned to Task Force Barker's contingent of military police as an intelligence liaison man, regularly called on the province and district intelligence agencies, picking up odd bits of information. Warren was originally scheduled to go into Pinkville with the task force, but was left behind at the last minute. Hanging around the TOC at Dottie, he heard the opening artillery barrage from the fire base at Uptight five miles away. He also listened over the radio to an angry Frank Barker criticizing the low weapons count in My Lai, complaining to whoever was on the other end of the conversation that the operation was moving too quickly. Because of this, Barker had said, the ground troops were missing the enemy weapons he was certain were there. Several times that morning the operations center tent was completely cleared of nonessential personnel. During a visit by the American Division commander, Maj. Gen. Samuel Koster, Warren was told to step outside.

Others had monitored helicopter pilots. "From up here it looks like a bloodbath—what the hell are you doing down there?" one exchange went. Another exchange—"If you shoot that man, I'm going to shoot you"—was heard over the air–ground net by an intelligence sergeant at Duc Pho. At midday Frank Barker called Medina on the Charlie Company net rather than the Task Force Barker frequency. This meant their conversation could not be monitored by commanders or staff officers at brigade HQ. Barker reported he had "a message from higher headquarters that there were civilians being killed." By this time Medina had ordered his men to cease fire. He said it wasn't his people doing the killing.

These were worrying developments for Charlie Company's commander but were nothing compared with what was to follow. Medina's antenna for trouble picked up real warning signals at about 3:30 PM, when a message was passed from brigade headquarters telling him to turn his men around and go back to My Lai 4. The executive officer at Dottie, Maj. Calhoun, told him to return and make a proper body count. He had to check exactly how every civilian had been killed. The instruction was monitored by a radio relay operator, Randal W. Roberts, at Uptight. Located in the mortar fire direction center, Roberts had been listening to four "Prick twenty-fives"—PRC-25 personal communication sets—which had a range of 11 miles. Subtropical atmospherics often interfered with the transmission quality of military radios in Vietnam, so Roberts was there to relay messages during the operation from the ground and air units back to LZ Dottie. He had heard talk of Vietnamese civilian casualties and also the message for Medina to check how many of them had been killed by small arms and artillery fire. He remembered Medina's reply: the combat assault was going so fast he didn't have time to check exactly how everyone died. Now, several hours later, Medina was being instructed officially to do the exact body count he earlier tried to avoid. Roberts overheard Medina say that he didn't want his men to return to My Lai 4; it was too dangerous with so many booby traps about.

Medina must have been all too aware what he would find if he returned to the village. He had seen the bodies but had already reported ninety enemy killed in a nonexistent firefight. Given that not a single shot had been fired at his men, his position was obviously compromised. But this difficult situation was saved by an intervention from on high.

Maj. Gen. Koster, flying over the area at 2,000 feet in his helicopter, call sign "Sabre-Six," *en route* to Chu Lai, broke in over the radio as Medina challenged the order to return to My Lai. Identifying himself, the general asked how many civilian dead there had been and how they had died. Medina lied. He responded that between twenty and twenty-eight had been killed by artillery fire. Koster seemed satisfied. "That seems about right," he replied, countermanding the order to return to the village and breaking off transmission. Koster believed that sending Charlie Company back didn't warrant the risks involved. He had seen plenty of corpses in Vietnam and couldn't tell what killed them most of the time. The civilians could just as easily have been killed by a single artillery shell or a gunship run or even in an exchange of crossfire. Koster continued his journey and Charlie Company pushed on northeast toward their rendezvous.

It was already running late and Medina's men were about to prepare a night defensive position. They had linked up with two platoons from Bravo Company who had been in a battle at My Khe, on a heavily fortified coastal strip beside the South China Sea. The two company commanders agreed on a rendezvous about one "klick" away from the scene of Bravo Company's fight at an inland peninsula. The location was near a hamlet marked on the military map as My Lai 1, wedged between the Diem Diem and

My Khe rivers. Brooks and LaCross organized their men in digging foxholes beside an old cemetery. They set up mortar positions and began preparing bivouacs and hot meals for the night. Calley's men were half a mile away. They formed a special night defensive perimeter for the rest of the company.

In the late afternoon a contingent of national police and a couple of South Vietnamese soldiers, wearing shoulder patches of the 2nd ARVN Division, arrived by helicopter from Quang Ngai. They were there to screen some of the thirty VC suspects Charlie and Bravo companies had gathered during the day. Leading them from the Huey was Eugene Kotouc, Task Force Barker's intelligence officer.

Kotouc needed quick tactical intelligence to locate mines and booby traps in the area, but he also wanted to find where the Viet Cong had gone. He began his interrogation of the VC suspects close to the Charlie Company bivouac. Officers from both companies were standing nearby. Some watched closely what Kotouc was doing; others were apparently unconcerned.

Sgt Phu, Medina's interpreter, talked with the national police from the local Son Tinh district headquarters, who had hitched a ride on Kotouc's helicopter. A delicate relationship existed between the Vietnamese and US troops. Although they often accompanied American units, the field police were not under the control of American officers. The Americans had been warned not to cause offense and loss of face by telling them what to do in their own country. While Kotouc questioned one suspect, the police guarded the others, who had been tied up, hooded, and left sitting in a squatting position close by. One of the policemen went along the line of prisoners pointing out suspects. They had with them their "black book" of local Viet Cong members, collated during Phoenix sweeps of known VC villages.

"He's VC!" they yelled in pidgin English. "Yes, this guy is definitely a VC. We know him, he is VC." The policemen repeatedly assured Kotouc that the suspects knew the location of booby-traps and weapons caches. The prisoners stayed silent in the face of Phu's translations of Kotouc's questions. Finally, in an attempt to scare one prisoner into answering, the bulky and sweating American drew his bowie knife and threatened to cut the man's finger off. This scene was observed by at least a dozen Americans, who were left in no doubt that Kotouc was torturing the kneeling prisoner. When the middle-aged man still refused to talk a board was wedged under the prisoner's hand and Kotouc tapped the blunt edge of his bowie knife across the man's fingers. Kotouc was becoming more and more frustrated at the prisoner's obstinacy. Several times he rapped the blunt edge of the blade sharply downward on the wooden block, occasionally striking the victim's hand itself. The prisoner remained silent. After several minutes of this cat-and-mouse game Kotouc cut off the little finger of the man's right hand near the knuckle. James Flynn saw the knife held against the back of the prisoner's neck. A six-inch-long cut began to bleed.

Another prisoner also refused to talk. Both men were grabbed by the national police and dragged away to a shallow ditch behind some bushes. One of the police drew a .38 pistol and began questioning the first prisoner again, threatening to shoot him. To those watching the man was clearly afraid but kept repeating "No" to their questions. The prisoner told the police they would have to kill him and was immediately shot in the back of the head. The policeman kicked him in the back and he rolled forward into a gully about two feet wide and two feet deep. Several yards away the sound of gunfire took John Smail by surprise. He had noticed earlier the prisoners being questioned by Kotouc but hadn't paid much attention. On hearing the shots he quickly wheeled around, thinking the position was under attack. Then he saw the man in the ditch.

The police started questioning the second prisoner. A carbine was held to his head. He refused to answer and the rifle was placed in his mouth. The questions were put more forcefully. When he failed to respond, the trigger was pulled, blowing part of his face away. The police then went to a third man, who immediately began talking.

The executions happened while Medina was in conversation with Captain Earl Michels, the commander of Bravo Company. When one of the national police came back from the execution site Medina went up to him. "Let's knock that off," he said angrily. "That's not the way we handle our people around here." Some of the other members of Charlie Company watching the executions from about ten yards away heard one of the prisoners moaning in the ditch after he had been shot. "Somebody should go and finish them off," a voice said. Another remarked how cruel the Vietnamese were to wound and not kill the suspects. John Paul, who had not witnessed the shooting, later went over and checked the bodies. They were both dead. Hein also saw the bodies in the shallow gully. One of them lay with his eyes open, staring upward. Hein went over to where Kotouc had questioned the prisoners. The short end of the little finger, severed between the middle and first joint, was still there on the block of wood. Hein picked it up and looked at it.

That evening, before he had his hot meal and went on guard duty, Thomas Partsch sat down with a pencil to write his last diary entry for March 16:

Our final destination is "The Pinkville." Supposed to be cement bunkers. We killed about 100 people. After a while they said not to kill women and children. It was pitiful seeing all those dead bodies lying there. Still couldn't look at them. Stop for chow about 13.00, we didn't do much after that. We are now setting up for the night. Two companies are with us. We set up in part of a village and rice paddies. We had to dig foxholes. Area is pretty level and our mortars are out with us. They are serving hot chow tonight. The names of the villages are My Lai 4, 5, 6. Am pulling guard for the night—one and a half hours. I am with the first squad, and the sky is a little cloudy, but it is warm out.

While they prepared the bivouac, Smail and some of the others could see a couple of men almost half a mile away. The men were carrying what appeared to be packs. Smail fired his machine gun and the men dropped down behind what looked like a dike. He never saw them again and didn't know whether he had hit them. He was in no mood to go and check them out.

Later that night in the darkness they could hear the shrill and distant sound of an old woman grieving loudly. It unsettled some of the soldiers as they tried fretfully to sleep. Charles West finally stood up and lobbed a grenade from an M-79 launcher in the direction of the noise. A couple of others fired their M-16s. The woman continued her mournful lament, wailing and crying throughout the whole night. It was an eerie, spooky sound, Smail later recalled.

In the darkness, a mile or so away, two young men in their early twenties, trained as medics by the Viet Cong, did their best to treat some of the injured. All had gunshot wounds. Tran Dau, a farmer, had been an active Viet Cong supporter for a year. He arrived in Tu Cung from Son My village at about 5 PM to discover a scene of utter devastation, death and injury on an overwhelming scale, far beyond his medical capabilities.

The villagers of My Lai and My Khe emerged from body-filled ditches, from destroyed shelters, from hiding places in paddy fields, to find that both hamlets had been completely destroyed. All animals had been slaughtered; foodstuffs had been burned along with their homes. For those survivors who escaped death, buried underneath bodies piled on top of them, their clothes were stained with blood. Chunks of flesh, the obliterated remains of what were once their children, mothers, wives, and friends, were stuck to their clothing. The pools of blood had begun to dry out in the late afternoon sun.

As Tran Dau tended the sick, children still groped frantically through rubble for their parents in the burned-out shells of what had once been their homes. Others searched among piles of corpses, already putrid in the tropical heat. Many of the youngsters wandered around in a complete daze, having witnessed scenes of total horror. The small world as they knew it had come to a complete stop. Nothing that was normal remained. The buildings had gone. The trees and vegetation had been burned or blown apart. Chickens and hens that strutted and pecked in the yards around every home had disappeared. Ducks, cows, calves, pigs, water buffalo—the economic lifeblood of every family—had all been slaughtered. Family, relatives, friends were all gone. And everywhere were the bodies. Hundreds and hundreds of bodies—in ones and twos, in groups small and large, in fives and tens, in thirties—and in the irrigation ditch the already rotting corpses of well over a hundred people.

Many of the survivors had severe injuries. Dang Thi, aged 21, had a limited knowledge of nursing care and had also joined the

Viet Cong the previous year. He tended three women and seven men before his medical supplies were exhausted. Although some ten or twelve survivors had by some means reached Quang Ngai City and managed to get medical attention from nuns or doctors working in the hospital administered by Canadian Quakers, many more died from their injuries for want of medical attention.

Many of the male heads of households had been working out in the fields when the Americans arrived. They, along with some of the survivors, began burying the dead—a task which was to continue for the next three days. The stories of what the American troops had done were not long in coming. Truong Ngu, 45, had crept back to his home from the paddies just as a soldier was escorting his family at gunpoint down the main trail. He stayed for hours listening to numerous bursts of gunfire before eventually coming out of hiding to discover his mother dead from wounds to the lower part of her body and his wife and three children also dead, shot in the head. Near them, just off the trail, were the bodies of his brother and sister-in-law and their four children. Ngu, working with another farmer called Do Hoa, placed fifteen people in one grave. Another farmer, Truong Lom, 49, managed to rescue two of his sons and take them to the safety of another village. He returned to the main trail and found his wife, Nguyen Thy Ting, 49, shot in the head, and their 3-year-old son, Thi, dead from stomach wounds. Ngu hired a man from the neighboring village of Son Hoi to help him bury his son in a field near his home. He took the remains of his wife back to Son Hoi, where he buried her the next day.

Phan Chot, 37, was working in the fields before first light and on hearing the helicopters ran to the rough dirt road leading to Quang Ngai and crossed over, hiding in the lee of a geographical feature the locals called Elephant Hill. The Americans labeled it Hill 85 on their maps, because that was its height in meters. Phan returned to the burned-out rubble of his home to find his daughter, Hai, shot in the back. Despite a long search he could not find the rest of his family. In the darkness he carried his daughter and buried her at the foot of Elephant Hill.

A number of mass graves were dug. Nguyen Quyen and Nguyen Phan, both aged 40, organized the burial of fifty people. A series of trenches were dug and three bodies were placed in each trench until all fifty were laid to rest. At the irrigation ditch, burial parties had to lift corpses out and carry them on their backs to a mass grave. The dead who were survived by a relative were buried in family plots—the rest were placed in the mass graves.

During the day the local market had been swept by rumors of a large number of killings at the hands of the Americans in Tu Cung, Binh Dong, and Binh Tay. People from neighboring villages slowly began to appear, both to see the truth for themselves and to offer help. Thi Nhung, 39, hired neighboring villagers to bury eleven relatives in the family vault, including her parents and four brothers and sisters. Nguyen Thi Tay, aged 17, paid two men to place her family in a grave hastily prepared in a rice field beside their home, close to the village pagoda destroyed in the shelling. Stories began going round about particular family losses, all of them tragic.

Several members of the local government committees who administered the village for the Viet Cong began trying to determine how many had been killed. The senior men were: Do Vien, 33, director of information and propagandist; Truong Qui, 40, chief of security; and Nguyen Co, also 40, the chief of administration. Their very rough total, cobbled together over the course of the next week, was that 370 had died in Tu Cung, Binh Tay, and Binh Dong. Working in the fields as a helicopter hovered overhead, Do Vien had escaped being shot by opening his shirt and throwing his hands in the air to show that he was not armed. There were only ten active Viet Cong supporters in the village and his chief task as propagandist had been to call village meetings and to give speeches to the villagers urging the people to donate money for the Viet Cong cause. His orders came from the Son My village information committee chairman, Pham Phan, 38, who received written instructions via messenger from the district committee, which also sent representatives to collect taxes. Security precautions were rigorous. When the orders were carried out they burned the messages. The district headquarters was moved constantly to avoid it being discovered.

Do Vien toured the village and saw the total destruction for himself. Amid the pitiful scenes were clear signs that many women and girls had been raped. Phuong Thi Moi, 13, and Do Thi Man,

12, were found inside their homes lying naked, their vaginas appearing to have been savagely ripped open. Pham Thi Nho, 19, had been shot in the stomach and had massive bruising on her legs. Some of the women had also been stabbed. Do Thi Nguyen, aged 10, was found in Ba Xam's house by her mother, Pham Thi Day, a 45-year-old widow who survived the killings. When Do Vien examined the little girl's body he could clearly see her clothes had been torn off. Her vagina had been ripped and there was blood all over the area. There were no bullet wounds or any other visible signs of injury. Miraculously one young woman, Tran Thi Hoa, 20, raped by several men at Binh Tay, had survived.

The stories the survivors told, and the evidence of Do Vien's own eyes, showed that destruction and butchery had occurred over a wide area and that many soldiers had taken part.

The artillery barrage on the northwestern portion of the hamlet had killed just one person, Do Tro. Truong Moi, an 18-year-old fisherman, was working at his nets in the river out in the paddies, seven hundred meters beyond the irrigation dike on the western side, when the Americans landed between him and the village. He had dropped his nets the previous evening and was up early at first light to check his catch and collect the fish. Soon after the shelling stopped, troops landed in waves about 500 meters away from his position. They then spread out before they entered the village, shooting as they went. He hid frightened behind a bush, worried that he might be shot but more concerned for his family, especially his mother. The helicopters continued firing around the edges of the paddies for half an hour. He could see smoke inside the village itself, coupled with explosions and a great deal of shooting. Trees were falling and homes were set on fire. In the afternoon he went back to the village and found the charred remains of his elderly mother who had been shot dead in their home. All the farm animals had been slaughtered.

He searched for the rest of his family. Along the paths and in the ditches beside the fields there were piles of bodies everywhere. Entire families had been killed. The throats of some of the children had been slit; others were disemboweled and completely naked. Moi's sense of horror and outrage was combined with a deep sense of injustice. His had been a very quiet and peaceful community, virtually untouched by the war, apart from the shelling and bombing. They saw few soldiers. The Americans had only been in the village twice—just before and just after Tet, less than two months previously. The troops asked the people for water and in exchange gave candy to the kids and cigarettes to the grown-ups. Sick people were given medicines. "How is it," he asked himself, "that they could come and do this to us, when we have done nothing to them?" After much searching Moi finally found the remaining members of his family at the foot of the watchtower, in the southern half of the village just off the main trail. His brother, his sister, and her two young children were all dead. He buried them. A total of twenty-four members of his immediate family were killed. His father, who had been working in the rice fields, escaped. Moi's younger brother had also been spared injury, hidden under several bodies which shielded him from the soldiers' bullets.

The children who survived had witnessed horrible scenes. Pham Thi Trinh, 10, watched her family being wiped out. Before the massacre hers was among the most wealthy families in the area. They lived at the northern end of the village in a large, well-built home with a veranda, sheltered by tall bamboo trees. When the shelling started the family hid in the tunnel underneath the house. The Americans arrived from the rear of the property and pulled them out of the tunnel, rounding them up outside. Three buffaloes in the stable were shot as Trinh hid behind her mother's skirt. When the troops turned their guns on the people she ran back into the house, and by some miracle the soldiers failed to spot her escape. A few minutes later she heard her sister, Mui, 14, shouting. Trinh peeked out from a window and saw Mui naked on the ground trying to force off an American who was on top of her. When he finished raping Mui the GI got up, pulled on his pants, and shot her. Their mother was lying seriously injured on the veranda, holding Trinh's seven-month-old brother in one arm, clutching her gaping wound with the other. There was blood on her legs. When she thought the Americans had gone Trinh went to assist her mother. In a whisper she told the child to flee: "Run away and hide, so you can live . . . as for me, I think I am going to die . . . I can't live much longer." Other members of the family were lying nearby. Inside the house her grandmother had climbed into a large cabinet to hide. Trinh found her dead in the closet. Her mother had crawled from the veranda into the middle of the yard. She suddenly called out that the house was on fire and urged Trinh: "Try to stay alive. I think I'm dying."

Trinh stayed hidden in another tunnel at the front of the house and remained there until she could hear no noise at all. When she came out she found her mother still cradling the baby in her arms. Like all the others her body had been burned by the fire and she was now lying horribly twisted in death. Trinh stood crying beside her mother's body. She later found herself walking away without thinking where she would go or what she would do. She felt she had lost her mind. All around her she could see that not a single home had been spared destruction; everywhere there were fallen trees and dead people. On coming upon a large pile of corpses she fainted. Later, people who had come to remove the corpses found her unconscious. They buried her family in a mass grave for thirty-two people.

Another 10-year-old, Truong Thi Lieu, was similarly badly traumatized. From a concealed place she had seen her mother, Truong Mieu, 38, shot in the neck at the door of their home in Binh Dong, when the soldiers arrived sometime between 9 AM and 10 AM. When she finally ventured out she found her father, Truong Le, 40, her sister Xi, 10, and her small brother, Cu, 3, all dead and the home burned. A girl the same age, Do Thi Phan, also from Binh Dong, came out of hiding and ran from house to house looking for her mother and father. In five separate homes she discovered the occupants—children with their parents, all shot dead, a total of nine adults and eighteen children. She later found her own mother and father in a field 200 meters away from her home. Both had been shot. There were no other bodies nearby.

Nine-year-old Tham Thi Lom's mother, Phung Thi Ly, and her sister, Xieu, aged twelve months, were killed at the irrigation ditch. Lom had been there with the others, guarded by about ten soldiers. When some of them opened fire, people fell dead on top of her, saving her life and that of her other sister, Xi, 7, and her 4-year-old brother. Wounded in the foot, she stayed in the ditch for several hours. When the Americans had gone, people came and called out to those who were still alive. Two days later her father found her in hospital in Quang Ngai.

Nguyen Dinh, 13, and his family were discovered hiding in their bunker by the soldiers. They forced out his father, Nguyen Da, 55, his mother, Pham Thi Lam, 47, his sister, Nguyen Thi Hoa, 29, and her sons, Do Tu, 6, and Do Lam, 3. Dinh's parents were shot outside their house in front of the children—the rest were marched to the main trail, where they were made to sit down. His nephew, Do Tu, was sitting with a group of people several yards away who were killed when the soldiers first opened fire. When they began shooting in his direction Dinh lay down and played dead until the soldiers had gone. He ran to a nearby village and later he met his sister, Hoa, carrying her son, Lam, on the coast road. They returned together to look for the family the next day, only to discover they had already been buried. Their small house and animal shed were burned down; three water buffalo and four pigs were shot dead.

Others managed to avoid being caught in the carnage. Nguyen Thi Bi, a 15-year-old farm girl, was drawing water from a well out in the rice paddy when the artillery rounds exploded. She watched as the shells hit the outskirts of the village, demolishing the Buddhist pagoda. Two helicopters landed and she ran to the neighboring hamlet of Son Hoa, only returning later that afternoon. Walking close to the main trail, she tried to avoid going near the bodies and made instead for the family home, which had been completely destroyed by fire. Three pigs were shot dead. Apart from her sister, Be, the family had all been out of the village. Be explained how she escaped from the home of their neighbor, Do Nguyen, before the soldiers arrived. Nguyen, 60, his wife, Day, 58, their daughter, and their twelve-month-old grandchild were all murdered. Her uncle Gap and his wife, Truong Thi Huyen, who were both in their forties, and their children Lanh, 10, and Tan, 6, were also dead. Her uncle Chuc, 55, her aunt Mai, 45, and three cousins were killed in their house on the eastern side of the village, along with another aunt, Ba Dao, 60, and her daughter-in-law and two-year-old grandchild. Her other uncle, Ky, was dead and burned in his house, but his wife, her aunt Doi, 50, survived.

Another teenager, Ba Do, 13, lived with his family close to the path that ran from the western side of the village to the north–south main trail. Their home was only 70 meters from where the helicopters landed. Ba Do stood rooted to the spot among the trees as the soldiers came into their yard, shooting the family animals, a pig and two cows. They grabbed him by the arms and took him to the trail, where he squatted down with the others gathered there. He had seen on the trail the bodies of Do Phu, the hamlet chief's mother, and two of her grandchildren. Ba Do sat there for an hour with his hands up behind his head, guarded by a group of American soldiers. Two—a Negro and a fair-haired soldier—suddenly began firing rifles at them. He was struck by bullets and fell unconscious, hit in the right side of the neck and right shoulder, and the index and middle fingers of his right hand. When he awoke it was late afternoon and he was lying underneath many bodies, surrounded by what he thought must be about a hundred people, all of them dead. They included his great-uncle, Do Ngo. Managing to hobble down the trail, he reached the highway, where he was found by an ARVN soldier who took him to hospital in Quang Ngai. He had two fingers amputated. His family had survived hidden beneath their home. So too did a distant relative, Do Ngu, 70, and his two nephews, despite being in the bunker of their house when it caved in around them. Two neighbors, Nguyen Thu, 40, and his wife, Thien, 50, were away at the market and returned to find their five children, three boys and two girls, shot and killed.

Ba Do's father, Do Cam, aged 40, was in the fields almost a mile from where the helicopters landed. When he heard shooting he ran to the next subhamlet, Theon An, and stayed there until the following day. Apart from Ba Do's injury, and the death of his greatuncle, his immediate family was safe. He helped others to bury their dead.

The mass executions had occurred in stages—principally at the main trail leading into the village and later at the irrigation ditch. One of those taken to the trail site was Truong Thi Le, aged 30, who lost nine members of her immediate family including her husband, mother, three brothers, and a 17-year-old daughter. When the shelling started, her mother and two of her children hid in a corner of their home. The Americans arrived and dragged them away and she became separated from them. Instead she was rounded up with her 6-year-old son, Do Ding Dung. When the shooting began she pushed him into the paddy field beside the trail and lay on top of his body, pressing him down, urging him not to cry. She wanted to see if they could save themselves. Two corpses were on top of her and when she raised her head slightly as the shooting stopped she could see soldiers still moving. They appeared to be pointing toward people on the ground. They began shooting those who were alive all over again. Eventually they left and Mrs Le walked along the path unable to believe her eyes—women and children were lying dead everywhere. Her three brothers were killed in a bomb crater, but most sad of all, her daughter was sitting dying, holding her grandmother, who was already dead. She said to Mrs Le: "Mother, I think I am very badly injured, maybe I'll die, I don't think I can survive. You have survived, you had better take little brother away. Please don't stay here as the Americans will shoot you." Mrs Le cried her heart out. Virtually her whole family was dead. She carried her son into the paddy field and lay down again to hide. The world had ended. Her husband had left for the rice fields at first light that morning and she never saw him again. Nine members of her family had died. When the troops left she carried her child home in her arms, but there was no home left. It was burned to cinders.

A soldier who kept shouting and using hand signals ordered Mrs Do Thi Nhan, 25, to leave her home. He then began beating her across the back with his rifle. Together with her husband, Nguyen Co, 40, her son, Hoang, aged 2, and her mother, Mrs Nguyen Thi Co, 40, she was taken to the trail and squatted for a while with other villagers. She noticed a white soldier, whom she thought hadn't shaved for a while, and a Negro. They began shooting the people with automatic fire. She fell underneath other bodies. Neither she nor her husband was hurt but her mother died, shot in the head and right arm. In this burst of fire only six people escaped injury—forty others were killed.

Sa Thi Quy, 43, lost three members of her family, including her aunt and nephew and her 22-year-old daughter, Do Thi So. She had been sorting through root vegetables for their midmorning meal when the troops arrived. Her husband had been trying to shoo a cow from their yard. Marched to the ditch, they were ordered to sit down. Everyone was too frightened to say no. The ditch contained over a foot of water and many women refused to get into it because the water was dirty. The Americans didn't understand what the women were saying and got angry and began shoving the women in forcibly. They kept telling the troops that there were no Viet Cong soldiers in the village. Do Con, a 35-year-old Buddhist monk who was Ba Do's uncle, had produced some papers for the troops to inspect. He was taken to one end of the ditch. He started to pray and the people began begging the soldiers to let him go. A soldier shot him and immediately the villagers jumped down into the ditch. To Mrs Quy they resembled ducks leaping into water. Some were crying out loud: "Oh, my God, please let me up!" "I haven't done anything!" "Have pity!" "They're shooting me, poor me!" "We're innocent people! Have pity."

There was silence.

Then more people came and the shooting began again.

"We're shot!" "Dear God!" "I'm hit. Have pity." "Let me out!"

Very young children crawled along the edge of the ditch looking for their mothers. Others who were still alive after the first volley of shots pleaded with the soldiers to let them come out of the ditch. Mrs Quy heard the soldiers fire again and then a third time. Underneath several bodies, she had been struck by a bullet in the buttocks. Unable to breathe because the people on top were crushing her, she felt she was going to die. The pain in her thighs and legs was unbearable. There was pressure on her head. When she was hit by the bullet she felt a hot, burning sensation which seemed to pass through her body. She started to shake . . . and then she fainted. About noon she awoke, in great pain and still shaking violently, to find the sun overhead. She crawled out of the ditch and found her way back to where her home had been. It had disappeared.

Mrs Pham Thi Tuu, 60, was shot in the wrist and side but continued to lie there in silence, in considerable pain, for many hours, until it was safe to get up.

Pham Thi Thuam, a 30-year-old widow caring for her 6-year-old daughter, lost six members of her family—father, sister, younger brother, and three nephews. She and her daughter were pushed into the ditch just before the firing started. Hiding underneath those dead on top of her, she pushed her child under her stomach. With bodies weighing her down she put her hand over her daughter's mouth and told her to keep quiet, not to cry, and to pretend to be dead. The soldiers waited to see if anyone moved and shot them again. They fired a second series of shots sometime later, and then a third. Much later, a long time after the shooting had ended, she pushed some of the corpses away to free herself. All around her were dead bodies curled up. She grabbed her daughter and ran across to a path. They were seen escaping and more shots were fired. Another woman running behind them was hit and fell down but Mrs Thuam just hung onto her daughter and did not stop. When she eventually came to a halt she discovered that her hair and neck were saturated with blood. There were lumps of flesh and pieces of brains from the people killed all over her, stuck to her body by drying blood. Suddenly overwhelmed by fear at the sight of this gore she ran frantically to the neighboring hamlet, crying hysterically, desperate to wash the blood and flesh from her body. Villagers came to help her and gave her clean clothes to wear.

Another who survived the ditch was a farmer, Pham Dat, aged 39, who lived 300 meters from where the carnage at the ditch happened. They were marched from their home after seeing their animals, four cows, three pigs, and ten ducks, shot. As he was being taken away Pham Dat looked back to see their home burning. No one had yet been killed when they reached the irrigation ditch. They stood there along with many other people guarded by about seven white soldiers and three Negroes. About an hour later two white soldiers began shooting them. He was struck in the left foot, left thigh, right thigh, and chin. He too lay for several hours pretending to be dead. His wife, Phung Thi Ly, 33, and daughter, Du, aged 3, both died. But some of his children survived. His daughter Lom, 12, was shot in the right thigh; another daughter, Chi, 8, was wounded in the lower right leg, and his son, Danh, 5, was shot in the left foot. Somehow he managed to get them to the highway, where a truck took them to hospital in Quang Ngai. In addition to his wife and daughter, seven other members of his family, including his parents, sister, brother, and three nephews and nieces, were murdered.

One elderly woman, 69-year-old Mrs Do Thi Don, used hand signals to ask one of the soldiers if she could sit at the back of the crowd. The soldier readily agreed. Some of those around her were squelching themselves down into the mud as far as they could at the bottom of the ditch, believing somehow it would protect them from the terror that was about to be unleashed. As soon as the firing started she threw herself on top of her grandchildren. Mrs Tran Thi Do, 34, also saved the lives of herself and her five children by making them fall down and play dead as soon as the firing began. So many people were crowded beside the ditch that the soldiers hadn't seen some people slip away into the paddy field and escape. Mrs Truong Thi Tung, 61, arrived at the ditch with a group of twenty people to find forty more gathered there, including many women carrying babies. Seated at the rear of the group, she slipped away into the long grass when the soldiers weren't looking. When she later returned to the village she met a young girl, Do Thi Tang, 13, whose entire family was killed. Mrs Tung adopted the child and took care of her.

Many parents made the ultimate sacrifice to save the lives of their children. Ten-year-old Nguyen Thi Tiet was saved because her father, Nguyen Gui, 45, and mother, Pham Thi An, 40, threw themselves on top of her and her sister, Thu, aged 9. Her other sister, Nguyet, aged 8, and brothers Thanh, 7, and Tai, 13, perished along with her parents in the irrigation ditch. Tiet fled to a neighboring hamlet—returning later to find the bodies of her family, all shot in the head. An elderly man helped her bury her family in a paddy field.

Only very rarely did the people encounter any Americans that morning who showed any compassion. Pham Ky, aged 34, his wife, Nguyen Thi Meo, 32, his 72-year-old mother, Vo Thi No, and his daughters Tuong, aged 8, Xiu, 4, and Pham Cu, 2, had hidden in a bunker as soon as they heard the sound of shells bursting on the village. They were discovered by a Negro and two white soldiers. The Negro ordered them out in Vietnamese and all three then took them to the southeastern edge of the village and told them to run for it: "Di, di mau!"—"Go, go quickly!" They fled across the fields to the coast road and ended up at the village of Son Hoi. On the way they saw the bodies of ten women and children. Another couple, Nguyen Thi Meo and her husband, Phong Ky, both aged 40, and their three children were escorted to the same road after their home was set on fire. They were told to run and hide.

In Binh Dong a Vietnamese soldier saved the life of a small boy aged 14 who was blind in one eye. The disability never bothered Quang Tan, who had been to school and could read and write. When the Americans landed he hid himself in the family bunker. The troops eventually searched the house and found him, but a Vietnamese soldier with them told him that because he was small and blind they would let him go. Tan later found his father, a widower, dead in the house.

After it was over, Mrs Le's uncle Chuc composed a lament:

> On March 16, at dawn,
> Birds twittered and hens called out to their chicks,
> Homes were burned to the ground and turned to cinders,
> The buffalo and the cow lay cold and twisted in their death,
> The people were all killed.
> Only the pig survived, all alone and helpless,
> Who's left alive to care and feed you, poor pig?

6. Aftermath

Those who managed to sleep were awoken at 6:30 AM. A low hanging mist off the South China Sea enveloped the bivouac site. Ninety minutes later Bravo and Charlie companies prepared to move out of their night defensive area. They spent the next two days tramping warily through the bush, continuing their pursuit of the 48th VC Local Force Battalion. It was a fruitless and frustrating effort and by the end of that day Medina was to discover the truth. The enemy was not at Pinkville—it was 40 kilometers away to the west, in the opposite direction to where they had been searching.

On paper at least, Barker's plan had seemed tactically shrewd, but it was always based on the assumption that the 48th was operating in the Batangan Peninsula. Alpha Company would stay where it was in its blocking position north of the Diem Diem River. In a two-company "push," Medina and Michels's men would move due south toward the mouth of the Song Tra Khuc River. At the point where it ran out into the South China Sea the river was over 1,000 meters wide. Any Viet Cong forces caught in the maneuver would be trapped by water on two sides.

Michels's men moved off first across a narrow bridge. They formed up a few hundred meters from the palm trees next to the sandy shoreline, which sloped steeply down to the sea. Medina's troops stayed inland. Both companies then moved down toward the river, keeping a distance of 1,000 meters between each other. The patrol took them across dried-out rice fields and through small deserted hamlets which they then burned.

Barker was concerned the Viet Cong might be hiding in large numbers in the secret tunnel complex they knew honeycombed the area. He feared they would suddenly launch an attack from the rear. As a precaution he wanted a platoon moved to the summit of

 ,hant Hill, the high point south of My Lai 4 that the military
 .beled Hill 85. From the top there was a perfect view across a
wide expanse of the fertile alluvial plain leading down to the South
China Sea. Since the time of the abortive French counterinsurgency
campaign against the Viet Minh fifteen years before, Hill 85 had
been the site of a small, well-prepared military position with dug-in
fortified defenses. Many years after the French abandoned the
country, Korean Marines and the South Vietnamese regional force
militia used the hill as an observation post. Both improved the
defenses in case of a sneak VC attack.

Calley's platoon, half a mile away from the rest of the company,
was the closest to Hill 85, an elongated feature with two gently
curving humps, one slightly higher than the other. From a distance
it resembled the head and back of an elephant. Medina gave strict
instructions over the radio not to go to the very top. There was a
danger of unmarked mines left by the South Vietnamese and
Koreans. He was being ultra-cautious. The company had paid a
high price when it made the mistake of wandering into the Korean
minefield three weeks earlier. Medina told Calley to go two-thirds
of the way up the hill, where they could observe the company's
rear. If the Viet Cong were spotted moving in on Michels's or
Medina's troops, Calley's men would be in a near-perfect position
to direct artillery fire with absolute precision.

After fifteen minutes Isaiah Cowan, the platoon sergeant, thought
they had gone far enough. He called out to halt the march, but
Calley took objection to receiving orders from his Negro sergeant
and snapped tersely that he was running the platoon, not Cowan.
It was typical of his immature behavior. The rest of the platoon
laughed among themselves. It was easy to see why Medina was
always on his back. Here was a classic example of Calley being
stupid, the little man trying to act the big guy. To demonstrate his
authority Calley took a squad of men further up the hill. They
included Meadlo, operating the mine sweeper. Calley said they
would clear a path which the others should follow, but Cowan and
the rest of the platoon defiantly held back and refused to proceed
any further.

Calley reached the top of the hill with Meadlo in tow. He
looked back to see that the others had completely ignored him.

The view was just as good from where Cowan had halted the men. Appearing rather ludicrous, Calley started down the hill again. Conti, another of those who climbed to the top of the hill, heard Calley tell Meadlo not to bother sweeping a path for mines on the way down, as it would take too long. He forcefully pushed the reluctant Meadlo back down in the direction they had come. A few minutes later Meadlo wandered slightly off the path. There was an explosion as a mine went off, throwing him and the mine sweeper up in the air. There was pandemonium for a while as the others moved forward carefully to assist. They discovered that Meadlo's left foot had been completely blown off. Ten feet behind, Calley had caught from the blast a glancing blow of shrapnel fragments on his face. Meadlo was screaming and shouting at Calley, who stood there completely dazed.

Already the men were blaming him for what happened. Sledge, a few feet behind the lieutenant when the mine exploded, radioed for a "dust-off,"* while Roy Wood and Lee, the platoon medic, bandaged the stump of Meadlo's leg. There were other injuries to his left hand and forehead. He writhed in agony until they administered a shot of morphine. The "dust-off" arrived twenty minutes later. As he was lifted on the stretcher Meadlo began to curse Calley. "Why did you do it?" he shouted angrily. "Why did you do it? This is God's punishment to me, Calley, but you'll get yours! God will punish you, Calley!"

Medina radioed for the platoon to rejoin the push down to the river. He halted the rest of the company while Calley's platoon caught up and for the rest of the day they proceeded through the fields and villages with great care. Most of the small hamlets were deserted but the area had been fortified with mines, booby traps, and bunkers as well as strengthened firing positions.

A small group of the South Vietnamese field police remained with them from the previous day. When civilians were found, the field police believed they had carte blanche to rough them up. Their usual tactic was to search military-age males for the telltale signs which indicated they were VC. Severe scratch marks on their lower legs suggested they had been walking through bushes and

---

* Medical evacuation helicopter.

undergrowth to avoid the paths and trails where mines were laid to trap the Americans. Heavy strap burns on their shoulders indicated they had been carrying packs or loads of mortar ammunition. In one hamlet a farmer cooperated and offered information voluntarily through an interpreter but after he finished talking one of the field police worked him over. The policeman went to the entrance of the man's hootch, picked up a large glass jar standing outside, and cracked it over the man's head for no apparent reason.

La Croix, the third squad leader in the 2nd Platoon, watched this with growing annoyance. Finally he lost his temper and butt-stroked the attacker in the face with his rifle. La Croix had stayed clear of the platoon's most vile excesses during the slaughter the previous day, although he had shot at least three civilians. The executions of the Viet Cong suspects the day before were still in his mind. He yelled at Stephen Brooks standing nearby: "If you want him along, you carry him." The platoon commander didn't reply.

La Croix's attitude toward the field police was typical of the deep ambivalence the Americans felt about the Vietnamese, a state of mind that revealed the cynicism of their own double standards. Among themselves GIs were able to rationalize their own brutal behavior by dismissing their victims as mere "gooks" or "dinks." "They were only VC," they said as a woman was raped or an old man tortured. Nevertheless many soldiers resented the way the field police behaved toward civilians, who were after all their own people. La Croix had not forgotten an earlier mission when one of the Vietnamese field police armed with a pistol went up to a child about 2 years old and shot it in the head. This scene had greatly disturbed him, and with everything else that had happened in the last twenty-four hours it all boiled over. Clubbing the policeman with his rifle relieved the tension.

Medina himself had once lost his temper and attemted to take a gun away from a man about to execute a VC suspect. He almost got shot in the process. Barker too was very reluctant to have the police on field operations, but it was virtually impossible to keep them away. They showed themselves to be totally ruthless. Only a few weeks previously newspapers had carried accounts of how, in Saigon during the Tet Offensive, the chief of the country's national police, Nguyen Ngoc Loan, had been filmed publicly shooting a

VC prisoner in the head with a pistol. A still photograph and television pictures of the scene appeared all over the world.*

Moving slowly toward the river mouth, two platoons were out in front, burning the hamlets. Medina followed Barker's scorched-earth policy to the letter and ordered each tiny collection of flimsy dwellings to be put to the torch. The rest of the company held back. Medina hoped to catch unawares any Viet Cong who came out of hiding and tried from the rear to pick off his forward troops with sniper fire or grenades. The tactic paid off. On the outskirts of My Khe 2 they scooped up three Viet Cong. Two men and a girl, believed to be a nurse, had been hiding in a hut and were captured when it was set on fire. They had stayed sheltering until the heat became unbearable. Conti, in a group of men bringing up the rear, saw three men and a girl run away from the burning house. He caught one and knocked him down. Simone struggled with a second man but the third person got away. Conti noticed the girl behind a tree and made a grab for her. As she fought him he lashed out and punched her in the head. She fell, apparently unconscious. All were strip searched and several documents were found. The nurse carried a small pack containing antibiotic drugs, a syringe, and some mild aspirin-type painkiller.

None of the other GIs was surprised when Conti carefully examined the pubic area around the woman's naked groin. He saw the vaginal area was infected with sores. Mockingly he complained to the others that she had every venereal disease possible and was probably a VC whore. "She's too dirty to screw," he said. In the melee the girl's white blouse had been ripped and torn, exposing her breasts. Conti using part of the blouse as a blindfold, picked her up, and carried her over his shoulder toward Medina's command group. The girl behaved as if she was sick and began bubbling and foaming at the mouth. Medina thought she was faking and asked the medic for an

---

* Westmoreland then complained to Gen. Cao Van Vien, Chief of the Joint General Staff of the RVN Armed Forces, about ill-treatment of POWs which caused "unfavorable public opinion." "We cannot permit our ethical standards and humane principles to be reduced to those of the enemy," he wrote on Feb. 21, 1968, "for it is his very brutality and lack of respect for the dignity of the individual that we most abhor."

ammonia capsule. He broke it open, placed it under her nose and
she immediately gained her senses. He gestured to one of the other
prisoners to remove his shirt and gave it to the girl to wear. By this
time the company had reached the river mouth and stopped on the
sandy shore in a coconut grove beside the wide expanse of water.
A stick from a banana tree was hacked off, placed between the
prisoners' wrists, and tied in the shape of a cross.

The river was busy with sailboats, junks transporting goods,
and fishing vessels passing by. The Tra Khuc River was an
important waterway which meandered across the whole of the
province, cutting it almost in two. It intersected Highway One—
the "Street without Joy"—at a strategic crossing point, the bridge
halfway between Quang Ngai City and the district headquarters of
Son Tinh, four kilometers away. The men relaxed and sat down,
watching the sailboats. They chopped down a bunch of green
coconuts and drank the milk. Some of them began looking at the
nurse with admiring glances. At one point the blindfold slipped
from around her neck and Hemming could see scratches around
her face. "I wouldn't mind laying her," he remarked to Hawkins.
Several other men felt the same and exchanged jokes among
themselves about raping the girl but they left her alone, discouraged
by Conti's verdict that she was a severe health risk. She was later
questioned by one of the field police, who slapped her very hard
across the face. Dennis Martin, a radio operator for one of the
forward observers from the artillery battalion, felt sorry for her.
He found a cloth, poured water over it and bathed her face. The
girl, Nguyen Thiu May, 21, turned out to be a cook for a VC
medical platoon. She claimed to have been pressed into service
against her will.

One of the two male Viet Cong suspects was much older than
the other. In the pockets of the younger man they found a small
piece of cloth embroidered with a Viet Cong slogan. Something
about the appearance of the older, middle-aged prisoner convinced
Medina and Sgt Phu he was not a farmer. When they started to
question him he shouted a warning to the other prisoners. Medina
told him angrily to "Shut up and keep quiet!" He slapped the man
fiercely across the forehead with the back of his hand, cracking
open the skin and causing the blood to run down his nose. A few

yards away one of the field police burned the younger prisoner with a cigarette and made him dig a hole.

Medina brought out a .38 revolver he had borrowed earlier from one of the field police, having first secretly removed the bullets. In a display of theatrics Medina played out a game of Russian roulette with the prisoner. His men watched this with some amusement, convinced he wouldn't actually kill the man. The charade seemed intended as much for the benefit of the troops as it was to encourage the man to talk. Phu warned Medina that the prisoner was certainly very important and urged him not to hand the man over to the field police. He feared they would execute him and it seemed obvious the prisoner had important intelligence information. Medina's performance, spinning the chamber of the pistol and pulling the trigger, failed to impress the prisoner, who stayed silent. Phu said they should shoot him anyway. Medina agreed and placed the man against a coconut tree. He then stepped back ten or fifteen meters, taking his M-16 with him. Phu, taking the role of Medina's straight man, urged the prisoner to talk, otherwise he was going to be executed. Medina took aim and fired his rifle. A bullet slammed into the tree eight inches above the man's head.

Medina walked back to the prisoner and Phu asked in Vietnamese if he wanted to talk. When he refused, Medina made great play of going through the same scene again, taking careful aim but this time placing the shot just a couple of inches lower. Again the prisoner had nothing to say. Medina returned, then pulled the prisoner around to look at the tree so he could see where the two previous rounds had struck. Spacing his index finger and thumb apart he measured the distance between the two holes. Then he moved his hand down so that the index finger down was in the lower hole. Medina's thumb now came level with the prisoner's eyes. His intention was clear. He propped the man, hands still tied, against the tree for a third time and, with a convincing appearance of someone clearly resolved as to what he was about to do, stepped back to his firing position. Just as Medina took aim, with the M-16 on "safety," the man began to talk. He blurted out that the 48th VC Battalion was many kilometers away on the western side of Highway One near the mountains. He had been in the Communist Party for many years and had been trained in Hanoi and infiltrated back into South Vietnam.

Medina was fascinated to know how the man was able to move around the area where the Americans operated yet still could be recognized as an important member of the Viet Cong by local villagers. The prisoner revealed that underneath his shirt he had a belt. When no Americans were around this was worn on the outside of his shirt. It showed he was an important official of the Viet Cong. When there were patrols in the area he simply lifted his shirt over the belt and kept it hidden.

The prisoner was Tran Van Quyet, aged 45, a local man from a small hamlet in Son Huong village, part of the Son Tinh district. Interrogated at length later in the POW compound at Chu Lai, his story showed the extent of the forward-planning organizational capability of the Viet Cong locally. Tran's job was to provide food for a special mobile medical platoon which treated local VC forces when they were injured. His involvement with the liberation cause dated back to 1946 when he fought as a sergeant with Viet Minh guerrillas against the French in Binh Dinh Province. He joined the Communist Party in 1950 and went to North Vietnam after the French left the country. Until 1963 he lived and worked in the North as a farmer and in August of that year he trained for a month in Hanoi as a unit food supplier. Back in the South he became commander of a food supply unit for VC fighting forces in Quang Ngai Province. The twenty men in this group came from all over South Vietnam and operated from a base near the Giang River in Son Ha district. They transported food from the rice-growing areas to storage depots in the mountains to the west of Highway One. Fighting units sent men to pick up supplies of food.

In July 1967, plans were being made to treat expected casualties in a major VC offensive planned for later in the year. Tran was put in charge of food supplies for the X-15 medical platoon which had fifteen medics and nurses. When there were no injured to treat they gathered rice from the fields. If they were unable to find food the local farmers' association was asked to provide it. Medical supplies came from a headquarters which controlled the whole of Quang Ngai Province. This command center was continually moved as a security measure, making it harder for the enemy to locate. Every three months the X-15 platoon leader, Hyunh Canh, traveled through various liaison stations to the provincial VC headquarters. Away for between three and five days, he took another helper with him if additional medical supplies were needed. The medical platoon too was kept on the move. VC casualties were brought to them for immediate treatment. Their patients were then carried on stretchers at night in groups of ten to a provincial hospital somewhere in the mountains. After the Tet Offensive the platoon received thirty casualties, injured with gunshot wounds. The medics and stretcher teams returned from the first run to the secret hospital in the mountains and another group was dispatched. In the first two weeks of March they received another twenty casualties suffering from injuries sustained in firefights. Tran had then taken leave to visit a cousin in My Khe 2, when he was captured by Charlie Company.

The younger male prisoner, Truong Quang Dung, aged 28, was a member of a local Young Men's Association, one of a myriad different VC organizations spawned to assist its cause. In his hamlet 70 males were involved. They were given political indoctrination, lectures on economics and taught the history of the life of Ho Chi Minh. They dug tunnels and spider holes, carried rice, and warned hamlet guerrillas if American troops were in the area. They had no weapons. The guerrillas who did the actual fighting lived in the tunnels where supplies of food and ammunition were stored. They kept their guns with them at all times. The tunnel system had several entrances, often a long way from the living quarters and supply areas.

The capture of the VC official was a real success for Medina, and the company stayed beside the river for an hour before heading back north again. The Vietnamese prisoners walked ahead as human mine sweepers tethered on ropes. Conti, ever ready to take the opportunity to lighten his load, made one of them carry his pack. After a mile, at about 6 PM, they stopped for the second overnight bivouac near My Khe 1. Barker flew in and picked up the prisoners, who were taken to LZ Dottie and then Chu Lai for further questioning.

The next day Charlie Company's mission was almost completed. They were scheduled to secure a landing zone for two lift helicopters and form a defensive perimeter before they could make the flight back to Dottie. The last hours before the end of a mission were nerve-racking for the ground troops. There was always the possibility of taking hits from a sniper or failing to spot a hidden mine. The closer they were to their R and R leave or point of departure for the United States, the worse the tension became.

Charlie Company's final kilometer march to the helicopter rendezvous ended in near tragedy. Two infantrymen, Gonzalez and Trevino, were caught in an explosion and suffered multiple leg and arm injuries. They were the last two men in line as the 2nd Platoon moved through a potato field and were saved from being killed by their flak jackets. Someone hidden close by had waited until the rest of the men cleared the area. A booby-trapped mine was then command-detonated. The explosion was the ticket home for Gonzalez, the more seriously injured of the two. He was hospitalized for three months. Flown to Japan and then to the United States, he never returned to Vietnam. From his hospital bed Gonzalez wrote his mother and wife about the events at My Lai. People back home, he told them, simply had no idea what was happening in the war. "What are we doing here?" he asked.

Forty-five minutes after Gonzalez and Trevino were hurt, Henderson flew out for an unexpected meeting with Medina. They spent nearly half an hour in close discussion as Henderson's regular pilot took off and circled the area. Lieutenant Colonel Richard K. Blackledge, the brigade intelligence officer, overheard the two men talking. Henderson wanted to know if some of the casualties the day before might have been noncombatants. "Were all those you reported as casualties military-aged males?" he asked. In the confusion of battle, Medina replied, it had been impossible for him to reach the center of combat. While a few people may have been caught in the battle zone, no deliberate or indiscriminate killing had occurred.

Medina then gave his version of how he came to shoot the woman in the paddy field, already aware from various radio messages and conversations with Barker that a helicopter pilot had made a complaint about this killing. He told Henderson there were so many helicopters popping off smoke to mark bodies that he didn't have enough men to inspect every incident, so he had gone to look at this woman himself. He thought she was dead but out of the corner of his eye when his back was turned he suddenly saw her move. Thinking she might have a grenade, he instinctively turned and shot her. Henderson relaxed. He understood how this could have happened. He told Medina to get on with lifting the men back to their fire base. When Henderson had gone, Medina walked across to some of the men, including Calley, and told them: "Well, it looks like I'm going to jail for twenty years." Later that day when Medina quizzed his platoon leaders about the shootings of civilians, Calley told him: "My God, I can still hear the scream-ing." Calley assured Medina that if there was an investigation he would take the blame because Medina had a family.

With only a pair of troop-carrying helicopters at their disposal, it took more than two hours to move the whole company back to Dottie. The first men to arrive at the fire base, where they felt relatively safe and secure, suddenly found themselves being questioned by Col. Henderson. He wanted to know about the Pinkville mission. Had they left a good impression during the operation? Jay Buchanon remembered Henderson asking whether the villagers would regard them as friends if they saw them coming again.

Buchanon and the others were on the way from the landing pad to their bunkers as the brigade commander was walking up to his helicopter. A dozen GIs pulled to attention as he approached. According to Henderson when he described the encounter later, the men looked proud: "Their heads were high. They were standing tall and in good spirits." Praising their efforts, he told them he appreciated the fine job they had done. It would be sometime before the 48th VC Battalion could mount another operation. However, he had heard that some civilians might have been killed without provocation by members of Charlie Company, so destroy-ing some of the mission's success. As commander he wanted them to know it was not the 11th Brigade's policy to kill civilians or to harm them in any way.

He then asked if they had seen anything unusual or any unneces-sary killings. The group, who included Haywood, Stanley, Grzesik, and Dursi from the 1st Platoon, remained quiet. He went to a handful of them and asked the question again. "Was there anything with this operation different from any other operation or were you ordered to shoot innocent civilians?" Each of them said: "No, sir." Henderson then turned to Jay Buchanon, the most senior man present: "What about you?" Buchanon's reply was an open invitation for more rigorous questions: "I would rather not answer that, sir." The troops admitted they had seen some civilians, particularly one family group, killed on the road, possibly by artillery or gunships. Henderson's way of judging whether the men had told the truth was to look each one directly in the eye. Since nobody turned away from his gaze he deduced they were being honest. "I think you have done a damn fine job and again I deeply appreciate everything," he said before finally dismissing them.

Medina arrived back at Dottie two hours later and quickly learned from Barker that Henderson had been questioning the men and was going to conduct an investigation into what had happened in the village. There were reports that a Negro sergeant had been firing at bodies. Medina offered to make his own inquiry but Barker turned him down. The investigation would proceed and Medina should get on with his normal duties.

At LZ Dottie that same afternoon Thompson recognized the infantry captain he had seen shoot the woman in the paddy field. Medina, though, did not identify Thompson as the pilot who had reported him. In the manner of a casual greeting to a fellow soldier he asked Thompson how everything was going. "Everything is going just fine," Thompson replied in a Southern drawl. He saluted Medina and walked away, not wishing to prolong the conversation further.

From the moment Charlie Company left My Lai 4 on March 16, the number of people with knowledge that something had gone badly wrong during the mission rapidly multiplied. They had picked up details from radio traffic, from eyewitness accounts of air crew, and from gossip in their quarters. Reports filtered back that between twenty and thirty civilians had died in the artillery preparation. Many had started questioning the body count. With only three weapons found, the official KIA of 128 seemed ludicrous. Others heard radio messages accusing ground troops of slaughtering civilians. It was impossible to keep quiet anything so serious and so unusual as one American unit threatening to attack another.

The word quickly spread to other battalions in the 11th Brigade. "Most of us in the brigade knew of the My Lai massacre, though we assigned it no such identification at the time," Tom Glen, a private with the mortar platoon of A Company, 4/3rd Infantry Battalion, remembered later. He was helping to unload a resupply helicopter when the door gunner asked him if he knew of the Charlie Company—1/20th—body count: "Over three hundred," he continued before Glen had time to answer.

"I immediately asked for the count every grunt knew really meant something: 'How many weapons [captured]?'" Glen said:

When the door gunner replied: "None," we exchanged knowing, sarcastic grins. We knew they had killed civilians. We chuckled among ourselves at the all too common cynicism and vicious hypocrisy of the Army's body count system, and then forgot about the incident. I thought no more about it until I was home and the story broke. I wasn't exactly a crusader.

In the aviation section details of some of the killings were spelled out by the pilots returning from the operation. The ripples spread ever wider. Before going to see his commander, Thompson spoke to a chaplain who was giving him confirmation classes prior to baptizing him. Captain Carl Creswell, a native of Kansas, had been an enlisted soldier before taking holy orders to become an Episcopalian army chaplain in 1964. Thompson often flew Creswell when the chaplain called on Americal Division units to give religious services. Occasionally Creswell provided pastoral care to young soldiers in combat who needed to talk about their emotions in circumstances that often left them shocked and feeling helpless. The pilot and the pastor became friends and it was natural that it was to Creswell that the much-troubled and still very distraught Thompson turned for help. Thompson described the incident of the infantry captain shooting the girl and how he landed his aircraft near the bunker to rescue the civilians. Creswell, seeing the pilot visibly traumatized, was concerned enough to pass these allegations on to his senior chaplain, Lieutenant Colonel Francis Lewis.

Later that day in the pilots' quarters, Thompson became distressed and emotional again when describing his experiences to another warrant officer, Charles Mansell. He sobbed as he told of saving the child from the ditch full of corpses. Mansell himself flew over My Lai 4 the following day when there were still a large number of bodies laying around unburied. Refugees trying to cross the Tra Khuc River were in danger of being attacked by the Navy Swift Boats patroling the waterway. He overheard the sailors radio the TOC, asking whether they should open fire. They were instructed only to keep observation.

On the evening of March 16, Brian Livingston, the high gunship pilot, wrote to his wife Betzy at their home in Indianapolis that he had never seen so many dead in an operation. A black sergeant had been shooting civilians in the head. Some of the aircrew mounted a rescue operation: "We had to do this while *we* [his emphasis] held machine guns on our own troops—American troops. I'll tell you something, it sure makes one wonder why we are here."

The same night, at the 5 PM briefing at the Americal Division headquarters 25 miles north in Chu Lai, the list of 128 KIA for the My Lai operation was announced. It was quickly followed by the news that only three weapons had been found. An audible murmur was heard and Lieutenant Colonel Charles Anistranski, the Americal Division civic affairs officer, said: "They were all women and children." Koster and his deputy were both present at the briefing. So was the senior chaplain, Francis Lewis, who confronted Barker the following day. Barker appeared totally unworried about the civilian deaths. "As far as I am concerned it was combat," he told Lewis, and added: "These [incidents] occur. It was tragic that we killed these women and children but it was in a combat operation and that is what I will report to Colonel Henderson."

Lewis, aged 51 and born in Seattle, Washington, saw Hugh Thompson a week later in the Artillery Club at Chu Lai. The pilot was still angry with himself because he participated in the My Lai operation. He wanted a thorough investigation.

Maj. Fred Watke, the commander of the aero scout company, chewed over the information his air crews had given him when they returned to base on March 16. He had taken the matter up with Barker straight away, but he was still bothered. The atmosphere had become especially fraught when Watke brought his men together for a briefing in the mess hall that same evening. A divisional staff intelligence officer went over the reported body count for the Pinkville operation. One of the fliers interrupted loudly: "You mean those women and children." The situation became rowdy and Watke intervened to calm the men down. One of the things worrying him was the effect the allegations would have on his own career. He pondered the matter still further, and late that same night, at about ten o'clock, he decided to find his battalion commander, Lieutenant Colonel John L. Holladay. He repeated what Thompson had told him, including the fact that the pilot had threatened to turn his guns on American ground troops.

By the time they finished talking it was past midnight, too late to take the matter further. First thing the following morning both Watke and Holladay found the assistant divisional commander, Brigadier General George H. Young. They explained Thompson's allegations of large numbers of civilians being killed, of bodies in a ditch, of the confrontation between the pilot and an infantry officer. It was this last revelation which peaked Young's interest. He seemed more bothered by the extraordinary scenario of a pilot threatening to kill American troops than anything else. That same day—it was a Sunday—Young had two meetings: one with Barker and Henderson, the other with the divisional commander, Maj. Gen. Koster. Thus, within twenty-four hours of Charlie Company leaving My Lai 4, two battalion commanders, the 11th Brigade commander, and two general officers knew of Thompson's very serious allegations. The best that can be said is that the full extent of the carnage in the village was not made clear to them. On their own admissions later, they knew that at least twenty civilians had been killed in My Lai. However, Thompson had seen upwards of one hundred civilians needlessly slaughtered.

An urgent meeting was arranged for 9 AM the following day—March 18—in the van Frank Barker used as his command post at LZ Dottie. Young and Henderson flew in for the crisis meeting with Barker, Watke, and Holladay. Brig. Gen. Young began by telling the others: "Only the five of us know about this." The implications seemed obvious: they should keep the allegations among themselves until they could be investigated.

But what stood in the way of Young demanding the most searching and far-reaching examination to get at the truth? Instead of calling the Adjutant General or the Inspector General's staff immediately, Young and Koster encouraged Henderson to investigate allegations concerning his own command. More than two decades later this still seems an act of almost unbelievable folly by two highly experienced soldiers.

Young had followed the classic route of officers heading for the top. The Army had been his life since he was a boy. He and Westmoreland shared a similar background. Both had been brought up in the South—Young at Pine Bluff, Arkansas; Westmoreland at Spartanburg, South Carolina. Seven years separated them as students at the South Carolina Military College, called The Citadel, a bastion of Southern pride and tradition. Young had led his infantry platoon ashore during the invasion of Sicily and took part in the landings on mainland Italy at Salerno. By the time he returned from the war in Korea, where he was a battalion commander, he was earmarked as a high flier. He was posted to the office of the Assistant Chief of Staff at the Department of the Army in Washington, DC. Then he went back to college and earned two masters degrees, one in civil engineering and the other in business administration.

Now here he was in South Vietnam, on his way for sure to a second star as a divisional commander. He had before him very serious allegations. Yet Young appeared more concerned with why charges had not been leveled against the helicopter pilot, rather than focusing his attention on the claims Thompson was making.

Young told Henderson to conduct an inquiry and have a reply ready within seventy-two hours. Later that morning Henderson began his investigation by taking notes at an interview with Thompson, who repeated his story for the umpteenth time. Henderson would later say he judged the pilot to be inexperienced in combat and emotionally upset. Thompson on the other hand recalled that he had been quite calm when retelling his story and had left nothing out. Henderson also questioned Thompson's door gunner Larry Colburn, who still wore the same bloodstained fatigues from when he carried the rescued child across his lap to hospital in Quang Ngai. Anxious to get matters straight, Henderson then flew immediately to see Medina, still out on patrol with his men. Returning to Dottie he questioned several members of Charlie Company just after they returned from their mission.

Henderson heard what he wanted to hear. Certainly he knew civilians had died; he had seen them himself. But instead of thoroughly probing Thompson's allegations, he took replies to his questions at face value, when logic and common sense should have told him to probe harder. Later it was said the motivation for his inaction was pure selfishness—the fear of jeopardizing his own advancement up the military hierarchy. He had wanted to be a general ever since he first enlisted as a machine gunner in the Indiana National Guard in April 1939 at the age of 18. Now, the very day after taking command of a brigade in Vietnam, men under his command, if the young pilot was to be believed, had gone berserk and killed many innocent people. Henderson could not, would not, let himself believe that this was true.

Alarming rumors of an investigation buzzed around Charlie Company, leading to much speculation. Some said Medina would be hung for mass murder and that the rest of them were going to jail for sure. Medina called his troops together and told them to cut out the idle talk. There was going to be an investigation and he would do the talking. The one loose cannon Medina worried about was Bernhardt, who in the past had spoken up when he thought injustices had occurred. At times Bernhardt made himself unpopular. Once he wrote to his Congressman to complain how supplies of personal items intended for general distribution among the whole company were being kept for select individuals. He complained about the beer ration and how he should be serving with a long-range reconn patrol, because of his special training with the LRRPs in Hawaii.

Medina made a point of telling Bernhardt that if he was thinking of writing to his Congressman about what had happened in the village, then he should forget it. Bernhardt heeded the warning and spent many weeks worrying whether he would get home alive. He was seriously concerned someone in the company might try to kill him to shut him up. He knew there was a rift between himself and most of the company. "I was considered the weak link in the chain," he said later:

It occurred to me I might get killed by my own people. Medina called me to the command post bunker; there were the platoon leaders, my platoon sergeant, and some others there. Medina asked me some questions about what I thought happened. Was I thinking of writing to my Congressman or was I going to tell anybody back home? It would be best if I let it alone. I was expecting this, I didn't think there was anything unusual in it. I told them I would do what I had to do and that I knew that I would do what I thought was right. I had to spend the rest of the tour, eight or nine months, with a company of men just about all of whom would be considered culpable and they knew it. I knew I had nobody else to rely on, nobody but me, because the Vietnamese weren't going to help, the Viet Cong were after me, and the company of men I was with probably would not be too unhappy if I didn't make it.

Partsch, when he arrived back at Dottie, wrote in his diary of the fuss caused by what had happened in the village. Questions were being asked. "There is going to be an investigation on Medina. We are not supposed to say anything. I didn't think it was right but we did it. At least I can say I didn't kill anybody."

For days the rumors went around about complaints a chopper pilot had made to divisional headquarters. Troops who stayed behind at Uptight and Dottie began asking questions. Many seemed willing to provide the answers. Some were particularly concerned children had been killed and said they were physically sick at some of the things they had seen. In Chu Lai, at the 2nd Surgical Hospital, Carter and Meadlo were placed in the same ward and discussed what had happened over and over. Meadlo remained convinced he was being punished by God. A couple of days later a few men from the company were passing through Chu Lai and called at the hospital to see them. They said a big investigation was being held into what happened. There was big trouble around the corner.

Three weeks later, on April 8, Thompson's crew chief Glenn Andreotta was fatally wounded by enemy fire. The same day, Task Force Barker's work was declared finished and the unit was officially disbanded. The mission seemed to have been a success, according to a series of "hero-grams" from the top brass. A message of congratulation for the Pinkville operation was received from Gen. Westmoreland himself. Koster added his own personal commendation for the teamwork and aggression exhibited by the companies involved. News of these plaudits reached Medina and his men via Henderson. In a postscript the brigade commander described the My Lai mission as having been an outstanding success. "The praiseworthy role of units of the 11th Infantry Brigade directly reflects your expert guidance, leadership, and devotion to duty," he wrote to Medina, copying the memo to Barker. "The quick response and professionalism displayed during this action has again enhanced the Brigade's image in the eyes of higher commands." It was enough to convince everyone in the company to stop worrying about what an inquiry would reveal. The message that gradually filtered down to the men in Charlie Company was that any investigation was now almost obliged to find a way to bury the truth.

With the task force disbanded, the three rifle companies under Barker's control returned to their parent battalions. Barker himself was reassigned to brigade headquarters as executive officer and Charlie Company went back out on patrol in an operation called Golden Fleece, intended to deny the rice harvest to the Viet Cong. They spent weeks in the bush and jungles and never went anywhere near My Lai again. A trickle of raw recruits joined as replacements for men who had been killed or injured. Those who had been there from the beginning called them "FNGs"—Fucking New Guys. The new men quickly heard how the company had killed hundreds of civilians at Pinkville. Tales ranged from 200 to 400 dead. Some veterans, like Torres, bragged about how many they personally accounted for. Boyce told one newcomer how he stabbed and killed a Vietnamese man and threw another down a well, dropping a grenade in after him. Leon Stevenson remembered vividly the manner in which some of the GIs described the operation. "It was the same as the stories of what the Germans did to the Jews," he said later. "There were a lot of them killed. The story was that it was deliberate. It sounded to me like a German blood bath, at least that is what came to my mind."

The accounts were so similar that few of the newcomers listening to Charlie Company's "war stories" were in any doubt that hundreds of people had indeed been slaughtered in the operation. It became part of unofficial folklore. They had little contact with the outside world and seemed to spend their time constantly on patrol, rarely returning to a fire base and with few opportunities for a decent meal or a hot shower.

Westmoreland's commendation had served only to push the truth of what had happened to the back of their minds. Perhaps the massacre hadn't happened after all. Their actions gained the illusion of legitimacy for Charlie Company when they read in the Army newspaper *Stars and Stripes* that they had, in fact, scored a stunning victory at Pinkville. An American Division newspaper, *Southern Cross*, ran a page feature complete with some of Haeberle's innocuous black-and-white pictures. Even the *New York Times* carried a wire report about the mission's success.

Background for the stories came from Frank Barker, who gave the details to Haeberle and Roberts, the photographer and reporter, when they stopped off at Dottie after the operation on the way back to their base at Duc Pho. They were about to be thrown out of the tactical operations center by Calhoun when Barker intervened and invited the two men inside. He took them over to a table and gave them an interview, using maps to explain the military concept of the operation. When Roberts mentioned that the operation had resulted in a large body count and small weapon count, Barker simply brushed the subject aside. Within a few hours the Army's PR machine was pumping out a colorful image of derring-do by American troops. Yet another body count was added to the meaningless volume of statistics of the war. The MACV communiqué, issued later the same day from Saigon, gave brief details of the operation, announcing that Americal Division forces had killed 128 enemy, six miles northeast of Quang Ngai City. "US TROOPS SURROUND REDS, KILL 128," was the headline printed in the Pacific edition of *Stars and Stripes* two days later. According to the story there had been a bloody battle in which a company of GIs was locked in heavy fighting with an unknown-size communist force. Less than twenty-four hours after Charlie Company left the village a mimeographed Americal newssheet was being churned out for the private consumption of the division's troops. This gave

Barker's men credit for a high enemy kill rate: gunships—4; aero scouts—2; Charlie Company—14; 6/11th Artillery Battalion—69; and Bravo Company—30. The official version of history had already been written. Among his other duties, Sergeant Jay Roberts was editor of the 11th Brigade journal, called *Trident*. His fictitious account of what had happened appeared with the headline: "TF BARKER CRUSHES ENEMY STRONGHOLD."

Roberts and Haeberle decided between themselves that they would keep quiet about what they had seen. They knew the Army information machine would bury the story and the photographs if they submitted an account of the massacre they had witnessed.

Haeberle later remembered their decision to stay silent:

On the return flight to our base camp Jay Roberts and I started talking. We knew we had something really hot, some very damaging evidence of an atrocity, but we decided we would not bring this out. We decided just to keep quiet about it, to let the soldiers or the officers above us bring it out. "They can talk about it . . . they can ask us some of the questions and then we'll supply them with the information."

We felt we were not going to break this story because we were part of it. We had other servicemen in the Public Information Office and Jay still had a year to go. Something could have happened if they knew we had ratted, broke the story. Something could have happened to one of the people in our office. Their lives would be in danger, easily disposed of, it's called "fragging." I had only a couple of weeks to go but something could have happened to one of them if they went on another mission with a camera. Everyone was afraid to tell the truth, including us. Look at what happened, it was covered up all the way from the top down. We definitely had a part in the cover-up, it's something we should have reported.

The 11th Brigade's senior officers were riding on a high when Gen. Westmoreland toured the 1 Corps area on April 20. He visited the Americal Division headquarters at Chu Lai and paid a flying visit to Duc Pho for a special briefing from the brigade's staff. When he met Westmoreland and Koster at the helicopter pad on their arrival at LZ Bronco, Henderson was still nursing a leg injury from a fragmentation grenade. Four weeks earlier his helicopter had been fired on and as he had landed to investigate a VC threw a grenade which exploded against the chopper, injuring both

Henderson and his gunner. Now walking with the aid of a cane, Henderson escorted the generals to the briefing tent. It was to be one of hundreds of similar briefings Westmoreland received during his time in South Vietnam. His only memory of the event several years later was a complaint by a Red Cross official about poor mail deliveries. The 11th Brigade briefing officer brought Westmoreland up to date on a number of operations, including the Pinkville mission. The official toll of 128 KIA was specifically mentioned. Significantly, MACV headquarters heard nothing of the civilian casualties at My Lai 4. Koster continued to stay silent about the matter during Westmoreland's visit.

The MACV commander's sojourn in Quang Ngai Province coincided with an announcement about Koster's future career. He was due to go stateside shortly, to return to the fortresslike stone buildings of West Point, 50 miles north of New York City. Westmoreland's visit only weeks before Koster was scheduled to leave South Vietnam was a significant personal moment for the two generals. Both were West Pointers. One was a former Superintendent; the other was about to take up the challenge. Koster, a graduate of the class of '42, was returning to the academy for the second time. He had been on the staff of the academy as the tactical officer until the Korean War intervened. Overseas he supervised guerrilla operations by the 8th Army against North Korea. Now he and his wife were going back to West Point to occupy Quarters 100—the Superintendent's house. There were few greater accolades for a former member of the academy. The appointment was a supreme moment in Koster's honorable career and signaled that further promotion to three-star general would almost certainly follow. He was still a young man and could have foreseen the possibility of promotion to the General Staff, perhaps eventually even to the job earmarked for Westmoreland himself, Chief of Staff of the US Army. The change of command at Chu Lai had already been decided. Major General C. M. Gettys would take over the Americal Division in June.

Nothing was allowed to mar the occasion of Westmoreland's visit to the Americal Division, and there were no revelations of large numbers or even relatively small numbers of civilian deaths. Koster knew Westmoreland's policy concerning civilian casualties meant that the figures had to be forwarded to MACV headquarters in Saigon, and he knew the reasoning behind it. Westmoreland believed this enforced reporting system would ensure that those in the chain of command would realize they were accountable for the actions of their subordinates and behave accordingly. The allegations about the Pinkville operation were still a subject of considerable discussion, gossip, and speculation at Chu Lai and Duc Pho, and Koster clearly had the chance to demonstrate frankly his apparent concern for noncombatants by taking Westmoreland to one side. Nothing could have demonstrated better his worthiness to be the true embodiment of the West Point motto: "Duty, Honor, Country." He promptly flunked the opportunity.

Koster and Henderson purposely avoided telling the commander-in-chief about a number of extremely serious reports circulating locally from South Vietnamese officials which claimed large numbers of civilians had been killed by American troops. US military intelligence had quickly picked up Viet Cong claims of a massive atrocity. News of the massacre had actually been reported to the South Vietnamese and American authorities at Son Tinh and Quang Ngai. Military intelligence had also intercepted Viet Cong communiqués and broadcasts about an incident at Son My village where they claimed five hundred civilians had been slaughtered by American troops in a bloodlust operation.

At the brigade intelligence cell at Duc Pho, Blackledge received intelligence reports from Vietnamese sources which indicated that the Viet Cong were making propaganda out of the Pinkville operation, describing it as an atrocity. They noted that VC soldiers were wearing red armbands which bore the slogan: "Resolve to avenge the atrocity at Son Tinh." The Viet Cong were saying that more than four hundred innocent women and children had been slaughtered. Henderson assured Blackledge he had already discussed these reports with the local Vietnamese authorities and that they had dismissed them out of hand as propaganda.

The Viet Cong special communiqué that contained these allegations was issued by the province People's Liberation Front Committee on March 28, 1968. It claimed hundreds of people had been slaughtered and named specific individuals who had been raped and murdered. At no time did US forces return to the village to check the accuracy of these statements. If, as was officially claimed, the VC had been routed at Pinkville, these reports could have been countered by the simple expedient of returning to the village and establishing the truth. No attempt was made to do this.

Within days of the massacre five separate internal reports about an atrocity at My Lai 4 began to circulate among South Vietnamese officials in Son Tinh and Quang Ngai. Translations were shown to Henderson and a network of American military and civilian staff in the province and district advisory headquarters. Many claimed later either not to have seen the South Vietnamese reports or to have dismissed the Viet Cong claims as propaganda.

The first detail of the carnage came out of the village on March 18, just two days after the slaughter. Throughout South Vietnam an official government reporting system called census grievance committees was established to administer civilian claims for loss of life and property. A minor official with the local census grievance team wrote a one-page report revealing that 320 civilians had been killed by American troops in one small hamlet—Tu Cung. He sent it to the committee's office in Quang Ngai.

On March 22, the chairman of the Son My village council, Dinh Luyen Do, reported in writing that hundreds of civilians had been killed at My Lai 4. A further ninety, he wrote, had been shot at a hamlet on the coast called Co Luy, where Bravo Company had operated. This letter was sent to the South Vietnamese Army officer in charge of the Son Tinh district headquarters, Lieutenant Tran Ngoc Tan. Almost a week elapsed before Tan forwarded his own report to his superior, the province chief in Quang Ngai, Lieutenant Colonel Ton That Khien. This stated that a great many civilians had been unavoidably killed in the American operation during a firefight with the VC after a sniper apparently opened fire. He warned that the Viet Cong might try to make propaganda out of the incident.

However, by April 11, Lt. Tan had completely changed his mind about an exchange of fire between American troops and the VC. He sent the province chief a second, follow-up letter stamped "Toi Khan"—"Top Priority." A letterhead proclaimed the slogan "Vung Len Diet Cong"—"Rise Up and Kill the Communists." In the intervening period Tan had investigated the incident further and now reported clear evidence of a massacre. He wrote: "the operational forces attacked the village, *assembled the people*, and shot and killed more than 400 people at Tu Cung hamlet and 90 more in Co Luy hamlet" (our italics).

He described the American action as an act of insane violence and requested the province chief to intervene on behalf of the people. Copies of this letter were forwarded to the headquarters of the 2nd ARVN Division and the MACV offices in Quang Ngai, where it was translated. As a result Lieutenant General Hoang Xuan Lam, the commanding general of the 1 Corps Tactical Zone, which covered the northern provinces of South Vietnam, heard of the allegations from the 2nd ARVN commander, Colonel Nguyen Van Toan. Col. Toan also spoke about Lt. Tan's letter with both Henderson and Koster. By mid-April, both men were aware of allegations that five hundred people had been killed at Pinkville. The Viet Cong were publicizing the Pinkville incident, which had been checked and verified by a government official.

One of the many Americans who met daily with Lt. Tan was Major David C. Gavin. He worked with the South Vietnamese authorities as senior advisor for Son Tinh district. On April 10, Gavin went on a brief R and R. In his absence his deputy, Captain Angel Rodriguez, prepared the official US reply to Tan's letter of April 11. On his return to his office six days later, Gavin was handed a file. It contained Tan's original letter and Rodriguez's response, which took the form of a statement about the atrocity involving 450 civilians. It set out the facts of how the allegations had come to be made and claimed that Lt. Tan had to rely for his information on the word of the village chief and others living in the area. It falsely claimed that Tan wasn't really sure whether the allegation was true.

In their bunker at the Son Tinh district headquarters Rodriguez and Gavin had a brief discussion about the killing of noncombatants. This conversation was overheard by a young intelligence officer, Lieutenant Clarence J. Dawkins, who worked in the same building. Dawkins interrupted them to mention an intelligence report he had received about many civilians being killed during an operation in which 90 percent of a village was destroyed. It was this last figure that caught his attention, and this was why he mentioned it.

Gavin later denied he ever received reports of a massacre. His only recollection was to have queried Viet Cong propaganda concerning American operations. Lt. Tan subsequently testified he gave Gavin the information about a massacre and discussed it with him.

The news spread to Chu Lai and Duc Pho, where the brigade civil affairs team believed a cataclysmic scandal was about to unfold. On a visit to divisional HQ in late March, Lt. Col. Anistranski confided to one of his colleagues, Captain Donald J. Keshel: "Task Force Barker is in big trouble, in fact the entire 11th Brigade might be in trouble. They [Quang Ngai] are up in the air about this and are having an inquiry, they want to get to the bottom of what happened in the Barker area." He tapped a white folder he was carrying: "Don't worry, it's all being taken care of."

Anistranski's belief that ARVN and US civilians working on the CORDS* pacification program in Quang Ngai were really concerned about the massacre was completely misplaced. A copy of the very first report giving details of the slaughter had arrived in the offices of the province advisory team, where Lieutenant Colonel William D. Guinn Jr was James May's deputy. Guinn showed the report to Henderson because May was away in Saigon arranging details of his impending marriage to a Vietnamese girl. Guinn was one of those who later claimed not to have taken the report of an atrocity seriously. Nevertheless, he passed on to Brig. Gen. Young details of Lt. Tan's letter of protest, which spelled out in unmistakable terms what had happened at My Lai 4. Young in turn appraised Maj. Gen. Koster, who then talked with Henderson and senior ARVN staff in Quang Ngai.

At every level in the chain of command—Americal Division, 11th Brigade, Task Force Barker, and Charlie Company—many officers were aware of the grave allegations about the Pinkville mission. The evidence was stacking up: a high body count and low weapons count; agents' reports that several hundred civilians had been slaughtered; Viet Cong communiqués and broadcasts; Thompson's allegations, confirmed by other air crew; and reports of eavesdropped radio communications about a blood bath.

* Civil Operation and Revolutionary Development Support.

Jesse Frosch, a military intelligence officer working in Quang Ngai with the province advisory team, later remembered how American officials ridiculed the official "after-action report" of the operation. They knew that Frank Barker had been spoon-fed intelligence about the 48th VC Battalion by Ramsdell, the newly arrived and somewhat gullible CIA agent in Quang Ngai. The idea that Barker's men could have killed 128 Viet Cong on the Batangan Peninsula was laughable, according to Frosch. Local intelligence experts had already warned Kotouc that there were only a few NVA stragglers left in the area.

"When we received the after-action report at Quang Ngai City we simply could not believe the count," Frosch wrote. "There weren't 128 Viet Cong troops in the village to be killed that day and it would have been impossible for that many Viet Cong to have been killed with so few weapons taken." When questioned by intelligence officers at Duc Pho about the low weapons count, one of Charlie Company's NCOs claimed the Viet Cong had doubled back to pick up the weapons while leaving the corpses behind.

"Although there was speculation that civilians had gotten in the way, nobody made much of it," Frosch continued. "The more accepted conclusion was that Task Force Barker had inflated its body count for good press coverage." Months later he was informed by an intelligence officer at Chu Lai that suspicions of a massacre were rampant in divisional headquarters. No specific place names were mentioned. Many believed that a large number of civilians had died—perhaps by artillery fire. Frosch added this caveat:

It can honestly be said that those who were expected to be in the know— those serving in intelligence—never knew exactly what had happened at My Lai. We had our ideas but there are a great many ways to kill large numbers of innocent people. We were never able to imagine a massacre, despite everything we had seen come and go in Quang Ngai Province.

No proper investigation was carried out even though not to do so was clearly against the Army's strict regulations concerning incidents involving civilian casualties. Westmoreland had laid down instructions at the series of meetings for senior officers regularly held at the 5th Special Forces headquarters in Nha Trang. Koster

was one of the twenty-five generals who were present at a
MACV commanders' conference on December 3, 1967, when
Westmoreland once again brought up the high rate of civilian
casualties. He wanted a maximum effort to reduce unnecessary
Vietnamese deaths. "Upon the occasion of an accident, the chain
of command should endorse the report all the way to MACV
level," the commander-in-chief emphasized. Civilian deaths were
officially regarded as a serious issue. By regulation there had to be
a proper inquiry that would involve taking signed statements and
sworn evidence from witnesses.

Koster recalled later he too had fundamental worries about the
behavior of US forces:

I put out directives about civilian casualties and the destruction of
villages, disallowing it. I felt very strongly about it as a matter of fact. I
banned the use of Agent Orange up in our area almost as soon as I got
there. I also banned a lot of indiscriminate night interdiction fire that
went on out in the countryside.

Westmoreland's warnings about unnecessary casualties had left
their mark. In the following months Koster made known down the
Americal Division's chain of command that unnecessary civilian
deaths were bad news for the United States' military effort in
Vietnam. He stated repeatedly that it harmed America's image.
Others, concerned for their own future, had concluded that a
searching and rigorous inquiry would cause the roof to fall in,
bringing an end to several promising careers. Instead of an investigation, more paperwork was churned out about the safeguarding of
noncombatants. A week after Thompson made his allegations,
Koster sent new Rules of Engagement to all his commanders: "It is
important that a thorough and continuing program be developed
at the lowest command level which will keep every soldier mindful
of the importance of safeguarding noncombatants, both from a
humanitarian standpoint as well as from the standpoint of *the
prestige of US forces and the Government of Vietnam*" (our
italics).

These rules stated that there had to be discriminate use of
firepower in built up areas; private property had to be safeguarded
and a plan developed to control civilians during military operations

in populated areas. Inhabitants should be warned of a forthcoming action by loudspeaker or given an access route to escape firefights. Wounded civilians had to have medical treatment. Koster added: "A concerned effort on the part of every soldier to minimize noncombatant battle casualties is essential if we are to gain the loyalty and cooperation of the people and create the conditions necessary to permit them to go about their normal lives in peace and security."

Four weeks later, even the term "search and destroy" was eliminated from the vocabulary of the Americal Division's official correspondence by order of the chief of staff, Colonel Nels A. Parson. Too much emphasis had been placed on the term "destroy." Now other phrases had to be used so as not to give the impression the Americal Division lacked compassion.

Despite—or because of—this new sensitivity regarding civilian casualties, Barker and Henderson completely ignored Thompson's allegations in their written reports on the Pinkville mission. Their deliberate deceit in the matter assisted in portraying the assault as a military victory and served to help prevent an official investigation into what had happened. Both reports had a very restricted circulation and contained references to the My Lai operation so totally fictitious they bordered on the farcical. Each was a grotesque and deliberate corruption of the truth.

Frank Akeley Barker Jr was a career combat soldier born and raised in New Haven, Connecticut, where his father was a businessman in the construction industry. A lieutenant colonel at the age of 40, Barker was on the ladder for promotion. It was only a matter of time before he made full colonel. He was not a pen pusher, nor was he interested in simply "having his ticket punched" with an obligatory combat tour in Vietnam as a necessary requirement for promotion. On leaving school at the age of 17, at the end of World War II, Barker joined the merchant marine. When the Korean War broke out, he was in the Army reserve and was called up for active duty. He made the Army his career and later served in Europe. In 1962 he joined the rush of infantry officers put through the US Special Forces School at Fort Bragg, North Carolina, as part of President John F. Kennedy's program to expand and develop

America's counterinsurgency capability. In his message to Congress on his first defense budget after he went to the White House, Kennedy had urged a rapid expansion of special forces. Three months later an increase of 3,000 men for counterinsurgency work was approved. Barker spent the next fourteen months as an advisor with the Green Berets in South Vietnam before returning to the United States. In October 1967, while serving on the staff of the CINCPAC* at Fort Smith, Hawaii, he was reassigned as commander of the 4th Battalion of the 3rd Infantry, part of the 11th Brigade, which was *en route* to Vietnam. Once there he was switched to the brigade headquarters as the S-3, staff planning officer.

Barker's posting to South Vietnam was a reflection of the speed with which infantry units were being hastily assembled to meet Westmoreland's demand for a rapid troop buildup. They needed experienced officers and Barker's knowledge of Vietnam was essential to the new 11th Infantry Brigade. On January 20, 1968, Brig. Gen. Andy Lipscomb gave him the job of leading a battalion-size task force to clear the VC from the eastern sector of Quang Ngai. Both Lipscomb and his deputy, Oran K. Henderson, had high regard for Barker's abilities. His experience with the Green Berets set him apart from the others and he was regarded as an outstanding officer, dedicated and enthusiastic.

Barker himself had clear ideas about taking the fight to the Viet Cong. "US forces fighting in Vietnam need only remember the basic principles and the basic premise of defensive tactics and offensive tactics," he declared in a personal commentary about the My Lai operation. Barker's observations, put onto tape a few days after the assault, provide a clear insight into his tactical thinking:

The big thing to remember in fighting the VC here in Vietnam is that it is no different today than it has ever been, and you fight offensively. You fight as you were taught in World War II and Korea; you fight the enemy offensively, using all support weapons available to you and using them properly.

When you defend against this enemy ... you dig in. You put out listening posts. You put out defensive positions with your artillery. I think the one thing you must all remember is that the Viet Cong is not

---

* Commander-in-Chief Pacific.

some unique exotic fighter that the American soldier cannot cope with. We have met soldiers like the Viet Cong many times before.

It is true the Viet Cong soldier can strike us at night at will, but so could Geronimo when he fought the US cavalry in the Western United States and he did this for eighteen years. We are wise to these types of soldiers and we can defeat them. Do not let the fear of the unknown keep you in your bases.

Barker's wife Dorothy continued to live in Hawaii with their children, a daughter and two sons. He named his fire-base headquarters "LZ Dottie" after her. He was a close family man, but the pressures of the job on the CINCPAC staff and later as a battalion commander meant that, by the time he returned to Vietnam, he hardly knew his youngest son, who was then eighteen months old.

Regarded as a loner, Barker had no close relationship with any of his company commanders and appeared somewhat detached from other officers, keeping himself very much to himself. A key benefit of the operational command of the task force was the tactical nature of its mission. It freed him from many of the administrative roles which went with normal command of a battalion. Barker was an aggressive infantry officer who tended to leave paperwork until the last moment before it was absolutely required, or until he was given a forcible reminder.

A signal had arrived from divisional headquarters on March 19, telling him to prepare urgently a combat after-action report about the My Lai operation. He had let a month go by and still had not yet written the after-action report about Alpha Company's earlier battle with the Viet Cong on February 23. He had had neither the time nor the inclination to write it up as regulations required. Now, suddenly, after-action reports were required by divisional headquarters for both the February 23 firefight and the Pinkville operation. Someone at division wanted the report urgently enough to have allowed only *three* days to elapse before requiring the formal paperwork to be completed.

Barker would not be hurried. He waited until March 28 to set down his version of what happened at My Lai 4. His official five-page report dramatized the operation as a successful assault on a heavily defended Viet Cong stronghold with a few administrative hiccups. However, a plausible reason had to be found to explain why there were so many bodies on the ground at My Lai. Barker's explanation was to blame the artillery fire, but the record had to be altered to suit the new facts. In his first radio message soon after Charlie Company landed near the village, Medina announced his men had accounted for fifteen enemy dead. This was followed forty minutes later by another report claiming sixty-nine more VC killed by *Charlie Company*. Yet at some point on March 16, the figure of sixty-nine KIA was altered in the 11th Brigade's official daily journal, so that it was credited not to Medina's company but instead to artillery fire. Moreover, the location was moved 600 meters outside the village, closer to the landing zone. Within hours of the GIs leaving My Lai 4, this fabrication became officially accepted as fact. It appeared in updated intelligence reports about Operation Muscatine, circulated every day to MACV HQ and the commanders of units all over South Vietnam.

Barker, already familiar with the serious allegations made about the mission, now enhanced the fiction with his own elaborately crafted additions. Charlie Company, he reported, had received enemy small arms fire as they pressed forward in their battle against the Viet Cong at Pinkville. Bravo Company was also involved in a particularly heavy firefight over toward the coastal area.

Six weeks later, Barker was dead, killed in a helicopter accident. His official report about what happened at My Lai 4 was a sad and dishonorable epitaph to what had been a promising career:

This operation was well planned, well executed, and successful. Friendly casualties were light and the enemy suffered heavily. On this operation the civilian population supporting the VC in the area numbered approximately 200. This created a problem in population control and medical care of those civilians caught in fire of the opposing forces. However, the infantry unit on the ground and helicopters were able to assist civilians in leaving the area and in caring for and/or evacuating the wounded.

Operations conducted in an area where large numbers of refugees might be generated should provide for civil affairs, psyops, medical, intelligence, and police teams to be brought to the area as early as practicable after the arrival of combat troops. This would facilitate population control and medical care, and would permit the sorting out of VC which have mingled among the population for cover. The presence of these teams would free infantry personnel for combat operations.

Barker was genuinely concerned that civilians be protected in future operations. And there was no way he could have known of the dreadful atrocity being committed by Charlie Company at the time it was happening. But it is clear he quickly became part of a coverup. He knew many civilians had died.

A conspiracy to conceal the massacre began the moment the brigade log was altered to credit artillery fire with a large number of enemy kills. The mission was portrayed as a triumph both for the task force and of course for Barker himself. Though Gen. Westmoreland was completely ignorant of the slaughter of civilians, once he sent his message of congratulation the fabricated version of events carried the imprimatur of the commander-in-chief. There was no way back for those in the chain of command and it would have been a brave man who decided to come clean and insist that truth be pursued.

The earliest strands in the web of deceit were woven during the initial combat assault when Medina reported the first civilians who were killed as being Viet Cong. When Thompson, aboard his helicopter, started complaining, a reason why so many civilians had been killed had to be found which would satisfy the command-ing general. Blaming artillery fire for the deaths of civilians was an acceptable solution because it was an unfortunate and regular occurrence in the war. The sixty-nine VC deaths attributed to the artillery barrage provided a plausible explanation why helicopter crews had reported seeing so many bodies in the village.

Immediately after the operation at My Lai, Henderson had told Koster that artillery fire was responsible for civilian casualties. This was the cover story which had come from Medina and Barker. Henderson continued to hold to this explanation in the face of the most damning evidence that something had gone terribly wrong. Later Koster asked him for a written report. But by allowing Henderson to investigate his own command, consciously or unconsciously, Koster enabled the truth to be concealed.

Henderson's investigation was equally as fraudulent as Barker's official account of the battle. He made no mention of Thompson's serious allegations and instead concentrated on the Viet Cong propaganda campaign. Moreover he lied when he claimed that the Son Tinh district chief, Lt. Tan, did not give the allegations of an atrocity any importance. Henderson's report concluded:

Twenty noncombatants were inadvertently killed when caught in the area of preparatory fire and in the crossfire of the US and VC forces on March 16, 1968. It is further concluded that no civilians were gathered together and shot by US soldiers. The allegation that US Forces shot and killed 450–500 civilians is obviously a Viet Cong propaganda move to discredit the United States in the eyes of the Vietnamese people.

Few people ever set eyes on this document. It was never logged in any of the official records at either the 11th Brigade HQ or the American Division, which would normally have been sent the original. Instead Henderson arranged for a copy to be placed in the safe of the intelligence section at Duc Pho. He later claimed personally to have carried the report to Chu Lai to show Koster. The truth was buried among the mass graves in the hamlets in My Lai 4.

The heat was off, but Charlie Company was never the same again. Whereas Medina had once been a strong disciplinarian who ruled the men with a rod of iron, he now began to let slide misdemeanors he would have previously pounced on. Soon his troops were completely lacking in leadership. When Charlie Company returned to the control of the 1/20th Infantry, the battalion commander, Lieutenant Colonel Edwin Beers, noticed immediately that morale had slipped. He saw Medina's troops behaving sloppily. Their appearance was not up to scratch and he found them drinking alcohol in the field. Beers chewed Medina out and insisted the company's standards be maintained. The troop's physical condition and general behavior had deteriorated to such an extent that Beers no longer regarded them as a top-notch company.

A battle-hardened first-class sergeant posted to Charlie Company in April quickly gained the same impression. James H. Raynor had done five combat tours in Korea and Vietnam. Soon after arriving at the company he heard alarming talk of the troops shooting women and children in cold blood during a killing spree. He was also seriously disturbed by the total lack of discipline he found. Raynor was on his third tour of duty in Vietnam and his wife was ill with tuberculosis in the United States. He undertook the latest posting only reluctantly and his experiences were so distressing that he quickly tried his utmost to get assigned to another outfit. In the four months it took him to achieve this objective the situation got steadily worse until there was virtually no discipline, leadership, or respect for those in command.

On patrols the men stubbornly threw down their gear and told junior officers: "I'm not going to carry it anymore, you carry it!" The men appeared in bad physical and mental shape and were frequently ill. The platoon sergeants were concerned to get the company back on its feet but Medina wouldn't back them up. The situation reached rock bottom when Raynor witnessed the insubordinate way some of the troops insulted officers: "What are you doing tonight at ten o'clock? You come by my bunk anytime, and I'll be ready for a blow job." One lieutenant, regarded as being slightly effeminate, was treated with total disdain: "Oh, boy, you put some lipstick on, sir, you would be good enough to kiss."

Charlie Company's task involved searches for Viet Cong weapons with the rest of the battalion as part of an operation called Norfolk Victory. They patrolled the foothills about eight miles southwest of Quang Ngai. The problems and hardships of continuous patrolling often rankled. The dangers of illness were never ending. Units were discouraged from keeping animals like dogs and monkeys in case they were infected with rabies. There was a constant fear of *vivax* malaria, common in the coastal region of Quang Ngai Province. In the high ground a more dangerous form of the disease, *palciparum* malaria, was rampant.

Calley continued to be particularly detested by his men, not least because of the way he tried to gain favor with Medina. He volunteered his platoon for dangerous work, always offering for them to go up front on point duty during patrols where they were likely to run into mines and booby traps before the others. The 1st Platoon finally put a bounty on Calley's head. Soon he was moved to the mortar platoon, where Sergeant Thomas Kinch, who

witnessed Calley's rough treatment of local people, found him hard
to get along with. At a fire base called LZ Ross, Calley vented his
anger on a couple of women. He kicked one in the stomach and
slapped another. "I could see no reason for it," said Kinch,
describing the scene later. Other members of the company were
equally brutal.

Some newcomers, however, reacted strongly to the vicious
behavior of their comrades. Among them was Johnnie Tunstall, who
arrived in Vietnam to begin his year-long tour on March 15. He
joined the company at LZ Dottie, four days later. At the end of April,
Tunstall got into a fight with another GI when he discovered him
trying to rape an elderly woman. Tunstall had to be restrained
from shooting him. They were searching hootches when he saw the
man throw the old woman on a bed. When he said he was going to
fuck the woman, Tunstall dragged him out of the hut. Later he
noticed that the GI was missing. He returned and checked the hut
again. The man had the woman on the bed once more. Tunstall
pulled him off and struck him across the face. A few minutes later
the soldier was missing yet again and when Tunstall went into the
hut for the third time the GI was raping the old woman. "He had
actually penetrated her this time," Tunstall recalled later. "I pulled
him off and was going to shoot him, but someone who had arrived
at the scene stopped me."

A few days later, on May 3, Thomas Partsch celebrated his
twenty-first birthday on patrol near Hill 953, well to the north of
My Lai. In a valley his squad fired on a group of people running
away. They were later found hiding in the undergrowth. Two men
and a woman had food and medical supplies on them. A few GIs
began abusing the girl while others searched a collection of huts
further along the valley. "We all ransacked the places and messed
with the girls, tore their clothes off and screwed one," Partsch
recorded in his diary.

Sgt Raynor hated being with Charlie Company because the men
reacted badly to his attempts to regain control. "Combat hasn't
ever bothered me but being in a unit like that made me try harder
to get out," he later recalled. "The men didn't give a damn." He
gradually became more and more worried about his personal safety
and knew there was a clear threat to him: "Some of them said I

would be better dead than alive. I would try to discipline them and they didn't like that."

Charlie Company's role in the war was to continue attempting to surprise and kill an enemy they rarely found but who they knew full well was all around them. Broken down into squad-size groups, Medina's troops tried to lay night ambushes as the Viet Cong ferried food supplies from the rice-growing areas back to their secret mountain depots. In the broader picture it appeared as if the Americans and the South Vietnamese were gaining the upper hand. Pacification, "revolutionary development" programs, and the relentless effort to destroy the Viet Cong infrastructure seemed to be having some success. Officially there were 25,000 people living in refugee camps in Quang Ngai but the real numbers of displaced people ran far higher. When their homes were obliterated, by either search and destroy operations, indiscriminate artillery fire, or aerial bombing missions, they were forced to move into special fortified camps, officially called "safe haven" villages. One was built close to Tu Cung hamlet at the foot of Elephant Hill. In April alone, the Quang Ngai pacification teams registered 1,200 people in their ID card program—an indication of the rate at which hamlets were being attacked and the civilian population made homeless. In these "safe haven" villages, the pacification teams drew up family census lists in an effort to identify those who had left to join the VC. American psyops units showed propaganda films and a theatrical troupe employed by the South Vietnamese government made a four-day tour of the refugee camps, trying to show the farmers who their real friends were. Measured by the number of incidents initiated by the Viet Cong, enemy activity was well down. The numbers of military and terrorist attacks in Quang Ngai declined to their lowest levels since the previous November. In February, there had been 94 incidents of varying kinds. In March there were 70, and in April only 34. But this merely reflected the fact that the Viet Cong's chief concern was the procurement of the rice harvest. During April the VC gathered an estimated 2,000 tons of rice in the eastern Quang Ngai area where the 11th Brigade operated, and transported it to their western base camps.

Viet Cong fighting units also managed assaults on the Tu Nghia district headquarters and the "safe haven" hamlet of Phuoc Thien in Binh Son district. These were both heavily defended targets and the VC attacks were repulsed but they demonstrated the Viet Cong's capacity to operate at several levels. Hanoi's concern was to keep harassing the South Vietnamese and their allies and show the local population that they retained control of the area. The North Vietnamese Army infiltrated several large units into Quang Ngai Province to buttress VC local force battalions. This brought forth greater demands from US commanders for more reliable intelligence. The Phoenix Program to root out and destroy the VC infrastructure moved into full swing.

The special branch training center at Da Nang, overseen by the CIA, sent 120 newly trained officers to Quang Ngai. They were then posted out into the districts to work with "revolutionary development" teams run and controlled by the Americans. By the end of April, they had more than seventy important Viet Cong undergoing questioning at the provincial interrogation center, where an additional sixty cells and three more interrogation rooms were being constructed. Among the American Division's successes was the capture of a man called Vo Thu, alias Gial Thu, aged 58, identified as the National Liberation Front's deputy province chairman. He proved very difficult to break but under intensive interrogation which frequently involved torture he eventually began to pass sensitive information about the Viet Cong's political and economic organization.

Another prisoner caught during this period was a senior economic official from the higher-echelon Inter-Zone V headquarters in Quang Tin. Huynh Diem Kang, aged 45, was sent into Quang Ngai specifically to ensure the 2,000 tons of rice was in store and ready for use by their fighting units by the end of April. The Viet Cong still got their rice, although an expected second Tet Offensive in the province never materialized. Senior US advisors in Quang Ngai reported that Task Force Barker deserved praise for its outstanding performance in clearing operations in Son Tinh and Binh Son districts.

But the next month, the harvest safely gathered in, the VC were back, more than doubling their military and terrorist attacks to ninety-six incidents, enough to keep the American Division, the 2nd

ARVN Division, and a number of South Vietnamese militia forces on their toes. Quang Ngai itself suffered a number of probing attacks accompanied by mortar fire. The 2nd ARVN HQ was a prime target, along with the jail, the radio station, and the power plant. Again and again the Viet Cong demonstrated their ability to penetrate secure areas.

However, on the pacification front the Phoenix Program was striking hard in the countryside. In Quang Ngai Province in the three-month period to mid-May 1968, CORDS officials estimated Phoenix had resulted in 796 civilian VC officials being either killed or captured. The official records showed well under half of these were being sent to the province interrogation center, which appears to indicate that the rest were summarily executed.

Charlie Company was sent on a series of long patrols. Often they spent weeks in the bush and jungle before being allowed back to their fire base. The longest period they were operating on their own was seventy-two days. GIs felt they were being sent out in the hope they might all be killed. Bernhardt later became so sick from tropical illness and jungle rot to his feet that he was evacuated to hospital at Chu Lai. "We were abused by the higher echelon—they wore us down to nothing," he said. "The supplies were not steady at all. You couldn't rely on them. As for the Vietnamese, the best we could do for them was leave them alone."

"They tried to bury us out there," Widmer bitterly remembered. "After My Lai we went out in the field for three months straight. We never came back into the villages. Our trips to the base camps were few and far between. They had a problem and they dealt with us by trying to hide us out in the jungle, hoping we'd all get killed. But we didn't."

On occasions the company was also thrown head-on into battle against the Viet Cong. For their pains in one confrontation they received five casualties but ended with two heroes. On May 12, they were conducting a combat assault against VC positions on Hill 378. This time intelligence reported the North Vietnamese Army was using the area as a base of operations. Moving up the hill at about 2:00 PM, they came under sudden and intense small arms fire. Jay Buchanon, the 2nd Platoon sergeant, and four of his men were seriously wounded by grenade fragments. Under the weight of Viet Cong automatic weapons and grenades they were forced to withdraw 100 meters back down the hill. Widmer stayed behind to provide covering fire while the rest of the platoon retreated. Clearly exposed to the enemy, Widmer then carefully and slowly backed down the hill, firing as he went until he used up all his ammunition. Buchanon was able to reach a safe position but then realized two men had been left behind, unable to move because of their injuries. Although wounded himself, Buchanon told his men to cover him. He began making his way back up the hill, running, dodging, and crawling until he reached the wounded troops. He picked one up and managed to carry him down to safety, then he returned for the other man. Meanwhile the platoon was running perilously short of ammunition. They had to have more if they were to provide cover for Buchanon's second rescue attempt. Again, exposed to hostile fire, Widmer made repeated trips down to the base of the hill to get more ammunition. Later both men were awarded the Silver Star—the United States' third highest award for gallantry in action. They had performed brave actions and thoroughly deserved their medals.

There was, however, a darker side to the way decorations were awarded in Vietnam. So many medals were doled out they became almost an institutional joke. The system was open to corruption. In soldiering terms an infantry unit without a high enemy kill rate to its credit was not considered effective by those higher up the chain of command. And if a unit had accounted for high numbers of enemy killed, and was therefore assumed to be effective, there had to be tales of derring-do. A unit couldn't possibly kill lots of Viet Cong and NVA without heroic actions on someone's part. Conversely, a combat outfit without medals must lack aggression and was not successful; its officers seen as incompetent. A commander of a company or battalion without medals was not a successful commander. It was rare for a battlefield commander in Vietnam to go home without at least a Silver Star for gallantry.

Frank Barker was awarded his Silver Star for intrepid actions during Alpha Company's battle near My Lai 4 on February 23. According to the citation he had remained close to the scene of action in his command-and-control helicopter, had landed amid hostile fire to pick up a wounded officer, and had returned four more times to rescue wounded soldiers.

In the first six years of the Vietnam conflict, nearly 1.3 million awards for bravery were given to American troops, almost as many as during World War II, when America had 10 million men in its armed forces. Before long medals for the fighting men in Vietnam—the "common grunts"—held very little meaning. All wars required heroes and Vietnam was no different. The deserving received decorations along with the undeserving. Accounts of bravery and gallantry were often inflated to provide a unit with the necessary citations to enhance the image of those in the chain of command. The Americal Division HQ in Chu Lai had an awards and decorations branch heavily overloaded by nominations for medals. Within twelve months of their arrival in the country they had processed 3,783 awards and nearly 2,000 general orders—which included citations for recipients of medals like the Bronze and Silver stars, or the Distinguished Flying Cross. Air Medals, awarded for so many flights in a combat zone, were dished out like confetti. Since the whole of Vietnam was a combat zone, they became meaningless. A battalion commander named Lieutenant Colonel Alexander Haig—the future US Secretary of State—came away from the Vietnam War with the equivalent of seventeen Air Medals. Oak Leaf Clusters were regarded with such contempt they became known as "rat turds." The Purple Heart was given to anyone who received an injury—whether it was as serious as having a foot amputated or so slight as to need only a band aid.

When he lost part of his foot in Charlie Company's minefield disaster, Robert Joel Van Leer was evacuated to a military hospital in the United States. There he was visited by a general who pinned a Purple Heart on Van Leer's bed-smock. Meadlo too received a Purple Heart for losing his foot on Hill 85, but so did Calley who had suffered only slight fragmentation injuries in the same incident.

Generals, armed with boxes of medals, would visit hospital wards where the wounded were being cared for. They followed a set procedure. A wound earned a Purple Heart. Loss of a limb, eyes or testicles also carried a promotion to the next rank. Two limbs lost brought the Purple Heart, a promotion, and a Bronze Star. For the top brass decorations were a means of rewarding the good soldier and encouraging the rest. But while Gen. Westmoreland agreed with Napoleon's view that a bolt of ribbon would win many battles, there were drawbacks, and he came to regret the effect that issuing so many Purple Hearts had on the official records. They skewed the statistics of American wounded, which played into the hands of people opposed to the war.

A great irony arising from the scandal of My Lai was that Hugh Thompson and his helicopter crew were given awards for gallantry for confronting Medina's troops and rescuing Vietnamese civilians during the massacre. Years later Thompson said of the troops on the ground: "They were the enemy then, I guess." And that is just what the official records showed. The award of Bronze Medals to Glenn Andreotta and Larry Colburn, and the Distinguished Flying Cross to Thompson, exposes the cynical nature of the conspiracy to cover up what really happened at My Lai 4. Barker's official report, most of which was fiction, described the crucial part helicopters had played in helping civilians leave the village. It was thus a noble action on the part of the helicopter crew and medals were bound to follow, particularly when one of them died.

On April 10, two days after Andreotta was killed as a result of hostile fire, his commanding officer wrote out a completely false citation for a posthumous award for his part in rescuing children at My Lai. Maj. Fred Watke said the children had been "hiding in a bunker located between friendly forces and hostile forces engaged in a heavy firefight." He continued: "Andreotta's willingness to risk his life for innocent children and his bravery in action reflect great credit upon himself, his unit, the Americal Division, and the United States Army." The irony was that Thompson and his crew were truly brave and noble soldiers, genuine heroes about whom America could justly feel proud if it had but known the truth. But the award was not only fraudulent, it was also a forgery. All recommendations for decorations had to come from unit commanders, countersigned by battalion commanders, and be accompanied by an eyewitness report. The signature on the eyewitness report accompanying the recommendation of a medal for Andreotta was forged as being that of Hugh Thompson.* Three

---

* Thompson is still emphatic that he never signed it.

days later, someone realized that Larry Colburn had also been a member of the crew and thought he should have a medal too. Thompson's signature was again forged on the eyewitness report. The award of Colburn's Bronze Medal with "V" device was announced in the Americal Division's general orders on May 14. And while it was going through channels, someone else discovered Hugh Thompson's efforts had gone completely unrecognized. Subsequently commended for his exceptionally valorous actions, he was awarded the Distinguished Flying Cross. The citation praised Thompson for taking to hospital a Vietnamese child "caught in intense crossfire," and said that the pilot's sound judgment "had greatly enhanced Vietnamese–American relations in the operational area." Thompson later threw the decoration away.

Bizarre as these awards were, they paled beside the hyperbole used to recommend honors for Ernest Medina, Frank Barker, and Oran Henderson. Barker decided Medina's actions as Charlie Company's commander were worthy of a major award. He penned the proposed citation on April 22, and heaped praise on the outstanding way Medina performed his duties:

Many times given only brief fragmentary orders, his outstanding tactical planning enabled him to gain and maintain contact with a most elusive enemy. His complete understanding of all tactical support available to him saved the lives of many of his men. The sound tactical decisions and recommendations he made, coupled with his coolness under fire, resulted in his unit killing 149 VC while only sustaining minor casualties within his own unit.

General William C. Westmoreland, COMUSMACV, sent a congratulatory message to Captain Medina and his company for outstanding action during the enemy contact in Operation Muscatine northwest of Quang Ngai City on 16th March 1968 in which the enemy was dealt a heavy blow. At the same time his unit was conducting combat operations, Captain Medina played a major part in the construction of two fire-bases within the area of operations. Captain Medina's extremely high state of discipline and esprit de corps found within his company is also indicative of outstanding leadership ability.

After the accomplishment of his mission, Captain Medina's utmost thoughts were the welfare of his own men. He continually sought ways to improve living conditions and rations, to provide clean clothing, entertainment, and many other comfort items beside religious activities which are vitally important to men living in a combat environment. In spite of the many difficulties he encountered, Captain Medina was able to keep his positive attitude and enthusiasm and was always an inspiration to his men.

The official verdict came on June 11, two days before Barker and five others were killed in a midair helicopter collision with a light observation plane. The Awards Board of the Americal Division and its commander, Maj. Gen. Koster, refused to give Medina the award Barker had recommended. Five weeks later, after Koster had departed to take up his job as Superintendent of West Point, Henderson put his signature to a second attempt to obtain Medina a decoration for gallantry. This time the citation concentrated on Medina's actions five months earlier in the minefield incident on February 25, when Medina had heroically completely disregarded the danger to himself in order to rescue his men. He received his Silver Star.

With Frank Barker's death came a shower of posthumous awards—the obligatory Purple Heart and an Oak Leaf Cluster for his Bronze Star for meritorious achievement while commanding Task Force Barker. The citation referred to the fact that the task force under Barker's "outstanding leadership and guidance" had been credited with killing 421 enemy soldiers. Next came an Air Medal and four Oak Leaf Clusters for making repeated aerial flights over hostile territory in his command-and-control helicopter. Finally Barker received the Legion of Merit for exceptionally meritorious conduct. Again the citation—approved by Henderson—made special mention of Task Force Barker's role. Henderson wrote to his widow expressing his sympathy: "By his actions he stood for compassion for his fellow man, pride in his country, and faith in his God. Knowing this, I pray that the love of God and good friends will console you." Early on June 13, Barker received a message that one of his companies was under enemy fire near Son My village. He flew off in his helicopter. A low-flying Army spotter plane brought down by VC machine-gun fire collided with Barker's aircraft. Six people perished instantly. The Government of Vietnam also awarded Barker the National Order of Vietnam (Fifth Class) and the Gallantry Cross with Palm.

Attempts were also in hand to get Henderson a top award for valor. Aged 47, he had already won several Purple Hearts and an Air Medal. The suggestion for an award for exceptional valor came from Henderson's own executive officer, Lt. Col. James A. Franklin. The eyewitnesses were a helicopter pilot and an infantry platoon commander. In mid-July near a VC position in the jungle-covered mountains a reconnaissance platoon wandered into a hornets' nest, a particularly hazardous feature in that part of South Vietnam. Within minutes the 27-man platoon was incapacitated by swarms of insects and was forced to summon medevac and gunship support. Henderson's helicopter appeared out of the sky to coordinate the rescue. Some of the injured men could not reach the dust-off helicopters and Henderson's aircraft ventured into the hornet-infested area, steeply sloping ground covered with trees and saplings. The pilot put his machine nose-first into the slope and Henderson unlocked his safety belt, leaned out of the aircraft, and assisted the men aboard. According to the recommended citation Henderson's efforts showed unquestionable valor and devotion to duty and resulted in saving many lives. The recommendation that Henderson receive the Distinguished Flying Cross was turned down.

By the time he left Vietnam, posted back to Schofield Barracks in October 1968, Henderson in any case wore the uniform of a brave combat soldier, decked with many ribbons including five Silver Stars, five Bronze Stars—two for valor—and four Purple Hearts. He was first wounded in action as a rifle platoon leader in the European theater in World War II. Having served also in Korea, Henderson had been in continuous Army service for nearly thirty years, since joining the Indiana National Guard at the age of 18 in April 1939. For his service in Vietnam he received the Legion of Merit, the Vietnamese Cross of Gallantry, and the Vietnamese Medal of Merit (Fifth Class).

Charlie Company were set to follow their brigade commander back to the shores of America a month after Henderson departed for Hawaii. The one date in the calendar etched in a GI's memory was his DEROS—Date Eligible for Return from Overseas. Since most of Charlie Company arrived in-country at the beginning of

December the previous year, by November 1968 they were all short-timers. They had thirty days or less to go before they could return to the United States. Some like Fred Widmer, who had been promoted to sergeant in May, chose to do another tour. Gruver, Doherty, and Terry had succeeded in getting transferred out of Charlie Company and into a LRRP unit a little more than a week after the My Lai operation. Medina went on leave and returned to a posting at Chu Lai with the 569th Intelligence Detachment. Calley in September extended his tour of duty in Vietnam for six months and was transferred to the 1/6th Infantry as the civic affairs officer. His commander, Lieutenant Colonel William D. Kelley, thought he had done a remarkable job, considering his lack of experience, establishing a good working relationship with his Vietnamese counterparts.

The great concern of everyone in their last few days was to stay well clear of Charlie Cong. They had to avoid at all costs being zapped by the VC now that the end was in sight. Some GIs in Vietnam carried short-timers' sticks and cut notches in them, counting the last few days before they were due to leave. When they finally came to climb up the steps to the "freedom bird" that would take them back home, a Pan Am or Continental Airlines Boeing 707, the Army presented them with a farewell memento. Each GI was given a magazine called *Tour 365* to commemorate their 365-day stay in South Vietnam. It contained statements from Presidents Eisenhower, Kennedy, and Johnson about the US commitment to South Vietnam and a series of articles about the history of the conflict, fully illustrated with color photos. Gen. Westmoreland, who in July had returned to the United States to take up an appointment as the Army's top soldier, the Chief of Staff, declared in a farewell message:

As veterans of this war, you can now look back with perspective on your experience and know the trying and difficult tasks inherent in fighting to protect the freedom of peace-loving people against Communist invaders. You know of the local Viet Cong terrorists who kill and maim their own neighbors, and appreciate the terror and destruction they spread. Having served here, you understand better than many of our countrymen, the meaning of aggression against South Vietnam.

The message struck a chord with one GI in the 11th Brigade,

Tom Glen. The 21-year-old mortarman with the 4/3rd Infantry had heard about Charlie Company's body count of several hundred dead with hardly any weapons found only the day after the massacre. Like all the others, he turned a blind eye to brutalities. He was considered by his battalion commander to be a fine soldier and hard worker, and by his associates to be extremely intelligent and likable. He came from a solidly hardworking family, the backbone of Middle America. Like many bright young men in Vietnam, Glen spent much of the war caught between the emotions of excitement, tension, and long periods of terminal boredom. His job with the mortar platoon meant he was often excused point and perimeter duties which the rifle platoons undertook but he and the others in the platoon were constantly on the move, carrying 81-mm mortar rounds. At the end of a patrol, they would find themselves at one of the fire bases with a proper roof over their head. At night they sat staring into the darkness, hoping to spot VC infiltrators before they reached the lethal zone from where they could throw satchel charges or grenades. Glen often thought of the fire bases as medieval castles, fortified hilltops complete with battlements. At one time he and his friends amused themselves, and the accompanying ARVN troops, by building a working catapult out of ammunition crates. There were infrequent idyllic moments, like their trips to LZ Charlie Brown down south on the narrow neck of coastline beside the South China Sea, an area almost like a resort back home where GIs could swim peacefully. But these moments were rare. More common were the horrors and the futilities of the war and the increasing number of mindless acts of ill-treatment of Vietnamese civilians.

Before he left Vietnam for his parents' home in Tucson, Glen sat down and wrote a long and eloquent letter to Westmoreland's successor as MACV commander, General Creighton Abrams. It was a remarkably powerful document for one so young, written from a troubled heart by a young man who truly cared for his country. Glen felt he had to speak out about something terribly wrong that was happening in South Vietnam. His letter showed that even the very youngest soldier in the Army of the United States could see what the generals failed to see: that its own fighting men and military policies were driving America to defeat.

His analysis went to the heart of the problem with extraordinary clarity as he spelled out the systematic ill-treatment he had seen of Vietnamese civilians during his tour—clear breaches of the Geneva Conventions which cried out for attention:

Upon finishing my tour in Vietnam as an 81-mm mortar crewman and based upon what I have seen during this year, I wish to bring to your attention that aspect of our army's role here which I feel to be truly a problem requiring attention.

In answering the government of South Vietnam's pleas for aid the United States has sent not only a military machine, but also a representation of a culture and nearly two hundred years of purported national ideals. We can act in no manner here that does not imply to the watchful world a statement of the purposes and designs of our national aspirations, a statement inherent in which is a belief in their correctness. Yet, the most motivatingly challenged and immediate of these ideals, a basic faith in Man's universal humanity and the fellowship of races, is in fact the one ideal least evidenced, or more correctly, most contradicted by American soldiers; for the average GI's attitude toward and treatment of the Vietnamese people all too often is a complete denial of all our country is attempting to accomplish in the realm of human relations.

Far beyond merely dismissing the Vietnamese as "slopes" or "gooks," in both deed and thought, too many American soldiers seem to discount their very humanity; and with this attitude inflict upon the Vietnamese citizenry humiliations, both psychological and physical, that can have only a debilitating effect upon efforts to unify the people in loyalty to the Saigon government, particularly when such acts are carried on at unit levels and thereby acquire the aspect of sanctioned policy.

If it is true that winning the confidence and loyalty of the people is as essential to creating a free, stable South Vietnamese Republic as is eliminating the National Liberation Front as an effective militant force, can it be wise to permit the work of Civic Affairs to be continually negated by troops in the field? Can it be of value to build a school for a Vietnamese child, if he returns from it to find his home burned to the ground?

Can confidence in the United States and its intention be instilled in a youth that has witnessed his grandfather being forced to climb into a well or to serve GIs as a slave? Can we hope for aid from a Vietnamese citizen whose mother has been beaten and humiliated by American soldiers?

And how can we obtain information from civilians that flee when an American unit approaches, being conditioned to soldiers that, apparently for mere pleasure, fire indiscriminately into Vietnamese homes and without provocation or justification shoot at the people themselves? Can we wonder that the Vietnamese often do not flock to the banner of an Army, the soldiers of which frequently make it obvious that they have no respect for their customs, that treat them as mere toys for sadistic pleasure, and in fact seem to consider them less than human? Can we kill or capture six Viet Cong, yet create of previously at least inactively neutral civilians a dozen Viet Cong sympathizers or activists, and call that progress?

But not only with Vietnamese civilians do American soldiers display a remarkable disregard for legislated and less factitious restraints upon irresponsibility. Captured Viet Cong operatives and "suspects" are frequent victims of more overtly vicious behavior. When confronted with prisoners completely at their mercy, American soldiers often seem to present a character completely contradictory to the image of Americans we would wish the world to accept. Fired with an emotionalism that belies unconscionable hatred, and armed with a vocabulary consisting of "You VC," soldiers commonly "interrogate" by means of torture that has been presented as the particular habit of the enemy.

Severe beatings and torture at knife point are usual means of questioning captives or of convincing a suspect that he is, indeed, a Viet Cong; and on occasion aroused scout dogs have been used to terrify prisoners. How admirable is a soldier who prides himself on beating a bound and helpless captive?

This mistreatment of prisoners is in direct violation of both MACV directives and the Geneva Conventions. How can we claim to honor these codes if we do not enforce them?

But tortures of prisoners and contempt for the welfare of an entire people violate codes far more sacred than those of MACV and the Geneva Conventions: those of moralistic humanity. When a GI murders, beats, or humiliates a Vietnamese citizen or burns his home simply to watch it in flames, he is quite plainly asking for the United States to eliminate racial intolerance in our own land. Does his presence in a combat zone and his possession of a rifle so absolve a soldier from moral responsibility?

It would indeed be terrible to find it necessary to believe that an American soldier that harbors such racial intolerance and disregard for justice and human feeling is a prototype of all American national character; yet the frequency of such soldiers lends credulity to such beliefs. Perhaps it is true; perhaps the only way to achieve our national ideals is to legislate them. The very fact that such a question arises here, where Americans are so clearly in the world's eye, implies a situation that could and should be improved.

If this conflict is to be resolved favorably, we must seek and obtain the aid of the Vietnamese people, yet American soldiers themselves make obtaining this more difficult, and perhaps more significantly practice here the intolerance which is so divisive of our country.

What has been outlined here I have seen not only in my own unit, but also in others we have worked with, and I fear it is universal. If this is indeed the case, it is a problem which cannot be overlooked, but can, through a more firm implementation of the codes of MACV and the Geneva Conventions, perhaps be eradicated. Thank you very much for your attention.

The letter provoked a series of messages from MACV HQ in Long Binh to American Division HQ in Chu Lai to the 11th Brigade at Duc Pho. "Who is Glen?" "What is he talking about?" His commanding officer, Lieutenant Colonel Albert L. Russell, believed Glen's ideals were the very ones the Americal Division upheld. Briefings had informed replacement troops that how they conducted themselves with local people could determine the outcome of the war. After praising the GI's character, education, and record as a soldier, Russell then proceeded to undermine Glen and show how he must be mistaken. Assigned to a weapons platoon, his duties had kept him at a fire support base, so, according to his commanding officer, Glen rarely came into contact with POWs. Members of his unit felt there was no possibility for Glen to have observed mistreatment of prisoners or local people, although there may have been isolated instances of maltreatment. Had the young GI spoken up and brought forward his evidence, there would have been prompt disciplinary action. "That he should write a letter charging violations couched in vague generalities after he had rotated makes his charges suspect and casts doubt on the moral courage he must possess to weather the onslaughts against the idealistic convictions he purportedly advocates," Russell concluded.

Brigadier General Howard H. Cooksey wrote to Glen, the idealistic young soldier, on behalf of the MACV commander. His reply would surely have been appreciated by Hugh C. Thompson Jr:

It is the duty of every American soldier to ensure that [the Geneva Conventions] are upheld, and the responsibility for violations rests in a certain measure upon those who do not report violations they have witnessed. You imply that this goes on at other than the individual level; yet, there is always a higher headquarters to which violations can be referred and channels exist through which these reports can be made. You ask: "Does his presence in a combat zone and his possession of a rifle absolve a soldier from moral responsibility?" The answer to that is, of course, No. But neither is a person who keeps silent when he witnesses a war crime absolved of responsibility for that crime merely because he did not actively participate in it.

In the headquarters staff of the Americal Division in Chu Lai that December, a reassuring memorandum was prepared for the Adjutant General by Major Colin Luther Powell, the assistant chief of staff (operations). All new soldiers arriving in South Vietnam, he wrote soothingly, received a ninety-minute lesson on civic affairs and the importance of treating the Vietnamese with courtesy and respect. Another hour-long course was given on their responsibilities under the Geneva Conventions concerning the proper treatment of prisoners. Showing all the signs of a soldier who had triumphed in the battle of military paperwork, Powell wrote what his superiors clearly wanted to hear. He described the Vietnamese people as being truly appreciative of the many civic improvement projects undertaken by Americal units and the direct interest the division's soldiers took in their welfare and the improvement of the Vietnamese people's standard of living. Maj. Powell, who twenty years later would briefly become President Reagan's National Security Advisor and subsequently the country's most important man in uniform as Chairman of the Joint Chiefs of Staff during the Middle East war with Iraq, concluded even more complacently: "Although there may be isolated cases of mistreatment of civilians and POWs this by no means reflects the general attitude throughout the division. In direct refutation of this portrayal [by Glen] is the fact that relations between American soldiers and the Vietnamese people are excellent."

7. Investigation

Toward the end of March 1969, another 11th Brigade GI just home from Vietnam was working in a popsicle factory in Phoenix, Arizona, waiting to go to college in California to study English literature. Ronald Ridenhour, then aged 22, had spent months anxiously wondering what he should do about something rather dark and bloody he heard had happened in a South Vietnamese village during the war.

Like Tom Glen, living across the state in Tucson, Ridenhour had completed a tour of duty with the 11th Infantry Brigade in Quang Ngai Province the previous December. The joy of being back among his close-knit family, feeling safe and secure in a familiar environment, was soon overshadowed by a deep sense of guilt. Ridenhour's family had been looking forward to welcoming home a hero. Instead they found a young man different to the one who had been drafted nearly two years earlier. Ridenhour was haunted by a shocking story he first heard nine months before, in April 1968. It had come from a soldier he had done LRRP training with in Hawaii.

Ridenhour had been one of a small group of newly trained infantrymen handpicked to spend several months during the latter half of 1967 living like animals in the jungle of the Kuhuku Mountains in the Pohakaloa military training area on the island of Oahu. They were all paratroopers, had 20/20 vision, were fairly intelligent, had higher scores than most with the rifle, and were good swimmers. Their task was to mount long-range reconnaissance patrols behind enemy lines. His LRRP detachment was disbanded at the end of November 1967—a week before the 11th Brigade went to Vietnam. Some of the others in the group, including Bernhardt, Conti, La Croix, Gruver, Doherty, and Terry, had been assigned to Charlie Company, 1/20th Infantry. Ridenhour was posted to the brigade's aviation section as a door gunner.

Four months later, toward the end of April, he met up with Gruver—the misfit—who along with Doherty and Terry had been reassigned on March 24 to a long-range patrol, Echo Company, 51st Infantry (LRP). They hadn't seen each other for several months and over a beer began catching up on what each had been doing. The conversation was barely a few minutes old before Gruver asked Ridenhour casually: "Did you hear about Pinkville?"

"No, what did you do at Pinkville?"

"We went in there and killed everybody."

"Killed everybody!" Ridenhour choked. "What do you mean?"

Gruver looked at him seriously. "We shot 'em," he replied. "Lined 'em up and shot 'em down. Three hundred, four hundred— I don't know how many."

Ridenhour was instantaneously revolted. He had many questions to ask. Gruver answered, describing in minute detail what had happened. Several times Ridenhour had to stop him to ask if they had killed *all* the people. Gruver replied that, yes, they were men, women, and children.

Ridenhour had seen GIs murder Vietnamese civilians before—in ones, twos, and threes—but Gruver's tale of horror was something entirely different, a scale which dwarfed everything Ridenhour had personally experienced. He thought to himself: "These no-good sons-of-bitches. Look at what they've gotten me into. Look what they've gotten us all into." He was left with a horrible choice: to find out what happened and turn in the people who did it, including his friends, or be part of a horrible crime. He felt he had no choice. The only way not to be part of the massacre was to discover the truth, to pursue it and let the chips fall wherever. That is what he set out to do, still hoping that Gruver was simply exaggerating. He still couldn't accept it, couldn't believe that so many young Americans had participated in such an act of sheer barbarism, and that their officers had condoned it.

But he had to be careful. If it appeared he was going public with the story the consequences for his own safety could be serious. He began to track down one by one other GIs he knew had been in Charlie Company. He never confronted them directly with allegations, but was prepared to bring the conversation around to what actually happened at Pinkville if necessary. Frequently, instead of him having to bring up the subject, the GIs he spoke to would mention it first. And from the moment he would say: "What happened, what did you do?" the story would come pouring out. Most of them seemed tortured by the facts. Far from contradicting Gruver's story, they confirmed it and added more bits of information. He heard that Terry and Doherty in the 3rd Platoon had come across many dead people, and that those who were still alive were sought out and shot. Nothing had been left alive.

Knowing Michael Terry's deeply held Mormon faith, his story of what happened in the village was deeply affecting. Ridenhour considered Terry to be honest, sincere, and decent—someone he was proud to call a friend. He felt chilled to his soul. Here Terry was telling how as the squad broke for lunch he and Doherty had taken part in the killings. "Billy and I started to get out our chow," Terry said, "but close to us were a bunch of Vietnamese in a heap and some of them were moaning. Calley's platoon had been through before us and all of them had been shot. But many weren't dead. It was obvious that they weren't going to get any medical attention, so Billy and I got up and went over to where they were. I guess we sort of finished them off." Then they returned to their packs and ate their lunch.

Several months went by before Ridenhour found any others who had more information. At the end of June he met up with Larry La Croix, a sergeant, in the USO at Chu Lai. By now Ridenhour thought he had a good grasp of what had happened in the village. But La Croix gave details which added a completely new dimension. Doherty and Terry had spoken of mass killings but La Croix filled in the details because he had seen what happened with the 2nd Platoon. "It was terrible," said La Croix. "They were slaughtering the villagers like so many sheep." Calley had ordered someone to fire his machine gun, but the machine gunner stopped after a while and refused to continue. Calley took over the M-60 and finished off the first group. When other civilians came along he did the job himself.

The facts almost overwhelmed Ridenhour, who had four months left to serve in Vietnam. These terrible stories played on his mind. He became determined to get back to the United States and somehow get the story out. But his neck was regularly on the line. At night he would take out his patrols, moving stealthily through the bush. Ridenhour and his men were not run-of-the mill grunts. They actively sought the excitement the dangerous missions brought. They looked at themselves as being special, different from other troops. They were part of an elite and knew they could rely on each member of the team not to let the others down.

This bond of mutual dependence added to Ridenhour's problems. He was presented with an agonizing moral dilemma. "The people who were involved in this, people who would be personally implicated, were not just friends, but good friends," he recalled later:

I was on deep jungle reconnaissance missions with them while I was trying to track down what happened in My Lai. Within these five- or six-man LRRP teams these were the people that, in theory at least, were ready to lay down their lives for me and I was prepared to do the same. At the same time I was tracking down the truth about My Lai, I was going to report it. It was a hard choice but I had to make the one that I had to live with.

A few weeks before going home to the States, Ridenhour heard that Michael Bernhardt had been taken to hospital at Chu Lai in pretty bad shape, suffering from jungle rot. Endless weeks out in the field had taken their toll. Bernhardt's health was at rock bottom and he was relieved to see Ridenhour, a fellow soldier he trusted absolutely. He poured his heart out. "I wasn't the only nut . . . I wasn't really crazy. Condemning what happened was the right thing." Ridenhour was delighted that Bernhardt had refused to participate. He was still stunned that men he would swear couldn't be involved in something so awful were indeed implicated. Yet here was Bernhardt, sick, half dead, appearing as steadfast as a rock. When Medina had gotten Charlie Company wound up with his little speech the night before the combat assault, Bernhardt told Ridenhour, he had realized what was going to happen and made sure to keep out of the way. He had refused to take part in the massacre. He thought it very strange the officers hadn't stopped it earlier. Later, he said, Medina had warned him not to write to his Congressman.

Both men were still left with the problem of what they should do with the knowledge they possessed. Bernhardt, only half joking in his weakened state, proposed returning to the States, tracking down the officers from Charlie Company, and shooting them one by one. Finally he made a pledge. If Ridenhour went public, he would testify openly about what had happened in My Lai 4.

This was the story Ridenhour relayed to his family. It profoundly disturbed them. Several times they watched the young man emotionally crumble in front of them as he told how some of his best friends had become mass murderers. Tears flooded down Ridenhour's cheeks as he told his mother, father, and sister how Michael Terry had actually murdered children: "I would have thought that before he would do such a thing, I would have done it myself."

Born in Oakland, California, Ridenhour was not a timid person. He'd been a defensive lineman on his school football team. Like many soldiers in war he could respect the bravery of his enemy. As a helicopter door gunner he admired the sheer reckless heroism of the way Viet Cong soldiers would sometimes defiantly break cover, stand up alone, and try to shoot his aircraft down with aging bolt-action carbines. He had taken long-range patrols on extraordinarily dangerous missions through the Vietnamese jungle at night. What traumatized him was not just the fact of the massacre itself but also the way he had uncovered the truth and the people he knew had been involved.

When Ridenhour suffered from a relapse of malaria and needed hospital treatment, his family were not agreed about his next course of action. "You must do what you've got to do," his mother and sister told him. However, his father was more cautious and very concerned about what exposing the massacre would bring down on the family. Ridenhour also talked it over with his friends, most of whom told him to forget it. But one said he should write to his local Democratic Congressman.

Mo Udall's antiwar views received wide publicity in a conservative state like Arizona. The skinny politician appeared an out-and-out radical to the traditional elites of the desert state. He was truly the antithesis of Arizona's most famous politician and senior Senator, the ultrahawkish Republican Barry Goldwater, unsuccessful GOP candidate against L.B.J. in the presidential election of 1964.

Determined that his future career lay in journalism when he finally finished college, Ridenhour decided to treat what he had learned as a writing assignment. He set down all he knew about the massacre, drafting and redrafting a statement to Udall. It was important to capture the attention of the reader quickly. Powerful men in Washington received hundreds of letters a week. His story had to stand out above the rest. Six weeks later it was ready.

Ridenhour posted the letter on April 2, 1969, to Udall and thirty prominent men in Washington, DC—including President Nixon, the Secretary of Defense, Melvin Laird, the Chairman of the Joint Chiefs of Staff, Edward Kennedy, Barry Goldwater, Eugene Mc-Carthy, and William Fulbright. He sent the letters registered mail, thinking that staff opening them would be bound to take the contents more seriously:

Gentlemen:

It was in late April 1968 that I first heard of "Pinkville" and what allegedly happened there. I received that first report with some skepticism but in the following months I was to hear similar stories from such a wide variety of people that it became impossible for me to disbelieve that something rather dark and bloody did indeed occur sometime in March 1968 in a village called "Pinkville" in the Republic of Vietnam.

The facts were laid out as Gruver, Doherty, Terry, La Croix, and Bernhardt had told them. The 1,500-word, three-page letter finally concluded:

Exactly what did in fact occur in the village of "Pinkville" in March 1968 I do not know for *certain*, but I am convinced that it was something very black indeed. I remain irrevocably persuaded that if you and I do truly believe in the principles of justice and the equality of every man, however humble, before the law, that form the very backbone that this country is founded on, then we must press forward a widespread and public investigation of this matter with all our combined efforts.

I think that it was Winston Churchill who once said: "A country without a conscience is a country without a soul, and a country without a soul is a country that cannot survive." I feel that I must take some positive action on this matter. I hope that you will launch an investigation immediately and keep me informed of your progress. If you cannot, then I don't know what other course of action to take.

I have considered sending this to newspapers, magazines, and broadcasting companies but I somehow feel that investigation and action by the Congress of the United States is the appropriate procedure, and as a conscientious citizen I have no desire to further besmirch the image of the American serviceman in the eyes of the world. I feel that this action, while probably it would promote attention, would not bring about the constructive actions that the direct actions of the Congress of the United States would.

Udall's office responded almost immediately. He wanted Ridenhour's permission to circulate the contents to members of the House Armed Services Committee on which he served. Udall personally pressured the committee chairman, Mendell Rivers, to request an investigation.

Although Ridenhour heard nothing official from the Department of the Army for two weeks, his letter had provoked an instant reaction. Within two days congressional staffers from four separate offices on Capitol Hill began calling their contacts at the Pentagon across the Potomac River. Copies of Ridenhour's letter were passed through the congressional liaison section of the Department of the Army. Another copy, sent to the Chairman of the Joint Chiefs, General Earle "Bus" Wheeler, was forwarded to the office of the Army Chief of Staff. Westmoreland found it impossible to believe American soldiers would engage in the mass murder and ordered an immediate inquiry.

The allegations were dynamite. At that very moment the new Nixon administration was trying to negotiate the start of secret peace talks in Paris with the North Vietnamese government. In a last-ditch effort to get a dialogue with Hanoi going before his presidency expired and thus help the Democratic candidate Hubert Humphrey, Lyndon Johnson had halted US bombing missions over North Vietnam. It was a tactic which ended in failure. Hanoi knew all the pressure was on Johnson. Moreover the new administration believed the bombing halt lessened the incentive for Hanoi to come to the negotiating table. Nixon's public strategy, masterminded by his National Security Advisor Henry Kissinger, was to show America as an honest broker anxious to resolve the war and produce an honorable peace. Kissinger, who prided himself on the use of subtlety and nuance in diplomacy, believed in the importance of sending the right signals to the North Vietnamese. Public opinion was crucial both inside and outside America. Hanoi had to be seen as the aggressor and the United States as fighting to defend the cause of freedom and justice.

By early 1969 the war had resulted in 31,000 American dead with no tangible benefits. A total of 14,592 Americans had died in combat in 1968. The war was costing the country $30 billion a year and two hundred young American lives every week. The other Nixon–Kissinger strategy to encourage Hanoi to start peace talks was secretly to bomb the NVA/VC sanctuaries in Cambodia from March 18. More and bigger raids followed. So crucial was it that America retain its public stance as peacemaker that these bombing missions, involving thousands of sorties by B-52s, were kept secret from the Congress and the American people. Westmoreland, in office as the Army's top soldier for less than a year, was enough of a politician to know that in these circumstances allegations of mass executions by American GIs needed careful handling, even though he personally found them hard to believe.

With immediate action promised, secret instructions were sent to Saigon requesting an urgent preliminary inquiry. The signal was sent via a back-channel communications system, the Digital Information Relay Center. Supervised by the National Security Agency, the system provided a secure message facility to the highest echelons of the military.

The section of the US Army that handles complaints and inquiries is the Office of the Inspector General. In South Vietnam IG officers made inspections and investigated complaints ranging from serious breaches of military regulations involving criminal offenses right down to petty gripes from malcontented soldiers. Often they had to deal with GIs' families complaining about whether their sons' companies had enough ballpoint pens or insect repellent.

Colonel Howard Whitaker, deputy IG at the headquarters of USARV at Long Binh, received his orders to investigate Ridenhour's extraordinary allegations on April 12. First thing the next morning he was in Chu Lai asking questions, wanting to see the files on Task Force Barker. The simplest means for Whitaker to determine quickly the veracity of Ridenhour's story was to check the paperwork. The list of names of so-called eyewitnesses mentioned in the letter had been phoned ahead to the Americal Division with orders to locate their current whereabouts. The Inspector General's staff at Chu Lai was given no reason for Whitaker's visit. The subject was too important to discuss on the telephone. Whitaker quickly discovered that certain facts did hang together, but he still could not believe that Ridenhour's preposterous story was true. However, the records did confirm that a significant military operation had occurred at My Lai on March 16 in an area known as Pinkville. The journals and log books of the 11th Brigade and the Americal Division gave a day-by-day, hour-by-hour, minute-by-minute breakdown of the operation. Whitaker also located Barker's after-action report, but found it made no mention of civilian casualties. There was no record of any investigation into mass killings.

All the names bar one mentioned by Ridenhour had served in Charlie Company but they were all were back in the United States. The exception was a Lt. "Kalley" (Ridenhour's letter misspelled Calley's name) who could not be traced. But none of the documents threw any light on the central allegation. At 3:30 PM the following day, Whitaker was on his way back south to Long Binh, firmly of the view that the letter looked like an elaborate hoax or a sick joke. For such an atrocity to have escaped official notice to this point would have involved a conspiracy of massive proportions. None of the available records substantiated Ridenhour's fantastic claims. Whitaker could only conclude he had grossly exaggerated his account of the military operation, but he signaled Washington that someone would have to interview the men from Charlie Company named in the letter.

At the IG headquarters in the Forrestal Building in Washington, DC, 45-year-old Colonel William V. Wilson, a native of North Carolina, was newly appointed to the staff. He could see a period of intense tedium ahead of him. He hated the idea of having to spend perhaps a year or more investigating the usual run-of-the-mill complaints passed on by members of Congress or the executive branch.

One week after Whitaker's signal, Wilson picked up Ridenhour's file. Wilson read it four times, thinking to himself that the story could not possibly be true. Because he was the only senior man on the IG staff with combat experience, Wilson volunteered to conduct the investigation. He had seen civilians killed in war but they had been accidents. And he was damn certain he knew the difference between an atrocity and the unfortunate effects of war. A Green Beret officer, trained in special forces and intelligence work, Wilson was a much-decorated veteran of the parachute invasions of France and Holland in World War II. Since then he had been involved constantly in highly secret work with special forces teams including the rescue of Americans during the trouble in the Congo in the early sixties.

Instead of the mundane work he imagined he would have to tackle when he was first posted to Washington, Wilson now found himself with a mission that would take him only God knew where and with what outcome. Describing the moment he took on the My Lai investigation, he later recalled: "If the Pinkville incident was true, it was cold-blooded murder. I hoped to God it was false, but if it wasn't I wanted the bastards exposed for what they'd done."

Wilson was to spend the next three months living in motel rooms all over the country with a stenographer, Albert F. "Smitty" Smith. During interviews with witnesses he wore his full uniform complete with all his decorations including his combat infantry-man's badge and the Purple Heart he won at Normandy in France. He wanted the men from Charlie Company to know he had been under fire, too—they might take him more seriously.

Less than four weeks after he had posted his letter, Ridenhour found himself telling Wilson his story in a downtown Phoenix hotel room on April 29. Smitty punched away on his machine. Ridenhour was "depressingly convincing," Wilson recalled later. The next day they moved on to Orem, Utah, to see Michael Terry, who was chastened by mental anguish over his actions in the village. He confirmed everything Ridenhour had said and readily admitted shooting wounded civilians. Wilson was inwardly outraged by the implications of this confession. The impossible was possible. The massacre had probably happened after all. But he still felt some compassion for the tortured young man telling him what he really didn't want to hear.

From Orem they proceeded to Fort Carson, Colorado, where on May 2 they interviewed Lawrence La Croix, who had been promoted sergeant with the Army Rangers. The previous day La Croix had broken two ribs in a severe fall on a training exercise and came directly from the hospital for the interview. Under oath La Croix's responses were a mixture of half-truths and outright lies. La Croix declined military counsel and said his squad had not killed needlessly. At first justifying the slaughter, he said:

The killing that we did I considered necessary if for no other reason than to stop them from moving around the way they were. When we have got from 50 to 100 people running around on the ground you can't control things at all and someone is going to put a weapon on you and start shooting. During the first part they were diving in tunnels, trying to get away, picking up grenades, ammo cans, and weapons; and in my opinion we had no choice.

Wilson knew from reports sent back from the IG office at Long Binh that hardly any weapons were found by Charlie Company in the village. But he refrained from challenging La Croix's suggestion that civilians had engaged in fighting the American troops. It was never his intention to treat the interviews as confrontations or to carry out courtroom-style cross-examinations. These people might be witnesses later, and he was merely gathering facts. The tactic worked. As La Croix tried to put the best light on the platoon's activities in the village, gradually he opened up and revealed that there had indeed been unnecessary killings. La Croix admitted he himself had shot three civilians with his M-16: a 13-year-old male with a grenade, a man aged 25 to 30 running away, and a man in a group of Vietnamese he claimed picked up garden tools as if to threaten members of his squad. "I am not going to let anything happen to one of my men if I can help it," he continued, at first defending his action but then conceding that killing the man might have been unnecessary: "I could have butt-stroked him."

La Croix thought 150 people might have been killed in the village. "Just an estimate," he emphasized, stating confidently that all 150 dead were Viet Cong supporters, as if this would legitimize the company's actions. Occasionally while telling his story La Croix wandered into the realms of fantasy, giving a detailed but completely fictitious account of how the company gave medical assistance to the wounded and how they picked up psyops leaflets which had been dropped before the operation warning the villagers to leave the area. The interview lasted two and three-quarter hours. The longer he was questioned the more vivid his picture of the massacre became. In his efforts to appear candid he suddenly divulged that a helicopter pilot threatened to report what happened: "He told our commanding officer that the view from upstairs was about as sickening as it could be, that he had never seen such a blood bath in his entire life, and that if we didn't cease murdering innocent civilians immediately he was going to fly back and get the division commander and bring him out."

Wilson: "What happened to this helicopter pilot? Do you know?"
La Croix: "No, sir, I don't."
Wilson: "Do you know who he was?"
La Croix: "No, sir, I just heard later talk that he was a warrant officer, that he didn't like the way we operated and was going to report us."
Wilson: "Did you consider this a blood bath?"
La Croix: "Well, in some ways it was, I guess. I mean, we weren't having that much return fire and most of the people we shot didn't have an actual weapon with them."

Realizing where this frank exchange was leading, La Croix began to fall back on the story of the civilians resisting, picking up weapons, carrying ammunition to the VC, or throwing grenades. This was why they had been shot, he said. Finally, near the end of the interview, Wilson asked why the attitude of the company on the Pinkville mission was different from any other operation they had been on. La Croix wanted him to understand what the men had been through: "When you lose twenty-one people in an hour's time in a minefield, you tend to want something back for it. We actually wanted heavy contact out there. We were hoping for it."

Three days later, Wilson and Smith were at Fort Hood, Texas, to see Doherty, who was immediately warned he was suspected of war crimes. He too refused military counsel. "I dream about it a lot," he said of the mass killings. "This had been the first village where there was quite a bit of killing and there was a lot of women and children killed. That is what I think about. They were just all over the place. We walked by it the next day and there was so many flies we covered our faces as we walked through it." Two hundred people died in the village at the hands of the company, he thought.

Doherty was reluctant to admit his part in the shootings.

"Did you fire on any wounded civilians?" Wilson probed.

Doherty answered:

Sir, I don't really remember much of that operation, the direct operations and I don't know—it was just almost all of it a total blank. I didn't pay any attention to it. I can't hardly remember—like I remember little things, like I remember a weapon and I remember the guy shooting himself in the foot. I remember they sat us down to lunch by a well, and they expected us to eat right in the middle of the village. I remember that. Almost all of this is a total blank.

Wilson pointed out that the law meant Doherty wasn't being asked to incriminate himself: "Did you eat lunch by these groups of dead people there?" Doherty wouldn't answer. "Were any of these people alive?"

Doherty: "There was a few people. I don't know whether they were alive or what."

Wilson: "Alive or what?"

Doherty: "Or whether it was their body nerves or what."

Wilson: "Because of movement."

Doherty: "Yes, sir."

Wilson: "Was there any sound."

Doherty: "No sound."

Wilson: "No sound. I will ask the question again. Did you fire at wounded civilians?"

Doherty: "Sir, I don't think I should answer that . . . I don't know what to say or do."

Doherty clearly needed legal advice. A lawyer from the Judge Advocate General's office on the base was brought in and Wilson left them to confer.

Wilson later resumed the interrogation. "The question was: Did you fire on any wounded civilians?"

Doherty: "Sir, I couldn't say. I really couldn't say. I don't remember. I really don't. I told you before that I have a very bad memory."

Instructed not to discuss the case with anyone, Doherty was concerned his company commander would ask him why he had been interviewed. Wilson insisted the investigation had to be kept on a need-to-know basis. If anyone started questioning him, Doherty should refer them to the Office of the Inspector General.

Back in his office in Washington, Wilson made clear to his superiors that Ridenhour's story had not been invented. The inquiry was going to take much longer. He didn't go into the details. The sheer awfulness of the killings turned Wilson's stomach. His stenographer, Smitty, who was nearing retirement, occasionally became depressed by the sordid testimony he had to listen to day after day. At times when the evidence was particularly gruesome he lost his appetite. He would sit staring into space with a blank expression as he took notes on his dictating machine. The list of potential witnesses grew larger. Each day meant a new interview in a new hotel or Army barracks in a different town. Smith's stenographic records, which still had to be transcribed, began to pile up.

At the end of the second week in May—six weeks after Ridenhour posted his letter—the team arrived at the huge Army base at Fort Benning, near Columbus, Georgia. Medina was living with his family in a redbrick apartment block on the post at 445 Craig Drive, attending a nine-month course at the Infantry Advanced Officers School. He and his wife had plans to move to Florida. The Army intended to enroll him as an undergraduate at the University of Tampa.

The interview with Medina was a long and tortuous affair lasting more than four and a half hours. It proved to be a sensation. Held in the Inspector General's office on the base, the questioning began at 7:50 AM. Informed he was suspected of committing war crimes, Medina wanted military counsel present. Wilson told the appointed counsel, JAG Captain Edwin J. Richards, that he was there solely to advise Medina, not to answer his questions for him. It was a sensitive case being conducted for the Army's Chief of Staff and was not to be discussed with anyone else.

Wilson detailed a number of allegations made about Charlie Company—the killing of between 300 and 400 people at Pinkville; the destruction of the village; the murder by his RTO of a 4-year-old wounded child; the mass execution of civilians by 2nd Lt. "Kalley" (which is how Ridenhour spelled the name); the finishing-off of wounded by Terry and Doherty; Medina ordering Bernhardt not to talk with his Congressman about the atrocities. Now Wilson wanted to know from Medina the names of officers and senior NCOs in the company. Confused, Medina appealed for a few minutes to think: "My mind is so cluttered up." He named the platoon commanders and sergeants and detailed Charlie Company's operations from the time of their arrival in Vietnam right to the end of the Pinkville mission. Barker had given permission to burn the village, Medina claimed, when he'd said: "It is the last time we are going into that place and we want it cleared out."

Medina guardedly claimed he hadn't seen too many civilian bodies during the mission. He volunteered that a helicopter pilot had been complaining. Determined to get more details about this incident, Wilson zeroed in with more questions. Medina became defensive and indignantly pointed out that Col. Henderson had already investigated the incident of killing the woman in the paddy field. Then, suddenly and dramatically, he stood up on the other side of the table from Wilson to explain exactly what happened. Holding his arms in a firing position he turned his body to demonstrate how he had shot her: "I turned around to walk away and as I turned around I caught a glimpse out of the corner of my eye of something in her hand underneath her and she started to move and the first thing that went through my mind was: 'You dumb bastard, you are dead.' I spun round and fired two or three times." Henderson, he said, had exonerated him of this when he flew out to the company's position in the field to investigate whether members of his company had murdered or killed civilians. Two other colonels were with Henderson when he conducted the investigation, according to Medina: Col. Blackledge and an artillery colonel called Luper.

It was a pivotal moment. Almost certainly a massacre had taken place in the village. Wilson now had it confirmed that a helicopter pilot had complained to Task Force Barker's HQ about a blood bath on the ground. Now he was being told by the self-assured infantry officer in front of him that at least one senior officer, a full colonel, possibly others, had investigated allegations of an atrocity. Yet none of the records in Chu Lai pointed to this. Military regulations dictated that if Henderson had conducted an inquiry it would have had to be a formal one. Evidence had to be taken on oath and signed statements produced. It was essential in a military inquiry that legal formalities were followed if testimony was to have any value in future legal proceedings.

Did Henderson give Medina an oath before he answered questions? Wilson asked. "I don't believe so, sir." The infantry captain had neither been asked to sign a statement nor been read his rights.

Then Medina dropped a bombshell. Wilson, anxious to locate any records that might have been missed in the search for documents at Chu Lai, casually inquired if Henderson's investigation resulted in any written document. "Colonel Henderson did say he was conducting the investigation at the direction of the divisional commander. I think that was his exact statement," Medina added. The implication of this was extraordinary. If true, it meant that the commanding general of the American Division—a two-star general—had known about allegations of an atrocity. If the matter had been investigated, it would have to have been documented by the Inspector General in Vietnam.

Wilson continued to tour the country interviewing witnesses, and had Henderson contacted at Schofield Barracks, Hawaii, where he was on the headquarters staff and scheduled to join the faculty of the Armed Forces Staff College at Norfolk, Virginia, in July. Henderson was making plans to leave Hawaii for the United States aboard the SS *Lurline* on June 16. Unknown to Wilson, Henderson telephoned Colonel John W. Donald, the American Division chief of staff, at Chu Lai. He said he had been ordered to report to Washington to give testimony about an alleged incident involving civilian casualties in a Task Force Barker operation and needed to refresh his memory before giving evidence. Could Donald locate a copy of an *informal* investigation he had carried out? Donald promptly ordered a thorough search of divisional and 11th Brigade files. On May 25, a search of the safe in the brigade intelligence section at Duc Pho by Master Sergeant Kenneth E. Camell turned up an unsigned carbon copy of Henderson's report. Donald telephoned Henderson with the news and announced that a copy was on its way to him and the Inspector General's department. The following day, Henderson reported to the Forrestal Building in Washington for his interview.

Henderson impressed Wilson and another IG colonel who was present with his confident answers. He was frank about the realities of operating in the Quang Ngai area, the problems with the ARVN forces refusing to engage the Viet Cong, the difficulties Barker's men had in pinning down the enemy in the Pinkville area which resulted in a large number of casualties. He mentioned Koster's strict policies against the destruction of villages and the harming of civilians. Henderson claimed to have seen 500 to 600 civilians moving along the road out of My Lai 4 toward Quang Ngai but only six or seven women and children dead in the village. Many of the Viet Cong reported killed in the village died in their fighting bunkers as a result of artillery and gunship fire.

Henderson then attempted to account for his handling of the original atrocity allegations by Thompson and what in effect was his complete failure to investigate civilian deaths properly. Henderson persisted in the view that he had simply followed up the helicopter pilot's story of seeing an infantry captain kill a woman unnecessarily. As for the other claims, he could find no evidence to justify them.

The contents of the report of investigation would not reach Wilson until sometime later. Henderson had gone on record as saying he knew twenty civilians had been killed by artillery fire because he mentioned this in his report of investigation. The incident should have been thoroughly probed in accordance with MACV and American Division regulations. It was Catch-22, and Henderson, whether he knew it or not, was digging a deep hole for himself by his answers. Failure to carry out a proper investigation was a grave breach of regulations. If he had investigated he would have discovered the truth of Thompson's allegations. There would also be a paper trail because the rules said testimony had to be gathered and statements on oath taken. The whole case should have been turned over to the Inspector General's department at either Duc Pho or Chu Lai. The very idea of a colonel investigating his own command was going to take some explaining.

Henderson's way of handling this problem was to claim he had made *two* investigations, one informal and the other formal, at the request of Maj. Gen. Koster. The informal investigation was into the helicopter pilot's claim that Medina had shot a girl in the paddy field. Later Koster ordered him to conduct a formal inquiry into Thompson's claims and Henderson told Wilson he passed this over to Frank Barker to conduct, before his death. Henderson went a stage further in his cover story. Not only had Barker carried out an investigation, before he died, Henderson claimed, but he had submitted a formal report that Henderson had seen and personally endorsed. He said he had forwarded the formal written report to Chu Lai two or three weeks after he had made his own informal investigation—the copy of which had been found in the brigade files. But he added that no copies were made of Barker's formal report. Henderson's claim that a formal investigation was made into the atrocity allegations subsequently resulted in fruitless searches through mountains of paperwork at Chu Lai and Duc Pho for a document which never in fact existed. At the time Wilson had no way of knowing whether this was a lie designed to conceal the coverup.

The evidence Wilson had so far accrued convinced him that a criminal investigation would have to follow. The weight of testimony heavily implicated the commander of the 1st Platoon, Lt. Calley, as the individual who both ordered and took part in mass executions. Having extended his tour of duty in Vietnam by six months, Calley was by now serving with a unit doing long-range patrols. Now he was suddenly recalled to the United States a month early. On June 5, he arrived back at Fort Benning, assigned to the student battalion. Calley was scheduled to return to civilian life in early September, three years after his enlistment, but now the Army took steps to ensure they would not lose jurisdiction over him. His personnel records were "flagged" to indicate he was suspected of serious offenses. He was not allowed his discharge from military service. On June 9, at the Forrestal Building in Washington, Calley was formally warned he was suspected of murder and war crimes by Colonel Norman T. Stanfield.

After consulting with a JAG officer, Calley tried to do a deal. He said he was willing to make a full disclosure of what happened in Pinkville but only if he were granted immunity from prosecution. Stanfield made clear that no such offer of immunity would be given, so Calley declined to be interviewed or make a statement. From that point on he refused each and every attempt to get him to tell his side of what happened. Calley was told to remain in Washington while other inquiries were made. Wilson believed he was getting close to finishing his inquiries. In the following two days he had two long interviews with Hugh Thompson lasting many hours. He went over Thompson's damning story in minute detail.

Thompson's gunner, Larry Colburn, and several other pilots and air crew also confirmed the details. They were unshakable. It was confirmed that Henderson had been made fully aware of Thompson's allegations, that the pilot had spent almost half an hour going over his story with the brigade commander. Thompson had been given leave to go to Washington from his job as an instructor at the Army Aviation School at Fort Rucker, Alabama, and was asked to report back to the IG headquarters for the third day running at 8:30 AM. On June 13, Calley also returned to the Forrestal Building. A lineup had been arranged. Thompson unhesitatingly picked out Calley as the infantry officer he argued with when he landed his helicopter at My Lai.

Wilson's search for more confirming evidence about the massacre continued for another four weeks. The last witness was the most crucial: Paul Meadlo, interviewed at New Goshen, near Terre Haute, Indiana, on July 16. Minus the foot he lost as a result of Calley's stupidity on Hill 85, Meadlo had returned a nervous, stuttering wreck to his young wife, who had been his childhood girlfriend in high school, and their year-old son. Discharged from Army service, he later got a blue-collar job at the Hercules Chemical Company, in Terre Haute. He worked eight hours a day and frequently felt searing pains in his leg. The job was important because he had a family to support and the government only gave him a veteran's disability pension of $197 a month, later reduced to $136 after the stump of his foot healed and he had an artificial lower leg fitted. The good-natured boy from the small Midwestern town, who had continually been teased in Charlie Company by the kids who were more street-wise, no longer laughed and joked. He had kept the story of the massacre secret from his family.

At the meeting with Wilson in Terre Haute, Meadlo was anxious to unburden himself. He had carried around the guilt of what had happened in the village for far too long and, besides, he felt angry at the Veterans Administration for reducing his benefits. He was anxious to get it all off his chest, when Wilson warned him that any statement he made could be used in a court of law.

"I don't care," he replied and he proceeded to explain how he and Calley and the others had executed dozens of people in the village. Wilson felt that something in himself also died as he sat there listening to Meadlo relive the scenes of the massacre. Here finally was the unvarnished truth. "I had prayed to God this thing was fiction and I knew now that it was fact," he later revealed.

The next day, Wilson wrote up his report. It was a damning document. The accompanying transcripts of evidence of thirty-six witnesses ran to well over 1,000 pages. It was clear there had been a massacre of more than a hundred civilians and that several members of Charlie Company were involved, but principally Lt. Calley. It was also extremely likely there had been a coverup involving dozens of officers, possibly right up to the rank of major general. On July 23, Wilson warned Colonel Jim D. Kiersey, chief of staff at the US Army Infantry Center at Fort Benning, that Lt. Calley should not be reassigned to another post.

Wilson had traveled tens of thousands of miles gathering his testimony. Now a more detailed inquiry would have to be conducted by the Provost Marshal General's department.

In and around the offices of the General Staff at the Department of the Army, Wilson's report carried with it the shock wave of a possible coverup. Westmoreland had had time to prepare himself for the worst because the Inspector General's staff had kept his office informed of Wilson's progress. The Army's relations with Congress would be crucial through the forthcoming crisis which would surely explode over the Pentagon when the story broke. Senators John Stennis, chairman of the Senate Armed Services Committee, and Barry Goldwater and Congressman Mendell Rivers were immediately briefed about Wilson's report by the Army's congressional liaison staff. Finally, on August 6, Richard Nixon, on vacation at the "Western White House"—his home in San Clemente, California—was warned that an infantry platoon commander would soon be charged with the mass murder of Vietnamese civilians.

The withering heat and high humidity of summers in the District of Columbia can be unbearable, but the process of government in Washington continues. In the middle of 1969, the hot news for political insiders in the nation's capital was the naming of a new Chief Justice of the Supreme Court, Warren Burger, the first of Richard Nixon's conservative appointments to the high tribunal. But the story which captured the attention of millions of people around the world lay much further afield in a dimension far removed from the concerns of Washington politics: America's astronauts aboard *Apollo 11* made the first manned moon landing on July 20. The world's problems, particularly the terrible war in Southeast Asia, were put aside momentarily as people celebrated and marveled at perhaps the most momentous achievement of their lifetime. All attention was focused on this magnificent technological feat by the United States. A plaque was left on the lunar surface containing sentiments which transcended national boundaries and rival political systems. It read: "We came in peace for all mankind."

Soon people would be talking of darker deeds. In several weeks the Army would formally charge Calley with murdering 109 "Oriental human beings" and by the middle of November America and the rest of the world would hear about the village of My Lai and some of the terrible things that had happened there.

In their air-conditioned suites on the third floor of the Pentagon, Westmoreland and his most intimate colleagues on the General Staff knew time was not on their side. Criminal charges arising from the now proven massacre at Pinkville were inevitable and sooner or later the story was going to break. They knew Calley would remain under Army jurisdiction until his scheduled discharge on September 6, but there were clear-cut rules which had to be followed to ensure that those in command of the Army had no influence in the legal process that lay ahead. The Adjutant General's department would take control of the case and the final charges would be determined by the appropriate military convening authority, in Calley's case the commanding general at Fort Benning. However, the ramifications of Wilson's report for the Army were many and the General Staff needed time to reflect and consider their response. Essentially Wilson had mounted only a preliminary inquiry to inform the Chief of Staff whether Ridenhour was telling the truth. It was obvious a sizable criminal investigation would have to follow. Hundreds of people had been murdered, though the full extent of what happened and who was implicated was unclear. It looked as if the 1st Platoon's leader had gone berserk. There was also the question of who knew about the atrocity and what they had done, or rather not done, about it. Wilson's evidence might be enough to charge Calley, but it was not enough to convict him or anyone else before a court-martial.

Even before the facts were made public, the enormity of the political damage which was bound to follow presented a major crisis for Westmoreland and the General Staff. In Southeast Asia they were about to reverse the strategy which Westmoreland had pleaded for as commander-in-chief. Now it was no longer a question of a troop buildup but troop cuts. The President, who had promised peace with honor in Vietnam, announced a reduction in troop strength of 25,000 men. The massacre became a major preoccupation for Westmoreland completely overshadowing another scandal which had only just broken in the media, resulting from a criminal investigation into the murder of a Viet Cong spy by a handful of Green Beret soldiers. Colonel Robert B. Rhealt's 5th Special Forces group at Nha Trang had been involved in Project Gamma, a highly clandestine intelligence-gathering operation across the Cambodian border. Special forces groups known as Daniel Boone teams had been operating inside Cambodia since 1967 in missions later codenamed Salem House. Covert cross-border penetrations had been a regular practice since the early 1960s and Westmoreland had been obsessed with Cambodia. The presence there of large numbers of enemy troops helped explain why his men could not win the war in South Vietnam.

Project Gamma's principal task was to discover MACV's equivalent of El Dorado—COSVN, the secret headquarters of the Viet Cong, the Central Office for South Vietnam. Rhealt's undercover troops, known as Detachment B57, spent months covertly trying to locate NVA/VC base areas inside Cambodia, in an effort to determine whether Prince Sihanouk's government was working secretly with the North Vietnamese. US special forces operations involved running large numbers of indigenous Khmer Serei guerrillas, dedicated to Sihanouk's overthrow, as secret agents under the codename Blackbeard. The whole of Project Gamma was supposed to be kept secret from the South Vietnamese government to prevent leaks. Eventually it was one of the Blackbeard secret agents, Thai Khac Chuyen, who was discovered to be passing information to the North Vietnamese. A Green Beret team found a roll of film and documents in a VC base area across the Cambodian border. When the film was processed it showed they had a double agent on their hands. One of the photographs pictured him meeting with NVA intelligence officers. Chuyen was secretly arrested, polygraphed, and interrogated for ten days. A CIA officer involved in Project Gamma said killing Chuyen might be the best way of dealing with the situation. The exposed agent was drugged with morphine, taken by boat out into the Nha Trang Bay, and subsequently executed. After being shot twice in the head he was thrown overboard, his body weighed down with chains and wheel rims. It was hoped that the blood from his wounds would bring sharks into the bay. Before he was shot, he was repeatedly struck on the head to draw more blood. Subsequently Chuyen's handler, a Green Beret sergeant called Alvin L. Smith Jr, took fright and thought his own life might be in danger.

The story of the spy's murder reached the MACV commander, Gen. Abrams, at Lonh Binh, who was already privy to the Pentagon's consternation over the results of the secret My Lai investigation. Abrams, not wanting another coverup on his hands, immediately ordered an investigation into the Green Beret case. As a result Rhealt and seven of his command were arrested, charged with premeditated murder, and held in the stockade. News of their incarceration created a sensation in America.

The Army was still deciding how to handle this debacle as Westmoreland absorbed the full implications of the Inspector General's report on My Lai. What was the law? As a signatory of the Geneva Conventions the United States was supposed to prosecute anyone perpetrating war crimes, but many members of Charlie Company had been discharged from military service; if they were involved, what jurisdiction did the Army have over them? And how should the General Staff handle the political crisis that was bound to develop when the story broke? Above all there was the public image of the Army, a major American institution, to reckon with. How would it emerge from the forthcoming scandal?

This latter question was of abiding importance for Westmoreland, a soldier of the old school with a strong sense of duty, who had dedicated a lifetime's service to his country. The son of a textile mill manager from South Carolina, he had a profound sense of the importance of honor in a soldier's life. Many in the era of flower power, acid trips, and antiwar demonstrations might have viewed Westmoreland's concept of honor as incongruous. To the tens of thousands protesting the war daily on campuses throughout America it was not honorable to send young men to fight in a far-off country. Westmoreland's sense of honor was a part of a vanished system of values from a bygone age, a cultural idea associated with the lost spirit of nineteenth-century Southern pride, truly a milieu that was "gone with the wind." But for the old soldier the importance of honor, the veracity of a soldier's word, was crucial. Now the unimaginable had happened. There were the strongest warning signs that Samuel Koster, the current West Point Superintendent and a two-star general, was somehow implicated in the My Lai scandal. The crisis needed careful handling.

There were, however, certain unavoidable priorities. Now that Ridenhour's allegations were confirmed an inquiry would have to be mounted by detectives from the Army's Criminal Investigation Division (CID), a branch of the Office of the Provost Marshal General. Over the next eight months, Chief Warrant Officer André C. R. Feher, aged 52, was to become steeped in the minutiae of the four hours Charlie Company spent in My Lai. Often following in Wilson's footsteps, he traveled tens of thousands of miles around the United States in an effort to discover the truth of what happened at Pinkville. Later he became one of the first American soldiers to reenter My Lai 4, nearly eighteen months after Charlie Company left the village and its people completely devastated.

*

Feher, a gray-haired stocky man, had an intriguing background. His parents were Hungarians. He was born in Mostar, Yugoslavia, in December 1916, where his father was a flight surgeon with the Austrian-Hungarian air force. The family later settled in the Dutch East Indies, but at the age of 18 Feher returned to Europe to complete his education before joining the merchant marine. When World War II finished, he was first officer aboard a tanker owned by the Pacific Tankers Corporation, a subsidiary of Standard Oil. Because he was not an American citizen the end of hostilities meant he could no longer sail as a foreign officer under an American flag. He switched to American-owned ships registered in Panama. Then on the spur of the moment in 1948 he joined the Army of the United States working as a translator. He then switched to military intelligence work and later skippered the Army Transportation Corps's harbor craft and seagoing tugs. Finally he became a military policeman and trained as a criminal investigator. He and his Austrian-born wife returned to Europe and the military garrison at Mannheim, Germany, a rough town recovering from the aftermath of war, where thousands of American GIs manned the NATO front line. The Army's detectives handled every conceivable kind of crime American troops could commit, from simple theft to murder.

Feher's very first case taught him a lesson he would remember for the rest of his time as a military detective. It involved a young second lieutenant, married with a child, who was accused of being a "Peeping Tom." Feher interrogated the officer and obtained a confession. He knew it would be a court-martial and certain dishonorable discharge from the Army. The day he obtained the confession Feher worried about what would happen to the lieutenant and his family. He stayed awake most of the night fretfully pacing the floor, feeling sorry for the man's predicament. Finally it got to be too much for Feher's wife. If he was going to become emotionally involved in every case he investigated, she said, it was better he leave the CID there and then. Feher heeded her advice and vowed never again to immerse himself emotionally in his work. "It was hard at first. Later it became second nature," he recalled later.

In 1967, Feher was operations officer with the 4th MP Detachment for the Military District of Washington, DC. His men worked out of Fort Myer, a vast nineteenth-century military garrison that straddled the northwestern boundary of the Arlington National Cemetery across the Potomac River from the Lincoln Memorial. In April 1968, Feher's men suddenly found themselves amid the burning streets of Washington's angry Negro ghettos. The city, along with eleven others across the nation, erupted in rioting and major outbreaks of violence following the murder in Memphis of the civil rights leader Martin Luther King Jr, just five days after Lyndon Johnson announced to a startled America that he would not be seeking reelection. Whole city blocks around 14th and U streets in the northeast section of the District of Columbia were aflame, and the Army was sent in to restore control. As armed troops patrolled the streets, CID agents provided security for high-ranking officers from the Pentagon who had come to assess the crisis. Two months later, Feher's detachment were involved in the aftermath of another assassination and helped man the security detail at the funeral of Robert Kennedy in Arlington Cemetery in June 1968. The following year saw him back across the Potomac River at the Office of the Provost Marshal, which on August 4 was handed responsibility for the criminal investigation of My Lai. As senior investigator Feher took over where Wilson left off, searching for hard evidence that could be used in court, obtaining sworn affidavits from soldiers who might themselves be charged or become witnesses.

After reading Wilson's report Feher still had a completely open mind about the case. Either people were going to be court-martialed or they were not—it didn't matter to him either way. If the evidence was there to be found, he would find it. If not, there would be no criminal charges. "To be honest, my real concern was that My Lai would make the Army's conduct of the Vietnam War look very bad in the eyes of the public and that many mothers would feel that this was not the place for their sons to be," he later recalled.

Three CID agents were assigned initially to the case on August 23; later another four were brought onto the team. A roster of Charlie Company was obtained and Army personnel records provided their home addresses at the time of enlistment. Feher spent the rest of August and most of September traveling around the country obtaining statements. The main focus was on 1st Platoon troops who could give evidence about Calley's actions. All the signs were that Calley was clearly involved—but the Army had decided it could not hold him beyond his discharge date unless there was evidence to charge him with some certainty that it would lead him before a jury at a court-martial. If the hard evidence was found, then Feher would go to South Vietnam to gather more evidence. His inquiry was treated as preliminary, and completely separate from Wilson's IG investigation, coordinated through the Washington headquarters of the CID. Feher's boss, Lieutenant Colonel Theodore Kanamene, gave him carte blanche to follow every lead he could.

Appointments were fixed in advance, and Feher worked out a rough itinerary that would take him on the road for five or six days at a time. He would leave his home late on Sunday night or first thing Monday, returning to Washington the following Friday. On the phone to headquarters daily he received updated information about the progress other agents were making and up-to-date addresses of potential witnesses to be included in his itinerary. Then the trips got longer and longer, sometimes taking him away for two weeks at a time. He used commercial flights and rented cars, and stayed in motels. Invariably affidavits had to be typed up in his motel room at night, often under a poor light. It was wearisome work. At the end of a long stint of waiting in airports, driving hundreds of miles, eating restaurant food, and living out of a suitcase, Feher, a devoted family man, yearned to get home to his wife's cooking. He was not a young man and above all he wanted to sleep in his own bed.

On one of his first trips on August 25, Feher interviewed an Army photographer who was now out of the service and living in Ridgeville, Ohio. The case file Feher carried contained press cuttings about the Pinkville operation from *Stars and Stripes* and the Americal Division newspaper *Southern Cross*. The criminal inquiry was still in its very earliest stages and building a complete picture of what happened in the village was a major priority in developing a case that might go to trial. Ronald Haeberle's black-and-white photographs, typical Army PR pictures recording Charlie

Lt.-Col. Frank A. Barker, commanding officer of Task Force Barker, which mounted the infantry assault on My Lai on March 16, 1968. He died three months later in a helicopter crash.

A soldier's life: snapshots from Fred Widmer's album. *Above left:* His official Army photograph on graduating, aged 18, from Fort Benning, Georgia. *Above:* "Bones" Widmer and buddy in their makeshift quarters at LZ Dottie. *Left:* Widmer (*top right*) poses with other members of Charlie Company, including their commander, Capt. Ernie Medina (*bottom right*).

Above: Charlie Company begins its combat assault on My Lai at 7.45 AM on March 16, 1968.
Right: Military intelligence officer Lt. Dennis H. Johnson and his interpreter, Sgt Duong Minn, interrogate a village elder in My Lai village.

The Zippo squad gets to
work in My Lai village.

The terrible evidence that convinced the world that a massacre had taken place at My Lai. These photographs were taken by US Army photographer Sgt Ronald Haeberle.

Charlie Company's only casualty at My Lai, Pte Herbert Carter, who shot himself in the foot, is carried to a waiting medical evacuation helicopter by Fred Widmer (*right*) and Robert Mauro (*left*).

Right: Charlie Company takes a lunch break on the trail inside My Lai village only yards from a pile of corpses. Seated from right to left are Roger Alaux, Leo M. Maroney, Martin Fagan, Nguyen Dinn, Sgt Phu and James H. Flynn.
Below: Viet Cong suspects—hooded and bound before their interrogation at My Khe.

Above: Army investigator André Feher was one of the first Americans to return to My Lai in November 1969 to question villagers about an alleged massacre. From left to right are Lt. John C. Wood, Do Chuc, Do Hoia, André Feher, and Denis Conti, one of the original members of Charlie Company, who volunteered to return to the village to assist in the investigation.
Below: Villagers indicate to André Feher the ditch where more than a hundred people were killed.

Searchers after truth. *Right:* Col. William V. Wilson, who conducted the Army's preliminary investigation into the massacre. *Below:* Lt.-Gen. William Peers, whose probing inquiry into the killings and their cover-up led to serious charges being leveled against nearly thirty officers.

Time of trial.
Left: William Calley receives a donation to his defense fund from an American Legion post in Columbus, Georgia, in February 1970.
Below: Calley (*right*) and his military counsel, Maj. Kenneth Raby, are pursued by press men at Fort Benning, Georgia, November 1969.

Among those who gave evidence at Calley's court-martial were: (*right*) Ronald Haeberle, (*below left*) Lawrence Colburn, a helicopter gunner, and (*below right*) Lt. Hugh C. Thompson, Jr, a helicopter pilot.

Many Army officers were charged with offenses connected with the aftermath of the massacre—none was ever convicted. Col. Oran Henderson was acquitted of dereliction of duty by a court-martial jury, and Capt. Eugene Kotouc was found not guilty of maiming a Viet Cong suspect during an interrogation. Charges against Maj. Robert McKnight (of making a false statement) and Maj. Charles Calhoun (of covering up the massacre) were dismissed by the Army before a court-martial was held.

Twenty years on
(*clockwise, from top left*):
Kenneth Hodges,
Ronald Ridenhour,
Michael Bernhardt,
Vernado Simpson,
and Fred Widmer.

Survivors from My Lai.
Top left: Pham Thi Thuam.
Left: Truong Thi Lee.
Below left: Truong
Muoi, standing beside a
stone marking the grave
site of 170 villagers.
Below: Vo Thi Lien (*right*)
and Pham Thi Trinh
standing in front of the
monument to the victims
of the massacre.

Twenty years on.
Above: Reunion—Hugh C. Thompson and his door gunner Larry Colburn met up again in Lafayette, Louisiana, in October 1988.
Below: Robert T'Souvas, who admitted killing five people at My Lai, was shot dead by his common-law wife while living rough in Pittsburgh in September 1988.

William Calley leaving his father-in-law's jewelry store in Columbus, Georgia, in 1991.

Company's combat assault, still had to be obtained from the 11th Brigade's public information office files at Duc Pho. They would be important evidence if Haeberle could remember where he had taken them and if the troops could be correctly identified. It would also help determine the sequence of events during the time Charlie Company was in the village.

Haeberle's sworn statement took hours to record. He gave an extraordinarily vivid account of his experiences in the village and appeared to have total recall. Some of the images etched in his memory were chillingly grotesque—women and children being shot, pieces of skull and bits of bone flying through the air, brains being blown out, a complete contrast to the broad facts which Wilson's inquiry elicited from those he interviewed. CID investigators were absorbed by minute detail. Haeberle told Feher that the GIs believed the villagers were all Viet Cong supporters or communist sympathizers. Three-quarters of the 150 or so people he thought had been killed were women and children. Feher asked who ordered the killing. Haeberle didn't know:

I figured out it must have come from higher up, since the soldiers just do not start killing civilians in the mass they were doing. This was the first time I have seen something like this . . . I heard later that the General of the American Division praised the Task Force for the operation. I take it that he was not told that most of the people killed were women and children.

Completely out of the blue, Haeberle announced he had some color slides of the massacre taken on his own camera. He had only handed in to the public information office at Duc Pho the black-and-white photos he had taken on the Army's Leica camera. The color pictures, shot on his own Nikon, were his own property but he was prepared to hand over copies to the government if they gave him a receipt. No one inside the Army knew anything about the color slides. Feher was astonished to hear that Haeberle had given a series of illustrated talks about the war to various groups in Ohio and had shown the slides to more than six hundred people at different venues: the Cleveland Optimist Club, the Kiwanis Club, two Jaycees clubs, a teachers' association, and a church youth club. They had even been seen by a group of high school students. Haeberle had shown the photographs so many times, in fact, that he was able to describe accurately to Feher the scenes they depicted: a close-up of a woman with her blown-out brains lying beside her; a large group of women and tiny children lying on a trail after they had been executed by small arms fire; two young children badly wounded; a group of women and children seconds before they were mown down. Haeberle remembered later:

I put together a slide show. It started off real nice with Hawaii, moved on to Vietnam, showed the villages, what our medical group did for the villagers and more shots of the children, and finally the My Lai massacre. I showed these slides to groups of different ages because I wanted to find the reaction these people would give me after viewing my slide show. It was mixed. Some people couldn't believe this actually happened. "Why would American GIs do this, especially to old men, women, and children?" A couple thought it had been done in Hollywood, that it was made up. They just didn't want to believe it. A lot wanted to know why. I didn't know.

He agreed to have dinner later that night at Feher's hotel and said he would bring the slides with him. Feher didn't know what to expect or even whether Haeberle would keep his promise and turn up, but he optimistically arranged to pick up a projector from the local Army CID office in nearby Cleveland and pinned up a sheet as a makeshift screen on the motel room wall. As a precaution he borrowed a Polaroid camera to take his own photographs of Haeberle's slides in case he refused to hand them over as promised. The photographer had been clearly unsettled while making the statement and had mixed feelings about giving evidence in court. He wouldn't positively commit himself to being a future witness, although he said on balance he might.

Haeberle did keep their meeting, and as Feher viewed the images projected on the wall of his room, he realized he had made an extraordinary breakthrough. The pictures were the first hard evidence a massacre had taken place, evidence that could be used in court. As Haeberle commented on each picture shown on the wall, Feher snapped away with the Polaroid camera, producing his own instant copies. He intended to show them to other witnesses during future interviews. The following day Haeberle returned to the motel with copies of the slides.

Feher quickly discovered that not all witnesses would be as

cooperative. He next flew to New York and drove down the New Jersey Turnpike to Trenton, where he'd arranged a couple of interviews with members of the 1st Platoon. In Bordentown, a suburb to the south of Trenton, Daniel Simone told him he had spent most of his time at My Lai with Alan Boyce and a kid from Kansas called Thomas Turner. "When I went in I had no intentions to shoot women and children . . . if it happened it happened behind us," he told Feher. Simone castigated Calley's lack of leadership, especially in the incident on Hill 85 when Meadlo lost his foot: "Calley is just gung-ho and has no common sense . . . He just kept on going in a stupid manner. He took no precautions . . . Because he is small he must have been pushed around all his life by bigger people. Once he got in the Army he found he had a lot of authority."

On several occasions Simone claimed he had definitely not seen women and children killed, an almost impossible achievement given the scale of the slaughter in the village. He insisted he only skirted the village and suggested the 3rd Platoon might have more information because they had come in behind the 1st Platoon. Feher showed him the Polaroid pictures of the scenes of carnage.

Simone: "If I had been there when the women and children were machine gunned, I might have protested."
Feher: "Would you testify in court when called upon?"
Simone: "I'd rather not. People might get the wrong impression and I have to live here. I did not do anything wrong. I did not see anybody firing on women and children. All I heard was that women and children were shot. But I did not like to listen to it."

He refused to sign a statement.

Allen Boyce was out of the Army and living at Bradley Beach, a few miles south of Asbury Park on the Atlantic coast, and agreed to be interviewed the next day. Boyce, married with a child, was a slight, blond-haired, kindly young man who spoke softly. He explained how Charlie Company had been "all psyched up" when they landed at the village because they wanted revenge for their fallen comrades. From a distance he had seen Calley and Meadlo shooting villagers. He said that Meadlo told him later that Calley had ordered him to do it: "It had broken Meadlo up because he did not want to shoot the villagers and to him it was a terrible thing. Meadlo was a farm boy and if he was ordered to do anything he just did it."

Boyce saw civilians shot by members of the 3rd Platoon for no apparent reason, and he thought that about one hundred people had been killed, eighty of them women and children. In contrast to Simone, Feher believed he had found another good witness. He wanted to know why the soldiers had killed so many women and children. Boyce, who denied killing them himself, said:

The war does a lot of things to people and you are miserable over there and you might want to take it out on them. I myself did not shoot any women or children. I fired my M-16 only a couple of times during this operation and I fired on people who were trying to get away, which was standard procedure ... From what I hear, Calley had ordered the shootings of the civilians. I cannot say that I heard Calley order the shootings. It has been such a long time ago and I want to blot this incident out of my mind. Ordinarily on combat operations we did not shoot women and children. From this I take it that men were ordered to shoot the villagers. We also shot the animals. I shot a few myself.

Boyce kept quiet about the incidents witnessed by his friend Harry Stanley—of killing an old man by stabbing him in the back, and throwing another man in the well. Feher had no knowledge of these at this stage. However, Boyce was willing to testify in court and finally told Feher: "I hope that they get to the bottom of this and find out what the cause was, to prevent any other incidents. Incidents like this are the reason why we cannot win the war. Because the civilians will help the Viet Cong."

The investigator was on the move once more. The next interview involved a six-hour flight across the United States to Seattle to interview Gregory Olsen, who had stayed on in the Army and was now a sergeant at Fort Lewis, Washington State. He had been at the ditch site and saw it full with bodies. The majority were dead, including babies, young children, old men, and women. Calley was also present and Olsen saw him walk over to a helicopter pilot who had landed nearby. "It looked to me like the pilot was angry because he was shaking his arms," he told Feher. He witnessed the platoon sergeant, David Mitchell, open fire on bodies in the ditch with his M-16 and watched as Boyce threw a prisoner in a bomb crater and then shot him twice: "The prisoner was not trying to escape. Why Boyce shot him is anybody's guess." Another GI called Conti, Olsen said, who had cut the hair off a Vietnamese girl, made a pony tail of it, and stuck it on his helmet, was going to screw a nurse they captured but then found she had VD.

Olsen too agreed to be a court witness if necessary. He admitted firing at a man on the tree line as soon as they got off the troop ship but said he adamantly refused to shoot women and children. His denial stuck out in Feher's mind years later:

If I had been told do so, like Meadlo was ordered by Lt. Calley, I would have refused because I know that it is a war crime. Even if General Westmoreland would have ordered me to shoot women and children I would have refused . . . It was a lot to bottle up and I feel better, now that I have talked about it. Even if I was not involved in the killing, I still have a feeling of guilt for not stopping it or for not reporting it to Col. Barker. I did not want to get Capt. Medina in trouble and I felt he was not responsible even though it was his company . . . I do not condone the shooting of the civilians by members of Company C. They should have refused. To this day I do not know what came over them by not refusing.

Feher's next appointment meant another long journey of 2,000 miles. He arrived two days later in Sardis, a poor farming community in Mississippi, to interview Calley's radio operator. Feher checked into the local Holiday Inn and arranged to conduct the interview with Charles Sledge in his motel room. Sledge had witnessed the first group of villagers killed at the intersection of the two trails and had been at the ditch site when Calley ordered Mitchell to push other civilians down the slope and began shooting them. He saw Calley kill the Buddhist monk and throw a tiny baby back into the ditch and shoot it.

Sledge proved to be a crucial witness because as the platoon commander's radio operator he had stayed beside Calley virtually the whole day on March 16. His recollection of events was so graphic it took Feher most of the day and part of the evening both to conduct the interview and to draw up Sledge's affidavit. He suggested they have lunch in the dining room, an event which immediately caused comment in the small Southern town, because Sledge was black.

Sardis, even in 1969, remained effectively a segregated town and

Sledge was the only Negro in the hotel apart from the domestic staff. They continued the interview about the events in the village after their lunch and Feher began to type up Sledge's seven-page affidavit at 5 PM. After three hours it still was not complete and the pair broke for another meal and returned to the dining room for dinner. Their close over-the-table conversation in the dining room and the hours spent closeted in Feher's room did not go unnoticed.

Next morning as Feher was having breakfast, he was approached by the local sheriff, who had checked the hotel registration card Feher signed on his arrival at the motel which gave his Washington, DC, address. The sheriff wanted to know what his business was in Sardis. "He might have thought I was a civil rights activist," Feher said later. "After I explained to him what I was doing in town and showed him my CID credentials all was well. He even offered me any assistance I might need."

It had been a rewarding week in terms of evidence. Feher now had a total of seven detailed statements as well as the Haeberle color pictures. He had established there were two principal groups of executions in which Calley was closely involved: one at the intersection of the two trails in the center of the village and one at the irrigation ditch about 100 meters to the eastern perimeter. Feher estimated that 120 women and children had been murdered. There was enough information for the Army to charge Calley. But it was obvious many others had been involved in the mass killings.

Calley had returned to Fort Benning on June 21, following the lineup at the Forrestal Building and his refusal to be questioned for the Inspector General's inquiry. His superiors were formally warned that one of their infantry instructors was suspected of involvement in a war crime. Calley was removed from contact with new recruits and given a job handling administration in the office of the deputy base commander. Colonel Talton W. Long, 54, a lanky, graying veteran of the 82nd Airborne Division in World War II, assigned Calley the job of planning a new system of car parking and working on a new letterhead for the infantry center's museum project. He occupied a small table behind the secretary's desk in Long's outer office on the third floor of Building 35. In addition to the secretary the only other person in the office was the colonel's driver.

On September 5, four days after Feher's interview with Sledge, the commanding general in charge of the huge military training area covering more than 200 square miles, Major General Orwin C. Talbot, charged the young lieutenant with multiple cases of murdering "Oriental human beings." Calley was to have been discharged from military service the following day.

8. Fallout

News that an infantry officer had been accused of murdering Vietnamese civilians made virtually no impact on the American public because hardly a newspaper or television station reported the fact in any detail. The Army made no announcement of the charges until a local reporter telephoned Fort Benning about a tip he had received.

The town of Columbus is four miles from the entrance to the huge military training area at Fort Benning, Georgia, officially designated the US Army Infantry Center. Its local paper, the *Ledger-Enquirer*, had a big readership among the soldiers at the base. The paper's associate editor Charles Black spent much of his time writing stories about military affairs and was particularly well informed. He was absent from the paper's 12th Street office on an assignment, working on the big story of the day, a bank robbery in which shots were fired. The tip about a mass murder charge was taken by David Leonard, a reporter in the newsroom. Immediately he called the information officer at Fort Benning, Lieutenant Colonel Douglas B. Tucker, who confirmed the basic facts and gave the name of the officer who had been charged as Lt. William Laws Calley.

Tucker had been prepared for a media onslaught for three weeks. Col. William Wilson had returned to Fort Benning on August 19 to brief him and a team of Army lawyers about the investigation. The final judgment on whether to charge Calley had been taken by Fort Benning's commanding general, Maj. Gen. Orwin C. Talbott, a 28-year career soldier who had only just returned from commanding the 1st Infantry Division in South Vietnam. In legal terms he was the convening authority. But the Army still had to follow a process known as an Article 32 hearing, a legal requirement under the Uniform Code of Military Justice in which the evidence is examined and a final decision taken on whether to proceed to a court-martial. In Calley's case it was the Army equivalent of a grand jury hearing. Again Talbott would make the final call. The decision rested with him, as the convening authority, because the country's system of military justice created structures specifically intended to prevent what was known as command influence. It was designed to rule out favoritism and prevent juries at courts-martial being manipulated by the highest ranks of the service in cases that might prove personally embarrassing to senior officers or in which they had a personal interest.

Local commanders were given total discretion to order courts-martial within their jurisdiction as convening authorities. Assisted by Army lawyers, they had a role similar to that of a district attorney. They assessed the evidence against an accused person before deciding whether charges should be brought. In this way the General Staff and the Department of the Army in Washington were meant to stay out of crucial legal decisions, especially in cases that could prove awkward to the Army.

The Army, fighting in a long and bloody conflict overseas, was now prepared to face a battle for public opinion at home. Talbott's public information staff had been in close contact with their counterparts at the Pentagon and prepared their responses to the news reporters they knew would be making inquiries the moment Calley's offenses were revealed.

David Leonard cobbled together a fourteen-inch story that ran under a double-column headline on the front page of the following day's *Ledger-Enquirer* on September 6. When the piece appeared Charles Black went to work among his Army contacts and learned the charges against Calley arose from an incident in South Vietnam on March 16 the previous year. He decided to check further and make calls among his friends at the infantry center to see if he could locate Calley and interview him. The administration and accommodation areas at Fort Benning, as at many other military bases, resembled a small town and there was virtually open access. Thousands of cars poured on and off the base every morning and evening as soldiers and civilian staff drove into work and back home again at night. Security was minimal and Black was a familiar visitor. He found Calley at home in the BOQ (bachelor officers' quarters), but Calley said he couldn't give an interview. Black, who had made five tours to Vietnam reporting the war, noticed that Calley was wearing the shoulder patch of the Americal Division—a blue background with the stars of the Southern Cross. He now knew where to look for more information and decided to dig away further. For the next two months he pored over Army newspapers, dug back through his own files, and interviewed soldiers who had been in Vietnam. In this way he landed on an operation which had occurred at a place called Pinkville, but he was anxious not to run the story before he had it sewn up. He didn't want everyone else jumping on board.

The *New York Times* buried a two-paragraph Associated Press wire story inside the paper and the expected flood of inquiries into the public information office at Fort Benning failed to materialize. Several reporters had good tips in later weeks about the case but failed to persuade their news bureaus to take it seriously enough to mount a major inquiry. Robert Goralski, working the Pentagon beat for NBC TV news, was trying instead to break the Green Berets' murder story when one of his contacts told him that he was wasting his time, he should contact Fort Benning, where a lieutenant had been charged with murdering a hundred civilians. Jerry ter Horst, Washington bureau chief of the *Detroit News*, got a tip but could not confirm the story. He stuck with the Green Berets charges.

For several months Ronald Ridenhour had been convinced that the Army would whitewash its investigation. He had heard nothing since Col. Wilson had come to see him in late April. Then, on September 7, he suddenly received a telephone call from someone in the military in Washington to say in guarded terms that Calley had been charged. Since the middle of June, Ridenhour had been trying to get the story published himself. From a writers' guide in the Phoenix public library he picked the name of Michael Cunningham, of Hartford, Connecticut, who listed himself as a literary agent.

Cunningham in fact worked full-time for a Hartford insurance

company and acted as an agent as a sideline. He tried to push
Ridenhour's story around several major newspapers in Boston and
New York as well as to the big television networks. "Everyone
Mike Cunningham talked to actively discouraged him," Ridenhour
said later. "Supposedly responsible people all said: 'What are you
associating yourself with something like this for?'" Ridenhour
wasn't trying to create a situation where America would have to
withdraw from Vietnam—he just wanted the story out.

When the Army told him that Calley had been charged,
Ridenhour feared they would use the platoon commander as a
scapegoat and put all responsibility on the shoulders of one
renegade junior officer. He knew for sure that many other members
of Charlie Company were involved in the massacre and that the
company had been ordered by Medina to destroy Pinkville. Following the phone call from Washington he decided to go public
himself and called the main office of the *Arizona Republic* newspaper in Phoenix, asking to speak to a reporter named Ben Cole.
He told Cole his story, but nothing appeared.

Six weeks later, on October 22, a freelance journalist in Washington
named Seymour Hersh was telephoned by a contact with sketchy
details about an officer at Fort Benning who had been charged
with killing seventy or eighty people. It appeared the Army was
hoping to keep a lid on the case but Hersh knew a story when he
saw one.

A former Chicago police reporter, Hersh had moved to
Washington and covered the Pentagon for the Associated Press,
later writing an exposé of the United States' military plans for
chemical and biological warfare. At the age of 30 he became
antiwar candidate Senator Eugene McCarthy's press secretary
during his unsuccessful bid for the Democratic presidential nomina-
tion. The job was a crown of thorns. Hersh was warned by friends
he might not be employable when it was all over if he tied his
colors to McCarthy's antiwar crusade. He quit following a bitter
row with local McCarthy campaigners over campaign tactics at the
end of March 1968. In the fall the following year he was planning
another book about the Pentagon. A natural ferreter of information,
his working life was based on the principle that if you *knew* the

story was out there, you followed it. The phone call about the officer at Fort Benning accused of multiple murders was just such a lead.

In winkling out a story a reporter often had to bluff his way through the early stages when there was only the initial hint of a scoop. The art was to make it appear you knew much more than you did. Hersh's telephone call to the information office at Fort Benning at midafternoon on October 23 began with a bluff and ended with him convinced he had a sensational story. Ultimately it would earn him a richly deserved Pulitzer Prize for his brilliant pieces of investigative journalism. His book on My Lai would be published two years before Woodward and Bernstein made investigative journalism fashionable.

His phone call to Tucker, the Fort Benning information officer, inquiring about "a classified trial" being held at Fort Benning, was a shot in the dark. Tucker told him no such trial was taking place. But Hersh clearly had some sort of lead on the Calley case and Tucker read him the two-paragraph item from the *New York Times*. The following morning Hersh was back on the phone after trying to locate Calley's home in Miami without success. Now he wanted Calley's official home of record from Army files and the name of his attorney. He learned that Calley lived at Waynesville, North Carolina, and that George W. Latimer of Utah, formerly a judge with the Court of US Military Appeals, had been retained as his civilian counsel. Latimer apparently had formed an immediate liking for the boyish Calley, whom he regarded almost as a son. Hersh also got in touch with the Pentagon, demanding as much information as the Department of Defense would provide. He was given the basic outline of the charges of first degree murder, the date, and the place of the offenses in Vietnam. Hersh promptly called Judge Latimer at his law offices in Salt Lake City and arranged an appointment for the following Monday.

That same evening Tucker spoke on the telephone with Latimer at his home. He had hoped they could talk on friendly terms, as a serving officer to a former officer. But the lawyer immediately began talking like a defense counsel. Latimer berated Tucker and said his client was being sacrificed by the Army. The evidence against Calley was based on unsubstantiated statements, he continued, and the case had only gone this far because of pressure from high places. "As high as Westmoreland," he said, aware the Chief of Staff had ordered the Inspector General's investigation. Latimer pointed out the Americal Division had praised the Pinkville operation and that a captain and sergeant were at least equally as involved as Calley. Then he brought up the case of Col. Rhealt and the Green Berets. Latimer had been briefed himself to defend one of those accused in the case. The previous month the government had dropped the charges, saying a fair trial would have been impossible because the CIA had refused to make any of its personnel available as witnesses in the interests of national security. Judge Latimer told Tucker he was thinking of contacting the Secretary of the Army to see if the Calley case couldn't be dropped along similar lines.

News of this conversation passed quickly along the grapevine to the Pentagon, and Army lawyers handling the Calley prosecution at Fort Benning were quietly comforted. They believed Latimer was trying to get the case dropped through media pressure because he knew the evidence against Calley was so strong.

Finally, on November 11, Hersh arrived in Columbus, where he interviewed Calley in his living quarters at Fort Benning, a one-room-combination bedroom and living room with a separate bathroom in the BOQ opposite Col. Long's office in Building 35. Over drinks at a party with some of Calley's friends, the young soldier confessed to Hersh how many people he was accused of killing. Hersh, a staunch critic of the sheer waste caused by the Vietnam War, thought of Calley as being as much a victim as the people he had slaughtered. Ready now to break the story, Hersh called *Life* and *Look* magazines but failed to interest them. Then he decided to hawk his article through a newly formed news agency in Washington called the Dispatch News Service, started by two young men keen to secure a wider audience for radical stories. The general manager was David Obst, aged 23, son of a Los Angeles advertising executive, who decided to push Hersh's story by calling fifty newspaper editors throughout the USA and Canada and making a sales pitch.

"I think I've got a story you'll be interested in," Obst said, asking only $100 as a fee if they ran the piece. He convinced thirty-five newspapers to carry the article on November 13, including the *Chicago Sun-Times*, the *St Louis Post-Dispatch*, and the *Milwaukee Journal*. The day the DNS article appeared in cities across the country, the *New York Times* also ran a story it had been researching. The *Alabama Journal* had gone with its own article the previous afternoon.

Hersh's was a superior piece of reporting. He included quotes from his interview with Calley as well as an accurate description from some of his sources of what happened when Charlie Company moved into the village. He described the trouble Task Force Barker had had in and around Pinkville and that Calley's platoon had suffered heavy casualties when it was repeatedly attacked from the rear. He quoted one unnamed member of Charlie Company: "They simply shot up this village and Calley was the leader of it. When one guy refused to do it, Calley took the rifle away and did the shooting himself." None of the men he had spoken to had denied women and children were shot but he quoted Latimer as saying: "You can't afford to guess whether a civilian is a Viet Cong or not. Either they shoot you or you shoot them. This case is going to be important—to what standard do you hold a combat officer in carrying out a mission?"

Finally the story was out, but its impact was slow to gather momentum. It took nearly another week for the dam to burst and for the deluge of information about My Lai to engulf an unsuspecting America. In a follow-up story on November 20, Hersh gave eyewitness accounts of the massacre. He found a shocked and humbled Michael Terry in Utah:

They just marched through shooting everybody . . . they had them in a group standing in front of a ditch, just like a Nazi-type thing. One officer ordered a kid to machine gun everybody down. But the kid just couldn't do it. He threw the machine gun down and the officer picked it up . . . I don't remember seeing many men in the ditch, mostly women and kids.

The Pentagon had been preparing for this moment for weeks. The Article 32 hearing* assessing the evidence against Calley had taken

* An Article 32 hearing is a closed hearing with no jury present where those with legal authority assess the overall evidence against an accused individual.

place toward the end of October at Fort Benning but no decision had been announced about a court-martial. The verdict of whether there would be a trial before a jury was still awaited but the Pentagon's brass was certain a court-martial was unavoidable. A second member of the 1st Platoon, Staff Sergeant David Mitchell, had been secretly charged at Fort Hood, Texas, with assault with intent to murder thirty Vietnamese civilians. Other charges were being prepared against Medina and Hutson.

In South Vietnam, a small group of newsmen reporting the war visited My Lai 4 on November 14, 1969, the day after Hersh's story broke. Henry Kamm of the *New York Times*, Paul Brinkley-Jones of *Newsweek*, and Don Baker of ABC TV were taken to the village under armed escort by American Division troops and found it deserted, completely laid flat, and overgrown. Several mounds were found which were thought to be mass graves. The villagers had been moved to a nearby refugee camp.

The generals in the Pentagon had known for months that culpability for the massacre went far beyond the few individuals who had so far been charged. These facts were still not public on November 21, when Westmoreland was pressed by news reporters to answer questions about My Lai. He was in Philadelphia, about to give a speech to the southeastern Pennsylvania chapter of the American Red Cross. Aware of accusations that command influence lay behind the decision to charge Calley, Westmoreland was anxious not to display personal knowledge of the case. Pressed for details of the massacre, he strived to distance himself from the legal processes that were underway:

Well, in justice to the individual, and to ensure that the procedures that will be involved after the investigation is completed are not jeopardized, I cannot comment on it, because I don't know whether there's a case there or not, so I don't want to give you the impression that an offense has been committed, I just don't know. I do not have the benefit of that information, and I do not want to prejudice the case by making assumptions.

The matter has been under investigation for quite some time and in order not to prejudice the case, the Army has not revealed details, and probably will not reveal details because it would prejudice the case and rights of the accused ... it would be imprudent for me to pass any premature judgment on whether there was an offense or not, and whether or not any individual was guilty of an offense.

That same day the legal complexities of the Uniform Code of Military Justice were being explained to a collection of reporters in a press room just off Correspondents' Corridor on the ground floor of the Pentagon's outer ring. The Army's General Counsel, Robert E. Jordan, sent in to take the heat, began a cat-and-mouse game with journalists determined to get information. Jordan quickly set the tone by telling them he wasn't going to make public any details about the case. The Army didn't want any future conviction reversed by the Court of Military Appeals because evidence was ruled inadmissible, though it was impossible to prevent some information coming out:

For example, some of you enterprising members of the press have been poking and digging around the last few days and you have identified some people that are identified in this and you've found out where they are and you've gone out and interviewed them. We don't consider it within our purview to order everybody who is in the Army not to talk to you.

The reporters, cynical about Jordan's motives, suspected that the Army was trying keep the nature of the exact charges secret and that eventually the government would drop the case, as it had done with Col. Rhealt and the Green Berets. Jordan found himself in a dilemma. To have confirmed the fact that a public trial would definitely be held would have given the impression the Pentagon *was* directly involved in the Army's judicial process. The rules against command influence prohibited this. Jordan emphasized there were Federal guidelines to prevent pretrial publicity; however, no reporter thought to ask him why then he had bothered to hold a press conference in the first place if he didn't have anything to say. The newsmen went to ingenious lengths to get him to budge from his position of silence about the facts of the case. Stories were already appearing about Calley and Mitchell. In fairness to them, one reporter pleaded, the Army should come out and give the specifics of the charges, otherwise they would "continue to get kicked around" by the press and television. When Jordan refused, one journalist sharply retorted: "The whole process lends itself to coverup—it has led to a coverup of this story for a year and a half. An investigation was made, nothing was ever said publicly about it, no results of that investigation were ever published, and the Pentagon was evidently was not informed of it either."

At the suggestion of a coverup Jordan went on the defensive and weakened on his pledge to give no information. The press obviously knew a great deal about the Henderson inquiry from their sources. When a reporter asked if other people were being investigated Jordan revealed that nine soldiers still in uniform were under investigation by half a dozen members of the CID in America and Vietnam. "These are just people whose names have come up and the CID people are looking at," he quickly added.

Reporter: "How many civilians are also being investigated? You said about nine still in the Army; how many out of uniform are also being investigated?"

Jordan: "There's a larger number, I think it's in the vicinity of fifteen or so people whose names have come up—recognize, now, that these are people who are not under military jurisdiction, or their term of active duty is over, or—"

Reporter: "What happens to them? What if cases can be made that they did commit murder in Vietnam in March 1968?"

Jordan: "There's some fairly difficult legal problems involved in answering that question. I'm not sure I can answer it yet. There are provisions in the Uniform Code for trying people for crimes committed while they were in service, after they get out of service under certain circumstances; namely, I think the crime has to be punishable I think by more than five years, and it can't be punishable in a civilian court; that is, no civilian court has jurisdiction, and so forth. That particular provision as applied to a particular case was held unconstitutional by the Supreme Court, in a habeas corpus action, and I believe that was a murder case, so this is kind of unchartered legal waters here, and as you know the Supreme Court has not been particularly favorably disposed toward the exercise of court-martial jurisdiction over civilians."

The reporters were angry that the Army had known about the murders since April 1968 and that only now were the details coming out in dribs and drabs. One of them shouted that My Lai had become a major international issue: "We're sitting here on a propaganda powder keg with our hands tied behind our backs," he moaned frustratedly.

Reporter: "Isn't the Army really trying to protect itself? Isn't the Army on trial? Why shouldn't we have the records of that period?"

Jordan: "Look, let's be realistic about this. Enough information has come out about this case . . ."

Reporter: "No thanks to the Pentagon."

Jordan: ". . . that any question about the Army protecting itself is really kind of silly, you know, the fat is in the fire. If you're talking about trying to cover up, we aren't trying to cover up and we haven't been trying to cover up."

The story was still building slowly in America—overseas, especially in Britain, it was receiving far more prominence. More information came as newspapers and TV stations across the United States sent teams of reporters to track down the men who had been at My Lai. GIs from Charlie Company suddenly found reporters on their doorsteps asking questions. When the newsmen left, wives and parents began to ask for answers.

Few GIs had spoken about the incident since arriving home. Infantryman Jack Birkhoffer heard about the massacre after joining Charlie Company in April 1968, and wrote to his parents about men being ordered to finish off women and children. When Birkhoffer returned to his home in Muscatine, Iowa, he found the letters he had written and burned them, along with his uniform. He didn't live long enough to celebrate his homecoming and died in a car accident on April 5, 1969.

Varnado Simpson reacted to the first spate of stories by immediately going public in his home town of Jackson, Mississippi, where he admitted killing ten civilians. He was still shocked by the discovery during the massacre that he had accidentally shot a woman carrying a child.

Some in the company, like Bernhardt, told their families of the horrors of My Lai to disabuse them of their fantasies. Arriving home Bernhardt found his father had no clue that the fighting in Southeast Asia was totally different from the war against Germany and Japan. A drill sergeant at Fort Dix, New Jersey, he was interviewed first by Hersh. When stories about the massacre began appearing Bernhardt kept his promise to Ridenhour and arranged a press conference. Bernhardt was within his rights to go public. Jordan, the Army's top lawyer, had announced the Army could not forbid soldiers to speak to the media. Accompanied by an Army information officer, with television cameras present, Bernhardt confirmed the details of the massacre. But the experience left him feeling slightly uncomfortable, as he later recalled.

When Ron Ridenhour visited me in hospital and asked me if I would be willing to testify, if I would be willing to make a statement or tell someone back home, I told him that I would. I didn't even hesitate. I had spent a couple of days in another environment [after weeks in the bush and jungle]—this was a military hospital, another world. But still, when the time came to do it, I was being asked to get specific about who did what ... I was asked to point the finger at certain individuals. I didn't feel really comfortable with that, and I'd spent a lot of time with these people. Even though they did all of that—I also knew their other side. We spent a long time over there—it was not one long string of abuse of Vietnamese, murdering Vietnamese civilians. Most of the time we did soldiering stuff, fighting and sweating and bleeding, just like soldiers do. That's what we did most of the time. Besides, by then I was with another military unit, and when you point the finger at some of your former comrades, these men you are now with begin to wonder about you too.

Ridenhour meanwhile was being interviewed over the telephone by a Canadian radio station, CKNW. He claimed Charlie Company had been instructed to destroy Pinkville, an order they interpreted quite literally. He wanted a full investigation, he told anchorman Art Findlay. This interview was quickly followed by two pivotal events that turned the story of the massacre into a global sensation.

In Ohio, Ronald Haeberle told a college friend, Joe Eszterhas, a reporter on the *Cleveland Plain Dealer*, that he had photos of the massacre. According to Eszterhas, when he called the Pentagon and, later, Fort Benning to check whether Haeberle had actually been at My Lai, an Army lawyer warned him off publishing the pictures. Haeberle had been in the village as an Army photographer, he was informed—the photos belonged to the Army. It was the confirmation Eszterhas needed to take the story to his night managing editor, Ted Princiotto, who was preoccupied with the news about the impending second American Moon landing. "We've got a world scoop," he eagerly announced.

"Fuck the scoop," Princiotto said, dismissing the reporter "we've got a Moon landing tomorrow."

Later the hardnosed executive ambled over to the photographic studios and looked at the startling images of death and carnage captured through Haeberle's camera lens.

"Jesus Christ!" he said. "Fuck, man, this is great stuff."

"Well," said Eszterhas, "what about Moon walk?"

"Fuck the Moon walk," replied Princiotto. "It's just a routine Moon walk."

On November 20, the paper slashed on its front page eight black-and-white photographs taken from Haeberle's transparencies and copyrighted under his name. It led to a frenzied scramble by the world's press to reproduce the pictures.

It was no coincidence that the following morning Robert Jordan went into the lions' den of the press room on the ground floor of the Pentagon.

The day the photographs appeared, CBS paid $500 and showed the *Plain Dealer*'s front page as the lead item on its nightly news show. A grave Walter Cronkite prepared his audience for a disturbing sight. The American public was stunned as the studio cameras slowly zoomed in on piles of bodies, and panned across scenes of small wounded children crawling on the ground and the haunted faces of half a dozen women and children seconds before they were slaughtered. Local Ohio Senator Stephen M. Young, a Democrat, said that the photographs evoked memories of Lidice, the Czechoslovak village destroyed by the Nazis. "It must be made crystal clear that Americans do not condone such conduct, war or no war," he added.

DNS had been busy marketing rights to Hersh's material. Hersh had closely questioned Paul Meadlo near Terre Haute, Indiana, and proposed that he go public to get his story out. On November 24, four nights after they ran Haeberle's pictures, CBS screened a sensational interview with Meadlo, who had traveled to the TV studios in New York at their expense. The deal was masterminded by Hersh, who arranged for the Dispatch News Service to collect a fee of $10,000 for delivering the former GI. CBS producers arranged for him to be cross-examined by one of America's foremost television interviewers, Mike Wallace. There was, of course, a moral dilemma. Meadlo's interview was bound to yield enormous publicity, which could endanger the process of justice and cause a mistrial in the Calley case when it came before the court-martial. Hersh's very firm view was that the American public had to learn the full implications of what happened in My Lai, and that the best person to convince them was a man who readily admitted his part in the mass executions and wanted to clear his conscience before the nation, live on TV. Before Meadlo agreed to the interview, DNS and Hersh arranged for him to be assured of his legal rights by an attorney working for a Washington law firm.

Round-faced and earnest looking, Meadlo had already made his confession on several occasions to different people. Nothing had prepared him for the highly charged atmosphere of a television studio and the relentless interviewing technique of Wallace. The hapless Meadlo appeared a sad and pathetic figure. His matter-of-fact answers, delivered with a flat Midwestern accent, made him appear as much a victim of the war as the people he had murdered.

Television was for most Americans quintessentially a medium of entertainment. Meadlo's confession was truly an extraordinary departure from the vapid diet of soap operas, comedy programs, and quiz shows. News, however, was important to American audiences—Walter Cronkite was a national institution. Meadlo's interview was delivered virtually without warning to an audience of millions of parents and children waiting excitedly for news of the *Apollo 12* astronauts' return from the moon and splashdown into the Pacific Ocean. Instead in their living rooms appeared the gawkish figure of the young man from Indiana. Meadlo brought to the audience a raw truth about the Vietnam War they would prefer not to have known. He chillingly described lining up the first group of villagers and shooting them down, expending four clips of ammunition in killing them. There were seventeen bullets to a clip, which meant, Wallace deduced, sixty-eight shots. At the ditch execution site Meadlo said he was ordered to fire single shots to conserve ammunition. Wallace wanted to know why he did it.

Meadlo: "Why did I do it? Because I felt like I was ordered to do it, and it seemed like that at the time I felt like I was doing the right thing, because I lost buddies, I lost a damn good buddy, Bobby Wilson, and it was on my conscience. So after I done it I felt good but later on that day it was gettin' to me."

Wallace: "You're married?"

Meadlo: "Right."

Wallace: "Children?"

Meadlo: "Two."

Wallace: "How old?"

Meadlo: "The boy is two and a half, and the little girl is a year and a half."

Wallace: "Well, obviously the question comes to mind . . . the father of two little kids like that . . . how can he shoot babies?"

Meadlo: "I didn't have the little girl, I just had the little boy at the time."

Wallace: "How do you shoot babies?"

Meadlo: "I don't know. It's just one of them things."

Wallace: "How many people would you imagine were killed that day?"

Meadlo: "I would say 370."

Wallace: "What did these civilians . . . these, particularly the women and children, the old men, what did they do? What did they say to you? They weren't begging or anything, 'No . . . no,' or . . .?"

Meadlo: "Right . . . They were begging and saying, 'No. No.' And their mothers were hugging their children, but they kept on firing. Well, we kept on firing. They was waving their arms and begging . . ."

Wallace: "Did you ever dream about all of this that went on in Pinkville?"

Meadlo: "Yes, I did . . . and I still dream about it."

Wallace: "What kind of dreams?"

Meadlo: "I see the women and children in my sleep. Some days . . . some nights, I can't sleep. I just lay there thinking about it."

CBS made a point of declaring they had not paid Meadlo a penny—merely traveling expenses. A company spokesman said: "The kid is getting absolutely zero." Meadlo had wanted to unburden his conscience. "We arranged for him to do so, after warning him that anything he said could be used against him later," Hersh said in a statement.

However, Meadlo himself was less happy with this arrangement. Publicity from his televised interview earned him a notoriety he didn't expect. His mother, Mrs Myrtle Meadlo, knew nothing of his part in the massacre until she saw the TV program. In a memorable interview she said that she had sent the Army a nice boy before he went to Vietnam, and they had turned him into a murderer. "He wasn't raised up like that," she told CBS news correspondent Ike Pappas, after listening to her son's confession. "I raised him up to be a good boy and I did everything I could. They come along and took him to the service. He fought for his country and look what they done to him—made a murderer out of him, to start with."

Many supporters of the war immediately went on the offensive. Senator Fritz Hollings of South Carolina claimed Meadlo was suffering from combat sickness. In a Senate speech he claimed the Army's decision to try Calley meant that all soldiers who committed "a mistake in judgment" under pressure of combat were "going to be tried as common criminals." "Are we going to take every helicopter pilot and every pilot of a B-52 that hits the wrong target and call him a murderer?" he asked. Senator Peter Dominick of Colorado attacked the broadcasters for interviewing someone who would obviously be a crucial witness in a murder trial. Widespread publicity would jeopardize Calley's right to a fair trial.

Meadlo was now completely disenchanted. Two days later he told a would-be interviewer he wanted money to talk: "I've already told my story. I feel I should be getting something out of it. I ain't talking to nobody now unless they pay."

Haeberle too decided there was cash to be earned. The day the *Plain Dealer* ran his pictures he and Eszterhas flew to New York and took a room at the Gotham Hotel in Manhattan. Bids were invited from media organizations for the rights to the color slides and Haeberle's own exclusive account of what happened in the village. The asking price was $100,000. One magazine editor said the pair must have known the photographs were the hottest property since the Zapruder film of President Kennedy's assassination. Eventually *Life* agreed to purchase the American rights in a deal that included hiring Eszterhas to work on the preparation of a ten-page layout. Separate deals were made with the London *Sunday Times* for $5,400 and *Stern* magazine in West Germany for $6,300. Time-Life eventually paid $19,550, and together with some ancillary fees from Sweden, Australia, and South Africa, the grand total came to $35,099.*

The publication of the photographs brought sharp criticism from the military judge appointed to oversee the Calley court-martial at Fort Benning. The hearings took place in Building 5, the rundown community service center across the pine-shaded street from the home of the base commander. The military defense counsel, Major Kenneth Raby, appointed to work alongside George Latimer, joined in a special plea with the prosecution to get a ban on interviews with witnesses. "All we are asking is that witnesses be allowed to come in court and testify first," he said, attacking the Army's General Counsel for having briefed reporters about the case the previous Friday. Capt. Aubrey M. Daniel, the prosecutor, said it was possibly the only time the two of them would agree in the case. The judge, Lieutenant Colonel Reid W. Kennedy, immediately ordered a ban on witness interviews, which was promptly ignored when several former members of Charlie Company told their stories. Charles West received several sums of $200 for talking to his local newspaper, the *Chicago Sun-Times* and other newspapers, magazines, and television companies. He and Ridenhour appeared together on a local CBS affiliate program, the *Chicago Show*; Raby said the selling of Haeberle's photographs meant the evidence in a case of mass murder had been auctioned.

Twenty years later the My Lai photographs bring Haeberle a steady income. Whenever they appear anywhere in the world he has to be paid a fee and thus continues to profit from the fact that he was present at the massacre, even though he did nothing to stop it and nothing to report it later.

In the Pentagon, the Army's congressional legislative liaison section was preparing briefings for the politicians on Capitol Hill. They began with the chairman and ranking minority members of the

---

* Eszterhas was subsequently dismissed from the *Cleveland Plain Dealer* in September 1971, after he wrote an article, "The Selling of the My Lai Massacre," in the *Evergreen Review*. He lost his appeal to be reinstated in binding arbitration in May 1972—see *New York Times* May 28, 1972, p. 6. Later, in 1991, he became one of the highest-paid screenplay writers in Hollywood, earning $3 million for his script *Basic Instinct*.

armed services and appropriations committees in the House of Representatives and the Senate. Now the Army itself was on trial. And in planning its defense the Army knew support from Congress was crucial. The Army, Navy, and Air Force went to great lengths not to alienate Senators and Congressmen, who traditionally support military spending programs.

My Lai, however, presented a different problem. Even friendly politicians were demanding to know the truth about the massacre. America's prestige was facing considerable damage at home and abroad. Countries around the world had condemned the atrocity. Journalists normally sympathetic to the interests of the United States labeled the massacre nauseating and inexcusable. Ronald Butt noted in the London *Sunday Times*: "If a fraction of the horror at Pinkville is proved, this military map reference will stand alongside Guernica, Hiroshima, and Sharpeville as one of the place names that have wholly changed the way that civilized men look at themselves." A significant number of senior politicians were already highly critical of the huge cost of the conflict in Southeast Asia in terms of loss of life and national resources. The antiwar movement at home was emerging as a powerful force that grew ever more hostile to government policy. In response to the political reaction at home, Nixon announced troop withdrawals, but the North Vietnamese had still not agreed to attend peace talks in Paris. The news of the massacre had come as a bombshell to the politicians, who every day were being bombarded with antiwar protests from constituents. The Army needed all the friends it had on Capitol Hill.

The job of sitting in the hot seat and taking the flak fell on the Secretary of the Army, Stanley Resor. Resor was widely respected. He was the only political appointee from Lyndon Johnson's presidency retained by Nixon. His senior officials warned him that if highly confidential information about the My Lai case was made public it would be a serious breach of Army regulations and of standards laid down by the Attorney General and the American Bar Association to avoid pretrial publicity. But the Army was facing accusations that it had covered up the murder of hundreds of civilians by GIs. Resor's staff reported to him in a confidential memorandum:

The testimony of witnesses, evaluated with available photography, strongly refutes any suggestion that C Company met ground resistance at My Lai 4 . . . It was clearly realized that no hostile action was directed at them. However, they continued to direct fire upon the hamlet and its unresisting civilian inhabitants. Testimony has consistently indicated that the victims were predominantly unarmed women and children; that they did not resist the combat force; that they were slain as they either fled the hamlet, sought refuge from assaulting small arms fire in huts and bunkers, or after they were collected into sizable controlled groups. And interpretation of the evidence assembled to date reveals that the number of victims at My Lai 4 totals about 350.

Resor was also told about "the possibility that the killing of noncombatants was known to responsible individuals and that efforts were made to conceal that information . . . That in addition to murder, other violations of the Uniform Code of Military Justice may have occurred at My Lai." However, the briefing paper drew back from mentioning that the "other violations" included wholesale rape, sodomy, and mutilations as Charlie Company rampaged through the village.

On November 26, Resor appeared in separate committee rooms in closed—confidential—hearings before the armed services committees of both the Senate and the House. The government was now under considerable pressure from powerful men wanting an inquiry into why the Army had waited so long to disclose the facts about My Lai. Resor announced that Lieutenant General William R. Peers was being appointed to head a small team to examine the adequacy of the original investigation. While Resor would not comment directly on the evidence in the case, he provided the committee with the known facts "about the tragic events that took place in the hamlet." He took them through the details, leaving out the fact that at least 350 civilians had been killed. The Henderson investigation, he said, was an extremely important and sensitive aspect of the case, which was why he and Westmoreland had decided a three-star general should hold an extra high-level inquiry. The Army had reviewed the case and was convinced the events in the hamlet were an isolated incident. "What apparently occurred at My Lai is wholly unrepresentative of the manner in which our forces conduct military operations in Vietnam," Resor said confidently.

The lights of the committee room were then darkened and a slide projector, operated by an Army technician, showed Haeberle's transparencies on a screen. Some of those present had seen the halftone pictures in the *Cleveland Plain Dealer* and fleetingly on television. But they were totally unprepared for what they now saw. The garish colours of the Kodak film gave the grisly photographs a shocking quality. The Senators stared in disbelief at unmistakable scenes of horrific butchery. The blood and gore of people blown apart by small arms fire turned stomachs as they looked at close-up pictures of bodies with their brains and intestines spilling out. When Resor crossed the Rotunda from the Senate to the House side of Congress to talk with the House committee members in secret session, there was the same stunned reaction. Republican Congressman Leslie C. Arends from Illinois found the sight of the carnage so awful he got up and left the room. "The pictures were pretty gruesome," he said afterward. "That's why I walked out. I can't take it, my stomach can't take it."

9. *Vietnam Revisited*

By the summer of 1969, a crucial shift had occurred in America's relationship with the South Vietnamese government. At a secret meeting in a Parisian apartment, Hanoi learned that the new US administration of Richard Nixon believed it no longer had an open-ended commitment to keep the anticommunist government of Nguyen Van Thieu, in Saigon, in power forever. The meeting had been called to emphasize to the North Vietnamese that Nixon sincerely wanted to find a formula to end the war in a manner that both sides would find acceptable. Hanoi interpreted this as a clear sign that its long struggle to liberate the whole of Vietnam would eventually succeed. It had only to keep up the pressure.

The US President was looking for a formula to extract America from an increasingly bloody and costly conflict without appearing to have capitulated. Any settlement had to produce "peace with honor." Nixon's predecessor, Lyndon Johnson, had started a war he was unable to finish; and on his very first day in office Nixon read with horror the daily cumulative totals of American casualties for 1968: 14,958 men killed and 95,798 wounded. Nixon had entered the White House full of optimism, with a vision of a new foreign policy for the United States, of building bridges with China as well as Moscow. But the Vietnam War was a huge obstacle in the way of these goals.

On March 12, 1969, Nixon's National Security Advisor, Dr Henry Kissinger, had sent a top secret memo—"National Security Study Memorandum 29"—to the secretaries of State and Defense and to the Director of Central Intelligence. It made clear that America's policy toward South Vietnam would soon be heading in a different direction. A new strategy was required to extricate the country from the Vietnamese quagmire.

In early April 1969, the new policy was ready: the war would be Vietnamized. American involvement would gradually be reduced; the South Vietnamese would take over the main role of prosecuting the conflict; and a start could be made on bringing home US troops. Secretary of Defense Melvin Laird was given overall responsibility for developing a plan that would put the South Vietnamese in the driving seat. Kissinger, in another highly secret memorandum, made clear that Laird should assume North Vietnamese as well as Viet Cong forces would continue fighting in South Vietnam. The starting date for the new policy was to be July 1, 1969, and it assumed that America would not be able to achieve a mutual withdrawal of forces with the North Vietnamese.

The official peace talks at the Majestic Hotel in Paris, begun during the Johnson administration, had completely stalled. By the time Nixon had moved into the White House these negotiations had come to nothing. Johnson had halted the bombing of the North and it had still not resumed. On August 4 secret talks with Hanoi were initiated by Kissinger to break the impasse—two days before the Pentagon informed the White House, through Kissinger's military aide, Col. Alexander Haig, that inquiries had confirmed mass executions by American troops at My Lai 4 and that a criminal investigation had been launched.

In the apartment of a former French diplomat and businessman, Jean Sainteny, overlooking the Tuileries Gardens in the Rue de Rivoli, Kissinger met with Xuan Thuy, a special advisor from the North Vietnamese foreign ministry in Hanoi, who had attended the unsuccessful peace talks. Sainteny had developed close links with the North Vietnamese as France's former delegate general in Hanoi. Kissinger's mission was to ensure that North Vietnam fully understood the new administration's desire to negotiate, providing both sides were willing to be flexible. He clearly spelled out to the North Vietnamese envoy for the first time America's willingness to shift away from its previously fixed position.

However, Kissinger's offer of negotiations to find a mutual path to peace was seen by Hanoi as a further sign of the USA's weariness with the war. Nixon had already reversed the previous administration's policy of sending reinforcements to South Vietnam and he was now committed to troop withdrawals, despite the private opposition of South Vietnam's President Nguyen Van Thieu. Nixon went ahead in June with an announcement of troop withdrawals and ignored the strong advice of the new MACV commander, Gen. Creighton Abrams. Typically, Nixon made it look as if the troop withdrawals had been Thieu's idea. Troops would be going home, he said, as a result of Thieu's recommendation and Abrams's assessment of the military situation. It was a lie, or in Nixon's terms a "diplomatic exaggeration." Thieu had been deeply troubled, realizing that the first American withdrawals would begin an irreversible process, the conclusion of which would be the departure of all Americans from Vietnam, as Nixon later admitted in his memoirs.

In a 45-minute monologue delivered at his Paris meeting with Kissinger, Xuan Thuy demanded Hanoi's total and absolute control over the South. President Thieu's removal from power was one of North Vietnam's preconditions for peace; the US Army had to leave; and a coalition government had to be established in Saigon.

Nixon found these conditions unacceptable because the noncommunist government in the South would be rendered impotent by the sudden and complete departure of US forces. Yet Kissinger's offer of a comprehensive peace plan in which the Viet Cong could stay in the South, following a deescalation of military operations, showed precisely where America was ultimately heading. Hanoi was prepared to bide its time, happy to see the United States continue its unilateral troop withdrawals. The North Vietnamese correctly read that Thieu's only chance of staying in power was to block any discussion of a coalition government involving the Communists in the South.

Nixon continued to leave the door to peace open to Hanoi, and as a sign of good faith the troop withdrawals continued. A further 40,000 GIs were scheduled to return by Christmas, making a total of 65,000 troops brought back since the summer.

It was against this background that the South Vietnamese government reacted to the first public news from America of a mass killing of unarmed civilians by US troops. Its attitude was uncompromising. It promptly denied there had been any massacre. An equally swift response came from the leader of the opposition,

Senator Tran Van Don, a retired general and former chief of staff and defense minister. The government's denial, he said, proved that Thieu was "the valet of the Americans, who are his sole support." Anxious not to hand a propaganda victory to the Viet Cong, Don—chairman of the South Vietnam Senate Defense Committee—said they would send their own investigators to the village to gather information.

The South Vietnamese authorities passed off the massacre as communist propaganda, just as they had done when local officials from Son Tinh district presented them with evidence of a large-scale atrocity the previous April. They ignored evidence of callous treatment of those living in areas controlled by the Viet Cong. This was nothing new. For several years government officials turned a blind eye to widespread civilian deaths throughout Quang Ngai Province. The additional news coverage caused by the of American reporters to My Lai 4 in response to Hersh's November 13 article, presented the South Vietnamese with few problems. Provincial administrators in Quang Ngai City offered soothing reassurances, despite the fact that villagers from My Lai 4 living in the nearby Truong An refugee camp at the foot of Elephant Hill had confirmed details of the massacre.

Government officials continued to claim that any civilians killed had been communists caught in the crossfire of an intense battle between American and Viet Cong forces. Either that or they were on the wrong end of artillery or helicopter gunship fire. Officials went to extraordinary lengths to play down the incident and portray a small number of civilian casualties as a mere accident of war, even though they were aware that US Army investigators already had confessions from members of Charlie Company admitting to a massacre. Faced with this direct evidence, the South Vietnamese officials persisted in arguing that the villagers had told lies in the hope that the Americans would pay them damages.

Col. Ton That Khien, the Quang Ngai province chief, wrote a secret and totally false report for President Thieu:

The communists boasted that the American Army killed women and children in order to claim they were communist regular casualties, the

VC propaganda creating hate among the populace toward the American Army in order to make the people forget their own hatred of the communists who rob and plunder and use the civilians as shields or as combat laborers for them.

When American reporters visited the village the local people told stories of many houses being burned and civilians killed because they hoped the Americans would compensate them for war damage.

Khien claimed to have organized an in-depth investigation when allegations of a massacre first arose eighteen months earlier. This was untrue. Khien was totally corrupt and had purchased the job of running the province from his previous position as chief of staff for the 2nd ARVN Division. He had already been the subject of two lengthy investigations by the Americans and had every reason to play down an atrocity. Before becoming province chief he had been accused of buying and selling both materiel and influence, though in the name of good relations the dossiers against him had been destroyed. It was also a matter of record that he had previously shown complete indifference to the peasants in the province because they had accepted Viet Cong control for so many years. Jesse Frosch, a military intelligence expert working in the province advisor's office in Quang Ngai, believed there was a simple explanation why Khien would ignore a massacre of his own people: "He did not want his highly lucrative financial operations sidetracked."

As senior figures in Washington, DC, heard the discomforting truth that more than 350 villagers had been murdered, government officials in South Vietnam gave the results of their own special investigation. They were able to confirm, beyond doubt, that only twenty-five civilians had been killed and five wounded. All but one of these casualties were from families who were communist supporters and whose children were active Viet Cong.

Lieutenant General Hoang Xuam Lam, the commanding general of ARVN's 1st Corps, conceived a bizarre explanation for the number of bodies seen in the village:

The people of Son My village have been under VC control since 1964 until August 1969. Therefore the large majority follow the communists. It can be said that the majority of those killed in the incident were communist cadre or agents. Moreover, after the battle in other areas, the VC intentionally brought all the corpses back to Son My to hold a propaganda ceremony to incite the people. For that reason we have been unable to find evidence to substantiate reports made by the people on numbers of people killed.

The worldwide explosion of publicity about the massacre caused the US Army's investigation to move into top gear. In late October, Feher had gone to South Vietnam to follow up inquiries. Then, in early December, a special CID task force was ordered to take over the entire investigation. The original team of three was swiftly increased as eight more CID investigators along with seven officers and a number of enlisted administrative personnel were assigned to the My Lai case. The number of former members of Charlie Company under serious investigation quickly increased to forty-six. The inquiry was widened still further when Feher uncovered strong evidence of a second massacre.

Resor's and Westmoreland's confident belief that My Lai was an isolated incident was now completely shattered. Questioning survivors of the atrocity, Feher discovered that, while Medina's men were rampaging through My Lai 4, another group of GIs from Bravo Company had been slaughtering ninety more civilians. It happened only a few miles away toward the coast, in a hamlet called Co Luy on an isthmus running beside the South China Sea. Feher found a woman from Co Luy being treated in the 91st Evacuation Hospital at Chu Lai. Nguyen Thi Bay, aged 46, had fled to Phi Tho in the Tu Nghia district of Quang Ngai. Shortly before Feher found her she was picked up as a Viet Cong suspect in a sweep by American troops. She told how thirty soldiers had come to Co Luy and started shooting, killing nearly 90 of the 100 people living in the hamlet. She took shelter with five others in an underground bunker. When the shooting stopped, American troops took her prisoner, holding her captive for two days while she was two months pregnant. She was repeatedly raped by two soldiers, causing a miscarriage. They later freed her and it was then she heard that more than three hundred villagers had also been killed in the neighboring village. Feher found two more women from Co Luy who made similar allegations.

The additional CID investigators who joined Feher immediately ran into problems when Vietnamese witnesses, who had earlier confirmed details about the massacre, suddenly changed their stories. The commanders of the task force were deeply concerned that South Vietnamese government denials were seriously obstructing attempts by the American investigators to uncover the truth. Gen. Abrams, the American Ambassador, and other senior US officials became involved. High-level negotiations took place involving a senior Army lawyer, Colonel Laurence H. Williams, from the Staff Judge Advocate's office at MACV headquarters and South Vietnam's Ministry of Defense. Williams took with him CID statements, Wilson's report for the Inspector General, and a copy of *Life* magazine, with its ten-page color spread of Haeberle's pictures, in an effort to convince the Vietnamese government of the truth. The Army was also anxious to clear the way for Lt. Gen. Peers to visit Vietnam as part of the separate top-level Pentagon inquiry into the coverup of the massacre by the 11th Brigade and the Americal Division. This would involve high-level interviews with senior government officials.

American investigators were faced with the bizarre situation of proving a massacre of Vietnamese civilians which their own government was saying never happened. Feher had traveled by helicopter to My Lai 4 in mid-November, two days after a group of reporters were escorted there. He spent the morning touring the village with an Army interpreter and Dennis Conti—a former member of Charlie Company's 1st Platoon, who had returned to Vietnam from a posting at the Hunter Army Airfield in Georgia and was stationed at Qui Nhon. Helping to retrace Charlie Company's passage through the village, Conti went unrecognized by two survivors who took Feher to the irrigation ditch and the trail site where hundreds of people had died. Do Hoia and Do Chuc pinpointed the mass graves. "The village was overgrown and deserted," Feher later recalled. "There was very little to see." The villagers had conducted a census of households and told Feher 370 people had been murdered. It was this revelation, relayed immediately back to Washington, which ensured that the investigation into what had happened at My Lai would have to be widened.

Villagers were shown enlargements of Haeberle's color pictures and the survivors quickly identified relatives and the exact location of the photographs. A former chief of the hamlet, Do Tan Nhon, 29, picked out his own daughter, Do Thi Kim Be, aged 7, as the terrified child wearing a white blouse, photographed seconds before her execution. The woman in the picture trying to protect her was his mother, Nguyen Thi Cung, aged 54. Nhon had been working away from the hamlet for the South Vietnamese authorities in Son Tinh when the massacre happened. He returned to learn the Americans had killed virtually everyone in the village.

Do Dinh Luyen, 41, the chief of Son My village, listened to this interview. He was one of the first to reveal to the authorities soon after the massacre that hundreds of villagers had been killed by American troops. But when Feher and his team returned to the village on November 25 to take formal statements, the Vietnamese accounts had changed. Nhon now denied there had been a massacre. Instead he claimed the villagers, including his mother and daughter, had been caught in the crossfire of a battle between Viet Cong and the Americans. The farmers who originally told him about the massacre, he said, were Viet Cong and had lied. Nhon appealed to Feher to halt the investigation. Even when told American troops had admitted their part in the massacre, he continued to insist it never happened. Luyen, the village chief, also accused the villagers of lying: "I am the village authority and what the farmers are saying I do not have any control over. They are not telling the truth."

Feher believed both men had been pressured by Vietnamese officials in Quang Ngai, who had sent Saigon reports completely at odds with his hard evidence of a major atrocity. When Feher briefed Colonel Nguyen Van Toan, the commander of the 2nd ARVN Division, he thought Toan appeared completely uninterested. At one point Toan more or less remarked: "So what? They were all Viet Cong." "It was as if to suggest the Americans were making a mountain out of a molehill," Feher later recalled.

It wasn't until mid-December that the Minister of Defense, General Vy, agreed to cooperate with the investigation. American pressure on Thieu resulted in a typical compromise. Without admitting they had been wrong, which would have involved considerable loss of face, the Vietnamese agreed that the deputy chief of cabinet in the Ministry of Defense, Colonel Do Tung, would accompany US Army investigators as an observer, acting as liaison with the Vietnamese authorities. It was a signal to everyone that the Vietnamese government now supported the Americans' investigation and that Col. Tung would inform all those the CID wanted to interview and make the necessary arrangements.

Meanwhile, the tracing and interrogation of former members of Charlie Company continued. Feher briefly traveled to South Korea to question a GI posted to the 2nd Infantry Division. He arrived at the CID offices in the 8th Army headquarters in Seoul to learn that Private Robert T'Souvas was in hospital suffering from a mysterious illness. T'Souvas was finally escorted to the interview the following day by a military police sergeant, Lewis Geis, who drove him into Seoul from their barracks 40 miles away. T'Souvas was not alert during the several hours it took to complete the interview and give his statement. Feher put it down to the fact the soldier was of low intelligence, unaware that T'Souvas was a habitual user of hard and soft drugs. Geis said nothing about the extraordinary journey into Seoul, when his passenger passed out several times and nearly tumbled out of his seat as the jeep sped along the main road into the city. The armed forces radio network announced over the vehicle's small loudspeaker that William Calley was due to face a court-martial in the United States for murdering civilians in South Vietnam. The radio reception was distorted. Geis couldn't hear the newscast properly, but T'Souvas apparently heard the platoon commander's name and asked whether Calley was the reason for the interview in Seoul. Geis said he didn't know.

During the interview with Feher, T'Souvas admitted the company had murdered four hundred unarmed civilians: "Just as if they had come to Seoul and started burning homes and killing people." He admitted himself shooting a girl aged about 15, among a group of five people. "She was sitting there completely torn apart," he explained. "I shot her to get her out of her misery." He killed four others who were wounded because they would not get medical treatment from the medics. He considered them "living dead."

T'Souvas, who refused the assistance of a military lawyer, thought he recognized the girl among a pile of bodies in one of Haeberle's photographs. "I wanted to talk about this for a long time and am glad now that it is off my chest," he said. "It is wrong. Even before it was investigated I wanted to write about it to my Senator, but I didn't know how to go about it."

At lunchtime Feher halted the interrogation and they took an hour-long break. Geis and T'Souvas walked to the Yongsan snackbar in the center of town and sat at a corner table about 20 feet from the door. T'Souvas, wearing an overcoat on top of his Class "A" uniform, remained subdued and complained of the cold. Geis tried to strike up a conversation and inquired about the Americal Division shoulder patch on T'Souvas's uniform, which was unfamiliar to him. T'Souvas immediately declared he had been at My Lai. He told the startled sergeant how he had killed five Vietnamese women and children, shooting them in the head and various parts of the body. Everyone in his platoon had gone completely berserk and started killing everything that moved. Geis asked if he had been on drugs. T'Souvas admitted smoking marijuana and taking pills for four or five years. After fifty minutes they finished their lunch and walked back to the CID office.

Two hours later the interrogation was over and T'Souvas signed a statement. As they prepared to make the hour-long drive back to their base Feher warned the military policeman that T'Souvas might be charged later. He should warn T'Souvas's platoon sergeant. During the drive back the passenger went over the details of the massacre again and again.

Because of his manner, facial expression, and general demeanor, Geis wondered whether T'Souvas was actually proud of what he had done. Geis began to wonder if he was safe driving him in the jeep or whether T'Souvas might go berserk and attempt to harm him, but he showed no signs of violence. He passed out several times, banging his head against the dashboard, drooling at the mouth. Geis struggled to keep control of the wheel. He stopped the vehicle, woke T'Souvas, and placed him in the rear seat. Soon his passenger fell into unconsciousness, and again Geis had to pull to a halt to wake him. He continued talking throughout the journey, trying desperately to keep the obviously sick passenger awake until they reached their base area. When they arrived, Geis immediately found T'Souvas's platoon sergeant and told him about his difficult journey. The NCO returned a few minutes later with a cloth armband which T'Souvas had worn on his uniform. Printed on it

were the words: "ASHAMED OF AMERICAL MURDER-
ERS."

T'Souvas spent the next five days recovering from a drug
overdose.

In Vietnam, the CID investigators faced a mammoth task. Over the
following few months they questioned more than a hundred witnesses
in Quang Ngai City, in Son My village, in refugee camps, and in
the prisoner-of-war enclosures at LZ Bayonet near Chu Lai. They
also talked to American civilians working for US government
agencies like AID and volunteer projects like the Vietnam Christian
Service. Every American they questioned claimed total ignorance of
the massacre—until the story broke in the newspapers.

Sgt Kenneth Hodges had been back in Vietnam for six months,
serving with another infantry battalion. He arrived in Saigon for
an interview with the CID task force just before noon on Christmas
Eve, and under questioning he denied seeing unarmed civilians
killed while leading the 2nd Platoon's first squad on the extreme
northern edge of My Lai 4. When the investigator brought up the
subject of rapes, Hodges fell silent, declining to answer any questions about sexual assaults in the tiny subhamlet of Binh Tay, to
the north of My Lai 4.

Army investigators questioning Vietnamese peasants had to learn
quickly the social anthropology of life in remote villages. They
were soon confronted with the realities of applying the strict rules
of evidence required by the American system of military justice to a
people living simple lives with no concept of maps, of time, or of
the difference between what they witnessed themselves and what
others had told them. To live in Son My village, even though it
was only 10 miles from the bustling environment of Quang Ngai
City, was to live in virtual cultural isolation. There had been no
school in the area until very recently and total illiteracy was the
rule rather than the exception for everyone other than adolescents.
The villagers also spoke a corrupted form of Vietnamese peculiar
to that tiny region of the Central Highlands; CID interpreters had
difficulty understanding them and frequently got facts wrong
which, when cross-checked, then had to be verified several times.
To please the investigators the villagers often said what they

thought the investigators would like them to say, which was how they dealt with all authority figures. Many had only an approximate idea of their own ages, and few records were kept. The only way they could conceive of time was through the position of the sun above the horizon. They had no concept of standard units of measurement for time or distance. Compass bearings meant nothing to them; sketch maps confused them. Often their insularity meant they knew only the details of their own family or very near neighbors, but nothing about villagers living only 50 or 60 meters away.

There was also confusion over names among the large extended families throughout Son My village. Frequently the investigators found that witnesses did not know their own given names but instead referred to themselves by nicknames or unofficial names commonly used throughout their lives. So when the CID talked to parents they were provided with names of their children and grandchildren at variance with those recorded in statements given by other people. Distant relatives might know a child by one name, close relatives by another.

Some women had two husbands still living; one or both might have been absent from the village for a considerable time. Some of their children bore one name, some another. Many Vietnamese men had two wives, one often considerably younger than the first who other residents thought of as the daughter of the head of a household, rather than a second wife; children of second wives they labeled grandchildren, rather than sons or daughters.

André Feher's upbringing in the Dutch East Indies and his later Army posting to Thailand with the CID gave him a valuable understanding of the cultural chasm his colleagues found in Southeast Asia. Sent in advance of the task force to brief Gen. Abrams about the investigation at MACV HQ, Feher frequently traveled alone throughout the country interviewing witnesses, and tracking down documents from the files of the Americal Division and the 11th Brigade. He searched daily logs, journals, and POW records. Two young CID trainees working with him proved completely out of their depth and he asked Washington for a more experienced investigator to join him.

Wayne Thorne, from Hawk Price Mountain, Alabama, had been

Feher's clerk typist in Washington, and had then trained as a criminal investigator. He and Feher were billeted in a compound in Quang Ngai City which had previously been a school and was shared with the province advisory team and the special forces. The other Americans in the compound took little interest in their inquiries. Feher and Thorne occasionally met them in their club for a drink. Many were initially skeptical about the massacre, though most of them had arrived in Vietnam long after it happened. In Quang Ngai City, Feher briefly met the former senior province advisor, James May, who kept referring to the massacre as an "alleged incident." After the third time Feher stopped him and said: "Look, there's nothing alleged about it. I've got sixty-three affidavits from soldiers who were there in my briefcase plus photographs in combat."

Feher and Thorne conducted their interviews with the Vietnamese in a detention center where former Viet Cong who had switched sides and taken advantage of the "Chieu Hoi" program were held. Vietnamese officials in Quang Ngai seemed totally uninterested in the American investigation. "I could not help but feel that they did not care one way or the other what had happened at My Lai," Feher said later:

Maybe they were masters at hiding their emotions and feelings. One thing that amazed me was that none of the Vietnamese I talked to during the investigation ever condemned the Americans' action at My Lai. In the detention center the officials were only interested in the rehabilitation and reeducation of their prisoners and paid us little attention. They never engaged us in conversation about My Lai.

Several small rooms were allotted to them around a small square inside the compound. Thorne's job was to type up statements as the interpreter translated replies to Feher's questions. He knew his chief's way of working so well that during an interview he frequently found himself anticipating Feher's next question. Each interviewee was photographed with a Polaroid camera to help with later identification of witnesses. Many villagers had never seen photographs of themselves. To break the ice, Thorne occasionally produced a second Polaroid for them to keep and had a souvenir picture of himself taken with Do Chuc, a 48-year-old farmer, who had been with a large group of villagers shot dead on the trail. Do Chuc survived after being shot in the leg and later helped bury the dead in mass graves.

Other witnesses began to identify more of the murdered victims from Haeberle's photographs. One scene showed a pile of bodies killed on the main trail. The former Viet Cong security agent, Truong Ngu, picked out his tiny daughter, Truong Thi Thu. Near her lay his niece, Truong Thi Bi, aged 13. He discovered their corpses when he returned to the village and was able to identify Thu from the photograph because she had been in the same position, lying face down, her buttocks exposed. His wife and mother had also been among those killed. Truong Ngu had joined the Viet Cong soon after the massacre and for eighteen months was the third member of the hamlet's security cell with security chief Nguyen Co and his assistant Truong Qui. He continued living in Son My and had returned to My Lai 4 to gather wood at the time American engineers began to survey the village for the criminal investigation. He was quickly captured and interrogated and began giving a detailed picture of life in the village before the massacre. He showed investigators where he had found his family, the sites of mass graves, and the rough location of where each of Haeberle's photographs had been taken. He helped the engineers construct a sketch showing the location of all the homes he could remember and then gave details of which family members survived and those who perished.

This evidence was cross-checked with another VC prisoner, Do Vien, the hamlet's propaganda chief. He had been captured while planting his crops in the paddy fields a few days before and was being held in the POW cage at LZ Bayonet near Chu Lai. When investigators showed him Haeberle's black-and-white and color photographs he was able to identify many of the figures. In a picture of a group of women and children taken just before they were killed he recognized the child held in the arms of his sister, Do Thi Cang, aged 23. It was his son, Do Hat, aged 6. The woman in the red shirt at the front, he said, was a merchant from the neighboring village of Son Hoa, called Ba So, aged 50, who had been selling fish sauce.

*

The CID investigation was heavily geared to discovering who exactly was involved in the massacre and producing hard evidence to sustain convictions. By the time the investigators finished they were able to pinpoint the routes each platoon had taken through My Lai. Army engineers spent a week surveying the village, producing a large-scale topographical map and a detailed plan of the 105 houses in the village. All Haeberle's photographs, color and black-and-white, were treated as forensic evidence. Magnified, some of the pictures showed the unit emblems on the liftships and gunships which ferried Charlie Company to My Lai. More interviews were then held with helicopter crews who had flown over the area on the day of the assault or who had been told about the massacre by Thompson when he returned to his base. Using engineers' maps, and by walking over the killing ground several times, the investigators, led by Maj. Thomas McGreevy, pinpointed exactly where each picture was taken. Eventually Haeberle's route through My Lai 4 and the locations where he took his photographs were mapped out on a large chart. The pictures were minutely examined to pinpoint particular features—for example, the corner of a building that remained standing after the demolition teams had been at work. Even a chunk of a large bamboo tree was sent back to laboratories in the United States for examination.

Although the pictures could not point to who killed particular individuals, through a process of identification and elimination investigators had a rough idea who was involved. They narrowed down those involved in shooting the group of women and children photographed by Haeberle seconds before their execution. The evidence pointed to two individuals from the 3rd Platoon. There were enough witnesses; at least six GIs had watched them open fire. Simpson had examined Haeberle's pictures and identified three of his own victims, picking out a photograph of a couple with a child: Nguyen Gap, aged 50, his wife, Truong Thi Huyen, aged 45, and their 6-year-old son, Nguyen Tan. Some of those photographed had survived. An elderly man, Truong Chau, aged 80, and his grandchildren, Ge (2) and Duc (4), now living in Saigon, were identified from the pictures. A search immediately began to find them but without success. Mot Lai (80)—discovered in a house by Medina's interpreter, Sgt Phu, and photographed with the company medic present—had perished.

The identification of Mot Lai's house when plotted on the map helped investigators follow Medina's exact movements through the village. They could trace the path he took from the time he shot the woman in the paddy field until his meeting in the late afternoon with the platoon commanders on the eastern side of the village. The evidence confirmed his story that he had not seen the ditch full of bodies—he had passed 100 yards to the north of the execution site as he left the village in the late afternoon. But there was conclusive proof that he was lying when he denied having seen piles of bodies on the main trail. Haeberle had photographed him among his command group as they took a lunch break. When the print was enlarged several times he was identified by the captain's bars on his camouflaged helmet. At the scene where Carter had shot himself in the foot, Medina was pictured in the background radioing for a dust-off chopper. Since the photographs were taken in sequence, Medina had to have crossed the trail at a particular point and must have seen the piles of bodies all around him, despite his continued denials.

Thirty-four survivors gave the CID investigators statements which identified particular individuals from Haeberle's photographs. Most recognized the same victims, but their testimony helped to establish the credibility of their story. Do Vien's interview was conducted over two and a half days. As the leading member of the information committee in the hamlet, he knew most of the people and where they lived. By the time he had finished and his information was checked and cross-checked with other survivors, the Army's detectives knew the names of 343 of Charlie Company's victims and where they had perished.

10. The Judgment of Peers

On New Year's Day, 1970, Hugh Thompson unexpectedly found himself back in a helicopter in South Vietnam, flying as copilot over the village of My Lai 4 on a low-level reconnaissance. Sitting in the observer's seat was the three-star general appointed to investigate mounting evidence of a coverup of the My Lai massacre by senior officers in the 11th Brigade and the Americal Division. Flying at treetop height, Thompson indicated the positions of the bodies he had seen and where he had landed to confront Calley. He and the general then flew down to the Tra Khuc River mouth for a wider perspective of the Pinkville area and to observe the ground covered by Task Force Barker's mission during those three March days nearly two years before.

Lt. Gen. William R. Peers specifically asked for the young pilot to join his inquiry team for the twelve-day trip to Vietnam. Accompanying them were ten other Army personnel and two top trial lawyers from New York who had been assigned as civilian counsel, sitting in on all interrogations. Thompson was happy to escape to Vietnam. For six weeks he had been in the limelight. His Army life, and actions in Vietnam, had been raked over and minutely examined by both the media and the rash of investigations being mounted into what was now being officially called the My Lai "incident." The word "massacre" was being actively discouraged by government and Army spokesmen. The media duly obliged.

In mid-November, Pentagon sources leaked the fact that Thompson and his crew had received medals for their part in the rescue of civilians at My Lai 4. After being given the broad details, reporters demanded to see the public record, quickly discerning that that the citations glossed over the fact that the "enemy on the ground" were American troops. Reporters pursued Thompson vigorously at Fort Rucker, Alabama, where he was instructing new pilots.

Summoned to Washington, DC, Thompson appeared before a special closed hearing of the House Armed Services Committee and received a severe mauling by Congressmen anxious to play down allegations of a massacre by American troops. It was a nerve-racking experience for him. Chief among his critics was the committee's chairman, Mendell Rivers, who was regarded as a good friend by the Pentagon for his staunch positions on national security issues and support of the armed forces.

However, when Thompson appeared before Peers's inquiry panel soon afterward he found an altogether different reception. Peers was impressed that Thompson had kept his integrity and hadn't been afraid to show that he knew right from wrong. He regarded Thompson's actions as the only good thing to come out of the bleak and depressing picture of My Lai that was slowly unfolding before him. The pilot had kept alive Peers's faith in the American soldier. He demanded that Thompson travel with him to Vietnam, and he took the young warrant officer under his wing.

Peers's inquiry team was received at Tan Son Nhut Airport, Saigon, on December 28, in the manner of a traveling potentate and his accompanying entourage. News reporters were out in force, and at an impromptu press conference Peers introduced the two lawyers on his team—Robert MacCrate, aged 50, and Jerry Walsh, a brilliant young trial attorney who had his own law office in New York City.

In Saigon, Peers went on a series of courtesy visits, including one to Theodore Shackley, the CIA station chief at the American Embassy. Two years earlier, during the Tet Offensive, Viet Cong commandos had tried to storm the embassy's CIA annex, a group of Quanset huts known as the "Norodom complex." The commandos were machine-gunned to death by a marine guard before they could reach their target. The Agency operated from the top three of the embassy's six floors. It had six hundred CIA personnel working in South Vietnam, the largest concentration of administrative staff, agent runners, and case officers outside its headquarters at Langley, Virginia.

Over lunch at the CIA station the day after his return to

Vietnam, Peers met up with Joseph E. Lazarsky, an old friend from his World War II days when he commanded an OSS guerrilla army called Detachment 101 behind the Japanese lines in northern Burma. They had only met twice since the war and Lazarsky was now the deputy chief of the CIA station. The next night, Lazarsky invited Peers back for dinner to the apartment he rented from the Standard Vacuum Oil Company near the cathedral, five blocks away from the embassy compound.

In the jungles of Burma, Detachment 101 had operated much the same way the Viet Cong were doing now. They also suffered many hardships. Peers occasionally told friends about the perils of leeches. While a colleague was asleep a leech had slithered into the tube of his penis. "When he awoke it was swollen to the point where he could not urinate," said Peers, describing the incident later. "It was becoming extremely painful and there seemed nothing they could do to remove the leech. When the pain became most excruciating he was actually thinking of gouging it out with a knife." Finally they constructed a forceps-shaped instrument from bamboo and pulled the leech out.

Lazarsky had learned of Peers's impending trip to Vietnam from a senior intelligence officer at MACV headquarters, a complex of bunkers five miles from the center of Saigon near the airport. It was a period when the agency was beginning to move away from running the huge CORDS pacification and antiterror programs. The commitment to hand over the running of the war to the South Vietnamese would in the long term mean a contraction of CIA personnel. Case officers strove to develop undercover spies among the communist forces but also concentrated on recruiting agents among the higher echelons of South Vietnam's government and armed forces. The CIA needed to ensure a stable political regime in Saigon if America was to hand over the war effort successfully.

Shackley and Lazarsky had little information to offer Peers. Privately they shared some of the Vietnamese concerns and believed the Army was making a lot of fuss about a relatively minor incident in the war. "While my colleagues in Saigon were not overly shocked by the My Lai incident when it first became public, they were concerned that too much was being made out of too little," Lazarsky later recalled.

*

Peers divided his Vietnamese investigation into two teams of inter-rogators. Peers and MacCrate interviewed a number of high-ranking Vietnamese officials, while Walsh probed the circumstances of Bravo Company's assault on the hamlet of Co Luy. Another team began poring over records. In Washington, DC, they had already taken testimony from Henderson and Koster, and Peers urgently wanted to locate copies of the formal investigation into civilian deaths at My Lai, which both men had said existed. He left behind his deputy, Bland West, to continue interviewing additional witnesses. West, a retired JAG colonel working on the staff of the Secretary of the Army as an assistant general counsel, was an able, sophis-ticated, and experienced staff officer, the perfect complement to Peers.

A priority on Peers's agenda in Vietnam was a visit to My Lai itself. No effort was spared by the Army in its preparations for his team and four other groups to tour the area in early January. A schedule was organized so the differing interests didn't trip over each other. The CID continued its investigation; a team of eighteen engineers wanted to map the hamlet, listing every house, pathway, and irrigation ditch; the press was badgering to go to the scene once more; and a group of Army lawyers, including the military prosecutor and defense counsel in the Calley court-martial, had arrived to examine Vietnamese witnesses and make an inspection of the killing ground.

For nearly two weeks around the turn of the year, My Lai 4 resembled a small American fire base. Nothing was left to chance. A special task force from the 198th Brigade moved in first to secure the area. It included a company of infantry, a troop of cavalry in armored personnel carriers, a reconnaissance platoon, a platoon of engineers, and mine-sniffing dogs and combat tracker teams. A perimeter was established around the entire village using barbed wire and bunkers. Pierced steel planking for a helicopter pad large enough for a Huey was brought in and several fortified bunkers were erected as shelter for visitors. The road from Quang Ngai—Route 521—leading to and from the village was closed. Check-points were set up by Vietnamese national and field police to control civilian traffic and all official visitors to the village had to enter and leave by helicopter. A pathfinder team controlled air movements and helicopters paused only long enough to disgorge their passengers.

Five helicopters from the air cavalry, including two gunships and one with an armed security team on board, flew overhead when Peers and eight of his team spent three hours in the village on the morning of January 3. The two interpreters who had been with Charlie Company on March 16, Sergeants Phu and Minh, took Peers around the village. That afternoon he questioned the ARVN officer, Lt. Tan, about his reports of the massacre when he was the Son Tinh district chief. The next day Thompson again flew his mentor over the area on a second air reconnaissance, a move strongly opposed by local commanders, but the general got his way. Peers had formed a strong liking for Thompson and his confidence in him demonstrated his approval of the pilot's strong moral courage. "He was very proud of Thompson," Jerry Walsh said later of the visit to My Lai. "He may have only been a high school boy from Georgia but he knew right from wrong and acted on it."

Close interest was shown in Washington and Saigon in the progress of Peers's investigation. Long signals were sent back to Washington. Among those kept informed on a regular basis was the MACV commander, Creighton Abrams, who was anxious to ensure that the Army acquitted itself well in the eyes of the watching world. Every move Peers made, every facility provided to him, every witness he or his team examined, was noted and recorded by his hosts and transmitted to the Pentagon, where a special team monitored the My Lai investigations for the Army's General Staff. The team's prime purpose was to coordinate requests for information from Congress and the White House. The same group reported to Westmoreland every day on Peers's progress in Vietnam.

Before leaving Vietnam, Peers had one last meal with his wartime colleague Lazarsky in Saigon, but he remained tight-lipped about his mission. Despite the CIA's reservations about the inquiry's purpose, Lazarsky was convinced there would be no coverup of the coverup. "If they wanted a whitewash then they definitely chose the wrong man," he said later. "Peers was intellectually honest and had high moral principles. I knew very well if a case could be made that a crime had been committed, Peers would spare no one, regardless of rank. There was very little gray area with Ray—it was one or the other, black was black and white was white."

One man who wanted to avoid a full inquiry into how the events at My Lai had remained a dark secret for so long was President Nixon. His advisors had been appalled by the political damage they anticipated would be caused by the revelations of a massacre. Whereas Westmoreland and Resor argued for a full inquiry, senior White House officials were anxious to let the matter drop. When Westmoreland learned of this obstruction from Alexander Haig, he threatened to exercise his prerogative as a member of the Joint Chiefs to go straight to the President and object. "That squelched any further pressure for a whitewash," he recorded in his memoirs.

His choice of Ray Peers to head the My Lai inquiry rested on two simple facts. Firstly, he was available. Stationed in the Pentagon and living with his wife in nearby general officers' quarters at Fort Myer, Virginia, he was chief of the Army's reserve forces and national guard. Consequently Peers had no direct command. More important was the fact that he was not a West Point graduate and thus could not be accused of coming under the influence of the fraternity of officers from the academy, a familiar criticism by non-West Pointers when decisions failed to go their way.

Another factor was Peers's reputation for fairness and objectivity as a commanding general in Vietnam. This was particularly important for Army morale if the rest of the officer corps was to believe the General Staff was not indulging in a witchhunt. When in subsequent months he made speeches throughout the country, particularly to military audiences, Westmoreland stressed the complete impartiality of the inquiries into the My Lai allegations. He continually emphasized the Army's respect for the due process rights of anyone accused of offenses arising out of "what was alleged to have happened" at My Lai.

Peers originally expected his investigation would last six weeks. He anticipated they would question only forty witnesses in the offices assigned to the inquiry, the small but secure Army operations center in a windowless basement of the Pentagon, two floors below ground level. The inquiry team met for the first time on November 27—three days after Westmoreland asked

Peers formally to take on the job. Peers had requested a small staff of thirteen, anticipating their work would be completed early in the New Year. But when he returned from Vietnam his investigation suddenly took off in a completely new direction. The number of Army personnel working on the project rapidly expanded until nearly eighty officers, enlisted men, and civilian staff were working full time against the tight deadline. The inquiry report had to be completed by March 14 because of the statute of limitations which covered the type of military offenses they were considering.

Peers now knew the coverup went far wider than a few junior officers at the lower end of the chain of command. He also knew that his team had only skimmed the surface of what had actually happened at Pinkville. As a result of Feher's and Walsh's inquiries in Vietnam, Peers was also convinced a second massacre occurred during Bravo Company's assault on My Khe. Following this new revelation, Resor and Westmoreland had little choice but to approve Peers's request for his terms of reference to be widened to include events that occurred throughout the whole of Son My village, including the hamlets of My Lai, My Khe, and Co Luy. Peers was determined to find out exactly what happened on March 16, 1968, as a precursor to deciding who had covered up the massacre.

He had deflected one oblique attempt to prejudge his inquiry in mid-December. He and Robert MacCrate had appeared together before the House Armed Services Committee, to answer questions about the scope of the investigation. Peers told them that, irrespective of the rank or position of any of the people involved in his inquiry, the chips would fall where they might. Their reception had been friendly and cordial. As Peers was leaving the room, the committee's chairman, Mendell Rivers, approached and invited him to a pre-breakfast meeting in his office.

When Peers arrived at the Rayburn Building two days later at 7:00 AM, his footsteps echoed along its vast, empty corridors as he walked to Rivers's office. The place was like a morgue, but even at that hour he found the committee chairman already hard at work, his desk covered in papers. Throughout their conversation Peers detected an effort to throw doubt in his way. Rivers mentioned the difficulty of soldiers being able to tell a VC if he was hidden among the local population, which was stating the obvious to someone like Peers who had only recently returned from commanding a division in Vietnam. As they discussed My Lai, Rivers's whole attitude was "that our boys would never do anything like that."

Peers was taken aback. He couldn't figure out whether this was a roundabout invitation to a whitewash or whether Rivers was really saying the allegations had been falsely reported. Peers spelled out some of the truths he had already learned about the massacre and left Rivers in no doubt that a large number of civilians had been killed in circumstances that could not be justified. The meeting never descended into acrimony and must have had an effect on Rivers, who, ten days later, directed a subcommittee under the chairmanship of Congressman F. Edward Hebert to explore the My Lai incident fully.

Hebert took this instruction at face value and demanded from the Army everything it had on My Lai—including all the evidence being scrutinized by Peers's panel. When all the witnesses and documents the subcommittee wanted were not forthcoming, there was a series of furious outbursts from Hebert, a Louisiana Congressman normally sympathetic to the Army. The Army was anxious not to jeopardize the future trials of My Lai suspects, but Hebert, keen to protect the integrity of his subcommittee, privately warned Westmoreland on several occasions he would not tolerate withholding any witnesses or documents:

We are going to get the witnesses, period . . . Don't force us to do what we don't want to do [the issuing of subpoenas] . . . We're right on the edge of a revolt . . . If this ever breaks out in the newspapers it will be a horrible mess. Mutual friends are putting pressure on me to hold a press conference . . . If I don't get these answers, I can't stop it . . . I sent a short, simple letter over there [to the Pentagon] and asked two simple questions and I get a lot of malarkey back instead of answers.

To a considerable extent Westmoreland shielded Peers from these concerns, although as head of the inquiry Peers occasionally met privately with Hebert to brief him. It was politic not to upset an influential member of Congress. Peers's main concern was his inquiry. It totally absorbed every waking hour. Throughout his life, firstly as a keen sportsman and then as a soldier, Peers was fiercely competitive. He was grimly determined to get to the truth about My Lai, no matter what. From the very beginning he knew it was a job that would earn him few friends.

Initially he resisted the civilian lawyers, MacCrate and Walsh, being imposed on him by Resor. He hadn't wanted them looking over his shoulder, raising questions that he thought might muddy the waters and slow down the inquiry. But Peers and MacCrate had a private meeting in the office of Thaddeus R. Beal, undersecretary of the Army, which broke the ice. He knew then they would work well together. A former naval reservist, MacCrate had served as law secretary to a Supreme Court judge for the state of New York, Justice David W. Peck, and from 1959 to 1962 had been Governor Nelson Rockefeller's counsel. It was the calm and reserved MacCrate who brought in Jerry Walsh. The tall lawyer from Kansas had left MacCrate's law firm of Sullivan & Cromwell a few years previously to go off on his own.

Although Peers admired MacCrate's brilliant mind and devastating skills at cross-examination, he formed a closer relationship with Walsh, who at 37 was nearly twenty years his junior. Walsh was a forceful and dynamic Irish-American with a good sense of humor, which matched that of the cigar-chewing general. They enjoyed a joke and a drink together and soon became close friends. The general regaled the young lawyer with stories from his military career. Walsh himself had served in the Army in the 1950s and was a platoon leader with the 82nd Airborne Division. In their private moments the three-star general told Walsh he still regarded himself as "a poor boy." Walsh could see Peers was a man clearly influenced by the hardships he endured as a child. He didn't just like cigars; he liked *big* cigars.

All three—MacCrate, Walsh, and Peers—shared a basic philosophy of sorts, a fundamental belief in truth as an absolute; they didn't think it possible to be just a little bit dishonest. Peers's belief that MacCrate and Walsh shared his view that white was white and black was black made them far easier to work with. Throughout his military career, Peers, while no intellectual, had little time for what he thought of as fuzzy thinking. It was a side of his character that did not always make him easy to get on with—not least for his own family.

Peers, like Walsh, originated from the Midwest. He was born in Stuart, Iowa, in June 1914. During the Depression his father moved the family to southern California to start a new life. At the age of 11 Ray Peers and his brother went to live with their mother in Covina, just outside Los Angeles, when his parents divorced. She remarried but was later killed in a tragic car accident. Ray Peers was unofficially adopted by the parents of his closest school friend in Covina. An all-round sportsman, Peers played football, rugby, and wrestled. He graduated from the College of Education at UCLA in 1937. Peers joked with Walsh that he joined the Army because it was the best job he could find at the time. In fact Army life suited his personality and general outlook. When he graduated he served as a reserve officer at the Presidio in San Francisco and in July 1938 the Army gave him a regular commission.

A year after the United States' entry into World War II, Peers was recruited into the Office of Strategic Services by an old Army friend and sent to North Burma with Detachment 101, initially as an operations and training officer, planning guerrilla missions, espionage, and sabotage. He was trained at a secret spy school—Camp B, in the Catoctin Mountains of Maryland, 70 miles from Washington. It was here that Peers first met Joe Lazarsky, who was one of the instructors. In Burma, Detachment 101 established a network of underground spies, saboteurs, and informers; they pinpointed Japanese positions and launched violent hit-and-run raids, constantly throwing the enemy off balance. Their aim was to help Gen. "Vinega" Joe Stilwell punch a path through Burma and into China. In 1943 Peers took over command, staying with Detachment 101 until July 1945, when he was switched to the China theater. As the commander of all OSS operations in China south of the Yangtze River, he organized and dispatched rescue teams to find US prisoners held in Japanese POW camps in China and North Korea, and led a Chinese parachute-commando unit into Nanking to occupy the city before the armistice.

His official record shows that in mid-1949 Peers was transferred to the CIA, where he planned and implemented the agency's first training program. Two years later, during the Korean War, he worked with Army intelligence at a classified overseas location. In fact, he was deeply involved in covert operations against mainland China, secretly training Nationalist Chinese guerrillas for operations on mainland China from a base in Chiang Kai-shek's island fortress of Formosa, now Taiwan, and in regrouping into a fighting force Chinese nationals who had escaped into northern Burma. In the early 1950s a number of incursions were mounted against Chinese troops from Burma, exactly the kind of work at which Peers had excelled against the Japanese.

During this period Peers faced another tragedy in his life. In 1947, immediately after the birth of their second daughter, his wife, Barbara, developed an infection of the pericardium, the tissue surrounding the heart. The infection lingered for several years and in 1952 she died while Peers was overseas. Within a year of his wife's death, Peers met and married his second wife, Rose Mary Rau. He knew he had found a woman who would both make him happy and be a good mother to his two girls. But always there was the Army and the next posting. At times, to his family, it always seemed he had things on his mind more important than they were. It could prove difficult.

His period at the Army War College after returning from China signaled Peers as a high flier. The next ten years saw him in a variety of staff jobs connected with intelligence and strategic planning. At the onset of the Vietnam War he was at the Pentagon, assistant deputy chief of staff for special operations; the next year he moved to the Office of the Joint Chiefs, where he was special assistant for counterinsurgency and special activities. Then, in January 1967, as a two-star general, he took over the 4th Infantry Division in the Central Highlands of South Vietnam. Fourteen months later he was promoted to command 1 Field Force with 50,000 US combat troops under his direct control, also coordinating four Vietnamese and two Korean divisions. The poor boy from Stuart, Iowa, had won his third general's star.

Peers's military philosophy as a field commander in Vietnam followed closely Stilwell's in Burma: find the enemy and destroy them. The Viet Cong guerrillas were using the same tactics he used twenty-five years before and he thought he knew what it took to beat them. "It takes small patrols, ambushes, tight security, you've got to beat him on his own ground," said Peers, describing his tactics while commander of the 1 Field Force, headquartered in Nha Trang. The strategy for dealing with the North Vietnamese regulars was different. The NVA operated more formalized battle tactics, similar to those of the Japanese—full-frontal banzai-style attacks. In several small-scale operations and two major set-piece battles his troops took them on and won. The first major battle was in the Highlands close to the Cambodian border in November 1967, at Dak To; the second success was at Duc Lap in August 1968: two battles where the odds were heavily in the enemy's favor. "They were out to win," Peers commented. "But so were we . . . we gave them a terrible mauling."

His style of command was to take problems to his staff for solving—rather than the other way round. "My job is one of rechecking to see if the problems have been solved satisfactorily," he observed. Peers's directions and questions were delivered in a concise, almost curt, manner with no possibility for misunderstanding. He spent much of his time traveling to every district within the Vietnamese II Corps region. He found little time for relaxation in Vietnam. Often at night, he wrote terse memos with a red felt-tip pen; their sharp tone caused his staff officers to label them, jokingly, "bloodstains."

Peers had seen much suffering during his military career but nothing prepared him for the personal anguish he endured during the My Lai investigation. There was absolutely nothing gray about either the massacre or its coverup. His acute sense of right and wrong left no room for doubt about a soldier's duty in a given situation. Charlie Company's actions could not be excused—neither could the behavior of people in the chain of command who knew something had gone wrong, whether or not they had precise knowledge of its scope. He was appalled by the killings with their overtones of grotesque ritualistic murder and sexual savagery. Everywhere he looked he could see flagrant breaches of the Army's rules, bad leadership, lies, and a deliberate conspiracy to cover up war crimes. He had known most of the commanders in Vietnam and had assumed they enforced the rules as rigidly as he did. He believed the United States had a moral obligation under the Hague and Geneva conventions to guarantee to safeguard noncombatants and to protect prisoners. If war crimes had been committed, then those responsible should be brought to proper justice. Some people had referred to the killing of 3,000 civilians in Hue by the Viet Cong during the Tet Offensive as if it somehow minimized Charlie Company's actions at My Lai, as if there could be any moral equivalence where mass murder was concerned. For Peers the important point was that America was supposed to represent civilized values; this was why it was fighting the war. But the regulations were only as good as the men prepared to enforce them.

The investigation, with all its complexities, took over his life. Six days a week he was at his desk early. The first of the morning meetings to review the previous day's testimony and plan the interrogation of new witnesses began at eight o'clock. His driver picked him up to return to Fort Myer for dinner with Rose Mary at 8 PM. MacCrate and Walsh usually took a short break for a meal and then returned to pore over the paperwork once more, frequently burning the midnight oil. On Saturday afternoons they dashed down the parkway to National Airport and took the late shuttle to New York, returning on the first plane back to Washington on Monday morning.

The full implications of what had happened during and after the massacre crept up on Peers. The day Westmoreland asked him to take the job he read Ridenhour's letter and initially refused to accept that the allegations were true. "I have to say quite frankly that I didn't believe his letter when I first read it," he said several years later. "I did not believe that this thing could have happened, but after I got into the inquiry and found that what he was saying was quite true, I ended up with a great deal of admiration for Ridenhour."

Several interrogation teams operated simultaneously in different basement rooms because the inquiry had to complete its work under a tight deadline. The offenses of negligence and dereliction of duty under the Uniform Code of Military Justice were covered by a two-year statute of limitations. This meant Peers's report had to be submitted by March 16, 1970, the day before if charges were to be laid. Then it was realized the international dateline meant

Washington, DC, was a day behind Vietnamese time. The deadline now was March 14.

By the end of the inquiry more than four hundred witnesses had been questioned and 20,000 pages of testimony taken. Hundreds of documents and photographs had been pored over. Witnesses were asked to take the interrogators through the route they had traveled with reference to the huge engineers' maps adorning the interview rooms. On some days as many as twelve witnesses were questioned. Peers headed one team of interrogators interviewing officers in the chain of command, while Bland West concentrated on members of Charlie Company. Jerry Walsh and Col. William Wilson, whom Peers drafted on his team because of the detailed knowledge he gathered during his Inspector General's inquiry, questioned nearly sixty members of Bravo Company in an effort to get to the truth about Co Luy.

During "B" Company's assault on the coastal hamlet, a platoon commander had been killed and seven men wounded by land mines. Walsh and Wilson centered their inquiries on the activities of the 1st Platoon, led by Lieutenant Thomas K. Willingham. Many in the company had poor memories of the event and eight former GIs who had left the Army refused to testify. These eight were thought primarily responsible for most of the ninety deaths in the village—two others had subsequently been killed. The body count officially reported was thirty-eight VC and the rate of firepower was so great that at midday Willingham had requested a helicopter resupply for more ammunition and TNT. Willingham himself refused to give evidence when he appeared before the inquiry on February 20, except to confirm he had not been interviewed about the operation until Wilson began his IG inquiry. Ten days earlier Willingham had been charged with murder when it was realized he was about to be discharged from Army service. Bravo Company's actions had been totally covered up and it would have remained that way but for Feher's fortuitous questioning of a woman from the hamlet and his search with Walsh for confirming evidence.

To Peers, the evidence was accumulating into a sorry picture, and a clear pattern of mistreatment of civilians by some members of Charlie Company well before the Pinkville operation. Sure, they had lost troops to booby traps and mines, but this was nothing exceptional, and the scale of the vengeful violence in the hamlets during the combat assault shocked Peers. He found the barbarous attacks on women especially difficult to comprehend. He could think of no instance either in World War I or II, the Korean War, or the Spanish–American War where soldiers had committed brutalities on a scale comparable with My Lai.

Each day when Peers reviewed volumes of testimony there was a new revelation, a new horror story. Thomas Partsch, who showed the inquiry team the diary he had written during his tour of duty in Vietnam, believed some of those involved in the murders took part out of curiosity to see what killing someone would be like. "As we went through there I don't think the guys realized what they did until after, when it hit them. Maybe some of them did—they were having a ball, but some of the guys were just like in a daze." Others, like Leonard Gonzalez of the 2nd Platoon, who had tried to help some of the wounded Vietnamese, were clear what the operation was about: "That day, it was just a massacre. Just plain right out, wiping out people."

Some former members of the company tried to hide the fact they were giving evidence to Peers's committee from their family, friends, and workmates. Tommy Lee Moss told his employer he needed the day off to go out of town on important business. He testified to seeing "guys . . . shooting old women, children, and men. Some of [the troops] were putting them in bunches and shooting them at the same time. Some of them were beating them and torturing them . . . I saw some guys had bayonets, sticking them in the back."

Again and again interrogators struggled to make sense of why the company had gone on its killing spree and why it had taken so long for the truth to come out. Herbert Carter, who had accidentally shot himself in the foot, appeared almost incoherent when he testified. None of the officers questioning him realized that he was stoned on heroin as he gave evidence. Carter, through his narcotic haze, said no one would believe what had really happened:

A lot of people have wondered why I didn't say something. Now who would believe me? You would call me a nut. You would think that nothing like that goes on in the United States. Just like I was in a bar a couple of weeks ago and there was a drunk in there reading the paper and he was asking me if I believed that things like that actually went on. I said: "I wouldn't know, pal." It was kind of weird.

. . . That day I tried my best to stay out of that whole mess. Some people might say that it was a cowardly act but I just tried to stay out of it. It's not my bag. I don't know how those guys can sleep. I can hardly sleep now and I didn't even participate in any of this mess. Something like that is hard to forget. It comes and it goes. I will be so glad when all this is over so I can forget it. They was rounding them up like cattle, they put them in big groups, they shot them. In this one incident I got kind of sick. I really got sick to my stomach.

If they had weapons it would have been a different deal. I wouldn't have thought twice about it. I would go down a tunnel in a minute and it doesn't bother me. A lot of these guys that did the killing are hurting inside but you'll never know about it. They won't say it. They will try and be a big man and say "It don't bother me" but it does. I haven't even participated in it and I can't sleep at night sometimes.

The behavior of the officers at the top of the 11th Brigade and the Americal Division caused Peers great anguish, not least because he had to scrutinize closely the actions of two generals he thought of as personal friends. He liked and respected Sam Koster and his deputy, George Young, now assistant commander of the 24th Infantry Division at Augsburg, West Germany. He knew the inquiry was certain to ruin their careers. In the mid-fifties Peers had had daily contact with both men for three years when they all served together in the plans and operations section of the Army General Staff. He considered both men outstanding officers and admired them greatly. But they were given no quarter when they faced his inquiry.

From early on it was apparent the coverup was so widespread it almost amounted to a conspiracy. Investigators discovered very quickly that many officers who had been in Quang Ngai had had a reunion at Cameron Station in Alexandria, Virginia, the day before Peers was due to begin taking evidence. The party was attended by officers from the 11th Brigade serving in the Washington, DC, area. Peers found it difficult to believe Henderson's assurance that My Lai had not been discussed at this gathering, since My Lai was

dominating the press and television headlines. He was further
disturbed when he learned of a series of telephone conversations
between Koster and Henderson about the questions Peers's team
had asked Henderson during his testimony. Then there had been
the selective destruction of the relevant files. MacCrate in particular
felt the purging of American Division and the Quang Ngai Province
advisory team's files was the result of a conspiracy. Pages had been
deliberately stripped from military logs, many other documents
had simply disappeared, and numerous witnesses had a collective
loss of memory.

Koster and Henderson made what Peers regarded as transparently
false claims that a formal investigation into Thompson's allegations
was carried out in accordance with the military regulations. They
had then asserted that this investigation had resulted in a formal
written report, complete with signed statements from various witnesses, including company commanders, platoon commanders,
platoon sergeants, and air crew. Henderson went even further and
claimed the statements had been made under oath, each man being
warned of his rights as Army regulations required. He said he had
given the job of investigating the allegations to Frank Barker, who
by now of course was long in his grave and unable to confirm or
deny these claims. Those said to have made signed statements
appeared before Peers and promptly denied they had been
interviewed about the events at My Lai. There had been no
investigation. They had made and signed no statements.

Even Calley, in an otherwise mute appearance before the inquiry,
denied he had been asked about civilian deaths. His counsel,
George Latimer, said Calley would stay silent because of the
serious charges against him. Peers then requested Calley at least to
say whether any investigation had been made immediately after the
My Lai operation. After a six-minute recess Calley returned to the
interview room:

Calley: "After conferring with counsel, I will make one statement
and only one statement here concerning this. That is that, to the
best of my knowledge and recollection, I was never asked questions
concerning the My Lai operation either by Col. Henderson or Lt.
Col. Barker."

Peers: "Would you be willing to go beyond that?"
Calley: "No, sir."

It was a classic Catch-22. For Henderson and Koster to have admitted there had not been a proper investigation would have meant they were both guilty of negligence and dereliction of duty, grave offenses under the Uniform Code. Their careers would be over. Peers believed they lied in order to save themselves, but in doing so they had dug a deeper hole. Their claims were easily disproved. Not only was their supposed report never found, but there was nothing to indicate to the inquiry that it ever existed. Two senior officers at the Americal Division headquarters at Chu Lai—George Young and Nels Parsons, the chief of staff—were said to have handled the spurious report. They promptly denied having done so. Koster and Henderson continued to stick to their story.

Henderson appeared to the inquiry team to have lied on numerous occasions during seven separate interviews. Whenever he spotted a possible trap while being closely questioned about his actions, he claimed to have acted in accordance with regulations. He claimed to have asked both a senior artillery officer and the commander of the gunship battalion to make strenuous inquiries about civilian deaths in the village. Both told the inquiry he had made no such request. Henderson denied having seen Barker's after-action report (which had made no mention of civilian casualties); moreover, he could not explain why only one copy of his own so-called "report of investigation," dated April 24, was ever found. Its hiding place, locked away in the intelligence section safe at brigade headquarters, was another factor that the inquiry found unusual. The original top copy of the document was never found; it would normally have been kept in a brigade central file which would have logged its title, date, and security classification. Henderson could not explain what happened to it. Neither were any logs or files discovered which would have shown how Henderson's report had been prepared, who typed it, and who was on the distribution list. Experienced officers interrogating him had never seen a military report written in this way. Incredibly, too, the report itself did not deal with the central issue: it made no mention at all of Thompson's very serious allegations, and it was Thompson's criticisms that had led to questions being asked. In any case, a commanding officer was not supposed to investigate his own unit.

Henderson denied emphatically that he knew of any massacre and spoke highly of Medina. Then, in a convoluted effort that left Peers completely unimpressed, he tried to protect himself once more. If killings had occurred, it was as a result of rash acts by members of Charlie Company: "Perhaps Captain Medina, then seeing that it had occurred, knowing he could not stop the thing once it had already happened—yes, a coverup. A coverup, I'm confident, was at that level if there was a coverup."

He disclosed that five telephone conversations occurred between himself and Koster, one three days after his first appearance before the inquiry despite Peers's specific warnings not to discuss his evidence with anyone. Peers was outraged and felt the telephone calls had given Henderson an opportunity to create impressions in Koster's mind that would influence his recall of events. "Some members of the inquiry felt even more strongly and saw these conversations as being very suspicious, even conspiratorial," he wrote later.

After Henderson was notified that he was being recalled to give further evidence, a truly extraordinary event occurred. The former brigade commander wrote privately to Westmoreland at the Pentagon, offering to take the whole blame for the initial failure to investigate properly what had happened at My Lai. It was a completely spurious gesture, clearly intended to halt the Peers inquiry in its tracks. In an apparent display of altruism tantamount to committing military suicide, Henderson offered symbolically to fall on his sword. He was willing to sacrifice himself because, he told Westmoreland, he believed a speedy decision about the findings of the Peers inquiry was urgently needed in the interests of strengthening the American people's confidence in its Army and to halt a growing disenchantment within the Army junior officer corps. He admitted advising Koster that irresponsible acts of killing noncombatants had not occurred, but incredibly, despite all the evidence to the contrary, his letter continued: "*I currently maintain that conviction* [our italics]. This judgment was mine alone and I am unwilling to share the responsibility with anyone . . . I continue to maintain the highest admiration, confidence, and faith in the integrity, fighting qualities, and courage of the officers and men, 11th Light Infantry Brigade, present during the alleged incident."

It was an embarrassingly transparent and shocking attempt by Henderson to appear magnanimously self-sacrificing. In effect he was trying to prevent his own negligence from being irrefutably proved by having the inquiry halted. He and Koster may not have known the awful truth of the massacre but they had, demonstrably, failed properly to investigate. Thompson's allegations, and when additional evidence emerged later of an atrocity they preferred to ignore it. Henderson's feeble attempt to take responsibility for command failures showed him to be a man of appallingly bad judgment and insensitivity. Had the offer been accepted Peers's inquiry would have appeared a complete whitewash. He told Westmoreland to do nothing about it and the Chief of Staff took his advice.

"Peers thought Henderson was stupid and probably lying as a result of a mistaken code of loyalty," Jerry Walsh reflected later. "He did not like us as civilians to see that someone as stupid as Henderson could have risen to the rank of Colonel. He was embarrassed by Henderson's idiotic effort as a loyal subordinate to 'take the blame' and thereby protect Koster."

For two days Koster, the Superintendent of West Point, faced an intense cross-examination. He too was suspected of negligence in failing to report war crimes and suppressing information about the unlawful killing of civilians at My Lai 4. Two months later, in mid-February, by which time the inquiry had interviewed 360 witnesses, Koster was recalled once more to the Pentagon basement. This time he was accused of lying during his original testimony and conspiring to withhold information.

Koster was challenged relentlessly about the information given to him by the Vietnamese authorities about the deaths of 400 people at My Lai and 90 at Co Luy. He had seen Lt. Tan's letter, he said, but thought the allegations were VC propaganda. He had not associated the report of an atrocity with a war crime because the allegations emanated from a Viet Cong area:

It did not jive with the information that we had developed as a result of the brigade CO's inquiry ... I felt if there was anyone that would give an honest opinion or make an honest inquiry it was Henderson. I knew him to be a brave individual and I thought a fairly strong leader, [though]

I wasn't sure that he was necessarily the most intelligent of the people I had commanding the brigades.

Peers remained convinced that the phone conversations with Henderson had conditioned Koster's memory of events. Yet Koster continued to insist he had seen a formal report of investigation complete with signed statements. Finally Peers turned on the man who had once been his friend:

Peers: "Well, we keep hearing, Gen. Koster, about a formal report. I say 'keep hearing'; that is erroneous. I must rephrase that. I can say that except for Col. Henderson and yourself, to my knowledge at the moment we have been able to turn up absolutely nothing concerning any formal report that was ever made."

Koster: "When I used the word 'formal report,' it was formal in the sense that these were written statements by a number of people who had been interrogated verbally prior to that time, and I know there was a sheaf of papers so big that it included these reports."

Peers: "We have talked to some of the people in command positions. They indicate that nobody ever talked to them. They made no signed statements. They gave no testimony under oath. We have talked to well over 70 people out of Charlie Company alone and we have yet to find one man who made a sworn statement or gave any testimony."

Koster: "I'm not positive that the statements were sworn but they were signed."

Peers: "They made no statements and to further compound the problem there is no record of such a report ever having arrived at HQ, Americal Division. There is no copy of the report available. There is no information whatsoever aside from that which you and Col. Henderson have indicated . . . we can find absolutely no one who has any knowledge of this report, including people who may have signed it, the people who may have prepared it, or any witnesses. We have talked to practically every individual who had any typing or preparation responsibility in the HQ of the 11th Brigade and we can find absolutely no reference to it."

Koster: "I can't explain that."

Peers: "So if you did receive such a report, the way the evidence would appear at the moment, it would have been a complete forgery."

For the three and a half months the inquiry lasted, Westmoreland and Resor continued to receive a steady drip-feed of information.

Public opinion about the affair was closely monitored within the Pentagon, which kept a running total of letters about My Lai. Fresh publicity inevitably led to a sudden increase in mail about the case. With serious charges pending against several infantrymen in Charlie Company, the Army was anxious to minimize prejudicial news coverage. The laying of charges against some individuals suspected of murder was deliberately delayed to reduce publicity.

News of an impending book about My Lai being written by Seymour Hersh also caused concern. In late January, Hersh met with senior Army officers at the Pentagon requesting information. He warned that the Army would not like his book. In confidential Army memos Hersh was accused of being connected by association with radical, anti Vietnam War elements, including people who had visited Hanoi. One senior officer commented: "I'm not sure just what we can do about [Hersh's book], but I certainly don't think the Army/DoD should be patsies for Hersh, Ridenhour and Co. There is some big money in My Lai [*Life* magazine fees to Haeberle] and it looks like this is an effort to get some of the $$$ . . . [We] should try to cut this guy's water off at the Pentagon end."

Five hundred letters a week were arriving at the Pentagon. By early February, the total had reached 4,500. Fifty percent continued to support Calley and servicemen generally. Ten percent attacked the press disclosures, and a quarter were against courts-martial in the case because of the effect it would have on the morale of the troops in Vietnam. There was a small crumb of comfort. The notion that the massacre might have been caused by troops high on drugs was ruled out. Each of the four hundred witnesses was routinely asked about drug taking, and there was simply no evidence that marijuana or other drugs had been used by members of Charlie Company when they stormed through the village.

One soldier who had a clear problem with drugs was Robert T'Souvas. He even appeared stoned during his testimony when he gave a long, rambling, and often completely incoherent account of his actions. When Colonel Robert Miller, a senior Army lawyer, had challenged him about his drug taking, T'Souvas became hostile and began arguing, unable to see a connection with the massacre. Miller was trying to unravel why none of the one hundred soldiers in the company had come forward at the time to expose what happened. He wanted to know about the armband T'Souvas had sewn on his uniform in Korea. The GI had it made in a tailor's shop because his conscience was bothering him and he wanted to express his feelings:

T'Souvas: "I guess it was like a dream in the back of my mind, it was a dream and it wouldn't come true, it would never come out into the open. And finally when it did and I realized it, I wanted to show my feelings toward it. I wanted to express what I knew, and I knew that it was wrong, but I didn't really know how to come (*sic*) about telling anybody. I was scared, you know, of getting in some kind of trouble . . . in my mind I knew it was wrong, I just kept it to myself."

Miller: "I think if one soldier had come forward, honestly and sincerely and gone to, let's say, the Inspector General or somebody, this would have been known. There are places a soldier can go and he can stand up and make his voice heard in something like this . . . you don't have to fear being punished for making a report like that."

T'Souvas: "I know right now, but now it's too late. I wish I could have done something ahead of time."

The final reckoning at the end of the inquiry was a document which had a devastating impact on Resor, Westmoreland, and the General Staff. In mid-February, Peers and MacCrate sent the Chief of Staff and Army Secretary an interim account to soften the blow of what was going to appear in the final report. It came like a bolt from the blue and they were immediately summoned to see the Army Secretary. Resor stressed he didn't want to control the final report, nor its central message, but he cautioned Peers and MacCrate about minimizing the use of undue emotionalism and over-strong language. In several passages in the interim report they had described the Vietnamese casualties as women, children, babies, and old men. Resor preferred the term "noncombatant casualties." Rapes had been fully described and he wanted a softer form of words for these as well.

"Resor asked me to tone down some of the language," Peers later revealed, long after he retired. "I had given him a preliminary report which was pretty brutal and a little bloody, some of the rapes were described in rather vivid detail. He could not tell me to soften down the report or do anything because of his position, he knew it would have violated Army procedure."

In several hundred pages, Peers's report set down the story of what had happened at My Lai and after. The crimes committed by Charlie and Bravo companies had included murders by groups and individuals, rape, sodomy, maiming, assault of noncombatants, and the destruction of several hamlets. Barker and Henderson had substantial knowledge of these war crimes, the report said, but did nothing about it. Henderson's inquiries were nothing more than a pretense to conceal the true enormity of the atrocities. "At every level within the Americal Division, actions were taken, both wittingly and unwittingly, which effectively suppressed information concerning the war crimes committed," the report said.

The report continued: "Henderson's actions appear to have been little more than a pretense of an investigation and had as their goal the suppression of the true facts concerning the events of 16th March." The most significant action to conceal the truth about the massacre was the deception used by Henderson to mislead Koster about the scope and findings of his investigation into Thompson's allegations. The deliberate efforts to withhold information had continued, the report said, while the Peers investigation took its testimony. "While Col. Henderson's later reports were false, and [Young and Koster] were negligent in having accepted them, they probably believed they were withholding information concerning a much less serious incident than the one that actually occurred." In trying to conceal the deaths of twenty to twenty-eight civilians at My Lai, the staff officers at Americal Division HQ effectively concealed the massacre.

For Peers a report alone was not enough. He hurled the Uniform Code of Military Justice at twenty-eight officers: two generals, four full colonels, four lieutenant colonels, four majors, six captains, and eight lieutenants. They were accused of a total of 224 serious military offenses, ranging from giving false testimony and failure to report war crimes, to conspiring to suppress information about war crimes and participating in those crimes or failing to prevent or report them.

Two days before the March 14 deadline for the submission of the report, Peers's team was rushing to complete the final chapter of its findings. Volume 1 contained the inquiry team's report and detailed analysis; Volume 2 had six books of documents; Volume 3 consisted of twenty-six books of testimony running to 20,000 pages; and in Volume 4 were statements taken by the CID. Four Army lawyers, assigned hastily to review the evidence, charged fourteen of the twenty-eight officers accused by Peers with court-martial offenses.

Having completed his Herculean task, Peers faced two more battles with the Army brass. Against his strong objections the Army Secretary refused to charge two Army chaplains—Lt. Col. Francis Lewis and Capt. Carl Creswell—for failing to ensure that Thompson's allegations were properly reported and investigated. Resor was concerned about the damage a court-martial would do to the chaplains' corps. He overrode Peers's view that when it came to reporting war crimes men of the cloth were no different from anyone else and in fact they had an even greater responsibility. Peers believed Lewis especially should have been court-martialed because he had been given a great deal of information about the massacre.

When the Pentagon called a press conference to give brief details of the results of the inquiry and the charges leveled against a number of officers, Peers became involved in a major row behind closed doors with the Army's chief of information, Major General Winant Sidle. Peers had shown Sidle a draft of a short statement he intended making to news reporters in which he referred to a "massacre" having occurred at My Lai 4 on March 16. Sidle wanted the word "massacre" removed from Peers's comments, fearing the damaging effect it would have on the Army's image. Suspecting this request originated with the Army Secretary, and feeling strongly that the public should not be deceived, Peers protested vehemently. The meeting with Sidle ended in deadlock and Peers was ready to boycott the press conference. "We were at it again the following morning, the day of the news conference," Peers wrote later. "I was not about to present a watered-down version and in effect said that if that was what they wanted, please leave me out."

With only hours to go before the public announcement, Robert MacCrate suggested a compromise. Peers, still irritated and apprehensive, agreed to using the words "a tragedy of major proportions" instead of "massacre." Even then Sidle had to check this out at the highest levels of the Pentagon. He gave the go-ahead only thirty minutes before the press conference was held.

Scant details of the report's contents were provided. Its 225 pages were heavily censored. The Army declined to give specific details of charges against the fourteen men accused as a result of the inquiry; they also declined to characterize the initial handling of the incident as a "coverup," and instead claimed information about the affair had simply "not been passed up the chain of command."

Peers himself delicately sidestepped awkward questions about a second massacre when asked questions about charges leveled against a young platoon commander, Thomas Willingham, who was not at My Lai 4. Peers had been placed in an awkward position. Though his report gave a very full account of what happened during Bravo Company's assault on Co Luy, the testimony was mostly hearsay evidence and the Army decided to keep it top secret. The CID was continuing its investigation into the second massacre because there had been a concerted effort by those involved to keep quiet; indeed, Peers's team had met with a virtual conspiracy of silence from the members of Bravo Company involved in the murder of ninety unarmed men, women, and children. It was another shocking revelation and one that the Army brass were desperate to keep the lid on. It utterly destroyed the argument that My Lai had been something completely out of the ordinary, an aberration committed by a rogue outfit. If this were so, how could it be that another company of American troops was carrying out, at precisely the same time, more brutal savagery on unarmed and defenseless civilians? Bravo Company was on the rampage only one and a half miles from the village which Charlie Company was destroying at My Lai. To the frustration of Peers's team, especially Jerry Walsh who had concentrated his efforts on unearthing what happened at Co Luy, Willingham was the only person charged as a result of the second massacre. Even so, charges against him were later dropped "in the interests of justice."

On the day of the press conference, several journalists were deliberately deceived by Pentagon briefers. Their questions about Willingham, when it was learned he was not a member of Charlie Company, were deflected. A second atrocity had been unearthed by the Peers inquiry, the briefers confided, but United States forces were not involved. The second atrocity had occurred at Son My village, they said, while American troops were at My Lai. The reporters learned nothing of Bravo Company's involvement. Instead South Vietnamese troops were blamed for what had happened to the civilians living in the coastal village of Co Luy.

The same day as the Pentagon press conference, nearly 250 miles north of Washington at West Point, Maj. Gen. Koster summoned the "Gentlemen of the Corps"—the academy's cadets. From the balcony overlooking the dining hall he announced he was requesting reassignment to save the academy from further publicity. He told them the cherished principles of West Point, "Duty, Honor, Country," had served as his constant guide throughout his military career. "I shall continue to follow these principles as long as I live," he continued. "Every one of you can have a wonderful experience in the military profession. To serve one's country true and faithfully is one of the highest callings. To this end, may good fortune and success come to all of you in the future." He then added the classic crude maxim appreciated by military men the world over: 'Don't let the bastards grind you down." It was an occasion fraught with emotion. The cadets suddenly leapt from their seats, cheering and clapping, and, without waiting to be dismissed, rushed from the dining hall to organize their farewells. They draped a banner in front of Washington Hall that said "DON'T LET 'EM GET YOU DOWN," then marched past Quarters 100—the Superintendent's house—in a final parade in the general's honour. Many of them were deeply critical of the media's reporting of My Lai and thought Koster was taking the blame for others. Koster himself never identified who the "bastards" were. His parting shot, he later claimed, was merely advice from an experienced soldier to a group of young men embarking on their military career. "I meant by it that there would be times when they felt that injustices had been rendered to them but that shouldn't be something they should look upon as being terminal or permanent," he said. "It's an adage that is true for any soldier in any country or even for life in general."

Publicity about My Lai continued to cause grave concern in military circles, especially with its effect on active combat units. In Vietnam, one of Koster's successors, as commanding general of the American Division at Chu Lai, Major General Robert Milloy, tested the effects of the case on the morale of his fighting troops. Milloy found them generally reluctant to believe the massacre had actually happened. My Lai had not basically changed how or where combat units operated, but senior commanders were more aware of the consequences resulting from the indiscriminate use of firepower. Milloy reported in an "eyes only" message to Lieutenant General Melvin Zais, the XXIV Corps commander at Phu Bai: "Junior leaders have developed a more cautious approach to combat operations with an attendant reduction in aggressiveness. They are reluctant to press an engagement in a populated area where supporting fire will not be available."

Milloy's men, the memorandum continued, were becoming increasingly frustrated about conducting combat operations in an area where the enemy was not easily identified. They felt intense resentment toward the Vietnamese in heavily booby-trapped areas. "Some soldiers feel that the enemy is getting more than an even break." Lower-level commanders on the ground were concerned they might be condemned for decisions they might take in good faith during combat. Milloy was worried about whether junior officers would want to stay in the Army because of the adverse publicity caused by My Lai. Senior officers and NCOs had expressed disappointment at the way soldiers allegedly involved at My Lai were apparently condemned prior to a thorough investigation. "They expressed a feeling of insecurity based on what was felt to be overreaction by the Army in response to the pressures of politicians and those vocal elements who condemn the involvement of the United States in Vietnam for any number of reasons."

Soon Westmoreland himself was sending "eyes only" messages to senior US Army commanders around the globe about a sensational and highly secret development that was causing him deep concern. Forty young officers *en route* to Vietnam had sent a round-robin letter to the White House pleading with the President to end the war, with a thinly veiled threat to mutiny if he did not. The forty lieutenants accepted that they were going to Vietnam, but they wanted Nixon as the Commander-in-Chief to be aware of their serious reservations about the war and their role in it. Their views, they wrote, were shared by a very large number of young men throughout the Army—officers and NCOs. America was not prepared to send the large numbers of troops required to win the war and public opinion had forced the President to limit the invasion of Cambodia.

"The country has been shocked and outraged by the My Lai and Col. Rhealt incidents of mass killing and assassination which are and have always been characteristic of warfare," they wrote. "The American people do not want to pay the terrible price of war; they don't want to see their own young men killed; and they don't want to face the brutal acts which these young men perform on people of another country."

The young officers found the continuation of the war difficult to justify, yet they were being asked to lead others who were unconvinced into a war in which few of them really believed. This left them with nothing but survival—"kill or be killed"—as a motivation to perform their missions. The letter then took an ominous turn:

If this is the only thing we have to keep us going, then those who force us into this position, the military, the leadership of the country, are perceived to be almost as much our enemies as the Viet Cong and the NVA. There is a great amount of bitterness toward both the military and America building up within the military forces.

The young soldiers, who all signed their names to the letter, found it hard to believe Nixon was not aware of the extent of the dissatisfaction among American troops, and if he was aware they wondered for how much longer he could force young men to go to war against their will. "As the war drags on, the troops will become increasingly opposed to the war and increasingly bitter about going. It seems very possible that if the war is allowed to continue much longer, young Americans in the military will simply refuse en masse to cooperate. This day is coming quickly, you must have us out of Vietnam by then."

In his speeches and news conferences Nixon had often contrasted the disaffection of the American student protesters with the devotion and patriotism of soldiers in Vietnam. But the letter warned:

"We want you to know that in many cases those 'protesters and troublemakers' are our younger brothers, and friends and girlfriends and wives. We share many common causes with them. Please get this country out of Vietnam before we too become completely disaffected."

The soldiers involved had not wanted to embarrass the President or the military and would not send copies of the letter to the press. But they did want Nixon to know that a large number of officers had misgivings about the war:

To this date officers have remained silent about their feelings but we think it important that you be informed of the widespread disaffection among us. We sign this letter knowing that it will be seen by your military staff before you ever see it—if it gets to you at all. We also know of punitive action taken by the Army to officers who have written similar letters to you. Nevertheless we must take chances to inform you of these feelings within the Army. Since you and the country have decided that Vietnam is not worth the awful price of Victory, we plead with you to get the country out of this half-hearted war at the earliest opportunity.

Westmoreland appealed to the Army's most senior commanders to treat the matter of the letter urgently on "a close-hold sensitive basis." He wanted to know if the Army was really facing a serious crisis and whether similar problems had manifested themselves in their commands. The signatories of the letter to President Nixon were a cross-section of young officers from different branches of the Army and were not substandard performers. "The extent to which this letter may represent the state of mind of many other young officers and men that you are receiving is of deep concern to me," he wrote. The fact that they had not had more trouble, Westmoreland said, given the criticism of the war in the country at large, was a tribute to the leadership of the officer corps. However, he was concerned about a trend which the Army staff had observed toward lack of motivation and increasing dissatisfaction among young officers and enlisted men. There had been a decline in the willingness of young soldiers to accept duty in Vietnam as an unquestioned obligation of their military service.

"These expressions are fraught with serious misconceptions

concerning the overall role of the Army, with particular emphasis on our efforts in Vietnam. What is now apparently dissatisfaction and lack of motivation could rapidly become disaffection," he warned.

11. . . . And Justice for All

"It's those dirty rotten Jews from New York who are behind it," an exasperated Richard Nixon kept repeating to a White House aide in late November 1969, as public reaction to the news of what happened at My Lai became more hostile. Opposition to the war in Vietnam grew louder and louder at home and abroad.

Overseas, United States ambassadors reported even sympathetic governments expressing skepticism about America's war aims in Southeast Asia. The foreign press condemned the outrage and in many towns and cities abroad young people took to the streets, drawing parallels between the atrocity at My Lai and the actions of the Nazis. Back home, Vietnam veterans were coming forward with further horror stories of ill-treatment of Vietnamese civilians and prisoners of war by American soldiers. A photograph was published of a Viet Cong prisoner being hurled to his death from an Army helicopter.

The publicity surrounding the revelations of what had happened at My Lai couldn't have come at a worse time in Nixon's view. By the fall of 1969 the ever-growing and vociferous antiwar movement in the United States had become the prime focus of his attention. When students scheduled an enormous antiwar protest on college campuses across the country for October 15, Nixon had fumed in the White House, demanding of his chief of staff Bob Haldeman: "It is absolutely essential that we react insurmountably and powerfully to blunt this attack." He was talking not of hordes of well-armed NVA troops but of American citizens, marching unarmed through the country's academic institutions.

Nixon's was a leave-nothing-to-chance White House, overseen by devoted aides from California, who had been schooled in campaign management by the J. Walter Thompson advertising agency. Men like Haldeman and John Ehrlichman were can-do fixers hypnotized by their own sense of power, who surrounded themselves with willing acolytes, anxious to do the President's bidding so as to keep his ear, until the Watergate scandal brought about their downfall. The seeds of that corruption and the subsequent humiliation and ruination of Richard Nixon lay in the siege mentality that existed within the White House about the opposition to the war. Nixon believed the media were responsible for turning the people against the war and that, from the time My Lai first became public, press and television commentators and the antiwar forces had used "the whole tragic episode to chip away at our efforts to build public support for our Vietnam objectives and policies." Redressing the balance was a key objective of the White House.

Manipulation of the media was nothing new in American political life. All the Presidents who fought their way into the White House wanted to be seen in the most favorable light. But the Nixon White House was different. The President stayed aloof from open and direct contact with editors and reporters because it made him appear vulnerable. Rather he immersed himself in maintaining the image of his presidency by using more underhand methods of swaying public opinion. This was essentially an exercise in deception. The mastery lay in not publicly being seen to be manipulating the media, which American society cherished as an almost sacredly independent institution, free of government control, a freedom enshrined in the constitution.

As Nixon became increasingly obsessed by what he saw as biased reports about the war he ordered his closest officials to go on the offensive. They monitored the activities of newspapers and television stations closely, mounting a swift counteraction if an antigovernment item appeared. There was outrage in the Oval Office when Senator George McGovern appeared on Johnny Carson's *Tonight* show and called for the immediate and unconditional withdrawal of all US forces from Vietnam. McGovern's onslaught came only days after the actress Shirley MacLaine had attacked the war on the same program. The White House responded by covertly targeting the NBC network for a letter-writing campaign, not from White House officials but from outsiders, trusted Republican Party supporters instructed to write to the network in protest. When a particular strategy required a strong show of support from the public, or if a counterattack needed mounting on a particular individual, Nixon took a close interest in the sordid details. He wanted critical articles planted in newspapers when Senator Edward Kennedy's antiwar stance was requoted in a statement by Hanoi. The President ordered a young aide, speechwriter Pat Buchanon, to begin a letter-writing campaign directed against Kennedy from Boston, the heart of his Massachusetts constituency.

The White House plan against the ever-growing American antiwar movement called for a counteroffensive starting with a Nixon "strategy for peace" speech to the nation on November 3, 1969. It was to be an appeal, delivered live on television, specifically designed to unleash what Nixon believed were the favorable prowar opinions of the silent majority. Aides were instructed to draw up a massive public relations/news management campaign to "demonstrate" the American people's support for the President's stance on the war. The US Information Agency sent to 104 countries around the world a fifteen-minute film called *The Silent Majority*, the theme of which was that most Americans supported the war; that dissenters might have the loudest voice but were not the ones to listen to. The Postmaster General, Winton Blount, declared that antiwar demonstrations were encouraging the communists to fight on. The protesters, he said, were having the effect of "killing American boys."

A secret plan was prepared within the White House to proclaim the huge support Nixon enjoyed across the country. It involved the careful planning of a series of "newsworthy events" at which the President could reemphasize the message. The campaign—which would run through mid-December—ranged from patriotic rallies to a barrage of telegrams and letters to the White House. Suitable quotations from these would be leaked to the media or revealed at special events. Antiwar protesters were targeted for attack by the Justice Department. The courts were to be used to gain injunctions against protesters who during their college moratorium had been reading in public the names of dead soldiers. Later the deputy attorney general, Richard Kleindienst, announced that the New Mobilization Committee to End the War in Vietnam was being investigated for a possible violation of federal conspiracy law.

Other items in the plan concerned the ways the moon mission could be exploited for the campaign. The President was scheduled to attend the *Apollo 12* takeoff at Cape Kennedy in Florida, and the White House seriously considered the possibility of seeing if it could write the script for the astronauts' message from the moon.

Nixon was desperate to show Hanoi that America was united. He believed that the more divided the country was, the less it was likely that the enemy would negotiate in Paris. During his network television speech on November 3, he crystallized his goal: "Let us be united for peace. Let us also be united against defeat. Because let us understand: North Vietnam cannot defeat or humiliate the United States. Only Americans can do that."

The obvious dichotomy between Nixon's appeal for unity and the administration's virulent attacks on hundreds of thousands of young Americans who opposed war seemed lost on the President. His appetite for the use of dirty tricks and deception in politics seemed matched only by his personal capacity for self-deception, a side of Nixon's character not fully understood during this first year of his presidency. Even in later years Nixon himself appeared never to have discovered much about his own character. When constructing his memoirs after his fall from grace, he wrote self-approvingly that the November 3 speech had influenced the course of history because 77 percent of Americans endorsed the speech and 68 percent gave him their personal approval. Telegrams and letters did indeed pour in—some spontaneously, but many as a result of action by White House staffers among Republican supporters across the country.

Nixon's rhetoric promised the American people a fair and honorable settlement and to continue the fight until the communists came to the negotiating table. The North Vietnamese saw it differently. The Nixon doctrine of withdrawing from a direct role in future foreign conflicts, by handing over to countries threatened by communism the means to defend themselves, was perceived by Hanoi as a sign that its relentless action in South Vietnam was gradually defeating the United States. It could only mean America's complete withdrawal at sometime in the future, and ultimately South Vietnam would have to stand alone. Hanoi was prepared to withstand threats of renewed bombing and continue the fight.

Lukewarm reaction in the media to Nixon's appeal for unity, however, resulted in more White House paranoia. Pat Buchanon's writing skills were employed once more to draft a speech attacking television and newspaper executives as the unelected elite. The central theme was that a small group of biased media executives was deciding what millions of Americans learned about events in the nation and the world. The attack coincided with publication of Hersh's revelations about My Lai. Vice President Spiro Agnew delivered the antimedia tirade, carried live by the three national networks, in Des Moines, Iowa, on November 13, the day Hersh's first article about My Lai appeared. The timing was coincidental.

Agnew's onslaught on the press and television executives shared the spotlight with *Apollo 12*'s astronauts who were scheduled the next day to blast off from Cape Kennedy for the second moon landing. Wide coverage was also given to the second moratorium of those opposing the war, held this time in Washington, DC. A quarter of a million antiwar protesters packed around the Washington Monument and the huge area of open parkland which runs along Constitution Avenue. The scene of this massive demonstration was Nixon's back yard. From a window behind the moat of security guards ringing the White House, Nixon could have easily observed the scene, but instead he watched a football game on television. Later his domestic policy advisor Ehrlichman brought four protesters into the Oval Office. Nixon's hapless and embarrassing attempts at humor to establish a rapport with the small group only made the complete gulf between them seem worse. "It was just awful," Ehrlichman said later. Further along Constitution Avenue at the intersection with 10th Street, protesters stormed the Justice Department building, tore down the Stars and Stripes from its mast, and raised the Viet Cong flag in its place.

It was against this background that the dreadful truth about My Lai unfolded. Through Alexander Haig, newly promoted to brigadier general, the Army kept the White House fully apprised of possible developments in the case. Kissinger in turn passed the information to Nixon via Haldeman. "Now that the cat is out of the bag," he wrote the chief of staff a few days before Calley was formally charged with capital offenses, "I recommend keeping the President and the White House out of the matter entirely."

Conflicting advice came from Daniel Patrick Moynihan, Councillor to the President, who found himself profoundly disturbed by Paul Meadlo's CBS television interview with Mike Wallace. Moynihan wrote a personal memo to Nixon expressing his fears:

It is clear that something hideous happened at My Lai . . . I would doubt the war effort can now be the same, nor the position of the military. Look if you will at the pictures in *Time* this week. As a father of sons about the age of those lying dead in that Vietnam ditch, I shuddered when I came to that page. How could it be that there could be such a thing to be looked at? I fear the answer of too many Americans will simply be that this is a hideous, corrupt society. I fear and dread what this will do to our society unless we try to understand it . . . I don't know with whom you talk on matters this serious but I would hope you might turn to them.

I think it would be a grave error for the Presidency to be silent while the Army and the Press pass judgment. For it is America that is being judged. And America will be condemned, unless we undertake some larger effort than can be had from a court-martial.

Moynihan was among many, including a group of law professors from universities throughout the country, who believed a special presidential commission ought to investigate the massacre. The sheer scale of the crime convinced many experts in jurisprudence that, under the Laws of War laid down by the 1949 Geneva Convention, America had binding obligations to prosecute war criminals, irrespective of whether they were still in military service. Some military lawyers believed Articles 18 and 21 of the Uniform Code of Military Justice could be used to ensure former members of Charlie Company were not beyond the reach of the law.

It was not clear whether America's highest legal body, the Supreme Court, would sanction such a move. In a 1955 ruling the court judged that a former Air Force sergeant charged with murder was entitled to the constitutional safeguards provided by a civilian trial. However, in a crucial 1946 decision involving the Japanese general Tomoyuki Yamashita, sentenced to death after being convicted of responsibility for war crimes committed by his troops in the Philippines, the Supreme Court upheld the jurisdiction of a US military commission. A similar commission in 1942 ordered the execution of eight Nazi saboteurs who landed secretly in the United States from a submarine.

What this held out for the White House was the awful specter of a huge war crimes trial—a Nuremberg-style hearing with two sets of defendants. The mass murderers of Charlie Company would be on trial but so clearly would the American government's military policies in South Vietnam. Kissinger was particularly worried about the effect the My Lai revelations would have on America's ability to fight the war. As Moynihan had said, it was America that was being judged.

Nixon's tactic, true to form, was to go on the attack, to turn the stories about My Lai on their head. He secretly demanded a special investigation of Ronald Ridenhour, whose letter about the massacre the previous April had been ignored by White House staff. At a meeting with Haldeman on December 1, the President secretly ordered that the campaign against media bias be kept boiling and that a covert offensive should be mounted on My Lai. Haldeman's personal notes of the meeting, which remain among Nixon's White House files in the National Archives, reveal the President's bidding: "Dirty tricks—not too high a level; discredit one witness, get out facts on Hue; admin line—may have to use a senator or two, so don't go off in different directions; keep working on the problem."

Nixon condemned the atrocity in public. But one night, according to a White House assistant, Alexander Butterfield, he spent two hours attacking the press for the My Lai publicity. The "dirty rotten Jews" in New York he complained of were most likely the editorial management of the *New York Times*, a constant critic of the government's war policies.

Nixon clutched at anything that offered a sympathetic view of the administration's position. A copy of a cartoon published in an Alabama newspaper struck a chord. Headlined: "For us . . . one time is too much," it showed a drawing of a GI with his hands dripping with blood and labeled: "Alleged village massacre." But the picture was dominated by the towering figure of an ugly thug whose rifle dripped blood, captioned: "Communist atrocities as standard operating procedure." In his own hand Nixon scrawled in the margin: "Good! Write him a note . . . Klein try to get this syndicated."

In public Nixon condemned the use of atrocities in war and promised that all the facts about the massacre would be investigated and the guilty punished. In the privacy of the Oval Office, however, he was particularly anxious that Ridenhour and Seymour Hersh should be targeted. Nixon wanted to know: "Who is backing Ridenhour?" Through John Ehrlichman, a special investigator began probing Ridenhour's background, possible criminal record, and political affiliations. The investigation revealed that Hersh had received $1,000 from the Edgar B. Stern Family Fund to help develop the My Lai story, and that Ridenhour was apparently incensed about it. In his view, Hersh had made money out of the tragedy. The President was told that Ridenhour, allegedly embarrassed and hurt by the affair, had considered consulting a lawyer to help bring legal action against Hersh. Nixon wanted the details secretly leaked to a journalist. Soon after his first articles revealed the massacre, Hersh was followed to work aboard a Washington commuter bus by a junior official in the National Security Agency, who sat behind the writer, eavesdropped on his conversations, and reported what he had learned to Alexander Haig.

The My Lai massacre had resulted in two separate inquiries. The CID looked at the crimes committed during the actual combat mission—murder, rape, and assault. Peers examined the aftermath, the possible coverup, and charges of negligence and dereliction of duty. Initially nearly eighty soldiers were under serious investigation as a result of both inquiries. But when it came for the military justice system to follow through with charges, its performance was lamentable. Nixon's pledge to ensure punishment of the guilty became an empty promise.

When the time came for the jury at Calley's court-martial to give its verdict at the end of March 1971, the young infantry officer did not stand in the dock alone. America's system of military justice was also on trial. Until that point it had failed completely and seemed to offer perfect proof of the belief of Clemenceau, the former French Prime Minister, who had declared in 1919 that military justice was to Justice what military music was to Music.

Peers's inquiry had recommended charges be brought against twenty-eight officers and two NCOs involved in the concealment of the massacre. He accused them of negligence and dereliction of duty. But Army lawyers decided that only fourteen officers should be charged. These included two generals and three colonels. Only one came to court, and he was subsequently acquitted.

The CID inquiry had yielded devastating results. Its investigation into the crimes committed on the day of the massacre involved a total of forty-five members of Charlie Company in addition to Capt. Eugene Kotouc, Task Force Barker's intelligence officer, and Lt. Thomas K. Willingham, a platoon commander with Bravo Company. Allegations ranged from murder and assault with intent to commit murder to violation of the rules of war, from rape to indecent assault. After a painstaking inquiry by the Army's trained criminal investigators, the CID concluded that there was sufficient evidence to charge thirty men with major crimes.

The allegations against the rest of the men either were unfounded or could not be proved or disproved. But Army legal staff decided to lay criminal charges against only those still in military service. There were four officers—Calley, Medina, Willingham, and Kotouc—and nine enlisted men. The cases against the remaining seventeen former soldiers were quietly dropped, even though many of those most closely involved with the case believed there was substantial evidence of their guilt. The departments of Justice and Defense could not agree on how to deal with these men. Some, like Varnado Simpson and Michael Terry, had actually confessed to killing unarmed Vietnamese civilians including women and children. Against others there was the clearest evidence of savage murder and sexual brutality.

Hundreds of people had been slaughtered in cold blood. The killers' identity was known. Yet through a simple bureaucratic decision to do nothing they had literally gotten away with murder. The pledge to bring the guilty to justice lay in tatters. Prime responsibility for this lay with the Nixon administration and its complete failure to establish a clear moral lead for the nation. By refusing calls for a presidential commission to investigate the massacre and its coverup the White House abrogated all responsibility for the conduct of American troops in a war whose very existence was a crucial plank of United States foreign policy. By leaving the prosecutions and judicial decisions in the hands of soldiers, the Nixon administration virtually ensured that there would be no justice for the victims of My Lai. Military law operated to serve the interests of America's armed forces as an institution, not justice, not international law, and certainly not moral leadership. It is true that senior officers like Westmoreland and the Judge Advocate General, Major General Kenneth Hodgson, were appalled and horrified by the killings. Within the constraints of the rules governing command influence they took great pains to ensure that the full force of military law was exercised. But to believe that justice might emerge from a system where the United States Army sat in judgment on itself in a matter so grave as My Lai was to expect too much.

It was precisely for this reason the group of thirty-four eminent lawyers and law professors, many of whom were experts in international and military law, had pleaded with Nixon to appoint a presidential commission soon after the revelations of My Lai were made public. It was not enough, they argued, simply to say, as Nixon had said, that the atrocities were abhorrent. "More is required to clear the conscience of the American people," Arthur J. Goldberg, the eminent lawyer and spokesman for the group, wrote to the President:

There is in this grave situation a paramount issue raised by the allegations of the massacre of civilians which cannot be laid to rest by a military court-martial of a few individuals. This issue is the extent to which the war in Vietnam is being conducted in a manner inconsistent with the minimum humanitarian standards established by the international law of war and incorporated in the general and military laws of the United States. We believe that this issue involves the good faith, humanity, dedication to law and moral leadership of the United States.

In the White House, chief among those firmly opposed to removing the investigation of My Lai from the military was Henry Kissinger, who earlier advised Nixon to reject Moynihan's plea for a special commission. Kissinger told the President to reject the lawyers' proposals:

You have already made your position clear on the incident and the public recognizes that you desire a full and impartial procedure under our laws to determine the facts, the possible guilt, and the necessary punishment for those involved. As events now appear, this will best be served by the scheduled courts-martial.

To do more at this time would primarily serve to focus additional and unneeded publicity on the incident [our italics] and would probably not be helpful in arriving at any clearer demonstration of facts. It might also conflict with the expressed desire of the responsible authorities to avoid further publicity on the incident lest the rights of the defendants and the position of the US Government be impaired.

Defense Secretary Melvin Laird, who turned down a similar request for a special commission from a US Senator, believed that "the Dept of Army should first have an opportunity to pursue its own investigation and criminal prosecutions to a just conclusion." A presidential commission would not be able to report until after the judicial process had been completed. Laird trusted that the public would better learn the truth of what actually happened at My Lai through the courts-martial that would follow charges against individuals.

It was a completely pious hope. The number of public trials was kept to an absolute minimum. There was no clearing of America's guilt, no large-scale Nuremberg-style judicial hearing at which the accused were put on trial for all the world to see. From the government's perspective this would have rendered its war aims in Southeast Asia untenable; and it would have been naive to expect otherwise.

A handful of soldiers charged with criminal offenses appeared at court-martial trials at different military bases around the country. A secret system of military justice dealt with many other accused behind closed doors. Pretrial hearings were privately held before two of America's highest-ranking Army officers, Lieutenant General Jonathan Seaman, commanding general of the 1st US Army, and Lieutenant General Albert O. Connor, commander of the 3rd US Army.

Of those officers accused by the Peers inquiry of being involved in concealing evidence of the massacre, only one individual—Col. Oran Henderson—was ever tried by a court-martial jury. Charges against the others of dereliction of duty and failure to obey lawful regulations (relating to the attempted coverup) were all dismissed before they could reach a jury. Charges against Brig. Gen. George H. Young, the assistant commander of the Americal Division, Col. Nels Parson, the Americal Division chief of staff, Col. Robert B.

Luper, the artillery battalion commander, and Major Robert W. McKnight, TF Barker's executive officer, were dismissed early on by Gen. Seaman for lack of evidence, on the advice of staff judge advocates. The remaining individuals who faced disciplinary offenses went through a more formal process held under Article 32 of the Uniform Code of Military Justice—a type of grand jury hearing that allowed evidence to be tested before a public trial, except that in this instance the "grand jury" was a general officer.

Koster's protracted Article 32 hearing was held by a one-star general who forwarded his recommendations to Lt. Gen. Seaman, former commander of the "Big Red One"—the 1st Infantry Division—during the early stages of the war. Brigadier General B. L. Evans found that while Koster had been remiss in not reporting the death of twenty civilians or ordering a proper investigation, all the charges against him should be dismissed. Specific mention was made of Koster's fine character and long career of outstanding service. Seaman duly obliged, although later Koster was demoted to brigadier general and the Army withdrew his Distinguished Service Medal. The Secretary of the Army also issued a formal letter of censure to Koster's deputy, George Young, who also lost his Distinguished Service Medal.

These actions, conducted in private, meant that the truth about the enormity of the coverup could be kept secret. This provoked strong criticism from those who had been intimately involved with the search for truth. Robert MacCrate, the New York lawyer attached to the Peers inquiry as civilian counsel, expressed his shock at Seaman's dismissal of the charges against Koster without even bothering to refer them for trial by court-martial. "In my opinion he has done a serious disservice to the Army," said MacCrate, who would later become president of the American Bar Association. "What is involved is a failure to recognize the Army's responsibility to the public at large and a failure to affirm to the Army itself the importance of acting in accordance with the rules of international law, the law of war and the principles of our constitution." Jerry Walsh, the other civilian lawyer on the Peers panel, was even more outspoken, calling Seaman's decision a "whitewash of the top man." "Generals are given great power and responsibility. They should be held strictly to account when they fail," he said. Congressman Sam Stratton, who served on F. Edward Hebert's subcommittee investigating the massacre, was equally outraged and claimed the dropping of charges against Koster was a grave miscarriage of justice deliberately committed by the Pentagon because it feared "a full public airing of the charges against Koster and of his incredible mismanagement of his command would make the Army look very, very bad."

To this day the sheer inconsistency surrounding Seaman's judgment of Koster's actions still fuels speculation about his true motives. Having decided that a public trial was not justified, Seaman then proceeded to mete out a particularly fatal form of military punishment that effectively halted the two-star general's once promising career dead in its tracks. Seaman, soon to retire from the Army to his home in South Carolina, sent Koster a letter of censure that line by line unstitched his reputation. The letter lambasted Koster's performance in relation to the My Lai operation, a performance that "did not meet the high standards expected of a division commander."

Koster, he wrote, was an experienced general who knew at least twenty civilians had been killed. This should have been reported:

I feel compelled, not only by time-honored command principles, but also by the peculiar facts of this case, to hold you personally responsible for the failure of the Americal Division to make the required report or to pass on in some other fashion information vital to and required by your superior commanders.

You knew on March 16, 1968 that a disturbingly high number of civilians had been killed. You knew that the count of 128 enemy killed in a brief battalion-size engagement was a near record success for your division . . . contrary to your normal practice you did not overfly or visit the scene of such a significant victory even though you were in the vicinity . . . at your division evening briefing you did not question the absence of information about civilian casualties even though you personally were aware that 20–30 civilians had been killed.

Seaman officially declared that Koster *was* fully aware of Hugh Thompson's allegations that ground troops had fired indiscriminately at civilians and that he had threatened to turn his own guns on American soldiers. However, Koster had merely accepted an oral report from Henderson that "the young excitable pilot had exaggerated":

Resolution of these allegations would have forced you to conclude either that the pilot was correct and further action against the offending troops was necessary; or that the pilot was incorrect and had blatantly interfered in a ground operation at grave risk to troops, the helicopter and the mission. In the latter case you should have taken action against the offending pilot.

It is my duly considered opinion that your failure to assure a proper and thorough initial investigation, despite the many clues of wrong-doing, is in part responsible for the fact that the full My Lai 4 events remained undisclosed for nearly two years.

Given the scathing nature of his private criticisms of Koster, the only conclusion to be made of Seaman's decision was that he wanted to avoid causing the Army embarrassment by having the former Superintendent of West Point Military Academy put on trial. Seaman was coming to the end of a distinguished military career; and this, his final mission, was to adjudicate in something so distasteful and painful to the Army's reputation as the actions of its officer corps in the aftermath of My Lai. A highly experienced battlefield commander who had enjoyed success in the Vietnamese campaign, he had, as the II Field Force commander, initiated one of the largest military operations of the war when more than 22,000 American and South Vietnamese troops battled for several weeks against the 9th Viet Cong Division and NVA regulars in Operation Attelboro, ending with 1,100 enemy killed. Now here he was with his last job for the institution he had served for more than thirty years. Could the Army afford the public trial of an officer in whom the General Staff had placed such great store? Had they not entrusted Koster with responsibility for nurturing a future genera-tion of generals, fit to climb to the highest echelon, from the students at West Point? A prolonged and open court-martial would without doubt have brought into question the very judgment of those who had backed Koster, and left an indelible stain. Given the extent of Seaman's true feelings about Koster, made fully public here for the first time, his decision not to proceed with a full court-martial seems illogical unless his primary concern was to protect the image of the Army as an institution.

The public learned little about the massacre from the first two public trials except that a court-martial jury would not easily hand down convictions over what happened at My Lai. A squad leader in Calley's platoon, Sgt David Mitchell, 28, son of a Baptist preacher from St Francisville, Louisiana, was acquitted of murder after the virtual collapse of the prosecution case at Fort Hood, Texas, in November 1970. Dozens of witnesses were expected to be called but the prosecution case was halted after only three members of Charlie Company gave evidence. Conti identified Mitchell as being at the ditch execution site when more than a hundred men, women, children, and babies were shot. Sledge positively identified Mitchell as being involved with Calley in carrying out the slaughter. Olsen testified seeing Mitchell take aim at the villagers in the ditch and open fire. But, incredibly, military judge Colonel George R. Robinson ruled that four helicopter crewmen who had been flying over the scene, including Hugh Thompson, could not give evidence of what they had witnessed. The four had appeared months previously in secret session before the congressional subcommittee investigating the massacre. Unless the committee was prepared to release their testimony to the defense the judge would not allow the four helicopter crew to give evidence. F. Edward Hebert, the subcommittee chairman, declared that the entire transcript of the one hundred witnesses would remain classified. Consequently a crucial part of the case against Mitchell was removed.

The tall handsome soldier was in tears when he testified he had not seen Americans kill any civilians in My Lai—which must have been a near physical impossibility. The prosecutor, summing up, described Mitchell's story as "inherently incredible." Yet the jury chose to believe Mitchell and he left the court a free man, smiling, in the arms of his wife. The Army even allowed him to continue serving as a soldier, though evidence that he had been involved in the ditch site executions with Calley continued to be stated as a fact by military lawyers at other trials.

A statement in which Charles Hutto readily admitted killing a group of unarmed civilians at My Lai with an M-60 machine gun was read out loud at Hutto's court-martial at Fort McPherson, Georgia, in early January 1971. Hutto, also from Louisiana, was one of six children brought up in a poor farming area near

Tullulah. He did not give evidence and the defense did not contest the fact that he had been involved in the killings. However, a clinical psychologist was called to show that Hutto did not adequately possess the capability to make the judgment on whether the order to kill civilians was legal. Dr Norman Reichenberg testified that Hutto's personality was marked by a total lack of creativity, a willingness to submit to orders from authority figures, and a willingness to believe in others. The jury, after considering the evidence for a total of two hours, found Hutto not guilty.*
Suddenly, what had appeared to be the clearest possible judgment of the war crimes trials at Nuremberg, that obeying orders was no defense to mass murder, had been blown apart. Hutto it seemed *had* only been obeying orders. If he was so suggestible as to be psychologically incapable of knowing right from wrong, what was he doing in the Army? It was a curious decision by the jury but perhaps not surprising to those who had observed all the proceedings at the trial. An infantry colonel had been allowed to remain on the jury despite telling the judge that he believed it might be proper to execute a prisoner of war in an unconventional conflict such as Vietnam.

The Hutto verdict had a cataclysmic effect on several other cases involving members of Charlie Company. Torres, Hutson, T'Souvas, and Smith had all been formally accused under military law of murdering Vietnamese civilians, but "in the best interest of justice" Lt. Gen. Connor dismissed the charges on the grounds that the case against each of them was not as strong as that against Hutto. Since Hutto had been acquitted, the charges against each of them should be dismissed. Yet was it to be argued that each of these men was also incapable of knowing right from wrong? The issue was never tested before a jury. Within weeks, murder charges against Scheil and Doherty, and accusations of rape and assault with intent to murder against Hodges, were also quietly dropped.

The trial of William Calley was not a hurried affair. It lasted seventy-seven days—four and a half months, starting in the fall of

---

* The US Manual of Courts-Martial says that a soldier must disobey an order that "a man of ordinary sense and understanding would know to be illegal."

1970 and finishing in the late spring of the following year. Once the initial media interest died away in what was to be the longest court-martial in military history, the judicial proceedings settled down to being a quiet, almost civilized affair, interspersed with occasional moments of high drama.

The setting for the trial was the small courthouse at Fort Benning, a low, white-painted, wooden building just across from a church. In a room about 30 feet square, with red carpet across the floor and blue curtains covering every wall, sat the principal players. The jury of six Army officers were all combat veterans, five of whom had served in Vietnam. They were chosen from among twenty-six potential jurors, who were called, then examined, and frequently challenged by both the prosecution and defense. On the very first day of jury selection an infantry colonel declared his belief, in response to questioning, that orders had to be obeyed in combat even if it resulted in the killing òf civilians. He was only challenged when he conceded he had been exposed to considerable publicity about the case.

An Army man for twenty-five years, Lieutenant Colonel Reid W. Kennedy, the silver-haired military judge from Spencer, Iowa, sat at one end of the room on a raised dais, wearing a formal black judge's gown. Two uniformed prosecuting counsel sat opposite him. Captain John Partin wore spectacles, while Capt. Aubrey Daniel looked somewhat young for the job and was dubbed by many of the women spectators the most handsome man in court. The son of a strip miner from Orange, Virginia, he frequently clashed with the judge. Once, after Daniel had made a string of seemingly petty objections, Kennedy finally snapped at him: "Don't be so thin-skinned."

The frequent cause of Daniel's frustration was the six-man defense team sitting at right angles to him, headed by George Latimer, the wily former military judge. And at one end of the defense table sat the figure who was, of course, the prime focus of attention: Calley himself, accused of the premeditated murder of 109 Vietnamese civilians, a violation of the Uniform Code of Military Justice, Article 118. The formal charges described those killed as "Oriental human beings, males and females, whose names are unknown, occupants of the village of My Lai 4." Those at the back of the room—the press and the public—struggled to view the accused soldier, only just able to see his head above the back of his chair. Despite his shortage of feet and inches, throughout it all Calley was a model of quiet, almost rigid, self-control. He continued to live in his bachelor quarters on post for which he paid $111 a month in rent. A red-haired former Red Cross nurse in her twenties called Anne Moore, whom the press described as his girlfriend, paid regular visits, as did other well-wishers. He held court in his small apartment, pouring drinks from behind the padded bar which fitted neatly into the corner of his living room. He'd cook them elaborate meals in his cramped kitchen area and tell how in Vietnam he would offer to construct banquets out of K-rations for his soldiers, if they dug his foxhole for him. He had so much mail from members of the public, many of whom had donated money to his legal defense fund, that he employed a secretary and spent $35 on an automatic letter opener.

Often, when the court sessions were over, Calley would be closeted in his quarters with a writer called John Sack who carried out prolonged tape-recorded interviews for a book to be published under Calley's name and serialized by *Esquire* magazine, for an advance of $150,000. Sack, protective of his property, sought to guard Calley from too many media questions. Among his self-appointed duties he oversaw access to the five courtroom seats allocated to the defendant. Frequently Sack filled them with pretty young women, many of whom had traveled from all over America to this obscure corner of the military universe in the curious hope of meeting the man on trial for his life. A select few were allowed to visit Calley's quarters for coffee. Some were invited back several times.

The inevitable media circus that surrounded the proceedings was managed by no less than seven full-time Army information officers. The public information office at Fort Benning, with the full approval of the Pentagon, spared no effort to ensure that not only was justice being done, it was *military* justice that was being seen to be done. Elaborate arrangements were made to cater for the 120 press and television reporters who requested a seat in the courtroom. Most of them faced the disappointment of not having a grandstand seat. Two-thirds of the 59 public seats were given over to reporters; the remaining 20 were allocated by ballot each morning to members of the public. Unclaimed seats were given to journalists.

Judge Kennedy proved to be courtesy itself. After initial warnings about the dangers of media interviews with potential witnesses, he provided every assistance to reporters. Keenly aware how important the trial was for the Army in public relations terms, he noted their deadlines and often allowed thirty-minute recesses in the late afternoon to allow them time to file their stories. An auxiliary press room in the courthouse had installed twenty-nine direct lines to long-distance operators at the telephone exchange in nearby Columbus, in addition to private lines for the television and radio networks and wire services.

Occasionally Judge Kennedy, who had earned his law degree from Drake University in Des Moines, Iowa, could be heard discreetly making arrangements to meet one of the reporters for a drink. He also allowed journalists to listen to court proceedings from a small room adjacent to the main courtroom, where witnesses' testimony was being taped. Speakers attached to a special circuit were installed for the purpose by technicians from the CBS television network. In an Army gymnasium a short distance from the courtroom, a special press center was established with space for two hundred reporters, photographers, and technicians, complete with a darkroom, extra phone and telex lines, and vending machines dispensing soft drinks, cigarettes, sandwiches, and coffee. At the steps near the entrance to the courthouse photographers were allowed to erect a tent, and they subsequently parked a camper trailer, where they could keep warm and take coffee breaks.

More than a hundred witnesses were photographed entering or leaving the courtroom during the course of the trial. Many gave evidence reluctantly about the events in My Lai but a few went to great lengths not to testify. Allen Boyce, who had taken part in the killing, cited the Fifth Amendment privilege against self-incrimination on eight occasions. He refused to answer any questions despite stern warnings from the judge. Paul Meadlo, on the advice of his lawyer, also refused to testify even after briefly being ordered into custody by Judge Kennedy, who recalled "the nauseating detail" with which Meadlo had described the killings on television. It was only when a writ was issued granting him immunity from prosecution under the Organized Crime Control Act that Meadlo went into the witness box and told how he and Calley had mown down a hundred villagers. Even then a US attorney and two federal marshals sat close by, ready to take him to jail if he refused to answer questions.

Only rarely did the jury hear of the wanton cruelty and savagery carried out by members of Charlie Company other than Calley, but by then journalistic interest in the trial had diminished and the details were not widely reported. An overseas observer noted that after Christmas 1970, with the honorable exception of the *Washington Post*, journalists were not reporting the nightmarish quality that had begun to infect the court proceedings. Thus the American public never understood the full horror of My Lai—the rapes, tortures, and mutilations that were committed. Among the evidence that passed by the public was the account given by Gonzalez and McBreen of how Roschevitz, in the 2nd Platoon, had forced a group of women to strip and then executed them by firing a special flechette round from his grenade launcher after they refused to have sex with him. Few outside the courtroom ever heard the appalling story of how Conti had tried to force a woman to perform oral sex on him by holding a gun to the head of her child until Calley came along and told him to pull up his pants and get on with the war.

The descriptions given in court of the mass killings were certainly gruesome but the details were mostly confined to Calley's actions during the course of the massacre, thus giving the impression that only a handful of men had gone berserk that morning. The evidence stacked up against Calley as a string of eyewitnesses described his actions, which included the killing of the priest and the little baby at the ditch. Conti graphically described the condition of the bodies:

They were pretty well messed up. There was a lot of heads had been shot off, pieces of heads, flesh of the . . . fleshy parts of the body, side and arms, pretty well messed up. I seen the recoil of the rifle and the muzzle flashes and as I looked down, I seen a woman try to get up. As she got up I saw Lt. Calley fire and hit the side of her head and blow the side of her head off. I left.

Calley's defense rested on his obedience to a lawful order given to him by a superior officer. The jury spent many hours out of the courtroom as Latimer tried numerous maneuvers to bring the trial to a complete halt—each of which was subsequently knocked down by Judge Kennedy. Latimer argued protracted points of law about pretrial publicity and undue command influence, and requested the testimony which F. Edward Hebert's congressional subcommittee had refused to declassify for the Mitchell court-martial. Many observers believed he was simply laying the grounds for a subsequent appeal. On one occasion his assistant angrily challenged the size of the blown-up colored photographs taken by Haeberle that the prosecution used in evidence, accusing Daniel of improperly trying to influence the jury.

During three days of testimony Calley agreed he had killed civilians but his defense for doing this was quite simple. At Latimer's prompting he described his instructions from Medina in a straightforward, almost bland fashion:

I was ordered to go in there and destroy the enemy. That was my job that day. That was the mission I was given. I did not sit down and think in terms of men, women and children. They were all classified the same, and that was the classification that we dealt with, just as enemy soldiers . . . I felt then and I still do that I acted as I was directed, and I carried out the orders that I was given and I do not feel wrong in doing so.

Calley privately regarded the people whose lives he was snuffing out as simply no more than animals, but this rationale was kept from the jury. He had given details of his inner thoughts and feelings to a team of military psychiatrists. In late January 1971, the trial was halted when the judge sent Calley as an outpatient for a psychiatric examination at the Walter Reed Army Hospital in Washington, DC. For a week he underwent a battery of tests including neurological and physical examinations. Then the military shrinks went to work, conducting twelve separate interviews each lasting an hour or two, sometimes with his military lawyer present but also on his own. The doctors applied the Wechsler Adult Intelligence Scale, the Rorschach Test, the Thematic Apperception Test, the Draw-a-person Test, the California Personality Inventory, the Strong Vocational Interest Blank, and several others. The results proved Calley was normal. They found no psychiatric disease and were certain their infamous patient knew the difference between right and wrong.

The psychiatrists' report shows Calley revealed far more about his real feelings to the doctors than he ever did to the jury, which was only shown a heavily censored copy. Included in the portion they did not see was the following:

On one occasion he allegedly kicked Meadlo to encourage him to follow orders and he alleges he had to stop one soldier from sexually molesting a Vietnamese female. *Lt. Calley states that he did not feel as if he were killing humans but rather that they were animals with whom one could not speak or reason* [our italics]. After the ditch incident other than a person crawling through a rice field whom Lt. Calley describes having killed then learned was a child, and an elderly man whom Lt. Calley alleges he killed, no further Vietnamese were encountered . . . During the events of the morning up to about noon Lt. Calley claims that he was "hyper" or "psyched up."

Calley had taken a positive attitude toward the doctors who examined him but occasionally became irritated when asked to repeat tedious tasks which he had previously undertaken for other psychologists or psychiatrists at the hospital. Anxious about the outcome of his trial, he gave the impression of confidence and even talked of his plans for the future. To the men in the white coats he exhibited a strong drive to achieve. He talked about his past, emphasizing his successes and ignoring his failures, continually striving to present the best possible image of himself. The doctors observed, however, that Calley failed to appreciate subtlety and tended to solve problems in a rather simplistic fashion. He had, for example, interpreted the proverb "People who live in glass houses should not throw rocks" as literally meaning: "If you don't want rocks thrown at you, don't throw rocks."

The psychiatrists finally concluded:

He tends to project himself as mature, intelligent, successful and confident and seems to be constantly striving to be outstanding. His style of thinking seems to allow him to miss finer discriminations of meaning, so that he tends to reduce subtle gradations of meaning to simple "either/or" concepts. He consciously rejects a dependent role, and one observed a tendency to avoid close relationships, yet he exhibits a strong need to be with people or to be accepted by them. One may postulate an underlying sense of insecurity which may be reflected in the thoughts and actions on the surface.

When the mass of witness testimony was finally completed, the jury took thirteen days to privately examine the evidence and consider each of the four charges.

"The defense would ask you to legalize murder," the military prosecutor told the jury in his final address, recalling Abraham Lincoln's order to the Union Army during the Civil War: "Men who take up arms against one another in public do not cease on this account to be moral human beings, responsible to one another and to God."

On March 29, 1971, after 79 hours and 58 minutes of deliberation, the jury returned to the courtroom and announced they had found Calley guilty of the premeditated murder of twenty-two of the villagers at My Lai. One of them said later that they had left no stone unturned in Calley's favor. Major Walter Kinard, a Vietnam veteran, declared they had "labored long and hard to find some way, some evidence, or some flaw in the testimony, so we could find Lt. Calley innocent." The jury then had to retire once more to determine whether he should hang for his crimes.

Latimer pleaded for the life of his client who, he said, had not killed for personal gain. Calley had been a "good boy until he got into that Oriental situation . . . You've been pretty well insulated," he told the jury, who for months had been continually warned by the judge not to read press reports of the trial or watch news coverage on television. "You'll find there's been no case in the history of military justice that has torn this country apart as this one," he added.

Calley then stood up and in a faltering voice, his eyes moist with tears, poured his heart out:

I'm not going to stand here and plead for my life or my freedom. I've never known a soldier, nor did I ever myself, wantonly kill a human being in my entire life. When my troops were getting massacred and mauled by an enemy I couldn't see, I couldn't feel and I couldn't touch, nobody in the military system ever described them as anything other than Communism. They didn't give it a race, they didn't give it a sex, they didn't give it an age. They never let me believe it was just a philosophy in a man's mind that was my enemy out there.

Yesterday, you stripped me of all my honor. Please, by your actions that you take here today, don't strip future soldiers of their honor—I beg of you.

As soon as he sat down, the military prosecutor, Daniel, was on his feet urgently responding: "You did not strip him of his honor. What he did stripped him of his honor. It is not honor, and never can be considered honor, to kill men, women, and children." Calley was taken away to a cell in the Fort Benning stockade.

Two days later, on March 31, after considering the matter for nearly seven hours, the jury returned to a crowded but hushed courtroom and declared that Calley should be confined at hard labor for the length of his natural life. Turning and saluting, the mass killer said he would do his best. He was then taken back to the stockade to await transfer to the Army's prison at Fort Leavenworth, Kansas. Army information officers arranged for his guards to escort Calley toward the cell blocks slowly but deliberately to ensure that photographers could get their pictures.

Even at that precise moment the rawest recruits to the United States Army were being instructed that there were to be no more My Lais. The message was being drummed home in special courses at the infantry training center at Fort Benning on how to deal with prisoners and civilians in the combat zone. Military lawyers taught the Law of Land Warfare to young second lieutenants bound for infantry battalions in Vietnam who were undergoing training as platoon commanders. What real effect this had is uncertain. The new grunts-in-the-making appeared just as eager to demonstrate the values instilled in them in training by their drill sergeants, most of whom were veterans of the war in Vietnam where soldiers at Khe Sahn had hastily raised a defiant sign—"'A' TROOP, 1st CAV, SALUTES LT. WILLIAM CALLEY"—after the court-martial verdict was announced. Artillerymen in the Ashau Valley labeled one of their guns "Calley's Avenger." The instructors had returned home to train their new charges in the savage arts, teaching them about warfare, staying alive, weapons drill, and the "spirit of the bayonet." They learned, as Charlie Company had learned, how to "Kill, kill, kill with cold blue steel." They also learned how to march in time. Route marches took the recruits along the narrow tree-lined roads that spread out from their company area, where they collapsed exhausted on bunks in barrack blocks and learned obedience to orders. In fair weather and foul they marched, helmeted, in heavy combat gear, carrying their weapons, strung out in long columns of threes. Beside them as they moved to or from the many firing ranges and assault courses that littered Fort Benning, drill sergeants badgered and hollered at them to keep time. And as they did so the trainees broke into a new marching chant they had learned, taught them by the senior noncoms, and sung out loud and clear to a regular foot-slogging rhythm:

> Calley . . . Calley . . . he's our man . . .
> If he can't do it, Medina can.

Three days later, Calley was out of the stockade under house arrest and back in his apartment at Fort Benning, freed for the time being by his Commander-in-Chief: the President. Nixon, vacationing at his home in San Clemente, California, wasted no time in agreeing to an utterly transparent display of political opportunism urged on him by his senior staff in the White House. Despite the troop withdrawals the war in Vietnam continued to be a deep wound in American life that would not heal. Now, with the verdict in the Calley trial, the wound burst open once more. To many Americans, Calley was a hero, and they believed that with the guilty verdict a great injustice had been perpetrated by the Army. These emotions were immediately exploited both inside and outside the White House. Disc jockeys at radio stations across America's southern states repeatedly aired a new recording on the Plantation label, by an instant Alabama vocal group called "C Company," about "a little boy who wanted to grow up and be a soldier and serve his country in whatever way he could":

My name is William Calley, I'm a soldier of this land,
I've vowed to do my duty and to gain the upper hand,
But they've made me out a villain; they have stamped me with a brand,
As we go marching on . . .

In the three days he had been behind bars "The Battle Hymn of Lt. Calley" had sold 200,000 copies and in South Vietnam the armed forces radio network in Saigon played it regularly until someone high up in MACV ordered them to stop. The sentiment of many GIs was expressed on a wall in the city: "Kill a Gook for Calley." These events coincided with the publication of a collection of essays about social destructiveness in a book named *Sanctions of Evil*, which touched on My Lai and why people took part in atrocities. The title of one chapter, "It Never Happened—Besides, They Deserved It," seemed perfectly to capture the attitude of many Americans who believed Calley was truly innocent. In an extraordinary wave of sympathy they sent 5,000 telegrams to the White House, running 100 to 1 in Calley's favor. On the political left those against the war saw Calley as a victim caught up in an immoral war. They wanted the generals and politicians put on trial for war crimes. Those on the right thought the verdict insulted all American troops fighting in Vietnam and were appalled at what their government was doing.

In Austin, Texas, a local newspaper ran a front-page editorial headlined: "Obituary US Army," and sold out the entire issue. "Free Calley" fender stickers appeared everywhere. On the second night Calley spent behind bars, waiting to see if he would be given the death penalty, a "Rally for Calley" was held in nearby Columbus, organized by the local branch of the American Legion. A local minister, Rev. Michael Lord, appeared to deify the newly convicted mass murderer: "There was a crucifixion 2,000 years ago of a man named Jesus Christ. I don't think we need another crucifixion of a man named Rusty Calley." Among the other speakers were Lester Maddox, lieutenant governor of Georgia, George Wallace, Governor of Alabama, and John Bell Williams, Governor of Mississippi. Governor Jimmy Carter organized an "American Fighting Men's Day," exhorting the citizens of Georgia to drive with their car headlights on and "honor the flag as 'Rusty' had done."

Resolutions urging the President to offer clemency to Calley were introduced in the state legislatures of North Carolina, Colorado, Kansas, Alabama, and Michigan. Draft boards in Athens, Georgia, and Huron County, Michigan, resigned. Local draft board No. 182 at Pittsfield, Illinois, protested to the President: "We do not believe that we can conscientiously ask our youth to serve their country under present conditions as would allow for such a court-martial verdict." At St Petersburg, Florida, many firms flew the US flag at half mast and a World War II veteran went into an Army recruiting office in Mobile, Alabama, to make an extraordinary request. He had flown bombing missions over Germany which had killed innocent civilians and wanted to be arrested for war crimes. A former Army sergeant, Furman Norwood, of Seattle, mailed his World War II medals—a Silver Star, three Bronze Stars, and two Purple Hearts—to the White House.

Others were equally incredulous at the extraordinary public reaction to Calley's conviction. "People aren't stopping to think," proclaimed Major Harvey Brown, 33, a member of the court-martial jury, after his wife and children in Matador, Texas, had received death threats. "They're letting their emotions rule their minds at this point. They haven't sat through four and a half months of a trial and heard the facts. When you conjure up a mental picture of men, old men, women, children, and babies—that was a rather harsh treatment, and a rather final treatment."

Nixon, satisfying public demand, announced that Calley would be freed from prison and remain under house arrest while his appeal was considered. He then went one stage further and injected an extralegal ingredient into the judicial proceedings. When all the appeals had been heard Nixon said he—as Commander-in-Chief—would finally review the case. For the second time in a few days the memory of Abraham Lincoln was invoked when the President recalled that during the Civil War Lincoln had personally shown clemency to a young soldier sentenced to death for falling asleep at his post while on guard duty.

It was a ludicrous comparison to make and one that totally ignored certain crucial facts. Calley was to remain in his comfortable quarters under house arrest while other convicted prisoners would have to serve out their time. They included a soldier in Fort

Leavenworth jailed for five years in 1970 for *pushing* a warrant officer and an Air Force colonel sent away for three years for smoking a marijuana cigarette. Almost eighty soldiers were serving time in Fort Leavenworth on murder charges that originated in Vietnam. Some of their victims were Americans, but most were Vietnamese. Some still had their appeals pending. *Time* magazine called the wave of sympathy for Calley "a sickening distortion of moral sensibility" but moral issues did not interest Nixon. What mattered to the White House was what the voters thought.

Across the world in the war zone, the policy of Vietnamization looked decidedly shaky in its first major military test. In February, a 5,000-man ARVN force had been sent into Laos to cut off the Ho Chi Minh Trail. Their efforts resulted in near disaster. After penetrating 11 miles they panicked when they came under sustained resistance including artillery fire. US forces had to bail them out.

So far it had been a disastrous year politically, as the President's poll rating among the public slipped lower and lower. From the high point of November 1969, when he had promised to bring American troops home from the war, Gallup showed him sliding month by month—56 percent at the beginning of 1971, 51 percent in February, 50 percent in March, and 49 percent in April. Moreover, his chief rival in the Democratic Party, Edmund Muskie, was leading him by an increasingly wide margin. Thus in the spring months when Calley's trial was drawing to a close, Nixon's popularity had fallen to a lower level than that of any President since Harry Truman at a comparable point in his administration.

Charles W. Colson, the President's special counsel—subsequently jailed for his part in the Watergate coverup—immediately saw the political capital to be gained from the adverse public reaction to Calley's conviction. If Calley was allowed to remain in his officer's apartment during the appeal process, he argued, "it would allow the President to capture public sentiment without foreclosing any future options." A civilian would be allowed the same rights, Colson argued, comparing Calley's case to that of the boxer Muhammad Ali "who made $5 million during the appeals of his draft case."

H. R. Haldeman, Nixon's chief of staff, watched as the President picked up the phone at the "western White House" in California and called Admiral Thomas H. Moorer, the Chairman of the Joint Chiefs of Staff at the Pentagon. He ordered Calley freed from jail and returned to his quarters.

"Yes, sir," Moorer replied to his Commander-in-Chief.

Nixon well knew the gravity, in legal terms, of the decision he had just taken. He turned to Haldeman and said, apparently contemptuously of Moorer: "Anyone else would have answered 'Yes—but.'"

Again the President was served with conflicting advice. Just as in late 1969 when he had refused pleas to appoint a special commission to investigate the massacre, he again made a decision that gave the greatest political advantage, resisting the call of his White House counsel, John Dean, to leave Calley alone. Dean had quickly boned up on military law and laid out the legal options, leaving Nixon's most senior advisors, Haldeman and Ehrlichman, in no doubt at all about Calley's role in the massacre:

There are several factors which militate against direct Presidential involvement with the case at this time. The facts show particularly aggravated conduct on the part of the accused. It appears that Lt. Calley and members of his unit secured the hamlet without a firefight, established complete control over the inhabitants who were unarmed, unresisting civilians, placed them in convenient groups and then shot them.

The conduct for which Lt. Calley has been convicted constitutes a gross violation of the customary law of war. Were it not for the fact that the victims were citizens of the Republic of Vietnam they would have been protected persons of the 1949 Geneva Convention and their murders would have constituted a grave breach which the US as a signatory to the convention was obliged to prosecute. Therefore Presidential involvement at this time could have an adverse effect on world opinion . . . it is my recommendation that the President should not intervene or become involved in this case at this time.

Once the decision was made to let Calley out of jail during his appeal process, the well-oiled news management machine at the White House swung into action. Leading lights in various veterans' organizations across the country were approached and asked to publicly endorse the President's action. Among those who obliged was Herbert Rainwater, national commander of the Veterans of

Foreign Wars: "Now for the first time in our history we have tried a soldier for performing his duty."

The only problem the Army had was whether Calley's release from secure military confinement would cause public relations problems. A senior military lawyer at the Pentagon warned the commanding general at Fort Benning that the White House had been consulted about the particular arrangements for keeping Calley under house arrest: "We could have him eat at the mess hall . . . I don't think you want him traipsing down to the local Safeway to buy food . . . I can't really see Calley going down to the Safeway and pushing his market basket around."

The most acerbic response to the President's decision came from an unexpected military source, the angry young Army lawyer who had just successfully prosecuted Calley. Capt. Aubrey Daniel wrote Nixon a letter which exploded with anger and dismay, causing severe embarrassment for the Army brass. Soon to leave the Army for a prestigious Washington law firm, Daniel told Nixon that those supporting Calley had not understood the evidence and were mistaken in their belief that he had simply been convicted for "killing the enemy." Shocked that so many had failed to see the basic moral issue, Daniel steadfastly reminded the President that it was *unlawful* for American soldiers to summarily execute unarmed and unresisting men, women, children, and babies. Daniel was appalled that America's political leaders were prepared to compromise the moral issue for political motives. The President, the letter continued, had damaged the military system of justice, had "helped enhance the image of Calley as a national hero," and had given support to those who had attacked "the six loyal soliders who served on the jury."

Rebuking Nixon, who was himself a lawyer, Daniel asked:

Have you considered those men in making your decisions, the men who, since rendering their verdict, have found themselves and their families the subject of vicious attacks upon their honor, integrity, and loyalty to this nation?

It would seem to me to be more appropriate for you as the President to have said something in their behalf and to remind the nation of the purpose of our legal system and the respect it should command. I would expect that the President of the United States, a man who I believed should and would provide the moral leadership for this nation, would stand fully behind the law of this land on a moral issue which is so clear and about which there can be no compromise. For this nation to condone the acts of Lt. Calley is to make us no better than our enemies and make any pleas by this nation for the humane treatment of our own prisoners meaningless.

The *New York Times* described Daniel's words as a magnificent expression of American idealism. However, the public hostility to the verdict did not die down and more and more draft boards across the country resigned. From an Atlanta-based organization calling itself Citizens of Georgia for Lt. Calley came an unusual gift for the President, delivered by plane to National Airport in Washington. Staff in the Air Express office contacted the White House about a billy goat which had arrived unaccompanied at the airport addressed to the President. It wore an Eisenhower jacket with red, white, and blue trimmings, and was labeled: "SCAPEGOAT." This message appeared to have more effect on Nixon's attitude than the pleas of those most intimately involved with the Calley case.

"Calley is not a scapegoat, nor a poor lieutenant singled out to bear the entire burden of a difficult war," declared a high-level Army memorandum circulating among senior staff at the White House. "His acts stand alone in infamy among known atrocities for the US forces in the war . . . if Calley is let go, or let off with a slap on the wrist, the message to all soldiers must read: 'anything goes.' The implications for the Army, let alone the nation, are incalculable but clearly intolerable."

The memo—classified "sensitive"—was sent by Melvin Laird to Haig to ensure the White House staff fully understood the implications of the Calley case, given that people had reacted to a misconception of the facts. The evidence showed the killings had not occurred in the heat of combat as many believed. "There was no battle and not a single casualty in Calley's platoon," the document emphasized. A presidential pardon or mitigation of Calley's sentence would endorse what had become known as "the mere gook rule"—the feeling that Asian life was not worthy of respect:

The President has no responsibility for what happened at My Lai . . .

[*but*] intervention could put him in the position of condoning it. No one should undertake to advise the President who is not fully informed of the sordid facts revealed by the trial and the Peers inquiry . . . There is no individual under investigation, charged or convicted, in any case, whose crime can *even remotely* [original italics] be said to equal that of Calley in terms of the number of human lives involved.

Opinion polls, however, interested the White House more than being confronted with the truth about the massacre or warnings against political exploitation of public sentiment toward Calley. In mid-April, Colson received advance results from the New York pollster Lou Harris of a survey about My Lai in which Nixon received an overall approval rating of 55 percent for his handling of the case. Colson wrote to Haldeman: "[Harris] therefore feels that is a very strong showing. On the question of whether the President went as far as he could to show sympathy for Calley, the positive/negative is 2 to 1. Harris further believes that with such a strong showing in the Calley case we are bound to be moving up significantly."

Nixon's intervention on Calley's behalf established a climate of opinion in which the crucial moral issues thrown up by the massacre and its aftermath could quickly be forgotten by most of America. The tortuous process of military justice dragged on through the rest of 1971 and nobody with any serious understanding of the issues involved could have been surprised at the outcome. By the end of the year three more defendants—Kotouc, Medina, and Henderson—had each been acquitted by the judgment of their peers, fellow officers on courts-martial juries.

Little wonder then at Kotouc's own verdict on the US Army when, a month after Calley's conviction, he was found not guilty of aggravated assault while interrogating a Viet Cong suspect by cutting off his little finger at Charlie Company's bivouac the afternoon of the massacre. An Army surgeon testified that this was an act requiring considerable force. Kotouc argued that the injury was an accident which occurred when he was "using an element of fear" to get the suspect to talk, as the US Army had trained him. The jury took less than an hour to find in his favor. As Kotouc left the courtroom he was asked if he would stay in the military: "Who

would want to get out of a system like this? . . . it's the best damn
army in the world," he said.

Three days earlier, the military judge had ordered the jury to
acquit Kotouc on the more serious charge of deliberately maiming
the prisoner. His final instruction to them had considerable influence; they had to be certain, he said, that Kotouc's actions were
carried out with intent to injure and were the result of negligence:

Unless you are satisfied beyond reasonable doubt that the cutting of the
alleged victim was not the result of an accident, you must acquit Capt.
Kotouc. The regulations and directives of the US Army with respect to
intelligence interrogation in force at the time of the alleged incident,
could well have led Capt. Kotouc to believe it was lawful for him to use
harsh and abusive language toward the victim and to threaten violence in
an attempt to get information. I must instruct you that if you find Capt.
Kotouc was merely *offering* [our italics] to do violence to the alleged
victim, such an act . . . would be legally justified.

It was a legal ruling completely at odds with the Geneva Conventions, which prohibit the use of violence or physical or mental
torture on POWs to get information. Indeed, when pictures were
shown on television of captured American and British fliers who
appeared to have been tortured during the war against Iraq in
1991, it caused outrage and indignation throughout the world.

Interpretations of military law and judicial rulings at Medina's
trial and other hearings were equally remarkable. Medina,
originally accused of taking part in the coverup, had dereliction
offenses against him dropped because of the statute of limitations.
He was instead charged with murdering 102 Vietnamese civilians.
An important tenet of military discipline lay at the heart of the
prosecution's case against Medina: command responsibility. As the
man in charge of Charlie Company, should he be held accountable
for the actions of his men? Hundreds of people had been needlessly
slaughtered. If he knew a massacre was taking place, or about to
take place, he had a duty to prevent it. If he didn't know, he
should have known.

Medina came to trial well versed in his account of what happened
since he had already given testimony to the Inspector General's
inquiry, to Peers, and at the Calley trial, as well as several other

hearings. Appearing before Congress he had defended his actions and those of Lt. Col. Frank Barker before Congressman Hebert's panel investigating My Lai. When he completed giving evidence in secret session the entire subcommittee rose as one man to applaud him. As they left the committee room each Congressman stood by the door and shook Medina's hand.

At his court-martial, eighteen months later, the highly skilled and somewhat flamboyant criminal lawyer from Boston, F. Lee Bailey, conducted a brilliant defense. He initially moved, unsuccessfully, for the charges to be dropped because of undue command influence, and attacked senior Army lawyers for alleged indirect threats against the two young JAG captains who were Medina's military lawyers. The military prosecutor, Major William Eckhardt, had already been defeated in the Hutto and Kotouc trials, and he was about to make it three in a row.

The government's case was that Medina knew what was happening in the village and failed to prevent it, thus abandoning his command responsibility. The prosecution got off to a rough start when Bailey managed to neutralize the testimony of Michael Bernhardt, a vital government witness who Medina had warned not to write to his Congressman about what he knew of the massacre. Outside the courtroom the evening before he was due to give evidence, Bernhardt ingenuously told Medina's military lawyers that he might be prepared to lie on oath in defense of a principle, a fact he readily confirmed the following day when Bailey challenged him in court. Eckhardt, acutely embarrassed, called for a recess and withdrew Bernhardt as a witness.

Ron Haeberle was allowed to give evidence about what he saw in the village, but Bailey successfully argued that his photographs should be kept from the jury.

During the trial Medina celebrated his thirty-fifth birthday. A cake complete with candles was brought into court, largely at the instigation of photographers, who snapped away. The judge, Colonel Kenneth Howard, joined in the media circus: "At the risk of poor taste we wish you a happy birthday."

In his own testimony Medina firmly denied knowing that his men had killed civilians and toward the end of the trial the judge reduced the murder charge to one of involuntary manslaughter of one hundred My Lai villagers. A charge of murdering a small boy was dropped, and it was left for the jury to decide whether Medina had unlawfully killed a Vietnamese woman in a paddy field. Exactly fifty-seven minutes after they retired, the jury returned and acquitted Medina of all charges. A few minutes later he professed never to have lost faith in the military system of justice.

Not long afterward Medina left the Army to work for a helicopter manufacturing company owned by F. Lee Bailey in Menomee, Michigan. He moved his family just across the state line to a small town called Marinette, Wisconsin, and they later took up residence in a large rambling timbered house on State Street where he still lives today. It wasn't until several months later, when he gave evidence at the trial of Col. Oran Henderson, that Medina finally confessed he had suppressed evidence and lied to his brigade commander about the numbers of civilians killed in My Lai. Medina had known all along that more than a hundred villagers had died and only now did he admit he was "not completely candid" in statements he had made under oath to Army investigators because of the disgrace it would bring the military, the United States, his family, and himself. Now out of the Army, he could not be tried for perjury.

Henderson's court-martial was the last of the My Lai trials. He was accused of covering up evidence of the massacre and making false statements to the Peers inquiry. During the 77-day hearing, in which a hundred witnesses gave evidence before a jury of two generals and five colonels, two pictures were painted of the former 11th Brigade commander. The prosecution claimed he had brought dishonor on his uniform. He had covered up the massacre out of a fear of losing his command and the apprehension he would not be promoted to general if it were known that his men had committed a war crime. The other image of Henderson was given by his civilian defense counsel, Henry Rothblatt, who portrayed him as "a great soldier" who had served his country well since 1939, suffering wounds in three major wars. But his lawyer had been most anxious to withhold some of the crucial evidence against his client. At pretrial hearings Rothblatt tried vigorously, but unsuccessfully, to prevent Henderson's previous testimony, given to the Inspector General's inquiry and to Peers, from being used against him.

On the stand, Henderson remained adamant that he never knew of any "excessive killings." The soldiers of Charlie Company told him no more than twenty civilians had been killed by artillery and gunship fire. However, he conceded he had not placed sufficient credence in Hugh Thompson's allegations; if he had known a hundred people had died, he would have conducted a formal investigation. After his acquittal he said the verdict "reaffirms the confidence any man can have in the military system." The *New York Times*, however, called it a debacle of military justice. One of the paper's writers reported nagging doubts about the case: "Those who have listened to the testimony of more than 100 witnesses believe that a number of high-ranking officers have not told the truth under oath, either to protect themselves or to avoid embarrassing the Army. There have been too many claims of 'I can't recall' for anyone to believe that the truth has been told."

Five days later, Henderson was at the Pentagon, having requested a personal interview with the Chief of Staff. Westmoreland did not relish the meeting, for the Henderson case had caused him much personal anguish. First there had been the letter in which Henderson had written to him offering to take the blame for the failure to investigate My Lai in the hope that the Peers inquiry would be halted. Then, after he was accused of coverup offenses, Henderson had claimed to journalists that other brigade-sized units in Vietnam had committed atrocities similar to My Lai but had not had a Ronald Ridenhour to make them public. This extraordinary outburst was immediately followed by a whining, self-serving letter from Henderson to the vice chief of staff announcing he was going to employ a civilian counsel because Army lawyers had obstructed the preparation of his defense. Finally, Westmoreland had received a pitiful personal letter from Henderson's 76-year-old mother, Mrs Mary Henderson, from her home on West Michigan Street, Indianapolis, in the middle of her son's court-martial:

We are Christian people and always tried to raise our six children to do what is right. We tried through the Depression to take care of them but it was very hard. We have known nothing but war for 34 years, for as soon as our four boys left high school they had to go in the Army. I feel we did our part giving all four.

We do feel our son, Col. Oran K., is being treated so unfair after 33 of his best years have been in the Army. He has always loved it and lived for it. He always told us he wanted to be a General . . . I do feel the Army are making a big mistake by doing the things they have to our wonderful soldier . . .

Henderson used his early morning interview with Westmoreland, three days before Christmas, 1971, to uphold his innocence stoutly, though he meekly conceded he might have made an error of judgment. In subsequent months the Army could have subjected Henderson to a special process of administrative review by which his performance as a soldier would have been assessed by military lawyers. Instead they decided to apply a double jeopardy rule because the court-martial jury had already passed judgment on Henderson's performance when they acquitted him of dereliction of duty.

Former members of Charlie Company, still in the Army, who had grave criminal charges against them dismissed before they came to trial found that the administrative review process was used to discharge them quietly from military service and bar them from reenlistment. Some officers accused of being involved in the coverup had their careers seriously damaged when they were issued letters of censure and had military decorations awarded for combat service in Vietnam removed. Yet the whole administrative review process seemed riddled with inconsistency to the extent that even the Army General Counsel described it in a confidential memorandum as a fiasco.

For example, in the case of Col. Robert Luper, commander of the artillery battalion which shelled My Lai, the Army did a complete somersault. Westmoreland initially recommended he should suffer a similar fate to that of Col. Nels Parson, the Americal Divison chief of staff, who was issued a letter of censure and had his Legion of Merit withdrawn. Mysteriously, after Luper formally objected to this proposed action, Westmoreland changed his mind. A note attached to Luper's case papers in the National Archives reveals there was pressure from members of Congress to leave Luper alone: "From a Congressional standpoint, OCLL [Office of Congressional Legislative Liaison] believes that in view of the acquittal by court-martial of Col. Henderson, Congressional criticism of the Army is more likely to occur if administrative action is taken in this case."

The Secretary of the Army instructed no further action was to be taken in Luper's case. Fiercely objecting to this, the Army's own General Counsel argued in a memorandum to the Secretary of the General Staff and the Judge Advocate General that Luper had a general obligation to report civilian deaths because he was the senior officer present with Henderson when they flew over My Lai the morning of the massacre. In a telling phrase, Berry conceded Henderson had been found not guilty: "but in my opinion one miscarriage of justice does not justify another."

Sgt Kenneth Hodges, a 2nd Platoon squad leader who had rape charges against him dismissed and thus avoided a court-martial, was one of the members of Charlie Company recommended for discharge from the Army and barred from future enlistment. Army lawyers remained convinced he had been involved in some kind of sexual frolic but Hodges fought against being forced out of the Army, insisting on his innocence. It proved one more public relations headache for the men at the Pentagon. Major General Winant Sidle—the man who forbade Peers to call what happened at My Lai a "massacre"—cautioned that there were several public affairs pitfalls to Hodges's case. From a legal standpoint, getting rid of him might be desirable, but it also threatened to put the My Lai story back on page one "after public interest seems to have waned":

The press is unaware of the results of any administrative actions against military personnel except in the earlier cases involving two general officers [Koster and Young]. This action risks lifting the lid and placing in plain view for public scrutiny and press exploitation the entire package of Son My administrative reviews.

Sgt Hodges's arguments, while perhaps not legally sufficient, have an emotional appeal. In media coverage he can be portrayed as another scapegoat and score points in his behalf with public and press while the Army is again placed at a disadvantage through prolonged media interest in a most unfavorable story.

Gradually, much to the satisfaction of the top brass in the Pentagon and of Nixon and his aides in the White House, the story of My Lai faded from the public consciousness. The troops were coming home from Vietnam, the numbers of combat casualties decreased, and America became caught up in a presidential election—one that saw a famous landslide victory for Nixon. Occasionally the massacre received passing mention, for example when Seymour Hersh obtained a copy of the secret Peers Report and exposed the full extent of the coverup, or when Lt. Gen. Peers retired from the Army without being granted a fourth star. It was said that he was being punished by some of his fellow generals who couldn't stomach the damage his report had caused Koster and the Army. Peers had been made deputy commander of US forces in Korea and many believed he would soon get the top job and promotion to full general. But by the time the post became vacant his friend Westmoreland had left the Pentagon and the position of commander in Korea went to someone else. Peers kept his dignity and his silence and retired to California.

Another soldier who by Army standards bore his punishment with good grace and dignity was William Calley, regarded as a model prisoner by those charged with his security while under continuing house arrest at Fort Benning. His sentence had been reduced on review to twenty years' hard labor, but George Latimer relentlessly argued his appeal through the military courts. The Army was anxious to keep Calley out of the public eye. There were no visits to the mess hall for his meals or trips to the Safeway supermarket to stock up his shopping trolley. Forbidden to communicate with fellow officers in the six-apartment BOQ complex on Arrowhead Road, he had to exercise in the fenced rear yard— he played badminton with one of his guards. His girlfriend, Anne Moore, bought food from a local supermarket. Calley was not allowed to go to the base cinema, gymnasium, or canteen; neither could he have visits from fellow prisoners. For recreation he built large gas-powered model airplanes and enrolled in several correspondence courses in accounting, history, and oceanography with the US Armed Forces Institute. For company he gathered around him a myna bird and a beagle, and purchased two aquariums, which he stocked with saltwater and tropical fish. Life under the oceans fascinated him and he idly expressed thoughts of being able to open a small resort in the Bahamas when he was finally released.

The isolation of his confinement, though, began to take its toll and Calley showed clear signs of depression, particularly after the long illness and subsequent death of his father. He became bored and unable to concentrate. The White House was warned that Army physicians were worried he might commit suicide. Unless moved quickly, his mental condition might deteriorate. He told visitors, including a psychiatrist, the President had done him no favors by placing him under house arrest at Fort Benning, where he was unable to socialize or take advantage of educational facilities that would have been available to him at the Leavenworth detention barracks in Kansas. He bitterly disliked being under constant guard and especially resented the armed escort which always accompanied him whenever he left his quarters. In the first eighteen months his only visits had been to the dentist and to his father when he was seriously ill. Because of the media circus it would have attracted, he refused to attend his father's funeral. He became increasingly tense when faced with crowds of curious onlookers who stopped outside his one-man gulag.

Calley's circumstances were again raised with the White House in February 1973, just as the scandal of Watergate was building steam. The country's attention was focused on welcoming home from Hanoi the first of the 591 US POWs held captive by the North Vietnamese. Nixon preferred not to pass a personal judgment on Calley just then. "To move on it now," he told Ehrlichman and Dean, "when people are primarily concerned with POW returns would be a mistake." Nixon also ignored a plea from a group of retired Army officers at Bowling Green, Kentucky, whose petition for clemency described Calley as "a prisoner of war of the United States rather than North Vietnam." In his isolation, watching the homecoming of US prisoners of war on television, Calley became increasingly bitter about the Army and more devoted to his civilian lawyers. An Army report, assessing his behavior in confinement, noted that he had come to see himself as "the last POW."

At the end of 1973, a special Army board recommended clemency but not parole and within a few months matters appeared to swing in Calley's favor. Having failed to win his client's freedom through the appeals process in the military courts, Latimer sought a writ of habeas corpus from a local judge in Columbus. The military authorities were getting ready finally to transfer Calley to Fort Leavenworth to complete his sentence. The district court judge, in a decision that was politically popular locally, gave Calley immediate bail of $1,000 and released him from house arrest in February of the following year. The government's response to the bail application took several weeks and Calley immediately moved into new officers' quarters at Fort Benning. Later, having become something of a celebrity locally, he rented an apartment in Columbus itself and changed his recreational pursuits. He drove around town in a white Mercedes, loaned to him by a well-wisher. Instead of building model airplanes he took flying lessons.

A few weeks later the Secretary of the Army, Howard Calloway, took a dramatic step and cut Calley's sentence by half—to ten years. It meant that within six months he would be eligible for parole. Calloway believed reducing the sentence would help place the "incident" (meaning the massacre) "once and for all in its historical perspective." Calley, he went on, may have sincerely believed he was acting on orders and not aware of his responsibility to refuse such orders.

On May 3, 1974, Nixon gave his final word on the case. Having reviewed the record, he decided he would take no further action. There was a certain irony in this; the President, for solely political reasons, had intervened in the judicial process three years earlier. In doing so he imposed on Calley a punishment worse than being sent to jail—the isolation of his own quarters wherein he became depressed and longed for the company of others. Now here was Nixon, himself isolated, lonely, and depressed within the Oval Office, a prisoner of the Watergate coverup, facing the certain denouement of impeachment for high crimes and misdemeanors.

Calley, however, was not yet completely home free; his freedom remained subject to a roller coaster of continued legal dispute within the civil courts as the government challenged the writ of habeas corpus. He had been out on bail enjoying life for several months when, on June 20, the Fifth US Circuit Court in New Orleans reversed the bail order. Calley turned himself in to the military stockade at Fort Benning. Six days later he was transferred under armed escort to the US disciplinary barracks at Fort Leavenworth, where he was given a job as a clerk-typist and formally began to start his sentence behind bars. His eventual freedom came four and a half months later on November 9, when the Army Secretary announced he would now be paroled.

But the process of justice had not been without further courtroom drama and the bizarre vagaries of judicial interpretation of the law. Six weeks before the government finally issued parole and actually freed Calley from prison, the judge in the civil district court in Columbus took it upon himself to overturn Calley's conviction completely and issue a writ of habeas corpus. In an extraordinary display of judicial eccentricity, Judge Robert Elliott invoked not only memories of the Civil War but also the Battle of Jericho in biblical times. Calley, he said in his written legal opinion, had not been given a fair trial; his country had denied him even a fair chance of a fair trial:

Keep in mind that war is war and it is not at all unusual for innocent civilians to be numbered among its victims. It has been so throughout recorded history. It was so when Joshua took Jericho in ancient Biblical times: "And they utterly destroyed all that was in the city, both man and woman, young and old . . . with the edge of the sword" [Joshua 6: 21].
Now Joshua did not have charges brought against him for the slaughter of the civilian population of Jericho. But then "the Lord was with Joshua" we are told.

General Sherman had ravished the Confederate state of Georgia and put the city of Atlanta to the torch, intent on slaying millions if necessary to achieve President Lincoln's war aims. He was not condemned, said Judge Elliott:

Sherman waged war with admitted calculated cruelty and he did so with the grateful blessings of his commander-in-chief [Lincoln] who did not suggest that he be court-martialed . . . and he was not condemned from the podium and the pulpit, but he was instead glorified, idolized, beatified, and sanctified. The point is that Sherman was absolutely right; not about what he did, but about the nature of war; War *is* Hell and when we take a young man into the Army and train him to kill and train him to take orders and send him into a strange foreign land to follow the flag, and he then in the wild confusion of combat commits an act which, long after the event, is made the basis of a capital criminal charge, simple justice demands that he be treated fairly by the press, by his government, and by the branch of the service which he served. Sadly, it must be admitted that Calley was not accorded such consideration. Quite the contrary.

A year later, the Federal Appeals Court in New Orleans restored Calley's conviction and overturned Elliott's habeas corpus ruling. At his trial, a majority of judges ruled, Calley had been fairly convicted of the premeditated murder of numerous Vietnamese civilians. By then Calley, aged 32, had been free for ten months, working for a Georgia construction company and courting Penny Vick, a 29-year-old buyer in her father's jewelry store in Columbus. They had met four and a half years previously not long after he had been charged with mass murder and they had kept a friendship going. They married at St Paul's Methodist Church in Columbus in May 1976, six weeks after the Supreme Court in Washington put an end to the legal argument surrounding his conviction. America's highest legal tribunal upheld the Calley trial verdict by refusing his lawyer's plea to hear the case. By this time Calley had gone to work at his father-in-law's jewelry store. In March 1975, he tried to earn money by joining the lecture circuit, and was paid $2,000 to address the students at Murray State University in Kentucky. A large banner held aloft by some of the students at the back of the lecture hall contained one word: "WHY?" He did not answer the question then and has never really answered it since.

12. Final Chapter

> The past is never dead. It's not even past.
>
> William Faulkner

Early on the morning of Sunday, September 4, 1988, Pittsburgh City Police were called to the banks of the Monongahela River where they discovered the half-clothed body of a homeless drifter. The dead man, in his late thirties or early forties, was lying on a gray sheet stretched out on a patch of earth amidst shrubs and garbage underneath the Smithfield Street Bridge. He looked not so much dead as in a stupor. His pale eyes were glazed and half open. Around the lips and dark beard, a frothing from the mouth had left a thin rim of stale bubbles. Except for a silver chain around the neck, the whole of the upper part of the body was naked, revealing several zoological motifs tattooed on his torso. A leaf from the overhanging shrubs had already fallen on the bald-headed bird of prey which was etched over most of his left arm above the elbow.

It was from the same man's arm, twenty years before in South Korea, that military police investigating the My Lai massacre had removed an armband which read: "Ashamed of Americal murderers." Then, Robert T'Souvas had just confessed to detectives in Seoul that he had killed five women and children at My Lai. His stupor that time had been drug induced; after five days he had recovered. This time he would not recover. But it was only at the city morgue that police found out why. Pathologists who examined the body discovered that Robert T'Souvas had been "acutely intoxicated" at the time of his death. They also found a .22-caliber bullet hole in the back of his head.

The murder of a drifter is no big story in a town like Pittsburgh.

Local newspapers soon reported that police had charged T'Souvas's 35-year-old wife with murder. But the story had one unusual twist. Kathleen T'Souvas had kept a diary in which homicide detectives found an account of the couple's life together. It seemed that they had been in the Pittsburgh area for about a year. At first they had lived in a van, using bathrooms in parking lots and service stations. When the van broke down, they built a shelter under the Smithfield Street Bridge. The T'Souvases had had a hard time the previous winter. They worked a little at casual jobs, caught fish in the river, and sold blood to make extra money. "[They] . . . put the needle in the wrong vein to make an overflow on Bob's vein," Kathleen wrote on October 16, 1988. "They only paid him $3." The nights, even at the beginning of winter, were cold. "Could only sleep off and on," read another entry.

Homicide detectives told the press that the couple had spent the previous Saturday drinking with another homeless man called Bozic. They spent time shooting at rats and cans with his revolver. Sometime in the late afternoon or early evening, after Bozic had gone off to get food, there was a quarrel over a bottle of vodka. Kathleen T'Souvas had shot her husband in the back of the head. According to police, she probably didn't even know that she had killed him. She was found the next day, a few feet from the body, sitting in the shelter with her head in her hands.

It took another full week before the press recognized in the murder of Robert T'Souvas a story with a moral for our times. By September 15, newspapers had begun to make the connection between the massacre at My Lai and the homeless drunk found dead under a bridge in Pittsburgh. Immediately the hand of Nemesis was seen to be at work. "For My Lai GI, A Private Hell Ends in Death," declared one headline that signaled the direction the story was to follow all over America.

"Another casualty in the My Lai incident has been recorded," announced the *Daily News* in a story that ran across two whole pages. "According to friends and relatives, the soul of T'Souvas had died at My Lai along with the bodies of more than 300 Vietnamese. It was only his corpse that was discovered 20 years later under the Smithfield St Bridge."

In another widely syndicated article from Associated Press, T'Souvas's father was quoted as saying: "He had problems with

Vietnam over and over. He didn't talk about it much. But he had problems with body counts, things like that. He lasted 20 years, but he was walking a tight line."

Although the police had already charged T'Souvas's wife, many press stories now indicated that his death had somehow been self-willed, the product of a long-suppressed pain. A pathologist was found who suggested that the wound was more consistent with suicide than homicide. T'Souvas's angst took on a spiritual dimension. "I could see the pain in Bob's eyes," said Sister Kathy Lehman, of the Sisters for a Christian Community, who helped to run a kitchen where the T'Souvases often ate. She told the press of a long conversation she had had with T'Souvas two weeks before his death: "He opened up a little. He wanted something so badly, he was reaching out so hard but he couldn't grasp anything." With bold, unfailing brushstrokes, the squalid death of Robert T'Souvas assumed tragic inevitability. There, in what one newspaper described as "his last bivouac . . . amid the squalor of empty booze bottles, weeds and rats," came an expiation of the act of blood committed twenty years before.

Yet the death of Robert T'Souvas was never to be more than tragedy in a minor key. Much newsprint was spent describing T'Souvas's incoherent lifestyle on the fringe of drugs, destitution, and criminality without any attempt to relate his disintegration as an individual with disorder in the wider world. Any possible wider implications of the massacre, any indications of social or political responsibility, were ignored altogether. As one newspaper reported: "It was a tragic end for a bit-part player in America's psycho-drama." An event on an historic scale had been reduced to a domestic drama. What once had been a national crisis of conscience had become the very "private hell" of a single very inadequate individual.

In Chapter XVI of the Book of Leviticus, God gave Moses instructions on how to go about making the very first scapegoat. It is unlikely that either the journalists who reported his death or Robert T'Souvas himself ever had any idea how well he followed the Mosaic scapegoat tradition. For the chosen goat, having had laid upon his head all the sins and trangressions of the Children of

Israel, was then led by a fit man "unto a land not inhabited." These original scapegoats did not merely take the blame for the sins of others; they were machines for forgetting, for transporting as far away as possible, out of sight and out of mind, the sins of the entire community. Only after they had bathed their flesh and washed their clothes were the men who led the scapegoats into the wilderness allowed back in camp. For the scapegoats themselves, however, there was no return. They were to remain forever in the wilderness, building their last bivouacs no doubt amidst whatever passed in biblical times for "empty booze bottles, weeds and rats."

Of course, men like T'Souvas, Calley, Meadlo, and the other veterans of My Lai serve so well as scapegoats because after all they were culpable. They did perpetrate the massacre. They were guilty of the most horrific murders. But by the time Robert T'Souvas was discovered dead in his little piece of wilderness near the Monongahela River, it had long been forgotten that responsibility for My Lai might extend beyond those who happened to be there. The massacre had become a matter for individual conscience alone.

For the man who exposed My Lai, this is a distortion of the truth that adds another tawdry dimension to the whole affair. It had been no part of Ronald Ridenhour's intention when he provided the Nixon administration with the first account of the massacre to project the entire responsibility onto the soldiers involved. For him it was not then, nor is it now, solely a matter of individual conscience. Today he expresses dismay at the place of My Lai in popular memory:

If you scratch most Americans today and say: "What about My Lai"—a lot of them would know about it; OK, a lot of them would not know about it. Those who were able to put it in a frame of reference would say: "Oh, yeah, that's when a crazy lieutenant—what was his name? Kelly, Calley, Cooley, something like that—yeah, that's when he went crazy, isn't it?"

Well no, it's not.

Calley and the others, Ridenhour argues, have received a "hugely

disproportionate" amount of the blame. Yes, of course, they committed terrible acts of savagery. Inexcusable acts. Yet the real
responsibility "didn't land where it belonged and where it continues
to belong."

In Ridenhour's picture of the men of Charlie Company there is
more sympathy than blame. The GIs at My Lai were young, naive,
impressionable, and afraid. They were away from home for the
first time; they were "following orders in a context in which they'd
been trained to follow orders." They make a wrong choice and
they realize a day later that "they have probably made the biggest
mistake of their lives." What has always bothered Ridenhour is
what made them make that mistake.

What he had hoped from the investigation was "some measure
of justice," which could only be achieved by extending the arc of
responsibility. Not only should the higher command of the Americal Division have been put on trial, but also the "architects of
policy," the people who had created the Vietnam strategy and
should have known where it would lead:

Certainly, people who'd made war and who'd been in war before had to
understand the implications, the consequences of body counts and kill
ratios and free-fire zones and search and destroy missions. There can
only be a limited number of consequences of those policies, and it has to
be that there are going to be large numbers of civilians murdered. You
don't have to be at war very long to figure that out. And certainly
anybody who was at war in Vietnam for very long knew that. These
people should have been on trial.

Thus Ron Ridenhour restated, in 1989, the familiar position of
most antiwar campaigners twenty years before. In effect, it was an
attack on the entire chain of command. As such it was feverishly
repudiated by the Army and the Nixon administration, for whom
such accusations came close to subversion. To many, the attempt
to spread responsibility was seen as a bid to get the men involved
off the hook. Guenter Lewy, for example, in his 1978 book,
America in Vietnam, described it as a repudiation of individual
responsibility. He drew attention to the fact that the policy, even at
My Lai, did not invariably, or even generally, lead to war crimes.
"Some individuals," he wrote, "under pressure and provocation,

committed atrocities while others successfully resisted these pressures and maintained their integrity. Instead of facing up to the harsh fact of individual moral failure it was easier to place 'the monkey' on the backs of the generals."

The question of responsibility split America. Whereas the moment of the exposure of My Lai had united the nation in an impulsive outcry of outrage and shame, grappling with the thorny issue of where to pin the blame quickly widened the deep fissures in American society that an unpopular war had already created. To those on the political right, to the White House, and to the Army, My Lai was an aberration, an embarrassment to policy. Management of it was considered a question of damage limitation. Consequently, responsibility was to be confined within very narrow limits. On no account was the massacre to be seen as representative of policy—or of policy makers. For the political left, on the other hand, and for the antiwar movement, this was precisely what the massacre represented. For them My Lai was more than just an isolated war crime; it was an opportunity to criminalize the whole war.

The question of responsibility was absolutely the right question. On its outcome depended not only what was going to constitute justice—who was going to take the blame—but also what was going to be done: would war policy change as a result? Remember, at the time there was widespread comment from abroad that the very fact of the massacre had left US policy in ruins. The political stakes were high. The war was still being fought. American boys were still dying in the thousands. With one side claiming that "America's citizens share in the responsibility for My Lai" and the other restricting guilt to "individual moral failure," My Lai quickly became an important political touchstone. Attitudes to My Lai became a test of loyalties and allegiances that went way beyond the facts of the massacre itself. There was an appeal to humanity. There was an appeal to the flag. Wounded radicals clashed with outraged patriots. The silent majority was called forth against protesters in the streets. Presidents were called murderers and murderers were called scapegoats. Soul searching gave way to sloganeering.

When the dust cleared, all that was left of that first clear call for justice and truth was the fact that Lt. Calley, who had been sentenced to life imprisonment with hard labor, had been transferred by the President to his home after only three days in jail. Moreover the telegrams arriving at the White House were running ten to one in favor of Nixon's action. As the Washington correspondent of the London *Times* wrote in 1971: "American attention has been deflected from the outset from the hard fact that ordinary men can commit murder at point blank range, something that, in fact, is easily identifiable as a war crime."

For a moment, in the first sharp shock of its exposure late in 1969, the My Lai massacre was seen as a crime on the nation's conscience. For a moment, it threatened the idea of what it was to be an American. It was at this point that Reinhold Niebuhr spoke of "illusions in the national history" about to be shattered. But conscience turned out to be a weak judge. Just as America's political and legal systems found indigestible all attempts to respond to My Lai with anything that would be commonly regarded as justice, there was no way that America's first anguished recognition of collective responsibility could find any lasting expression.

It was therefore somewhat premature of the French news magazine *L'Express* to write, with undisguised *Schadenfreude*, in 1969: "The Americans have learned that in Vietnam they have become the equals of the French in Indochina, Madagascar, Algeria, and the Germans at Oradour." Such assessments underestimated the resilience of a national myth in which American moral superiority was taken for granted, and war crimes, like famine, leprosy, and plague, were something visited upon, and perpetrated by, uncivilized foreigners.

On July 15, 1970, an investigating subcommittee of the House Armed Services Committee issued a heavily censored report of its inquiries into the massacre. "What obviously happened at My Lai was wrong," the report concluded. "In fact, it was so wrong and so foreign to the normal character and actions of our military forces as to immediately raise a question as to the legal sanity at the time of those men involved." The conclusion is unsurprising. Long before 1970 the reassuring nostrums of national history had been shown to be entirely unassailable by mere fact.

Take, by way of example, the following: "The American soldier in officially sanctioned wrath is a thing so ugly and dangerous that it would take a Kipling to describe him." Not a description of My Lai, but the observation of James H. Blount, a young lieutenant, later to become a judge, on the behavior of troops in the Philippines—sixty years before Vietnam. Here too, American soldiers found themselves fighting a guerrilla war in the face of overwhelming opposition from the native population. As in Vietnam, the exhortation to pursue the enemy with "the utmost vigor" was given brutal interpretation in the field. Soldiers' contemptuous slang for the Filipinos was "goo-goos," and similar difficulties in discriminating between civilians and combatants resulted in similar remedies for dealing with them. On November 11, 1901, the *Philadelphia Ledger* printed an officer's letter that could just as easily have been written by Greg Olsen or Brian Livingston from their fire bases in Quang Ngai. "Our men have been relentless, have killed to exterminate men, women and children, prisoners and captives, active insurgents and suspected people, from lads of ten up, an idea prevailing that the Filipino was little better than a dog."

The records of hearings on the conduct of the war held in camera before Senator Henry Cabot Lodge's Committee on the Philippines in 1902 reveal testimony that would not have been unfamiliar to General Peers: search and destroy operations; burnt villages; torture; body counts that gave clear evidence of ruthless slaughter. Courts-martial of officers who too conspicuously overstepped the mark resulted in acquittals or gentle wrist-slapping. According to Elihu Root, the Secretary of War, the "actual conduct of military operations in Samar," one of the Philippine Islands where particularly brutal repression had taken place, could be justified by the "history and conditions of warfare with the cruel and treacherous savages who inhabited the island." He used historical precedent to bolster his claim. In 1866, after an ambush by Sioux Indians had wiped out a detachment of troops from Fort Phil Kearny in the Dakotas, General William Tecumseh Sherman had written to General Ulysses S. Grant: "We must act with vindictive earnestness against the Sioux, even to the extermination, men, women and children. Nothing else will reach the root of the case."

As many field commanders had been old Indian fighters, it is unsurprising that in the Philippines habits acquired in the Indian Wars spilled over into the new century.

In case the Philippines conflict seems too distant and arcane, here is an example from another, more recent war:

What kind of a war do civilians suppose we fought anyway? We shot prisoners in cold blood, wiped out hospitals, strafed lifeboats, killed or mistreated enemy civilians, finished off the enemy wounded, tossed the dying into a hole with the dead, and in the Pacific boiled the flesh off enemy skulls to make table ornaments for sweethearts or carved their bones into letter openers.

Again, this is not My Lai, or even Vietnam. This is from the "good war." It is a horrifying account, written by American war correspondent Edward L. Jones, of the behavior of American troops fighting in the Pacific during World War II. It was published in the February 1946 edition of the magazine *The Atlantic*.

Evidence abounds to substantiate such an account. The May 22, 1944, edition of *Life* magazine published a full-page picture of a "conspicuously decent and middle-class" girl writing a thank-you letter to her sailor boyfriend who had thoughtfully sent her the Japanese skull resting on the desk before her.

In April 1943, the *Baltimore Sun* ran a story about a local mother who had petitioned the authorities to permit her son to send her an ear he had cut off a Japanese soldier in the South Pacific.

On August 9, 1944, President Roosevelt announced that he had declined to accept the gift, sent to him by a serviceman in the Pacific, of a letter opener fashioned from a Japanese thighbone. The celebrated aviator Charles Lindbergh, a national hero ever since his 1927 flight in the *Spirit of St Louis* from New York to Paris, spent four months as a civilian observer with US forces in New Guinea recording in his diary a disturbing commentary on the American atrocities he witnessed. When finally he returned to Hawaii, he was asked by customs men whether he was carrying any bones in his luggage. It was a routine question.

As in Vietnam, American servicemen in the Pacific were fighting a horrendous war against an enemy who himself did not shrink from atrocity. But both wars produced American as well as enemy atrocities, as has every significant conflict since the Indian Wars. Atrocity has been as much a part of the American experience of war as of any other nation. For senior officers, dealing with that fact of atrocity was something that came with command. Compare these two directives issued twenty-five years apart. The first, issued in September 1942, from the commander-in-chief of the Pacific Fleet: "No part of the enemy's body may be used as a souvenir. Unit commanders will take stern disciplinary action." The second, issued by General Westmoreland on October 13, 1967, condemns the practice of cutting off ears as "contrary to all policy and below the standards of human decency."*

Likewise, dealing with the fact of their own or their comrades' atrocities is one of the things ordinary soldiers have had to live with. The circumstances may change from conflict to conflict, but the experience of atrocity is remarkably consistent. The two following accounts are both reactions from essentially decent young men to the brutality they witnessed all around them. They reflect not only the horror, but the moral disorientation produced by situations in which atrocities have become commonplace.

The first, from the Pacific War, is the account of Eugene B. Sledge, a former marine and a veteran of the battles of Peleliu and Okinawa: "Time had no meaning, life had no meaning. The fierce struggle for survival . . . eroded the veneer of civilization and made savages of us all. We existed in an environment totally incomprehensible to men behind the lines—service troops and civilians."

The second is Greg Olsen's version of how the moral certainties of his Mormon upbringing crumbled in the face of what he saw in Charlie Company: "We believed this behavior was pretty commonplace. I didn't think we were doing anything different from

---

* There were many cases of GIs shipping home body parts illegally from Vietnam. In August 1971, the US Army CID agency was forced to outline to its component organizations an official policy on how to handle customs seizures of severed body parts—ears, fingers, skulls. Previously the details had been confined to military intelligence reports; in future the CID would pursue war crimes cases against those involved. See memoranda, "Policy on Suspected War Crimes," from Col. Henry H. Tufts, USACID Agency, Washington, DC, Aug. 30, 1971.

any other unit. You really do lose your sense ... not of right or
wrong, but your degree of wrong changes ... A different set of
rules and I don't think that any of us quite knew what those rules
were."

To these testimonies could be added Michael Bernhardt's experience that in an isolated unit like Charlie Company the laws back
home didn't make any difference anymore. Charlie Company "was
the whole world. What they thought was right was right. And
what they thought was wrong was wrong. The definitions for
things were turned around." Or Fred Widmer's account of his own
brutalization: "Something happened to me ... you reach a point
over there where you snap ... Somebody flicks a switch and you
are a completely different person. There is a culture of violence, of
brutality, with people around you doing the same thing. It is
something which occurred more and more frequently and there
came a point where nothing mattered anymore."

These are dispatches from the front line in the battle to retain
human values. Not all these eyewitnesses emerged victorious. These
moral battlefields, familiar to soldiers throughout the ages, have
been almost completely ignored by military historians. Yet without
attempts to explore such accounts of the moral conflict that has
existed side by side with military campaigns, it is difficult to see
how we can put what Lewy calls the "harsh facts of individual
moral failure" into any useful ethical framework.

By the time of the Japanese war, the "goo-goos" of the Philippines War had already become "gooks," an expression whose
usefulness survived infamously throughout the wars in Korea and
Vietnam. The word "gook" itself was like a marker on a transmission belt down which unseemly aspects of military life passed,
unnoticed by military historians and staff colleges, to reappear in
conflict after conflict as predictably as sandbags or howitzers.
Likewise, from one war to another, atrocity and the experience of
atrocity pass similarly down channels hidden from view. This does
not necessarily mean that atrocities happen in all combat situations,
or that at any one time they have involved more than a small
minority of those under arms. Rather that atrocity is like a virus
known to strike soldiers in combat and that surprisingly little has
been done to protect against it or find out more about it. Instead,

the tendency has been to deny its existence, or more absurdly, to suggest that it doesn't affect "our" men.

In his account of conflict in the Pacific, *War without Mercy*, John Dower notes

such behavior was offered as confirmation of the innately inferior and immoral nature of the enemy—a reflection of national character—when, in fact, the pages of history everywhere are stained with cruelty and unbridled savagery. The "civilization" which both the Allies and the Japanese claimed to be defending had failed to stem these impulses ... Allied propagandists were not distorting the history of Japan when they pointed to much that was cruel in the Japanese past. They had to romanticize or simply forget their own history, however, to turn such behavior into something uniquely Japanese.

By the time of the Vietnam War, this aspect of the war against the Japanese had simply been forgotten. Allied atrocities played little or no part in the popular picture of World War II. A whole raft of experience had once again disappeared underground. When, during Calley's trial, prominent veterans of the "good war" emerged to say that they too had committed atrocities, and that atrocities were inevitable in war, these revelations were greeted with astonishment.

Why was My Lai so shocking? Historical forgetfulness plays an understandable and important role in nation building. It is natural that after a trauma like war, people want to look to the future and leave wartime divisions and horror behind. But there is a price to be paid if convalescence becomes a full retreat into innocence and naivety. Turning a blind eye to the abundant evidence of how people actually behave in the extremity of combat simply leaves each generation of soldiers with old lessons to be learned from scratch. Before the chances of civilized behavior can be improved, the potential for savagery must be understood. And remembered.

Two ways were found of avoiding the shock of My Lai. The first blamed individuals. The second blamed everybody. In the first case, explanations were sought in deviance, in eccentricity, in aberration, or in irrationality. The search for explanation began and ended with the individuals involved. In the second case, "war" took the blame, or "human nature," something big and grand but difficult to bring to trial.

The one found expression in phrases like "the harsh facts of individual moral failure" or "a question of the legal sanity of those involved"; or in the "isolated incident" of Nixon's press conference on December 9, 1969. The other was expressed in Calley's surpassingly laconic: No big deal; or perhaps in the results of an opinion poll published by *Time* magazine early in January 1970, which showed that "surprisingly Americans are not particularly disturbed by the disclosure that United States troops apparently massacred several hundred South Vietnamese civilians, reasoning that incidents such as this are bound to happen in a war."

On paper it might appear difficult to hold both of these viewpoints at the same time. In practice, faced with the massive blow to national pride represented by My Lai, a great many people had little problem. Both ideas were wonderful remedies for shock.

The question "Why was it shocking?" was asked by an American journalist at a festival showing of the film *Four Hours in My Lai*. The film had the effect of reminding people of the shock of the massacre. The journalist's question was a reminder of how it had come to seem not so shocking after all. He explained that he had been a correspondent in Vietnam during the war and everyone there knew that these things were taking place all the time. What was surprising to him was not so much that My Lai happened but that people should be so upset by it. War is hell, he said. Atrocities are inevitable. Moral reactions that might seem appropriate to civilian audiences watching documentaries had little meaning in a combat zone. The rest of us were just hiding from ourselves the awful truth. There wasn't much point after twenty years in making such a fuss about My Lai. It was not going to change anything.

But people were demonstrably shocked by the Ridenhour/Hersh revelations of My Lai in 1969. They were shocked by Ron Haeberle's pictures in *Life* magazine, and Paul Meadlo's appearance on television. If the journalist is right, if atrocities like My Lai are unavoidable, then the American people were shocked because they felt deceived. The war was completely different from the war the government told them they were fighting. No one had ever considered soldiers to be on leave from humanity. Certainly the

Army advertising for recruits, or the government sending young people off to battle, had never suggested that they were marching into a moral vacuum.

On the contrary, soldiers were assumed to carry the values of the community at large with them into the battlefield. American soldiers, in Vietnam, for example, were assumed to be the military expression of the American ideal. It was said often enough that it was this ideal they were fighting for. People knew that war was hell, but they also thought that "there was a moral world in the midst of hell." My Lai threatened that world. That's why people were shocked. The military also knew it was threatened—that's why they tried the coverup. The question "Why was it shocking?" not only threatened this world but was an attempt to deny its existence.

Yet this "moral world" was shared by the public and the soldiers themselves. In becoming soldiers they did not think they were becoming murderers. They thought they were the "good guys—the men in white hats." As Ridenhour said:

Most of them had never been away from home before they went into the service. And they end up in Vietnam, going there many of them because they thought they were going to do something courageous on behalf of their country and they thought they were going to do something which they thought was in the American ideal—whatever that meant.

But it didn't mean slaughtering whole villages of women and children, innocent people. Or even people who weren't innocent. It didn't involve that . . . One of my friends when he told me about it said: "You know, it was this Nazi kind of thing." And that's exactly right. It was this Nazi kind of thing. We didn't go there to be Nazis. At least none of the people I knew went there to be Nazis. I didn't go there to be a Nazi.

Even those My Lai veterans who have attempted to justify the massacre have never pretended that it took place outside any moral frame of reference. Instead they struggled to create a competing moral world in which even the most hideous deeds could be given a moral context. The most obvious example was the idea that the military was a moral realm unto itself in which the only imperative was to follow orders. This is the reason given by the former sergeant, Kenneth Hodges, who even today insists that there was no crime committed at My Lai:

As a professional soldier I had been taught and instructed to carry out the orders that were issued by the superiors—my lieutenant, my commanding officer, the captain. At no time did it ever cross my mind to disobey or to refuse to carry out an order that was issued by my superiors. I felt that they [Charlie Company] were able to carry out the assigned task, the orders, that meant killing small kids, killing women, because they were soldiers, they were trained that way. I feel that we carried out the orders in a moral fashion, and the orders of destroying the village, of killing the people in the village, and I feel we did not violate any moral standards.

Alternatively, Calley, who of course also argued that he was only following orders, created a world in which ideological struggle took precedence over everything. In Calley's memoir *Body Count*, he asserts:

We weren't in My Lai to kill human beings, really. We were there to kill ideology that is carried by—I don't know. Pawns. Blobs. Pieces of flesh. And I wasn't in My Lai to destroy intelligent men. I was there to destroy an intangible idea. To destroy communism . . . I looked at communism as a southerner looks at a Negro, supposedly. It's evil. It's bad.

This moral perspective didn't leave Calley entirely scruple free. Elsewhere in *Body Count* he recalls an incident in which during the massacre itself he rebuked a GI (Conti) who was in the process of sexually assaulting a young Vietnamese woman. Rape in Vietnam, he told himself, was a very common thing. Why was he being so saintly about it? "Because: if a GI is getting a blow job, he isn't doing his job. He isn't destroying communism . . . he isn't doing what we are paying him for. He isn't combat effective."

In another place, Calley constructs a moral case on the basis of military necessity: "And babies. On babies everyone's really hung up. 'But babies! The little innocent babies!' Of course, we've been in Vietnam for ten years now. If we're in Vietnam another ten, if your son is killed by those babies you'll cry at me, 'Why didn't you kill those babies that day?'"

Calley's moral encephalitis never extended to most of the men. Most My Lai GIs never tried to pretend to themselves. "We all came from the same place," Harry Stanley, one of the men who refused to take part in the killings, has said. "I know that they all had to have the same values as I had somewhere along the line." Sooner or later those values caught up with the men of Charlie Company, and usually when that happened they were left bewildered, disgusted, mystified, and shamed. Ridenhour described their reaction when he sought them out in their camps and fire bases to talk to them about My Lai: "You'd ask them and it would be like popping a boil . . . just come gushing out. Ah, it was a horrifying experience for them. And for most of them the recollection that they had made the wrong choice came too late. And they realized it."

A year later, when military investigators were retracing Ridenhour's footsteps they heard a large number of the My Lai veterans recall the curse of Paul Meadlo after he had stepped on a mine the day after the massacre: "This is God's punishment to me Calley, but you'll get yours. God will punish you, Calley." They all knew what he meant.

For most men from Charlie Company, claims of following orders, or military necessity, have been no defense against the pervading sense of transgression. Even among those not involved with the killing, the experience of standing powerless while the veneer of civilization was stripped away has left a deep mark. Harry Stanley, who refused Calley's direct order to shoot, still feels guilty: "Even though I didn't participate I was there and I feel like I'm just as guilty as anybody that was there. Because there was nothing I could do about the things that they did."

For Michael Bernhardt, the loss of the moral world in the midst of hell resulted in a loss of faith in the moral world of home:

I had seen people who looked like everybody else—normal people— doing atrocious things, and I really wasn't sure how anyone would have acted in the same situation. I thought I knew human nature. I thought that people were basically good and that they couldn't do this. I thought most of the values people held were pretty solid, that when we defined things as being good or bad, that they were good or bad, and that we would know when something was really bad. But I had seen that was not the case. I wasn't sure that I could trust anyone again. I wasn't sure I could ever get close to anyone, or confide in anyone very closely, because of what I'd seen over there.

That loss had been Ridenhour's starting point. His object in tracking down the truth through the fire bases and hospitals of Quang Ngai had much to do with making good that loss. It is there in his original letter. "I remain irrevocably persuaded," he wrote,

that if you and I do truly believe in the principles of justice and the equality of every man, however humble, before the law, that form the very backbone that this country is founded on, then we must press forward with a widespread investigation ... I think it was Winston Churchill who once said: "A country without a conscience is a country without a soul, and a country without a soul is a country that cannot survive.

Twenty years after that letter, Ridenhour described his first reaction to hearing of the massacre in equally far-reaching terms: "My immediate reaction, you know, these no-good sons-of-bitches, look at what they have gotten me into, look at what they've gotten us all into."

Had Ronald Ridenhour, then aged 21—a young man who had been in Vietnam long enough to see many terrible things—believed that what his comrades were telling him was merely one of those incidents "that are bound to happen in war," or that they could be explained by the "harsh fact of individual moral failure," the world would almost certainly never have heard of My Lai. For Ridenhour, "the harsh fact of individual moral failure" was an inadequate explanation for why the vast majority of Charlie Company had turned into killers. His investigations had begun among ordinary men who had committed murder. There is still, in his conversation today, a sense of his shock at the discovery that some of his closest friends—decent men—had made the wrong choice and been involved in the killings.

At My Lai, he concluded, common decency had become exceptional. Common humanity had become heroic. Normal moral behavior was beyond the reach of normal people:

Only a few people in those circumstances had the presence of mind and the strength of their own character that would see them through. Most people didn't. Only an extraordinary few could withstand the pressures and maintain their moral beings in that awful place, in those terrible conditions. The extraordinary few somehow did withstand it. But we shouldn't—our society shouldn't be structured, ought not to be structured, so that only the extraordinary few can conduct themselves in a moral fashion.

When the military take their armor into extreme conditions, they take steps to ensure that it will still function. If they go to the desert, they make it sandproof. In the Arctic, they protect it against snow and ice. In Vietnam, the Americans tried to proof their weapons against the effects of high temperatures and humidity. Every soldier knows that in extreme conditions, kit goes wrong, and good soldiering involves taking steps to anticipate this.

No piece of kit, throughout history, has been as sensitive to its environment as that which, in its Vietnam manifestation, came to be known as the "common grunt." Almost all his training has been designed to stamp out his unpredictability and improve his efficiency as an instrument of policy. But nothing has so far been discovered that can guarantee the quality—or the character—of his performance. What is known is that throughout history, besides the courage, loyalty, perseverance, resourcefulness, and all the other sterling qualities for which he has been rightly praised, lurking in the background there has been an enduring propensity toward cruelty and injustice. Given the extremities of his working environment, there is always the danger that these lower impulses will be given brutal expression. It might therefore be assumed that good soldiering involves taking steps to anticipate this.

What steps were taken early in 1968, among the men of Charlie Company, part of Task Force Barker, in Quang Ngai Province, in the 1st Corps Military Region, in the Republic of South Vietnam? The whole story of My Lai gives its murmuring answer: *Not many*.

What steps were taken to halt the run of beatings, thefts, rapes, tortures, and murder which prodded Charlie Company down the road to My Lai? *None*.

Who, among the chain of command that found on its bottom rung Lt. William Calley and rose through Medina, Barker, Henderson, and Koster, gave any kind of moral lead or example that might have prevented the moral destruction of the company? *No one*.

In place of clear leadership, there was paper leadership: the rules of engagement, numerous codes of conduct and other directives, all of which contained the loftiest intentions. There was nothing wrong with these regulations; in spirit they were a recognizable expression of the American ideal at war—a blueprint for moral order in the midst of hell. They simply never became part of the soldiers' reality because they were never seriously enforced, and without emphatic enforcement they corresponded as much to the world of the "common grunt" as road maps of Mars.

In his long survey of the morality of war, *Just and Unjust Wars*, Michael Walzer makes the point that anyone seeking to regulate the conduct of war "must come to grips with the fact that his rules are often violated or ignored—and the deeper realization that to men at war the rules don't seem relevant to the extremity of the situation." Relevance diminishes even faster if, day by day, soldiers see the rules flouted with impunity. That is what happened in Charlie Company in the days leading to My Lai. The invisibility of codes that derived from the Western liberal tradition left a vacuum that was filled with behavior springing from other impulses. It is true, as individuals they were morally autonomous. They were also morally alone.

This is what was meant by Bernhardt's "the laws back home don't make any difference. This group of people that they were with was all that mattered. It was the whole world." With the virtual abandonment of the rules of engagement, the company had lost a vital moral compass. Strong enforcement would have offered not just a safeguard to Vietnamese civilians and prisoners of war, but a brake on the more brutal and vengeful instincts of a confused and dejected company.

Medina, in common with the entire chain of command, was unwilling to allow his obligations under the Law of Land Warfare to interfere with his intention to use his troops with maximum violence. Instead of regarding the wrathful mood of the company as a danger signal, Medina exploited it and then did absolutely nothing to moderate the results.

"The struggle of man against power," wrote Milan Kundera, "is the struggle of memory against forgetting."

Behind the pages of this book there have been many voices

raised in that struggle. The voices of Vietnamese survivors of the massacre who lost everything and for whom forgetting is impossible. The veterans of Charlie Company who returned safely to their homes and loved ones, but who lost something that they cannot define and cannot forget. The voice, curiously, of Robert T'Souvas, on the telephone a few months before he died. There are also the voices of American journalists and writers who twenty years ago struggled against the condition of their craft to lift the massacre out of the newsprint world of "incidents" and into genuine significance.

On December 20, 1969, Jonathan Schell, who had chronicled the destruction of Quang Ngai Province in previous reports, wrote an article in the *New Yorker* in which the claims of memory are championed with desperate urgency:

When we look at the photographs published in *Life* and see the bodies of children and women in piles, and look into the faces of an old woman and a young girl who [we are told] are about to be shot, we feel a kind of violence is being done to our feelings, and that the massacre threatens to overpower us. To block it out, we may freeze. If we face the massacre for what it is, we are torn by almost unbearable grief, but if we turn away and let the rationalizations crowd into our minds to protect us, we are degraded. We want to go on with our daily lives, and we may wonder, Why should my life be interrupted by this? Why should I take on this suffering on behalf of these victims? However much we may resist it, the choice has been made for us, irrevocably. Whether we manage to bear the grief or whether we freeze, the massacre enters into us and becomes a part of us. The massacre calls for self-examination and for action, but if we deny the call and try to go on as before, as though nothing had happened, our knowledge, which can never leave us once we have acquired it, will bring about an unnoticed but crucial alteration in us, numbing our most precious faculties and withering our souls. For if we learn to accept this, there is nothing we will not accept.

Jonathan Schell's article appeared midway between the original revelations about My Lai and the publication in *Time* magazine of the poll that showed that most Americans believed the massacre to have been just one of those things that are bound to happen in war.

Today, there is about My Lai an overwhelming sense of

unfinished business. Hopes that what was so demonstrably wrong could be demonstrably righted have never been fulfilled. Ridenhour's call for justice was answered with a farrago of legal process. Schell's fears that, even if people knew the truth, they would shrug it off as if they had never been told, have turned out to be well founded. Today, the Tree of Knowledge has become the supermarket of news. Massacre has a short shelf life. The tension between the barbarity of My Lai and the national myths has been resolved in favor of the myths. "Thank God," George Bush said after the Gulf War in 1991, "the Vietnam syndrome is buried forever." If, as Walzer says, "the moral reality of war is not fixed by the actual activities of soldiers but by the opinions of mankind," then public opinion is as little ready to define or defend its ideals now as in 1968. Once again the darker side of war has gone underground. My Lai is no longer a public burden or concern. The burden of guilt and the burden of responsibility have fallen onto the soldiers themselves. "Shit," the men of Charlie Company used to tell each other, "rolls downhill."

How can you forgive? I can't forgive myself for the things—even though I know that it was something that I was told to do. But how can I forget that—or forgive? It's easy for you to say: Well, you go ahead with your life. But how can you go ahead with your life when this is holding you back? I can't put my mind to anything . . . Yes, I'm ashamed, I'm sorry, I'm guilty. But I did it. You know. What else can I tell you? It happened.

These words are a last glimpse into the "private hell" of Varnado Simpson as he sits, shaking from side to side in his chair, alone in his house in Jackson, Mississippi. Until we learn to share Varnado's bleak, existential cry, we cannot begin to hope that something like My Lai will never happen again.

Chronology

1962	12,000 US forces in South Vietnam as advisors; 31 US deaths. US government denies troops are involved in combat.
1963	15,000 US advisors; 77 deaths.
1964	
February 1	President Johnson approves covert operations against North Vietnam. Operation Plan 34A raids begin.
August 7	Tonkin Gulf resolution passes through both Houses of Congress, gives the President authority to take all necessary steps to prevent attacks on US forces.
1965	
February 11	US barracks at Qui Nhon attacked.
February 13	Operation Rolling Thunder—the sustained air war against North Vietnam—launched.
March 8	Two battalions of US Marines land near Da Nang.
July 28	Johnson sends 50,000 extra men.
September	Operation Pirana—first US sweep of Batangan Peninsula, Quang Ngai Province.
December 24	USA suspends bombing of North Vietnam.

December 25	185,000 US troops in South Vietnam.

1966
July 1	1/20th Infantry Battalion assigned to newly reactivated 11th Infantry Brigade at Schofield Barracks, Hawaii, assigned to the Pacific Reserve.
December 19	Capt. Ernest Medina takes over Charlie Company, 1/20th Infantry. 389,000 US troops in Vietnam.

1967
April 20	Task Force Oregon based at Chu Lai becomes operational—search and destroy operations take place throughout Quang Ngai Province.
July 29	11th Brigade redesignated a light infantry brigade on notice to go to Vietnam as part of Westmoreland's rapid buildup of troops.
November 27	Troops from Charlie Company depart for Vietnam. Advance party arrives Duc Pho.
December 25	Charlie Company spend Christmas at LZ Charlie Brown on Gilligan's Island. 463,000 US troops in Vietnam.

1968
January 1	Task Force Barker activated. Charlie Company move to LZ Dottie.
January 28	C Company's first casualty—from a booby trap.
January 31	Tet Offensive. Charlie Company observes VC attack on Quang Ngai City from Hill 102.
February 25	Charlie Company lose two dead and thirteen injured in minefield.

March 14	Sgt Cox killed when booby-trapped shell explodes.
March 15	Col. Henderson takes command of 11th Brigade. Barker briefs commanders about Pinkville operation. Medina briefs Charlie Company about their assault on My Lai 4. Prayers for Sgt Cox.
March 16	Charlie and Bravo companies assault My Lai 4 and My Khe.
March 28	Lt. Col. Barker's after-action report goes to Henderson, no report made of civilian casualties.
April 8	Task Force Barker disbanded.
April 24	Henderson's report of investigation says twenty noncombatants killed inadvertently.
November 1	US halts bombing of North Vietnam.
November 4	Nixon beats Hubert Humphrey in presidential election.
December 1	Original members of Charlie Company return to the USA. 495,000 US troops in Vietnam.

1969

April 9	Chairman of Joint Chiefs forwards Ridenhour letter to Army Chief of Staff's office. US troops in Vietnam at peak of 543,000.
June 5	Calley recalled to the USA; identified as a potential suspect in mass murder inquiry.
June 8	US troop cuts of 25,000 announced.
July 30	Inspector General recommends criminal investigation into My Lai.
September 3	Ho Chi Minh dies in Hanoi.

September 6	William Calley charged at Fort Benning with 109 murders of "Oriental human beings."
September 16	Sgt David Mitchell suspected of murder/ attempted murder.
October 28	Mitchell charged with assault with intent to murder thirty Vietnamese civilians.
November 24	Lt. Gen. William R. Peers appointed to head Army inquiry into scope of original investigation into massacre.
December 2	Ten possible suspects for My Lai killings identified by the Army. 541,000 US troops in Vietnam.
December 5	Calley appears before Peers—refuses to testify.

1970

January 8	PFC Gerald Smith charged with murder and indecent assault. Sgt Charles Hutto charged with rape, murder, and assault to commit murder.
January 22	Army suspects thirty-three individuals implicated in massacre—nineteen of them civilians.
March 10	Charges announced against Kotouc, Medina, Sgt Hodges, Sgt Esequiel Torres, PFC Max Hutson.
March 17	Findings of Peers inquiry announced.
March 25	Charges of premeditated murder preferred against SP4 William Doherty, Cpl Kenneth Schiel, and SP4 Robert T'Souvas.
March 31	Medina charged with murder of 175 Vietnamese civilians.
September 4	Charges of rape and murder against Charles Hutto dismissed.

November 17	Calley's court-martial convened.
November 20	Mitchell acquitted of all charges. US casualty rate halved as troop levels drop to 334,600.

1971

January 5	Hutto's trial begins.
January 14	Hutto found not guilty.
January 21	Charges against Doherty dismissed.
January 22	Lt. Gen. Albert O. Connor, commanding general, 3rd US Army, dismisses charges against Smith, Hutson, Torres, and T'Souvas.
January 29	Lt. Gen. Seaman, the day before he retires from the Army, dismisses charges against Maj. Gen. Koster.
March 29	Calley found guilty of murder of twenty-two Vietnamese civilians and assault with intent to murder a Vietnamese child.
April 1	President Nixon orders Calley to be released from the stockade pending his appeal.
April 29	Kotouc found not guilty of maiming a civilian.
August 16	Medina court-martial begins.
August 20	Calley's sentenced reduced to twenty years' hard labor on review by commanding general, 3rd US Army.
August 23	Henderson's court-martial begins.
September 22	Medina found not guilty of all charges.
October 15	Medina resigns from US Army.
December 17	Henderson found not guilty of all charges. US troop levels in Vietnam fall to 156,800.

1972

April 30   US troop levels at 69,000.

December 7   Army and Air Force Clemency Board and
                  Parole Board makes recommendation for
                  clemency for Calley.

1973

April 2   US Army Court of Military Review affirms
                  sentence in Calley case and denies a new trial.

May 14   Secretary of the Army denies Calley clemency.

May 23   Petition granted for a review of *US* v. *Calley.*

December 21   US Court of Military Appeals affirms decision
                  of the US Army Court of Military Review in
                  US v. *Calley.*

1974

February 11   Calley's counsel files petition for writ of
                  habeas corpus and an application for bail in
                  US District Court in Georgia.

February 27   Calley freed on bail of $1,000 by district judge.

March 8   US government files motion for revocation of
                  bail with US District Court in Georgia.

April 15   Secretary of the Army reduces Calley's
                  confinement to hard labor for ten years.

May 3   Nixon announces he will take no further
                  action in Calley case.

May 10   US government files appeal of bail and
                  restraining order granted by US District Court
                  with Fifth US Court of Appeals.

June 13   Court of Appeals reverses District Court bail
                  order and rescinds restraining order against
                  Army.

June 20	Calley held in stockade at Fort Benning pending hearing on merits of a habeas corpus petition.
June 25	Arguments for habeas corpus petition held at US District Court (Middle District of Georgia). Supreme Court upholds Court of Appeals order sending Calley back into confinement.
August 9	Nixon resigns as result of Watergate scandal.
September 25	District Court orders Calley's release on bond, following writ for habeas corpus.
November 9	Secretary of the Army announces Calley is to be parolled after completing one-third of his sentence. Calley is a free man.

Notes on Sources

In researching what happened at My Lai and afterward we have traced and talked with many people, former members of Charlie Company, survivors from the village of My Lai in Vietnam, and those involved in the subsequent coverup and investigation. Some were able to provide many original documents. Fred Widmer in the course of several long interviews was able to remember extensive details of his military life and subsequently unearthed a treasure trove of original documents relating to his personal history in and out of the military, as well as magazine and newspaper articles and a vast collection of photographs. Hugh Thompson loaned us his personal scrapbook; Mrs Dorothy Barker found original correspondence and other documents relating to her late husband, Lt. Col. Frank Barker; and Mrs Christina Peers Neely's search of her home brought forth many gems, including a tape recording of a two-hour-long interview her father gave to a radio station in San Francisco in 1979. Telephone interviews were conducted with many people including Samuel Koster and Eugene Kotouc. In the summer of 1988 Ernest Medina kindly agreed to an off-the-record interview at his home in Marinette, Wisconsin. Some did not wish to talk—William Calley does not give interviews. However, his wife, Penny, once engaged an English visitor making a purchase of a $50 watch at their jewelry store in Columbus, Georgia, in conversation and revealed that her husband's family originated from Wales. His grandfather was an ostler who emigrated to the United States at the end of the nineteenth century.

Documentary and archive research was conducted as follows:

The *US Army Crime Records Center*, Baltimore, Maryland, made available for the first time the complete archive of the CID investigation into the My Lai massacre, files nos 69-CID011-00014, 69-CID011-00068/00074, 70-CID011-00001/00016, and 00043. These included the full and unsanitized CID statements taken from US military personnel, ARVN, forces, and a hundred survivors from the village of My Lai, as well as polygraph tests, case reports of the CID investigators, engineers' maps of My Lai village giving the location of every family, and a forensic photographic record showing the identity of people in Ronald Haeberle's pictures. Robert A. Brisentine Jr, who had conducted many of the original polygraph tests at the time of the My Lai investigation, was director of the Crime Records Center when we asked for permission to consult the files. Now retired, he remains one of the world's foremost authorities on polygraph examinations. Through him we were able to correspond with CID investigators Wayne D. Thorne and André C. Feher. We received a thirty-page handwritten, detailed account of the CID investigation prepared specially for us by Mr Feher, and obtained from the National Archives a daily journal for the CID Task Force.

US Army Center of Military History, Washington, DC. Those of Gen. William C. Westmoreland's papers that covered the period of the Vietnam War he donated to the L. B. Johnson Library, in Texas. Most of these are now at the Center of Military History, record group 319. File N3-407-86-1 provided a detailed finding aid of Westmoreland's papers, which include many backchannel messages classified as "sensitive" and "eyes only." We were particularly interested in historical files in boxes 35 and 36, records of telephone conversations in box 26, especially folder 455, and various backchannel messages in boxes 18–20.

US Marine Corps History and Museums Division, Washington Navy Yard, provided many useful documents concerning the early US military involvement in Quang Ngai Province and several volumes of the history of the US Marine Corps in Vietnam, as well as memoranda on psychological operations.

Federal Records Center and National Archives, Suitland, Maryland. Record group 338-77-0983 covered files of the 23rd Infantry Division (Americal) and contained background files relating to Charlie Company, the 11th Infantry Brigade, and the Americal Division, including unit reports, intelligence reports (for example a lengthy analysis of the 48th VC Battalion), after-action reports, interrogation reports, biographies of personalities, and documents relating to the investigation of My Lai after Ronald Ridenhour had written his letter.

Accession number 338-33-0983 contains historical background material on the My Lai investigation including the US Army's administrative reviews of the performance of those military personnel accused of offenses resulting from either the criminal investigation or the Peers inquiry.

Accession number 319-78-0051 yielded many more documents from the various appeals by William Calley against conviction and sentence. Among them were the documents relating to his welfare while serving his sentence including papers relating to his Clemency Disposition Board hearings which contained the full psychiatric analysis of Calley conducted by Army psychiatrists at the Walter Reed Army Hospital during his trial in 1971, and further examinations carried out in 1972 and 1973.

Also located within the record group 319 file no. N3-338-87-1 were a mass of papers from the US Army's Vietnam War Crimes Working Group, which operated within the Discipline and Order Division of the Directorate of Discipline and Drug Policies, Office of the Deputy Chief of Staff for Personnel. This working group was formed in 1970, as the senior echelons in the Army became alarmed at the public and political response to the My Lai case. They analyzed 246 separate Vietnam war crimes allegations. My Lai was one of the separate specialized series of case files we examined.

Record group 159-78-0183 contained some 7 linear feet of files of Col. William V. Wilson's investigation of the My Lai massacre. One of the most disappointing features of our research was that some sections of the US Army continue to act as the guardians of secrecy which still pervades the massacre and its investigation. Our Freedom of Information Act request for Col. Wilson's final report proved difficult. Finally a copy was sent to us. However, on the orders of the acting Inspector General, Maj. Gen. Bobby F. Brashears, all names contained within the report, various conclusions, and the final recommendations had been censored, on the grounds that it was "normal practice." This was twenty-two years after the event. We were fortunate, however, that in various archives we had already obtained original copies of uncensored transcripts of evidence taken during the original inquiry by Col. Wilson for the Inspector General and included as an appendix in his final report. We also came across a long and fascinating article in *American Heritage* magazine written by Col. Wilson about his experiences and were able to engage in personal correspondence with him.

My Lai Trial Records. The US Army Judge Advocate General's Office gave us excellent cooperation. Through the courtesy of Col. William Fulton, the clerk of the Court at Military Review, Falls Church, Virginia, and especially his deputy, Mary B. Dennis, we were able to review trial records in what for researchers were almost perfect conditions. The complete archive records of the courts-martial of Calley, Medina, and Henderson were obtained on our behalf from the Federal Records Center at Suitland. These included the full trial transcripts and collection of exhibits, now stored at the National Archives in record group 153. The full accession number of the records of the Calley trial is NN3-153-89-1. It runs to 30 boxes and forms more than 12 linear feet of documents. The complete collection of 64 sound tapes of Calley's trial are now in the National Archives' motion picture, sound, and video branch. We were able to listen to them at our leisure at the Court of Military Review. We also obtained a copy of the tape recording made by Capt. Charles Lewellen in the task force operations center of the operational radio traffic as Charlie Company landed at My Lai on March 16, 1968.

Peers inquiry. The *Department of Army Review of the Preliminary Investigations into the My Lai Incident*, in four volumes, was a major source of material. Vol. 1 is the Report of the Investigation; Vol. 2 is the verbatim testimony to the inquiry from four hundred witnesses which runs to 33 books and some 20,000 pages; Vol. 3 consists of exhibits collected for the inquiry in seven books, which include directives, reports, correspondence, statements, and photographs; and Vol. 4 contains CID statements. We viewed these initially at the National Archives at Suitland, accession number 319-79-053, boxes 17–20. A complete copy of the Peers Report was also found in the Pentagon Library, where we were given facilities to review and photocopy the report, courtesy of Col. William Mulvey, chief of the media relations division of Army Public Affairs, who believed that after twenty years the story of My Lai deserved to be told. The transcripts of evidence to the Peers inquiry remain sanitized to protect the identity of those giving evidence who had not been publicly named. Still censored from the original testimony are many details relating to intelligence matters and details which could have severely embarrassed the US government, particularly in its relations with South Vietnam. However, in 1975 a key giving the identification codes of 123 witnesses was made available, but the identity of the remaining witnesses continues to be secret, though by cross referencing from other sources it was possible in many cases to break the codes and identify the witnesses.

Records of legal hearings connected with the My Lai trials, principally for Calley's appeal, contained unsanitized and uncensored transcripts of evidence from twenty-one witnesses to the Peers inquiry. These files (319/20/181–202) were located in the Federal Records Center. They were particularly helpful, for example, in reconstructing the role of Capt. Eugene Kotouc, Task Force Barker's intelligence officer. The Pentagon Library contained many Rand Corporation assessments written in the 1960s about the Viet Cong and the North Vietnamese Army.

White House files. These came from the National Archives' Nixon Project at 845 South Picket Road, Alexandria, Virginia. Nixon and his lawyers pulled many files out of the public domain after he left office, on the basis that they were private documents. Many hundreds of thousands of these are still the subject of much legal argument between Nixon's lawyers and the appropriate guardians of America's documentary heritage within the National Archives. Many White House papers relating to My Lai, including the covert investigation of Ronald Ridenhour at the request of Richard Nixon, were withdrawn by the former President's advisors. Nevertheless a careful examination of the White House special files, central files, files containing the President's handwriting, and the files of his closest aides, provided a helpful insight into the President's concerns about the issue.

The Library of Congress has the complete edition of the Pentagon Papers, which we drew on in part, as well as the evidence and final report of the House Armed Services Committee's investigation of My Lai, chaired by Congressman F. Edward Hebert, which was finally published in 1976, call number KF 27.A752 1970a in the Law Library.

Notes on the Text

1. INTRODUCTION

p. 9 *Lloyd George:* Quoted in Philip Knightley, *The First Casualty*, London, Deutsch, 1975, p. 109.

p. 11 *"... concealed ... true nature of war":* Col. Harry G. Summers Jr, *On Strategy: A Critical Analysis of the Vietnam War*, New York, Dell, 1984, p. 63.

p. 11 *"Fuck you, John Wayne":* Charles Anderson, "The Grunts," quoted in Jeffrey Walsh and James Aulich (eds.), *Vietnam Images: War and Representation*, London, Macmillan, 1989, p. 19.

p. 12 *reported from Washington:* London *Times*, Nov. 26, 1969.

p. 14 *Schell report from Quang Ngai:* Jonathan Schell, *Observing the Nixon Years*, New York, Vintage, 1990, p. 18.

p. 15 *Gen. Weyand:* "Vietnam Myths and American Military Realities," *Commander's Call*, Jul./Aug. 1976, quoted in Summers, *On Strategy*, p. 68.

p. 16 *Taylor on rules of engagement:* James W. Gibson, *The Perfect War*, New York, Vintage, 1988.

p. 17 *medical staff shocked not surprised:* Interview in Vancouver with Claire Culhaine, former administrator with a Canadian medical mission in Quang Ngai City in 1967–8; telephone interview (1990) with Dr Alje Vennema, former director of Canadian Medical Assistance in Quang Ngai City.

p. 18 *Westmoreland's strategy:* Philip Caputo, *A Rumor of War*, New York, Ballantine, 1988, p. xix.

pp. 18–19 *"... what it eventually turned into":* Michael Bernhardt, personal interview.

p. 20 *"... So do we all":* Ronald Ridenhour, personal interview.

2. THE WAR

p. 29 *Vann: "... discrimination in killing":* Neil Sheehan, *A Bright Shining Lie*, London, Picador, 1990, p. 317.

p. 30 *Vann: "... shooting at everything":* Ibid., p. 383.

p. 30 *"... clever mixture ...":* Gen. Bruce Palmer Jr, *The 25-Year War,* Louisville, University of Kentucky Press, 1984, p. 176.

p. 31 *Mao on guerrillas:* Mao Tse Tung, *"Yu chi chan,"* trans. as "Guerrilla warfare" by S. B. Griffith, *Marine Corps Gazette,* 1940; quoted in Robert B. Asprey, *War in the Shadows,* New York, Doubleday, 1975.

p. 31 *"... people's soldiers":* Frances FitzGerald, *Fire in the Lake,* New York, Vintage, 1989, p. 201.

p. 32 *Westmoreland: " ... police up":* Quoted in James W. Gibson, *The Perfect War,* New York, Vintage, 1988, p. 103.

p. 32 *McNamara memorandum:* Sheehan, *Bright Shining Lie,* p. 685.

p. 33 *Gen. DePuy:* Ibid., p. 619.

p. 33 *Search and destroy:* Pentagon Papers, p. 463.

p. 34 *"... how can you tell?":* Varnado Simpson, personal interview.

p. 35 *Lawler: " ... it's gone":* Al Saltoli, *Everything We Had,* New York, Ballantine, 1981, p. 177.

p. 35 *Westmoreland: "... other dangers":* FitzGerald, *Fire in the Lake,* p. 430.

p. 36 *Sheehan: "... victims of the war":* *New York Times,* Oct. 9, 1966.

p. 37 *MACV directive:* Force SA 1 corps order 30403, Dec. 13, 1966.

pp. 39–40 *"... couldn't trust anybody":* Fred Widmer, personal interview.

pp. 41–2 *Gellhorn's articles:* The extract is from "A new kind of war," London *Guardian,* Sept. 1966; reprinted in Martha Gellhorn, *The Face of War,* London, Virago, 1986. "My articles on the Vietnam war ... were published in the *Guardian,* London," Gellhorn recalls in an essay accompanying the reprinted articles, "unsuitable for American readers." Philip Knightley, *The First Casualty,* London, Deutsch, 1975, which examines the work of war correspondents, also notes that "no newspaper in the United States" would publish Gellhorn's articles; Knightley quotes Gellhorn as saying: "Everywhere I was told that they were too tough for American readers. After their publication, Gellhorn was blacklisted by the South Vietnamese authorities and despite many attempts was unable to visit the country again during the war.

p. 42 *McNamara to President:* Pentagon Papers.

p. 43 *McNamara from McNaughton:* Ibid.

3. THE COMPANY

p. 51 *Project 100,000:* The Armed Forces Qualification Tests classified all volunteers and draftees into five categories. Categories I–III were automatically taken. Category V were automatically rejected. During peacetime, the Army rejected most of the men whose test results put them in category IV. This changed when the ground war in Vietnam began in earnest in 1965. A special remedial education program was set up for large numbers of category IV men who now entered the armed services. Secretary of Defense Robert McNamara called it Project 100,000; and from 1966 to 1968, 240,000 category IV men were registered on the program. See James W. Gibson, *The Perfect War*, New York, Vintage, 1988. Of Charlie Company, the Peers Report stated: "About 8 percent of the enlisted personnel, less noncommissioned officers, fell into the Project One Hundred Thousand category and were in the lowest mental group. The percentage of this group was lower than the Army-wide accession figure of 12 percent."

p. 51 "*. . . cross section of American youth . . .*": Peers Report.

p. 54 *Calley: ". . . everyone's bad"*: John Sack, *Body Count: Lt. Calley's Story as Told to John Sack*, London, Hutchinson, 1971, p. 28.

p. 59 *Operation Benton summary:* Jonathan Schell, *The Military Half: An Account of Destruction in Quang Ngai and Quang Tin*, New York, Vintage, 1968.

p. 65 *Lipscomb: "top officers"*: Henderson, testimony to Peers.

pp. 70–71 "*. . . We were abused . . .*": Michael Bernhardt, personal interview.

p. 71 "*GI firing into Vietnamese family:* Seymour Hersh, *My Lai 4: A Report on the Massacre and its Aftermath*, New York, Random House, 1970.

p. 71 "*. . . Just lost it*": Greg Olsen, personal interview.

p. 72 *Calley's later admission:* Sack, *Body Count*, p. 56.

p. 72 *Calley on Body Count:* Richard Hammer, *The Court Martial of Lt. Calley*, New York, Coward-McCann, 1971, p. 258.

p. 73 *Trinkle's recollection:* Trinkle, CID statement, Nov. 24, 1969.

p. 79 *Calley and Carter with old man in well:* Stanley, CID statement.

p. 80 "*. . . culture of violence . . .*": Fred Widmer, personal interview.

pp. 81–2 *rapes:* Gonzalez, testimony to Peers.

p. 83 "*. . . buddies . . . getting killed*": Charles Hutto, personal interview.

p. 86 *Lipscomb "almost in disgust"*: Henderson, testimony, to Inspector General.

pp. 87–8 *Kotouc:* See William E. Hawkins, in *Pittsburgh Post-Gazette*, Feb. 26, 1971, p. 27.

p. 89 *Dr Nelson on torture:* Seymour Hersh, *Cover-Up: The Army's Secret Investigation of the Massacre at My Lai 4*, New York, Vintage, 1972, p. 91.

p. 89 *CIA men disapprove of violence:* See William E. Colby, *Honorable Men: My Life in the CIA*, New York, Simon & Schuster, 1978.

p. 91 *intelligence roundup:* "Memorandum for: Army Staff Monitor, My Lai. Subject: Analysis of Enemy Intelligence of My Lai Area."

p. 92 *Calley on Medina:* Sack, *Body Count*, p. 87.

p. 94 *Kotouc on Barker:* Kotouk, testimony to Peers.

p. 96 "*. . . in the target area*": Peers Report, ch. 5, s. F.

p. 98 "*. . . do not kill women and children . . .*": Medina, testimony at Calley trial.

pp. 98–9 *Hodges's recollection:* personal interview with author 1989.

p. 99 *men heard order to kill everyone:* Testimony to Peers; evidence at Calley trial.

pp. 100–101 *Olsen's recollection:* Greg Olsen, personal interview.

4. MY LAI, MARCH 16, 1968: AM

p. 106 *250,000th round:* Jonathan Schell, *The Real War*, London, Corgi, 1989, p. 161.

p. 108 *Smail angry with West:* Smail, CID statement, Dec. 14, 1969, p. 2.

p. 111 *elderly woman shot in hip:* Olsen, CID statement, Aug. 30, 1969, p. 3.

p. 111 *trophy ears:* Robert J. Lifton, *Home from the War*, London, Wildwood House, 1974, p. 44; Seymour Hersh, *My Lai 4: A Report on the Massacre and its Aftermath*, New York, Random House, 1970, p. 23.

p. 112 *killed cow:* Lee, CID statement, Sep. 17, 1969, p. 3.

p. 112 Boyce, personal interview, and CID statement, Oct. 14, 1969, pp. 2–3; Olsen, CID statement, p. 6; Grzesik, unsworn CID interview, Feb. 9, 1970, p. 1.

p. 113 *Conti: oral sex at gunpoint:* See Calley's own testimony, Calley trial transcript, p. 3813, National Archives.

p. 114 *Medina's false body count:* Peers Report, ch. 6; J. Goldstein, B. Marshall, and J. Schwartz (eds), *The My Lai Massacre and its Cover-Up*, New York, Free Press, 1976, p. 135.

p. 114 *killing of villagers:* Bunning, CID statement, Dec. 7, 1969, p. 1.

p. 115 *woman in tunnel:* Hutson, CID statement, Oct. 28, 1969, pp. 1–2.

p. 115 *Hutto and Torres swap:* Hutto, CID statement, Nov. 17, 1969, p. 2.

pp. 115–16 *on Brooks and Crossley:* Partsch, CID statement, Oct. 21, 1969, p. 2, and testimony to Peers, Jan. 30, 1970, vol. 3, bk 26, p. 24.

pp. 117–18 *killing of villagers:* Gonzalez, CID statement, Feb. 27, 1970, p. 2, and testimony to Peers, Jan. 21, 1970, vol. 3, bk 26, p. 13.

p. 119 *guarding villagers:* Conti, testimony to Peers, Jan. 2, 1970, vol. 3, bk 24, pp. 32–3.

pp. 120–21 *Meadlo and Calley kill villagers:* Conti, CID statement, Oct. 30, 1969, p. 1, and testimony to Peers, pp. 32–3.

p. 121 *Conti's venereal disease:* Nick Capezza, personal interview.

p. 123 *on Dursi:* Olsen, CID statement, pp. 4–5.

p. 124 *". . . everyone was part of it . . .":* Ronald Haeberle, personal interview.

pp. 124–5 *LaCross and Glimpse:* Smail, CID statement, Dec. 14, 1969, p. 3.

pp. 125–6 *Minh and Johnson:* Minh, deposition, Oct. 30, 1970; Lt. Johnson's administrative action papers.

pp. 126–7 *Medina shoots woman:* CID statements: Bernhardt, Nov. 20, 1969, p. 2; Flynn, Mar. 6, 1970, p. 2; testimony to Inspector General's inquiry: Thompson, Jun. 11, 1969, Washington, DC, pp. 593–603; Colburn, Jun. 19, 1969, Ft Hood, Tex., p. 766.

p. 127 *Medina's expression:* Hemming, CID statement, Feb. 21, 1970, p. 3.

p. 129 *mutilation of women:* See William R. Peers, *The My Lai Inquiry*, New York, Norton, 1979.

p. 129 *Vietnamese killed while greeting GIs:* Moss, testimony to Peers, vol. 2, bk 26, p. 10.

p. 129 *company "signature" and Ace of Spades:* Fagan, testimony to Peers, Jan. 6, 1970, vol. 2, bk 28, p. 36.

pp. 130–31 *". . . I just started killing . . .":* Varnado Simpson, personal interview.

p. 131 *multiple rape:* Gonzalez, testimony to Peers, p. 19.

p. 132 *Roschevitz kills women; raped girl:* Ibid.; but see also various CID statements and court-martial testimony at Calley trial, e.g. McBreen p. 2790 and Gonzalez p. 2672.

p. 133 *". . . It was an atrocity . . .":* Ronald Haeberle, personal interview.

p. 134 *shared beer:* Kern, quoted in statement by CID investigator Thomas Porter, Dec. 10, 1969, p. 2.

p. 137 *Thompson radio warning:* Hill CID statement, Mar. 14, 1970, p. 1.

p. 137 *injured woman:* Hugh Thompson, personal interview.

p. 137 *infantry captain kills woman:* Ibid., and Thompson, testimony to Inspector General; Peers, *My Lai Inquiry*; Lawrence Colburn, testimony to Inspector General cited above, and personal interview.

p. 138 *Calley: ". . . I'm the boss here":* Evidence cited in US v. Calley, Court of Military Review, CM 426402, Feb. 16, 1973.

p. 138 *GI shoots bodies in ditch:* Livingston, CID statement, Dec. 4, 1969, p. 1.

5. MY LAI, MARCH 16, 1968: PM

pp. 143–4 *Partsch and Bernhardt:* Partsch, CID reinterview, Mar. 7, 1970, p. 1, and testimony to Peers cited above, p. 27.

p. 145 *Warren at Dottie:* See summary of CID evidence prepared by CID investigator Robert N. Zaza, Washington, DC, Jul. 20, 1970, p. 17 (hereafter "Zaza file").

p. 145 *pilots: ". . . like a blood bath . . .":* Peers Report, ch. 10, p. 238; in J. Goldstein, B. Marshall, and J. Schwartz (eds), *The My Lai Massacre and its Cover-Up*, New York, Free Press, 1976.

p. 145 *Barker calls Medina on company net:* Peers Report, ch. 10, p. 238.

p. 146 *Koster–Medina radio con.:* Medina, testimony to Inspector General, May 13, 1969, p. 266, Ft Benning, Ga, and to Peers, Dec. 4, 1969, p. 44; Adcock, CID statement, Mar. 24, 1970, p. 4; Koster, testimony to Peers, Feb. 18, 1970, pp. 175–7.

p. 146 *Koster's reasoning:* Koster, testimony to Peers cited above, p. 25.

p. 147 *"He's VC":* Medina, testimony to Inspector General cited above, p. 270.

pp. 147–8 *Kotouc: torture with knife:* See Grimes and Flynn, Article 32 evidence against Kotouc, quoted in the memorandum of law papers of Kotouc's administrative review.

p. 148 *rifle in mouth:* Kern, CID interview notes cited above, p. 4.

pp. 148–9 *Medina: "knock that off":* Kotouc, testimony to Peers, p. 31.

p. 149 *". . . finish them off":* Martin, CID statement, Oct. 16, 1969, p. 4.

p. 149 *picked up finger:* See Hein, CID statement, Dec. 16, 1969, p. 2.

p. 149 *Mar. 16 diary entry:* Partsch, testimony to Peers cited above, p. 24.

pp. 149–50 *woman's lament:* Smail, CID statement cited above, p. 5.

pp. 150–62 Vietnamese accounts of the massacre based on CID notes of interviews with survivors in My Lai file at US Army Crime Record Center, Baltimore, Md, and on personal interviews with Vo Thi Lien, Truong Muoi, Truong Thihe, Sa Thi Quy, Pham Dung, Pham Thi Tham, and Pham Thi Trinh.

6. AFTERMATH

p. 163 *C Company awake, prepare to move out:* Thomas Partsch, diary entry for Sun., Mar. 17, 1968, given in Peers testimony cited above.

p. 165 *hamlets deserted and fortified:* Medina, testimony to Peers, Dec. 4, 1969, p. 56.

p. 166 *La Croix to Brooks:* La Croix, testimony to Inspector General, May 2, 1969, Fort Carson, Colo., p. 57.

p. 166 *La Croix clubs policeman:* Ibid., p. 59.

p. 167 *prisoners:* Fagan, testimony to Peers cited above, p. 29.

p. 168 *jokes about VC nurse:* Ibid., also Hemming, CID statement, Feb. 21, 1970, p. 5.

p. 168 *VC woman's claim:* 52nd MID interrogation report no. 52-262-68, PW no. 210-3-11, Mar. 20, 1968, in 11th Infantry Brigade files, National Archives.

p. 169 *Phu's warning:* Medina, testimony to Peers p. 58.

p. 170 *VC prisoner's belt:* Ibid., p. 60.

p. 171 *statement by younger prisoner:* See 52nd MID interrogation reports nos. 52-230-68, PW no. 372-3-11, Mar. 21, 1968, and 52-276-68, PW no. 335-3-11, Mar. 29, 1968, in 11th Infantry Brigade files, National Archives.

p. 172 *"What are we doing here?":* Gonzalez, testimony to Peers cited above, p. 34.

p. 172 *". . . no deliberate or indiscriminate killing . . .":* Blackledge, CID statement, Oct. 16, 1969, p. 1.

p. 173 *Henderson "understood":* See Medina, testimony to Peers, p. 61.

p. 173 *". . . I'm going to jail . . .":* Calley, testimony at his court-martial, R3839, National Archives.

p. 173 *Calley "would take the blame":* See report of Medina's testimony at Calley's court-martial, *New York Times*, Mar. 11, 1971, p. 24, col. 1; similar evidence was given in Medina's own trial in the absence of the jury. Se F. Lee Bailey, *For the Defense*, New York, Atheneum, 1975, p. 133.

pp. 173–4 *questioned by Henderson:* Buchanon, Dursi, and Haywood, CID statements. See William R. Peers, *The My Lai Inquiry*, New York, Norton,

1979, p. 57; Henderson, testimony to Inspector General, May 26, 1969, p. 458; Peers exhibits S-3 and S-4, statement and draft question and answer statement prepared by Henderson, Dec. 5, 1969, for appearance before a congressional committee, which he handed to the Peers inquiry; Peers Report, vol. 3, Bk 5, pp. 737–64; and Peers, *The My Lai Inquiry*, p. 1101.

p. 174 *Thompson–Medina exchange:* See Thompson, testimony to Inspector General, Washington, DC, Jun. 11, 1969, p. 606.

p. 175 *no crusader:* Tom Glen, personal correspondence.

p. 176 *5 PM briefing:* Peers, *My Lai Inquiry*, p. 130.

p. 176 *Thompson still angry:* Lewis, CID statement, Dec. 29, 1969, p. 1.

p. 177 *Watke air crew briefing:* Peers, *My Lai Inquiry*, p. 100.

p. 177 *Young bothered:* Holladay, CID statement, Dec. 10, 1969, p. 1.

p. 177 *two generals knew:* See Peers Report, ch. 10, p. 246.

p. 177 *Young ignores Thompson claims:* Peers, *My Lai Inquiry*, pp. 99, 116.

p. 178 *Henderson–Thompson interview:* See ibid., p. 73.

p. 179 *rumors of investigation:* Conti, testimony to Peers, p. 40; Oliver, CID statement, Mar. 6, 1970, p. 3.

p. 179 *Medina "would do the talking":* Flynn, CID statement, Mar. 6, 1970, p. 2.

p. 180 *". . . killed by my own people . . .":* Michael Bernhardt, personal interview.

pp. 180–81 *hero-grams from top brass:* The original carbon copies of these messages were loaned to us by Barker's widow, Mrs Dorothy Barker.

p. 181 *veterans' boasts:* See Glazier, CID statement, Jan. 6, 1970, p. 2.

p. 181 *". . . German bloodbath . . .":* Stevenson, CID statement, Nov. 3, 1969, p. 4.

p. 182 *brushed aside by Barker:* See Roberts, CID statement.

pp. 182–3 *fictitious account: Trident* 11th Brigade journal, Mar. 22, 1968, vol. 1, no. 7 (Peers exhibit M-17); *Americal Division* news sheet, Mar. 17, 1968, vol. 1, no. 332 (PE M-23); *Stars and Stripes;* Pacific edn, Mar. 18, 1968 (PE M-88).

p. 183 *". . . something we should have reported":* Ronald Haeberle, personal interview.

p. 184 *his only memory:* See William C. Westmoreland, *A Soldier Reports*, New York, Doubleday, 1976; also Peers's account in *My Lai Inquiry*, p. 207.

p. 185 *Henderson on "VC propaganda":* Blackledge, CID statement, Oct. 17, 1969, p. 2.

p. 186 *minor official's report:* We have a copy of the translation obtained from the National Archives, headed "Republic of Vietnam"—letter/report, Mar. 18, 1968, by Cadreman Phung Duc (last name not legible).

p. 186 *village chairman's letter:* Copy in Peers, *My Lai Inquiry*.

p. 186 *report to province chief:* Ibid.

p. 186 *"top priority" follow-up letter:* We have a copy of a translation from the National Archives: "Letter from District Chief Son Tinh to Lt. Col. Province Chief, Quang Ngai. Subject: Allied operation at Son My assembled and killed civilians," dated Son Tinh, Apr. 11, 1968; ref. 190/CT/ST.

p. 188 *Gavin's recollection:* See Gavin's administrative review papers, p. 2.

p. 188 *Tan's subsequent testimony:* Peers, *My Lai Inquiry*.

p. 188 *". . . all being taken care of":* Ibid., p. 155.

p. 189 *"never able to imagine a massacre . . .":* See Jesse Frosch, "The Anatomy of a Massacre," *Playboy,* Jul. 1970, p. 192.

p. 190 *on civilian deaths:* See notes on Westmoreland's comments at MACV commanders' conference, 5th Special Forces HQ, Nha Trang, at 0930 hrs, Dec. 3, 1967, in memorandum "Summary of Remarks by COMUSMACV Relating to Noncombatant Casualties," for CoS, Gen. Westmoreland, Dec. 24, 1969—Westmoreland Papers.

p. 190 *". . . directives about civilian casualties":* Samuel W. Koster, telephone interview.

p. 190 *fear of inquiry:* Watke in testimony to Peers said he was worried about his career; Medina admitted at Calley's court-martial he was worried about the repercussions for himself; and the prosecutor at Henderson's trial said he had refused to act out of fear he wouldn't get his general's star.

p. 191 *term "search and destroy" eliminated:* See American Division memorandum, Maj. Gen. S. W. Koster, Mar. 24, 1968, "The Safeguarding of Noncombatants"; and Col. Nels A. Parson, Apr. 13, 1968, "Administrative Correspondence"—National Archives.

p. 192 *Kennedy expands special forces:* See Shelby L. Stanton, *Green Berets at War: US Special Forces in SE Asia 1956–75,* Novato, Calif., Presidio Press, 1985, p. 12.

p. 192 *high regard for Barker:* See Peers Report, ch. 8, p. 200.

pp. 192–3 *Barker's taped commentary:* This taped commentary was subsequently posted to Barker's wife Dorothy at her home in Hawaii. On the tape Barker continued to claim that 128 VC had been killed in the My Lai operation, many of them by helicopter gunships whose "rockets and miniguns struck the enemy forces who were trying to stop the movement of Company C. The gunships exacted quite a toll on the enemy." The tape was played at the trial of Col. Oran Henderson, on Nov. 22, 1971, as defense exhibit M. See the tape transcript in the record of trial p. 5466, in the National Archives.

p. 193 *report urgently demanded:* Memorandum from 1st Lt. R. H. Genel, AGC American Div., to CO, 11th LIB, Mar. 19, 1968, from National Archives (Peers exhibit R-13).

pp. 193–5 *Barker's reports:* The original carbon copies of Frank Barker's two after-action reports, for Feb. 23 and Mar. 16, were shown to us by his widow.

p. 197 *troops insult officers:* Raynor, CID statement, Dec. 11, 1969, pp. 1–3.

p. 197 *bounty on Calley's head:* Smail, CID statement.

p. 198 *Calley mistreats women:* Kinch, CID statement, Nov. 28, 1969, p. 6.

p. 198 *Tunstall and another GI:* Tunstall, CID statement, Nov. 25, 1969, p. 2.

p. 199 *fewer VC attacks:* Province Monthly Report, Apr. 30, 1968, p. 3, Office of the Quang Ngai Province Senior Advisor (Peers exhibit R-15).

p. 200 *Phoenix results:* Province Monthly Report, May 31, 1968, p. 5, Office of the Quang Ngai Province Senior Advisor (Peers exhibit R-16). For a more detailed official US explanation of Phoenix and its problems, see "Southeast Asia Analysis Report," Dec. 1968, a secret report prepared by ADASD(SA)SEA Programs, ASD/SA Control no. 8-5303, pp. 51–64, in the declassified documents section of the Library of Congress. The program was thought to be especially effective against low-level membership of the Viet Cong infrastructure, whereas high-level success rates were put at about one percent of all Phoenix "eliminations." It was, however, quite apparent that the official statistics being quoted had grossly underestimated the numbers of deaths under the program at the hands of the national police. The official report for 1968 contained a projected cumulative total of 13,000 VC infrastructure eliminated of whom 9,214 were said to have been captured, 1,656 to have joined the Chieu Hoi program, and 1,692 to have been killed. Within only a few years the total number of deaths attributed under the program was officially given as being in excess of 20,000. The figure was given by William Colby at a congressional hearing in 1971; although he never intended to suggest they had been assassinated, it was widely assumed this was what had happened. "They assassinated a lot of the wrong damn people," John Ranelagh quotes one former CIA analyst as saying—*The Agency*, London, Weidenfeld & Nicolson, 1986, p. 439. The official account of the Phoenix Program for 1968 suggested the people running the show included in their list of VCI eliminated too many Vietnamese who were not members of the Viet Cong infrastructure, so much so that the CIA were discounting the reported figures by between 29 and 36 percent.

p. 201 "*. . . leave them alone*": Michael Bernhardt, personal interview.

p. 202 *medals system corruption:* See William E. Hawkins, in *Pittsburgh Post-Gazette*, Feb. 26, 1971, p. 27.

pp. 202–3 *Barker gallantry citation:* American Division general orders no. 1835, Apr. 8, 1968.

p. 203 *Haig's medals:* Roger Morris, *Haig: The General's Progress*, London, Robson, 1982, p. 87.

p. 203 *set medals procedure:* See William Broyles, writing of the procedure in the US Marine Corps, *Brothers in Arms: A Journey from War to Peace*, New York, Knopf, 1986, p. 171, who adds: "Nothing extra was gained from the loss of three or more limbs." Also Westmoreland, *A Soldier Reports*, pp. 273, 306.

p. 204 *Thompson's DFC:* Hugh Thompson, personal interview.

p. 206 *Henderson's letter:* Letter from Col. Oran Henderson to Mrs Dorothy Barker, dated Jun. 27, 1968. The original citations for her husband's medals were loaned to us also by Mrs Barker along with the correspondence from his brigade commander and notification of his Vietnamese decorations.

pp. 204–7 *medal citations:* American Division general orders: 2137, Apr. 23, 1968 (Andreotta); 2585, May 14, 1968 (Colburn); 3601, Jul. 1, 1968 (Thompson); 5139, Aug. 5, 1968 (Buchanon); 5393, Aug. 9, 1968 (Widmer);

6242, Aug. 22, 1968 (Medina); recommendation for Col. Oran K. Henderson, DFC and eyewitness statements; Oran K. Henderson, US Army biography, 1970—all from Modern Military Records Branch, National Archives. Orders and related papers for awards to Colburn, Andreotta, and Henderson, plus accompanying eyewitness statements and draft citations, Peers Report, vol. 111, bk 4, pp. 185–210, exhibits M-42, M-43, M-44.

p. 208 *Kelley's approval:*   Peers, *My Lai Inquiry*, p. 125.

p. 208 *Westmoreland's farewell message:*   *Tour 365*, USARV returnee magazine, spring/summer 1968.

pp. 208–9 *Glen's recollections:*   Tom Glen, personal correspondence.

pp. 209–12 *Glen's letter:*   Letter from Tom Glen to Gen. Creighton Abrams, Nov. 27, 1968, National Archives.

7. INVESTIGATION

p. 215 *Ridenhour's meeting with Gruver:*   Ronald Ridenhour, personal interview.

p. 216 *La Croix to Ridenhour:*   Larry La Croix, letter to Ronald Ridenhour.

p. 217 *". . . hard choice . . .":*   Ronald Ridenhour, personal interview.

p. 217 *Bernhardt in hospital:*   Robert J. Lifton, *Home from the War*, London, Wildwood House, 1974, p. 59.

pp. 219–20 *letter to Udall:*   Alexander Cockburn, "He Did Not Stand Idly By," *The Nation*, Mar. 26, 1988, pp. 402–3.

p. 220 *Westmoreland's reaction:*   William C. Westmoreland, *A Soldier Reports*, New York, Doubleday, 1976, p. 375.

p. 222 *Whitaker's call:*   Record of telephone conversation, Col. H. Whitaker, USARV deputy IG to Lt. Col. Eli P. Howard Jr, Americal Div. IG, Apr. 12, 1969, National Archives.

p. 222 *Whitaker's conclusions:*   Memorandum for the record, Apr. 17, 1969, "Preliminary Inquiry Concerning Alleged Massacre of All Vietnamese Residents of My Lai by US Soldiers," Col. Howard K. Whitaker IG; Peers Report, vol. 111, bk 4, pp. 359–62, exhibit M-98.

p. 223 *Wilson's recollection:*   See William Wilson's own excellent account of his inquiry, "I Had Prayed to God that This Thing Was Fiction," *American Heritage*, Feb. 1990, pp. 44–52.

p. 224 *". . . we had no choice":*   La Croix, testimony to Inspector General, May 2, 1969, p. 63.

p. 225 *". . . never seen such a blood bath . . .":*   Ibid., p. 84.

pp. 225–6 *dreams of killings:*   Doherty, testimony to Inspector General, May 5, 1969, p. 136.

p. 226 *". . . so many flies . . .":*   Ibid., p. 139.

p. 226 *". . . a total blank":*   Ibid., p. 153.

p. 227 *Wilson's stenographer:*   Wilson, in *American Heritage*, p. 49.

p. 228 "... *we want it cleared out*": Medina, testimony to Inspector General, May 13, 1969, p. 254.

p. 229 "... *his exact statement*": Ibid., p. 272.

p. 231 *"two investigations"*: Henderson, testimony to Inspector General, May 26, 1969, p. 479.

p. 232 *Calley deal offer refused:* Zaza file, cited above, p. 10.

p. 232 *Henderson knew Thompson allegations:* Wilson, in *American Heritage*, p. 51.

pp. 232–3 *Meadlo's background:* *Washington Post Magazine*, Oct. 22, 1978, p. 22.

p. 233 "... *prayed to God* ...": Wilson, in *American Heritage*, p. 53.

p. 235 *special forces in Cambodia:* See William Shawcross, *Sideshow: Kissinger, Nixon and the Destruction of Cambodia*, London, Fontana, 1980, pp. 24–6, 63–5.

pp. 235–6 *Project Gamma:* See Shelby L. Stanton, *Green Berets at War: US Special Forces in SE Asia 1956–75*, Novato, Calif., Presidio Press, 1985, pp. 187–9; Seymour Hersh, *Kissinger: The Price of Power*, London, Faber, 1983, pp. 178–9.

p. 238 *Feher's first case:* André Feher, personal correspondence.

p. 239 *Washington riots:* See Wayne D. Thorne, personal correspondence; see Lewis Chester, Geoffrey Hodgson, and Bruce Page, *An American Melodrama: The Presidential Campaign of 1968*, London, Deutsch, 1969, pp. 4, 15–16.

p. 239 "... *not the place for their sons* ...": André Feher, personal correspondence.

p. 241 "... *most of the people killed* ...": Haeberle, CID statement, Aug. 25, 1969, pp. 4–5.

p. 242 *"I put together a slide show* ...": Ronald Haeberle, personal interview.

p. 242 *mixed feelings:* Haeberle, CID statement cited above, p. 7.

p. 244 "... *why we cannot win the war* ...": Boyce, CID statement, Aug. 28, 1969, pp. 2–7.

p. 245 *"They should have refused* ...": Olsen, CID statement cited above, p. 8.

pp. 245–6 *Sardis hotel incident:* André Feher, personal correspondence.

8. FALLOUT

p. 250 *Black visits Calley:* See Columbus, Georgia, *Sunday Ledger-Enquirer*, Dec. 7, 1969.

pp. 250–51 *Ridenhour's story:* See Christopher Lydon, "Pinkville Gadfly," *New York Times*, Nov. 29, 1969; also Seymour Hersh, *My Lai 4: A Report on the Massacre and its Aftermath*, New York, Random House, 1970, p. 115.

p. 251 *Hersh's background:* See *The Nation*, Mar. 26, 1988, p. 403.

p. 252 *lead on Calley case:* See Hersh, *My Lai 4*, p. 122.

p. 253 *Army lawyers comforted:* See memorandum for the record, Douglas C. Tucker, "Calley Case," Oct. 27, 1969, Office of the Information Officer, Ft Benning, Georgia.

p. 253 *Calley as victim:*   See Hersh, *My Lai 4*, p. 134.

pp. 253–4 *Obst sells story:*   See *Time* magazine, Dec. 5, 1969, p. 75.

pp. 256–8 *news conference:*   Text of Pennsylvanian news conference, Nov. 21, 1969, from an index of Gen. Westmoreland's public statements about My Lai, among his personal papers in the National Archives.

p. 258 *Birkhoffer:*   Zaza file, cited above, p. 19.

p. 259 *". . . wonder about you too":*   Michael Bernhardt, personal interview.

p. 259 *on Canadian radio:*   Interview with Ronald Ridenhour, Vancouver radio station CKNW, Nov. 18, 1969.

pp. 259–60 *Eszterhas:*   See Hersh, *My Lai 4*, p. 137.

p. 260 *Sen. Young:*   *Washington Post*, Nov. 25, 1969.

pp. 260–61 *Meadlo's TV confession:*   Recordings of all the television broadcasts about My Lai were used as evidence in legal arguments over prejudical publicity at Calley's court-martial. We viewed many hours of them on June 15, 1988, at the invitation of the Judge Advocate General's Dept, US Court of Military Review, Falls Church, Virginia. They are now stored at the National Archives audiovisual center in Washington, DC.

p. 262 *Meadlo–Wallace interview:*   See *The Scotsman*, Nov. 26, 1969.

p. 262 *Hersh statement*:   See *New York Times*, Nov. 23, 1969.

p. 263 *Mrs Meadlo's statement:*   CBS Evening News, Nov. 25, 1969.

p. 263 *Sen. Hollings speech:*   *Washington Post*, Nov. 26, 1969, p. 8.

pp. 263–4 *Haeberle and Eszterhas take bids:*   See ibid.; also *Newsweek*, Dec. 1, 1969, p. 57.

p. 264 *Haeberle's income from photos:*   See Report of House Armed Services Committee, *Investigation of the My Lai Incident*, 1970, p. 46. The Armed Services investigating subcommittee, chaired by F. Edward Hebert of Louisiana, was highly critical of Haeberle's actions and the Army in letting him get away with it. He had to produce his financial records for the subcommittee when he gave evidence on Apr. 23, 1970. The Army responded by changing its regulations to prevent soldiers in future claiming copyright on photos taken in combat. The Justice Department considered whether it could reclaim the money Haeberle made from the sale of the photographs. See memorandum, "Proposed Civil Action against Ronald L. Haeberle," by Robert E. Jordan III, Army General Counsel, Dec. 3, 1970; and letter from William D. Ruckelshaus, assistant attorney general, US Justice Dept, to Robert Jordan, Nov. 24, 1970. The subcommittee's transcript of testimony was classified for six years, until Apr. 13, 1976, and only released when Calley's appeal process had been exhausted.

p. 266 *memo to Resor:*   See memorandum for the Secretary of the Army, "Information for Members of Congress: Alleged Murder of Noncombatant Civilians in the Hamlet of My Lai (4), Republic of Vietnam," approved by the Vice Chief of Staff, Nov. 24, 1969; and separate paper, undated in the same file: "My Lai Investigation."

p. 266 *Resor statement:*   Statement by Hon. Stanley R. Resor, Secretary of the Army, First Session, 91st Congress, Nov. 26, 1969—in papers of War Crimes

Working Group, Modern Military Records Branch, National Archives.

p. 267 *Arends leaves room:* *Columbus Enquirer*, Nov. 27, 1969, p. 1.

9. VIETNAM REVISITED

p. 268 *new strategy required:* See National Security Council document, from Henry A. Kissinger, National Security Study Memorandum 29, dated Mar. 12, 1969—declassified document in Library of Congress.

p. 269 *Kissinger to Laird:* See NSC document, from Henry A. Kissinger, National Security Study Memorandum 36, dated Apr. 10, 1969—declassified document in Library of Congress.

p. 270 *troop withdrawals continued:* Seymour Hersh, *Kissinger: The Price of Power*, London, Faber, 1983, pp. 168–74; Richard Nixon, *The Memoirs of Richard Nixon*, London, Sidgwick & Jackson, 1978, pp. 390–414; Henry Kissinger, *The White House Years*, London, Weidenfeld & Nicolson and Michael Joseph, 1979, pp. 277–88; Bruce Oudes (ed.), *From the President: Richard Nixon's Secret Files*, London, Deutsch, 1989, pp. 59–69.

p. 271 *Don's response:* *Atlanta Constitution*, Nov. 26, 1969.

pp. 271–2 *Khien to Thieu:* Memorandum to the President of the Republic of Vietnam, "Concerning the Military Operation on 16/3/68 at Tu Cung," 736/SD2/TM2/K, Nov. 20, 1969.

p. 272 *"simple explanation":* See Jesse Frosch, "The Anatomy of a Massacre," *Playboy*, Jul. 1970, p. 192.

pp. 272–3 *Lam's explanation:* Report to Minister of Defense from Lt. Gen. Hoang Xuan Lam, Dec. 3, 1969.

p. 273 *allegations to Feher:* See confidential interrogation report on Nguyen Thi Bay, Dec. 16, 1969, by Capt. Boudewijn W. van Pamelen, Interrogation Section, Military Intelligence Det., American Division; and CID Agency RVN Task Force daily journal, Dec. 17, 1969, entry no. 8.

p. 274 *villagers shown enlargements:* Statement by CW4 Andre C. Feher, Nov. 16, 1969, My Lai CID Archives, US Army Crime Records Center, Baltimore, Md.

p. 275 *". . . not telling the truth":* See unsworn statements of Do Dinh Luyen and Do Tan Nhon, Nov. 25, 1969, US Army Crime Records Center, Baltimore, Md.

pp. 276–7 *later recollections:* André Feher, personal correspondence.

p. 278 *Hodges's denial and refusal:* See Task Force daily journal, Dec. 24, 1969, entry no. 9; "Hodges refused comment on whether he observed any rapes in the sub-hamlet NW of My Lai (4) and further refused comment on whether or not he raped anyone . . . Hodges declined to furnish a written statement"; also entry no. 13: "Hodges did not deny the allegation, he merely refused to discuss the matter."

p. 280 *Feher–May exchange:* See May, testimony to Peers, second interview, Feb. 17, 1970, p. 7. May was subsequently accused in a congressional subcommittee report of being involved in covering up information about the massacre. Later he was posted as a diplomat to the US Embassy in Somalia as an administrative officer. An official State Dept investigation cleared him of being involved in a coverup, after Cong. Sam Stratton tried to prevent his promotion.

p. 280 *". . . never engaged us in conversation . . .":* André Feher, personal correspondence.

10. THE JUDGMENT OF PEERS

p. 285 *Thompson impresses Peers:* See William R. Peers, *The My Lai Inquiry*, New York, Norton, 1979, p. 158.

p. 285 *CIA in South Vietnam:* Frank Snepp, *Decent Interval: The American Debacle in Vietnam and the Fall of Saigon*, London, Penguin, 1980.

p. 286 *Peers in Burma:* William R. Peers and Dean Brelis, *Behind the Burma Road*, London, Hale, 1964, p. 84.

p. 286 *CIA efforts:* Snepp, *Decent Interval*, pp. 25–6.

p. 286 *". . . too much . . . out of too little":* Joseph Lazarsky, personal correspondence.

p. 288 *". . . knew right from wrong . . .":* Jerry Walsh, personal correspondence.

p. 288 *reports on Peers:* See CoS memorandum, "Army Staff Monitor, My Lai," Nov. 28, 1969, Westmoreland Papers, file "CS 091 Vietnam."

p. 289 *pressure for whitewash:* William C. Westmoreland, *A Soldier Reports*, New York, Doubleday, 1976, p. 376; Peers, *My Lai Inquiry*, p. 3.

p. 289 *respect for due process rights:* See e.g. Westmoreland's speech to the Utah National Guard officers' club, Fort Douglas, Utah, Feb. 19, 1970—in "Index of Public Statements on Son My Incident," Westmoreland Papers, National Archives; and memorandum for the record by Lt. Col. F. A. Hart, Westmoreland's aide, "CSA Discussion of Son My at Armed Forces Staff College," May 21, 1970.

p. 290 *Peers determined:* See memoranda between Peers and Secretary of the Army and Chief of Staff, Dept of Army, Nov. 26 and 30, 1969, and Jan. 21 and Feb. 2, 1970—enclosures in Peers Report, vol. 1.

p. 290 *chips would fall:* See Seymour Hersh, *Cover-Up: The Army's Secret Investigation of the Massacre at My Lai*, New York, Vintage, 1972, p. 233.

p. 291 *Rivers's attitude:* See Peers, *My Lai Inquiry*, p. 21.

p. 291 *Hebert to Westmoreland:* See records of CoS fonecon with Cong. Hebert, Dec. 15, 17, and 23, 1969, in Westmoreland Papers, National Archives. The conversation of Dec. 23 was marked "sensitive."

p. 293 *Peers in Burma:* See Peers and Brelis, *Behind the Burma Road*, p. 32.

p. 294 *Chinese incursions:* See John Ranelagh, *The Agency: The Decline and Rise of the CIA*, London: Weidenfeld & Nicolson, 1986, p. 217; also William Blum, *The CIA—a Forgotten History*, Atlantic Highlands, NJ, Zed Books, 1986, p. 18.

pp. 294–5 *Peers's tactics:* Typhoon (1 Field Force), vol. 3, no. 3, Mar. 1969, p. 4.

p. 295 *Peers's command style:* Ibid., p. 6.

p. 296 *civilized values . . . regulations:* Radio interview with William Peers, *The Art Findlay Program*, Station KGO, San Francisco, Jun. 18, 1979.

p. 296 "*. . . admiration for him*": Ibid.

p. 297 *Bravo Company's assault:* Peers, *My Lai Inquiry*, pp. 184–95.

p. 297 *Willingham at inquiry:* See Willingham, testimony to Peers, Feb. 20, 1970, p. 5.

p. 298 *Peers shocked, uncomprehending:* Peers, *My Lai Inquiry*, p. 175.

p. 298 "*. . . just like in a daze*": Partsch, testimony to Peers, Jan. 30, 1970, p. 5—Peers Report, vol. 3, bk 26.

p. 298 "*. . . wiping out people*": Gonzalez, testimony to Peers, Jan. 21, 1970, p. 32—Peers Report, vol. 3, bk 26.

p. 298 "*. . . guys had bayonets . . .*": Moss, testimony to Peers, Jan. 5, 1970, p. 10—Peers Report, vol. 3, bk. 26.

pp. 298–9 "*. . . can't sleep at night sometimes*": See Carter, testimony at Medina's Article 32 hearing under the UCMJ, quoted in F. Lee Bailey, *For the Defense*, New York, Atheneum, 1975; and Carter, testimony to Peers, Jan. 2, 1970, pp. 28–47 passim—Peers Report, vol. 3, bk 24.

p. 299 *no quarter given:* Peers, *My Lai Inquiry*, p. 113.

p. 300 *loss of evidence:* Ibid., p. 143.

p. 301 *spurious report:* Lt. Col. Barney Brannen told a pretrial military hearing into disciplinary charges against Koster in Sept. 1970 that while serving at the Americal Division HQ in 1969 he had seen Frank Barker's original report, complete with several statements that appeared to have been written by the same individual. No one else claimed to have seen the report and it was never found. See Hersh, *Cover-Up*, pp. 220–6.

p. 302 *Henderson on coverup:* Peers, *My Lai Inquiry*, p. 64.

p. 302 "*. . . even conspiratorial*": Ibid., p. 110.

p. 302 *Henderson to Westmoreland:* Oran K. Henderson, letter to Army Chief of Staff, Dec. 10, 1969, Westmoreland Papers, National Archives (and Peers exhibit M-13).

p. 303 *Peers's advice:* Peers, *My Lai Inquiry*, p. 112.

p. 303 *Peers embarrassed:* Jerry Walsh, personal correspondence.

p. 304 "*. . . a complete forgery*": Koster, testimony to Peers, Feb. 18, 1970, pp. 151–3—Peers Report, vol. 3, bk 3.

p. 305 *charges delayed: Army Staff Monitor* summary, Jan. 7, 1970.

p. 305 "*. . . cut this guy's water off . . .*": *Army Staff Monitor*, Jan. 27, 1970.

p. 305 *support for Calley: Army Staff Monitor* summary, Jan. 23, 1970; War Crimes Working Party papers, National Archives.

p. 306 "*. . . ahead of time*": T'Souvas, testimony to Peers, Jan. 31, 1970, pp. 28–39 passim—Peers Report, vol. 3, bk 28.

p. 306 "*. . . violated Army procedure*": Peers, *My Lai Inquiry*, p. 210; also Peers radio interview, San Francisco, cited above.

p. 307 "... *suppressed information* ...": Peers Report, vol. 1, ch. 12 "Findings and Recommendations," p. 3.

p. 307 "*Henderson's actions* ...": Peers Report, vol. 1, ch. 2 summary of report, p. 7.

p. 307 *efforts to withhold information:* Ibid., pp. 9, 11.

p. 308 *Peers on Lewis:* Peers, *My Lai Inquiry*, p. 215.

p. 308 *ready to boycott press conference:* Ibid., p. 217.

p. 309 *Peers sidesteps questions:* See Hersh, *Cover-Up*, p. 251.

p. 309 *Bravo atrocity hushed up:* See Peers Report, vol. 1, ch. 7; and *New York Times*, Mar. 18, 1970, p. 17.

p. 310 *Koster's address to cadets:* "US Generals Charged over My Lai," London *Times*, Mar. 18, 1970.

p. 310 *cadets' farewell to Koster:* See Joseph Ellis and Robert Moore, *School for Soldiers: West Point and the Profession of Arms*, New York, Oxford University Press, 1972, pp. 163–9.

p. 310 "... *life in general*": Sam Koster, personal telephone interview.

p. 311 *Milloy's worry:* "Eyes only" message from Maj. Gen. Milloy, CG Americal Div., Chu Lai, to Lt. Gen. Zais, CG XXIV Corps, Phu Bai, Apr. 30, 1970—War Crimes Working Party papers, National Archives.

pp. 313–14 *Westmoreland's warning:* Confidential KRA 3466 "eyes only" message, from Gen. Westmoreland, Chief of Staff, to Generals Polk, Woolnough, Haines, and Chesarek, Sep. 3, 1970—Westmoreland Papers, National Archives.

11. ... AND JUSTICE FOR ALL

p. 315 "*dirty rotten Jews from New York*": Quoted in Seymour Hersh, *Kissinger: The Price of Power*, London, Faber, 1983, p. 135.

p. 315 *VC prisoner hurled to death:* See "Photos Allege Copter Killing," *Baltimore Sun*, Nov. 29, 1969, detailing a story printed the day before in the *Chicago Sun-Times*.

p. 315 *Nixon:* "... *blunt this attack*": Bruce Oudes (ed.), *From the President: Richard Nixon's Secret Files*, London, Deutsch, 1989, p. 45.

p. 316 "... *whole tragic episode* ...": Richard Nixon, *The Memoirs of Richard Nixon*, London, Sidgwick & Jackson, 1978, p. 500.

p. 317 *Buchanon's letter-writing campaign:* Oudes, *From the President*, pp. 44–5.

p. 317 *antiwar protesters targeted:* *Time* magazine, Nov. 28, 1969, p. 19.

p. 318 *astronauts' "script":* See Oudes, *From the President*, pp. 65–9.

p. 319 *protesters in Oval Office:* See Michael Maclear, *Vietnam—the Ten Thousand Day War*, London, Thames–Mandarin, 1981, p. 396.

p. 319 "... *out of the matter entirely*": Kissinger, memorandum to Haldeman, Nov. 21, 1969, National Archives Nixon Project.

p. 320 "*. . . America will be condemned . . .*": Memorandum to the President, Daniel Patrick Moynihan, Nov. 25, 1969, National Archives Nixon Project.

p. 320 *obligation to prosecute war criminals:* The US Army first set down its rules of warfare, known as the Lieber Code, in 1863. President Lincoln commissioned Prof. Francis Lieber, whose son was to become Judge Advocate General, to draw up a code to deal with prisoners of war. The Code was used against Capt. Henry Wirz of the Confederate Army, charged with allowing 14,000 Union prisoners to die in Andersonville prison camp. He was hanged in 1865.

p. 321 "*Dirty tricks . . .*": Haldeman's account of his conversation with the President, dated Dec. 1, 1969, is in the White House Special Files, labeled "Haldeman Notes July–December, 1969," National Archives Nixon Project.

p. 321 *Butterfield on Nixon:* See Hersh, *Kissinger*, p. 135.

p. 321 *Alabama cartoon:* Nixon's copy of the cartoon published in the *Birmingham News*, Nov. 26, 1969, is in the White House Special Files box no. 3, "President's Handwriting 6th November–30th November, 1969," National Archives Nixon Project.

p. 322 *Hersh's movements watched:* Hersh, *Kissinger*, p. 1325; also various White House memoranda, e.g. John R. Brown III to Alex Butterfield, Dec. 10, 1969; Butterfield to the President, Dec. 17, 1969; Butterfield to Brown, Dec. 19, 1969, National Archives Nixon Project.

p. 324 *Goldberg to President:* Goldberg's letter to President Nixon, dated Dec. 5, 1969, is in the White House Central Files, National Archives Nixon Project: WHCF ND 18–4: war crimes trials 69–70; in subject files: confidential files 1969–74 box 43.

pp. 324–5 *Kissinger to President:* Kissinger's undated memorandum to the President, "Proposal for a Presidential Commission to Investigate Alleged US Atrocities in Vietnam," is in the same file.

p. 325 *Laird's trust in judicial process:* See letter from Melvin Laird to Sen. Robert Packwood, Dec. 12, 1969, in the same file.

p. 326 *MacCrate statement:* *New York Times* interview, quoted in William R. Peers, *The My Lai Inquiry*, New York, Norton, 1979, p. 224.

pp. 326–7 *Walsh statement:* Ibid.

p. 327 *Stratton statement:* Congressional Record, Feb. 4, 1971.

pp. 327–8 *Seaman's decision:* See William C. Westmoreland on Seaman, *A Soldier Reports*, New York, Doubleday, 1976, p. 180; also Seaman's letter of censure to Maj. Gen. Koster, Jan. 28, 1971, among the papers of the Army's administrative review of his case, in the Modern Military Records Branch, National Archives.

p. 330 *charges dropped after Hutto verdict:* See *New York Times*, Jan. 23, 1971, p. 1; and JAG administrative review papers in the cases against all four individuals, in the Modern Military Records Branch, National Archives.

p. 331 *Kennedy–Daniel exchange:* See *Time* magazine, Apr. 19, 1971, p. 16.

p. 333 *Courthouse arrangements:* Undated memorandum, "Public Affairs

Aspects of the Calley Court Martial," Office of the Information Center, HQUSAIC, Fort Benning, Georgia, in the Modern Military Records Branch, National Archives.

p. 334 *overseas observer:* Stephen Fay, in London *Sunday Times*, Mar. 21, 1971.

pp. 334–5 *". . . I left":* Conti testimony, Calley trial transcript R 1814, 1817.

p. 335 *". . . I do not feel wrong . . .":* Calley testimony, Calley trial transcript R 3833–4.

p. 337 *". . . actions on the surface":* "Report of Psychiatric Evaluation—Lt. William L. Calley Jr," Walter Reed Army Medical Center, Feb. 12, 1971, Modern Military Records Branch, National Archives.

p. 337 *". . . find Lt. Calley innocent":* London *Daily Telegraph*, Apr. 2, 1971; *Time* magazine, Apr. 12, 1971, p. 15.

p. 338 *Daniel's response:* See *Newsweek*, Apr. 12, 1971, p. 30. The entire sound recording of Calley's trial is stored in the audiovisual department of the National Archives.

p. 341 *Nixon invokes Lincoln's memory:* London *Sunday Times*, Apr. 4, 1971.

p. 341 *other prisoners:* See also William Greider, in *Washington Post*, Apr. 5, 1971.

p. 342 *Nixon's popularity:* See Theodore H. White, *The Making of the President 1972*, London, Cape, 1974, pp. 58–9. For a rosier version of the ARVN operation in Laos, see Nixon, *Memoirs*, p. 498.

p. 342 *Colson on Calley:* See memorandum from Lawrence Higby to H. R. Haldeman, Apr. 1, 1971, in White House Special Files, National Archives.

p. 343 *Nixon to Haldeman:* White, *Making of the President*, p. 59.

p. 343 *Dean on Calley:* See John Dean, *Blind Ambition: The White House Years*, London W. H. Allen, 1977, p. 44; and White House memorandum for John Ehrlichman and H. R. Haldeman from Dean, Apr. 1, 1971—National Archives Nixon Project.

pp. 343–4 *White House news management:* See memorandum for Charles W. Colson from Henry C. Cassem III, "President's Planned Announcement re Calley Case," Apr. 3, 1971—White House Special Files, alpha subject box 115, National Archives; and *Newsweek*, Apr. 12, 1971, p. 24.

p. 344 *Pentagon lawyer's warning:* Memorandum for the record, Apr. 1, 1971, "Extract of Telephone Conversation," Maj. Gen. Talbot, Commanding General USAIC (Fort Benning), and Brig. Gen. Parker, Deputy TJAG, 19.15 hrs.

pp. 344–5 *"Have you considered . . .":* Letter from Capt. Aubrey M. Daniel III to Richard Nixon, Apr. 3, 1971—National Archives Nixon Project. See also Haig's memorandum to Ehrlichman, Apr. 7, 1971, about the Army's grave embarrassment at the young officer's action. "It was done completely without their knowledge."

p. 346 *Colson to Haldeman:* See Colson's memorandum, Apr. 19, 1971, National Archives Nixon Project.

pp. 346–7 "... *best damn army in the world*": *New York Times*, Apr. 20, 1971, p. 1.

p. 347 *judge instructs jury:* See Kotouc's administrative review papers, National Archives.

p. 348 *Medina before Congress:* F. Lee Bailey, *For the Defense*, New York, Atheneum, 1975, p. 61.

pp. 348–9 *Medina's trial:* See ibid., pp. 26–143; also Col. William G. Eckhardt, "Command Criminal Responsibility: A Plea for a Workable Standard," US Army War College, Carlisle Barracks, Pennsylvania, May 1982, which considered some of the detailed legal arguments surrounding Medina's trial.

p. 349 *Medina at Henderson trial:* See *New York Times*, Nov. 16, 1971, p. 1.

p. 349 *Henderson's court-martial:* *New York Times*, Dec. 16, 1971, p. 4.

p. 349 *Rothblatt at pretrial hearings:* See talking paper, "Son My Cases," TJAG/Military Justice Division, May 29, 1971, in National Archives.

p. 350 "... *too many claims of 'I can't recall'* ...": See Douglas Robinson, "Henderson Trial: More Is Involved than a Colonel," *New York Times*, Nov. 29, 1971.

pp. 350–51 "... *being so mistreated*": Letter from Mrs Mary Henderson, Oct. 17, 1971, in Westmoreland Papers, National Archives.

p. 351 *pressure from members of Congress:* See Luper's Army administrative review file, National Archives.

p. 352 "... *one miscarriage of justice* ...": See Berry's letter to SGS and TJAG, Apr. 24, 1972, National Archives.

p. 352 "... *most unfavorable story*": Memorandum for the Asst. Dep. Ch. of Staff for Personnel, "Administrative Review of Son My Cases," Maj. Gen. Winant Sidle, chief of information, Feb. 14, 1972.

p. 354 *Calley's circumstances raised at White House:* See White House memoranda, John Dean to Ehrlichman and Haig, Dec. 22, 1972; and Dean to the President, Feb. 16, 1973—in White House Special Files, National Archives Nixon Project; letter and petition from the Cumberland Trace Chater, Retired Officers' Association, Bowling Green, Kentucky, Mar. 8, 1983, National Archives.

p. 354 "*Last POW*": See papers concerning Calley's case before the Army and Air Force Clemency and Parole Board, Sep. 18, 1972, and Nov. 15, 1973; and William L. Calley Jr, "Prisoner's Progress Summary Data," Jul. 31, 1973, National Archives.

p. 355 *Calloway:* London *Sunday Times*, Apr. 21, 1974.

p. 355 *Nixon's final word on Calley:* See Nixon's memorandum re Calley, May 3, 1974, in White House Special Files, National Archives Nixon Project; and B. Woodward and C. Bernstein, *The Final Days*, London, Secker & Warburg, 1976, p. 404.

pp. 356–7 *Judge Elliott:* Quoted in J. Goldstein, B. Marshall, and J. Schwartz (eds), *The My Lai Massacre and its Cover-Up*, New York, Free Press, 1976, p. 555.

12. FINAL CHAPTER

pp. 362–3 *"... backs of the generals"*: Guenter Lewy, *America in Vietnam*, New York, Oxford University Press, 1978, p. 316.

p. 363 *"... share in the responsibility ..."*: See Norman Podhoretz, *Why We Were in Vietnam*, New York, Simon & Schuster, 1982, p. 189.

p. 364 *"The Americans have learned ..."*: Quoted in Richard Hammer, *One Morning in the War: The Tragedy at Pinkville*, London, Hart-Davis, 1970, p. 174.

p. 364 *House committee report*: Quoted in Richard Drinnon, *Facing West: Indian Hating and Empire Building*, New York, Schocken, 1990, p. 452.

p. 365 *"... it would take a Kipling ..."*: Quoted in Robert B. Asprey, *War in the Shadows: The Guerrilla in History*, New York, Doubleday, 1975.

p. 365 *1901 officer's letter*: Drinnon, *Facing West*, p. 315.

p. 365 *Sherman to Grant*: Ibid., p. 329.

p. 366 *"... bones into letter openers"*: Paul Fussell, *Killing in Verse and Prose*, London, Bellew, 1988; John Dower, *War without Mercy*, London, Faber, 1986, p. 64.

p. 366 *Japanese soldier's ear*: Dower, *War without Mercy*, p. 65.

p. 366 *Lindbergh and customs men*: Ibid., pp. 70–71.

p. 367 *"... stern disciplinary action"*: Quoted in Fussell, *Killing in Verse and Prose*, p. 26.

p. 367 *Westmoreland's directive*: Quoted in Lewy, *America in Vietnam*, p. 329.

p. 367 *"Time had no meaning ..."*: Quoted in Dower, *War without Mercy*, p. 61.

p. 369 *"... something uniquely Japanese"*: Ibid., pp. 72–3.

p. 370 *"... bound to happen in a war"*: Quoted in Hammer, *One Morning in the War*.

p. 371 *"... in the midst of hell"*: Michael Walzer, *Just and Unjust Wars*, New York, Basic Books, 1977.

p. 372 *"... It's bad"*: John Sack, *Body Count: Lt. Calley's Story as Told to John Sack*, London, Hutchinson, 1971, p. 103.

p. 372 *"... He isn't combat effective"*: Ibid., p. 100.

p. 372 *"And babies ..."*: Ibid., p. 103.

Bibliography

Adair, Gilbert, *Hollywood's Vietnam*, London, Heinemann, 1989.

Asprey, Robert B., *War in the Shadows: The Guerrilla in History*, 2 vols, New York, Doubleday, 1975.

Bailey, F. Lee, *For the Defense*, New York, Atheneum, 1975.

Barker, Mark, *Nam: The Vietnam War in the Words of the Soldiers Who Fought There*, New York, Berkley Books, 1983.

Blum, William, *The CIA—a Forgotten History*, Atlantic Highlands, NJ, Zed Books, 1986.

Caputo, Philip, *A Rumor of War*, New York, Ballantine, 1988.

Carrier, J. M. and Thompson, C. A. H., *Viet Cong Motivation and Morale: The Special Case of Chu Hoi*, Calif., Rand Corp., May 1966.

Chester, Lewis, Hodgson, Geoffrey, and Page, Bruce, *An American Melodrama: The Presidential Campaign of 1968*, London, Deutsch, 1969.

Chomsky, Noam, *American Power and the New Mandarins*, Harmondsworth, Pelican, 1969.

——, *At War with Asia*, London, Fontana, 1971.

——, *The Backroom Boys*, London, Fontana, 1973.

Clare, Michael T., *War without End: American Planning for the Next Vietnams*, New York, Vintage, 1972.

Clausewitz, Carl von, *On War*, ed. Anatol Rapoport, Harmondsworth, Penguin, 1968.

Colby, William E., *Honorable Men: My Life in the CIA*, New York, Simon & Schuster, 1978.

Culhane, Clare, *Why Is Canada in Vietnam?*, Toronto, NC Press, 1972.

Cutler, Thomas J., *Brown Water, Black Berets*, New York, Pocket Books, 1988.

Davison, W. P., *Some Observations on Viet Cong Operations in the Villages*, Calif., Rand Corp., July 1967.

——, *User's Guide to the Rand Interviews in Vietnam*, Calif., Rand Corp., November 1972.

Davison, W. P. and Zasloff, J. J., *Profile of Viet Cong Cadres*, Calif., Rand Corp., March 1967.

Dean, John, *Blind Ambition: The White House Years*, London, W. H. Allen, 1977.

Denton, Frank H., *Some Effects of Military Operations on Viet Cong Attitudes*, Calif., Rand Corp., November 1966.

Department of the Army, *The Law of Land Warfare: Field Manual FM 21–10*, Washington, DC, US Government Printing Office, 1956.

——, *The Department of Army Review of the Preliminary Investigations into the My Lai Incident*, vols 1–4, Washington, DC, Department of the Army, 1971.

Donnell, John C., *Viet Cong Recruitment: Why Men Join*, Calif., Rand Corp., December 1967.

Donovan, David, *Once a Warrior King*, London, Corgi, 1987.

Dower, John, *War without Mercy*, London, Faber, 1986.

Drinnon, Richard, *Facing West: Indian Hating and Empire Building*, New York, Schocken, 1990.

Elliott, David W. P. and Elliott, Mai, *Documents of an Elite Viet Cong Delta Unit: The Demolition Platoon of the 514th Battalion*, Calif., Rand Corp., May 1969.

Ellis, Joseph and Moore, Robert, *School for Soldiers: West Point and the Profession of Arms*, New York, Oxford University Press, 1972.

Fall, Bernard B., *Street without Joy: Insurgency in Indochina, 1946–63*, New York, Schocken, 1975.

FitzGerald, Frances, *Fire in the Lake*, New York Vintage, 1989.

Fussell, Paul, *Killing in Verse and Prose*, London, Bellew, 1988.

——, *Wartime*, Oxford, Oxford University Press, 1989.

Garland, Albert N., *Infantry in Vietnam: Small Unit Actions in the Early Days, 1965–66*. Nashville, Tenn., Battery Press, 1982.

Gershen, Martin, *Destroy or Die: The True Story of My Lai*, New Rochelle, NY, Arlington House, 1971.

Gibson, James W., *The Perfect War*, New York, Vintage, 1988.

Goldman, Peter and Fuller, Tony, *Charlie Company: What Vietnam Did to Us*, New York, Ballantine, 1984.

Goldstein, J., Marshall, B., and Schwartz J. (eds), *The My Lai Massacre and its Cover-Up: Beyond the Reach of the Law*, New York, Free Press, 1976.

Goldston, Robert, *The Vietnamese Revolution*, New York, Bobbs-Merrill, 1972.

Goure, Leon, *Some Impressions of the Effects of Military Operations on Viet Cong Behavior*, Calif., Rand Corp., August 1965.

Goure, L., Russo, A. J., and Scott, D., *Some Findings of the Viet Cong Motivation and Morale Study: June–December, 1965*, Calif., Rand Corp., February 1966.

Goure, Leon and Thompson, C. A. H., *Some Impressions of Viet Cong Vulnerabilities: An Interim Report*, Calif., Rand Corp., August 1965.

Hallin, Daniel C., *The Uncensored War: The Media and Vietnam*, Berkeley, University of California Press, 1989.

Hammer, Richard, *One Morning in the War: The Tragedy at Pinkville*, London, Hart-Davis, 1970.

——, *The Court Martial of Lt. Calley*, New York, Coward–McCann, 1971.

Henry, William E. and Sanford, Navit (eds), *Sanctions of Evil: Sources of Social Destructiveness*, San Francisco, Jossey-Bass, 1971.

Herman, Edward S., *Atrocities in Vietnam*, Philadelphia, Pa, Pilgrim Press, 1970.

Hersh, Seymour, *My Lai 4: A Report on the Massacre and its Aftermath*, New York: Random House, 1970.

——, *Cover-Up: The Army's Secret Investigation of the Massacre at My Lai 4*, New York, Vintage, 1972.

——, *Kissinger: The Price of Power*, London, Faber, 1983.

Hirsch, Phil (ed.), *Vietnam Combat: Brutal Stories of Men Fighting a Dirty War*, New York, Pyramid Books, 1967.

Jenkins, Brian M., *Why the North Vietnamese Will Keep Fighting*, Calif., Rand Corp., 1969.

Johnson, James T., *Can Modern War Be Just?*, New Haven, Yale University Press, 1984.

Kalb, Marvin and Kalb, Bernard, *Kissinger*, London, Hutchinson, 1974.

Karnow, Stanley, *Vietnam: A History*, London, Penguin, 1984.

Kellen, Konrad, *Conversations with Enemy Soldiers in Late 1968: A Study in Motivation and Morale*, Calif., Rand Corp., September 1970.

Kissinger, Henry, *The White House Years*, London, Weidenfeld & Nicolson and Michael Joseph, 1979.

Klein, Joe, *Playback: Five Marines and Vietnam*, New York, Ballantine, 1984.

Knightley, Philip, *The First Casualty*, London, Deutsch, 1975.

Lewy, Guenter, *America in Vietnam*, New York, Oxford University Press, 1978.

Lifton, Robert J., *Home from the War*, London, Wildwood House, 1974.

Maclear, Michael, *Vietnam—the Ten Thousand Day War*, London, Thames-Mandarin, 1981.

Marchetti, Victor and Marks, John, *The CIA and the Cult of Intelligence*, London, Cape, 1974.

Martin, Earl S., *Reaching the Other Side*, New York, Crown, 1978.

Mason, Robert, *Chickenhawk*, London, Corgi, 1984.

Miller, Merle, *Lyndon: An Oral Biography*, New York, Ballantine, 1980.

Morris, Roger, *Haig: The General's Progress*, London, Robson, 1982.

Newman, Bernard, *Background to Vietnam*, New York, Signet, 1965.

Oudes, Bruce (ed.), *From the President: Richard Nixon's Secret Files*, London, Deutsch, 1989.

Page, Tim, *Page after Page*, London, Sidgwick & Jackson, 1988.

Page, Tim and Pimlott, John, *'Nam: The Vietnam Experience 1965–75*, London, Hamlyn, 1988.

Palmer, Gen. Bruce Jr., *The 25-Year War: America's Military Role in Vietnam*, Louisville, University Press of Kentucky, 1984.

Peers, William R., *The My Lai Inquiry*, New York, Norton, 1979.

Peers, William R. and Brelis, Dean, *Behind the Burma Road*, London, Hale, 1964.

Podhoretz, Norman, *Why We Were in Vietnam*, New York, Simon & Schuster, 1982.

Powers, Thomas, *The Man Who Kept Secrets: Richard Helms and the CIA*, New York, Pocket Books, 1979.

Pye, Lucien W., *Observations on the Chu Hoi Program*, Calif., Rand Corp., January 1966.

Ranelagh, John, *The Agency: The Decline and Rise of the CIA*, London, Weidenfeld & Nicolson, 1986.

Sack, John, *Body Count: Lt. Calley's Story as Told to John Sack*, London, Hutchinson, 1971.

Saltoli, Al, *Everything We Had*, New York, Ballantine, 1981.

——, *To Bear Any Burden*, New York, Ballantine, 1985.

Schell, Jonathan, *The Military Half: An Account of Destruction in Quang Ngai and Quang Tin*, New York, Vintage, 1968.

——, *The Real War*, London, Corgi, 1989.

——, *Observing the Nixon Years*, New York, Vintage, 1990.

Shawcross, William, *Sideshow: Kissinger, Nixon and the Destruction of Cambodia*, London, Fontana, 1980.

Sheehan, Neil, *A Bright Shining Lie*, London, Picador, 1990.

Sheehan, Neil, Smith, Hedrick, *et al.*, *The Pentagon Papers*, New York, Bantam, 1971.

Shulimson, Jack, *The US Marines in Vietnam: An Expanding War, 1966*, Washington, DC, History and Museums Division, HQ US Marine Corps, 1982.

——, *Tet—1968: The Illustrated History of the Vietnam War*, New York, Bantam, 1988.

Shulimson, Jack and Johnson, Maj. Charles M., *The US Marines in Vietnam: The Landing and the Buildup, 1965*, Washington, DC, History and Museums Division, HQ US Marine Corps, 1978.

Simpson, Charles M., *Inside the Green Berets*, New York, Berkley Books, 1984.

Smith, Bradley F., *The Shadow Warriors: OSS and the Origins of the CIA*, New York, Basic Books, 1983.

Snepp, Frank, *Decent Interval: The American Debacle in Vietnam and the Fall of Saigon*, London, Penguin, 1980.

Stanton, Shelby L., *Green Berets at War: US Special Forces in SE Asia 1956–75*, Novato, Calif., Presidio, 1985.

Stavins, R., Burnet, R. J., and Raskin, M. G., *Washington Plans an Aggressive War: A Documented Account of the US Adventure in Indochina*, New York, Random House, 1971.

Summers, Col. Harry G. Jr, *On Strategy: A Critical Analysis of the Vietnam War*, New York, Dell, 1984.

——, *Vietnam War Almanac*, New York, 1985.

Sweetland, Anders, *Rallying Potential among the North Vietnamese Armed Forces*, Calif., Rand Corp., December 1970.

Telfer, Maj. Gary L., Rogers, Lt. Col. Lane, and Fleming, V. Keith Jr, *US Marines in Vietnam: Fighting the North Vietnamese, 1967*, Washington, DC, History and Museums Division, HQ US Marine Corps, 1984.

Thayer, Thomas C., *War without Fronts: The American Experience in Vietnam*, London, Westview Press, 1985.

Walsh, Jeffrey and Aulich, James (eds), *Vietnam Images: War and Representation*, London, Macmillan, 1989.

Walzer, Michael, *Just and Unjust Wars*, New York, Basic Books, 1977.

Westmoreland, William C., *A Soldier Reports*, New York, Doubleday, 1976.

White, Theodore H., *The Making of the President 1972*, London, Cape, 1974.

Woodward, B. and Bernstein, C., *The Final Days*, London, Secker & Warburg, 1976.

Index

FOR THE BEST IN PAPERBACKS, LOOK FOR THE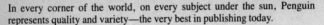

In every corner of the world, on every subject under the sun, Penguin represents quality and variety—the very best in publishing today.

For complete information about books available from Penguin—including Pelicans, Puffins, Peregrines, and Penguin Classics—and how to order them, write to us at the appropriate address below. Please note that for copyright reasons the selection of books varies from country to country.

In the United Kingdom: For a complete list of books available from Penguin in the U.K., please write to *Dept E.P., Penguin Books Ltd, Harmondsworth, Middlesex, UB7 0DA.*

In the United States: For a complete list of books available from Penguin in the U.S., please write to *Dept BA, Penguin,* Box 120, Bergenfield, New Jersey 07621-0120.

In Canada: For a complete list of books available from Penguin in Canada, please write to *Penguin Books Canada Ltd, 10 Alcorn Avenue, Suite 300, Toronto, Ontario, Canada M4V 3B2.*

In Australia: For a complete list of books available from Penguin in Australia, please write to the *Marketing Department, Penguin Books Ltd, P.O. Box 257, Ringwood, Victoria 3134.*

In New Zealand: For a complete list of books available from Penguin in New Zealand, please write to the *Marketing Department, Penguin Books (NZ) Ltd, Private Bag, Takapuna, Auckland 9.*

In India: For a complete list of books available from Penguin, please write to *Penguin Overseas Ltd, 706 Eros Apartments, 56 Nehru Place, New Delhi, 110019.*

In Holland: For a complete list of books available from Penguin in Holland, please write to *Penguin Books Nederland B.V., Postbus 195, NL-1380AD Weesp, Netherlands.*

In Germany: For a complete list of books available from Penguin, please write to *Penguin Books Ltd, Friedrichstrasse 10-12, D-6000 Frankfurt Main 1, Federal Republic of Germany.*

In Spain: For a complete list of books available from Penguin in Spain, please write to *Longman, Penguin España, Calle San Nicolas 15, E-28013 Madrid, Spain.*

In Japan: For a complete list of books available from Penguin in Japan, please write to *Longman Penguin Japan Co Ltd, Yamaguchi Building, 2-12-9 Kanda Jimbocho, Chiyoda-Ku, Tokyo 101, Japan.*